Build Strong Homes

For Strong Churches and A Strong Nation

Edited By

Mike Willis

ISBN 10: 1-58427-375-5

ISBN 13: 978-1-58427-3752

Guardian of Truth Foundation
CEI Bookstore
220 S. Marion St., Athens, AL 35611
1-855-49BOOKS or 1-855-492-6657
www.CEIbooks.com

Table of Contents

Introduction

Build Strong Homes

Mike Willis

The American home is in trouble. However, a generation has arisen that has seen nothing except what twenty-first century American culture shows them and may be unaware of how significantly our society has changed in the last fifty years. This introduction to the series presented in this book is designed to (a) give a subjective and personal look at the changes in American culture over the past fifty years as a way of relating to our contemporaries that what we see in the American home does not have to be the way it is; (b) to call attention to some of the causes and effects of the breakdown of the nuclear family in America and the forces that are undermining the home in the American culture; (c) to make us aware of how the reshaping of the American family is also affecting churches. In order to have a strong nation and strong churches, Americans must build strong homes.

Personal Observations

I turn sixty-six this year and have lived through a dramatic shift in our

---

Mike Willis was born on July 22, 1947, the sixth of seven children born to Onan J. and Wilhelmina Willis. All four of their sons became gospel preachers (Cecil, Don, Lewis). In 1966, Mike married Sandra Carol Parson and to their marriage were born two children, Jennifer Lynette (Mann) and Corey Michael. Mike received the B.A. degree from Butler University and M.A. degrees from Christian Theological Seminary and Indiana University. He is the author of commentaries on 1 Corinthians and Galatians in the *Truth Commentary* series, of which he is also the editor. He has over twenty titles of adult workbooks in print. He has been editor of *Truth Magazine* since December 1976. Mike has done full-time preaching at Alexandria, Indiana, several churches in the Indianapolis area, Knollwood in Xenia, Ohio, and Franklin, Kentucky. He has led tours to the Bible Lands since the early 1990s. In 2005, he participated as a volunteer in the archaeological dig at Beth-shemesh, Israel while a graduate student at Indiana University.

culture. We live in an age of violence. Chicago had 500 homicides in 2012.[1] Detroit had 411.[2] New York City had 414.[3] Each of us was shocked by the astounding act of violence that occurred on December 14, 2012 at the Sandy Hook Elementary School in Newton, CT which took the lives of twenty first graders and six adults.

My childhood was not marked by such widespread violence. My parents lived in Woodlake, a rural community in East Texas; we children attended grade school in Groveton. As was typical of communities in that area, most of the men hunted for both recreation and food. Guns were a part of our lives. When a young man was coming of age, he got his first gun and was allowed to join the deer or squirrel hunts with his father. Many men drove a pickup and carried their .30-.30 Winchester Rifles in a gun rack in their pickup, just in case they saw a deer (mostly in deer season, but not always!) or coyote or other varmint. They parked their pickups on the town square with their rifles in the gun rack, left the doors of their trucks unlocked and the windows were rolled down (Texas is hot, especially during the summer months), and went about their business without concern that

---

[1] "Chicago reached 'a tragic number' today, according to Police Superintendent Garry McCarthy: Its homicide total for the year hit 500, the highest annual total since 2008" (*Chicago Tribune* reporters, Jeremy Gorner and Peter Nickeas, "Chicago police confirm 'tragic number' of 500 homicides," December 28, 2012, *http://articles.chicagotribune.com/2012-12-28/news/chi-chicago-2012-homicide-toll-20121228_1_latest-homicide-500th-homicide-tragic-number*, accessed 2/19/2013).

[2] *Detroit Free Press* reporter Ron Rancinto wrote, "Detroit reported 411 homicides in 2012, 25 of them deemed "justifiable" by FBI crime reporting standards. Still, the remaining 386 represent 54.6 homicides per 100,000 residents, according to the *Detroit Free Press*. In 1993 the rate was 57.6 homicides per 100,000 residents" (January 4, 2013, "Detroit reports highest homicide rate in 20 years," *http://news.yahoo.com/detroit-reports-highest-homicide-rate-in-20-years-192557311.html*, accessed 2/19/2013).

[3] NBC News reporter, Max Alan Johnson wrote, "New York Mayor Michael Bloomberg was crowing.

"'The number of murders this year will be lower than any time in recorded city history,' Bloomberg said Friday in a statement announcing that homicides in the city this year had fallen to 414 — the fewest since it started keeping such statistics in 1963" (*http://usnews.nbcnews.com/_news/2012/12/29/16218098-tale-of-two-cities-homicides-plummet-in-new-york-leap-in-chicago?lite*, accessed 2/19/2013).

their guns might be stolen or that they might be used in violence against another citizen.

The "streets" (we lived on a dirt road) were safe then. Mom would let us "go out to play" after breakfast and we may not see her till noon. After lunch, we went out to play and came home in time for supper. We rode our bicycles wherever we wanted without fear of sexual predators or kidnappers.[4] When I witness how closely parents watch over their children today, I mourn the loss of such a safe environment in which to rear our children.

When our family left home for church or anywhere else, for that matter, we closed the screen door on our home and never bothered with locking our home or our cars. We were more concerned about keeping out the flies than thieves. Perhaps one might think that we did not have anything worth stealing, which was mostly true, but the society in which we lived was not a threat to one's possessions.

School began each day with the principal reading a portion of Scripture over the intercom. This was followed by prayer and the children standing to say the "Pledge of Allegiance." I remembered how honored I felt when I was given the class assignment to raise and lower the United States flag. I was taught how to fold the flag properly, never allow the flag to touch the ground, to take it down during the rain, and otherwise to show respect for it.

We prayed before football games and basketball games, had a baccalaureate service at a local denomination,[5] invited denominational preachers to speak to the weekly assembly, had Christmas plays, and observed Easter. Though some[6] in those days wished that secular schools would not allow

---

[4] I am not sure that a Mom with seven children would have ransomed anyone of her seven children, although she used to say, "I wouldn't give a nickel for another child, but wouldn't take a million dollars for any one of them!" Paying a ransom for one of us might have been a different story!

[5] For those who have never experienced a baccalaureate service, it is a celebration which honors a graduating senior class from a college or high school. The event is typically a Christianity-based interdenominational service that challenges the new graduates to live an honorable life before God and men.

[6] Members of the churches of Christ believe that Christmas and Easter are unauthorized religious holy days, developed centuries after the New Testament was written and recognized as an authoritative document for the church. Most did not participate in the religious observances of such "holy days," though they saw nothing wrong with the secular observance of Halloween, Christmas, Easter, etc.

denominational preachers access to their children to perpetrate their denominational doctrines and unauthorized religious holy days, no one thought of bringing a lawsuit against the school to remove all references to God from the schools and political arena. Christ and His word were respected throughout the American society.

Before birth control, most people had rather large families. Mom and Dad had seven children, four boys and three girls. The families were quite stable. In the little community of Woodlake, I can only remember one divorced family – a divorced woman who was rearing her daughters. Another broken family was a widowed grandmother who was caring for her unruly grandchildren, whose parents had deserted them. We were allowed to play with these children only at our house, where Mother could supervise us. When we asked why we could not go to the other family's house to play, we were told that their parents were *divorced* – a word that conveyed the idea of failure in the most basic and fundamental obligation of life – family. Mom and Dad wanted to protect their children from their influence.

We only received one channel on our television and, anyone fortunate enough to live in or near a town that received several channels had to get out of his chair to change the channels. In good weather, we could sometimes pick up the Houston stations, if someone went outside and redirected the antennae. What we saw on television was clean and wholesome entertainment: *The Lone Ranger* (1949-1957), *Sky King* (1951-1962), *The Roy Rogers Show* (1951-1957), *Leave It To Beaver* (1957-1963), *I Love Lucy* (1951-1957), *Father Knows Best* (1954-1960), *The Andy Griffin Show* (1960-1968), etc. Our favorite cartoon characters were Bugs Bunny, Road Runner, Mickey Mouse, and their accompanying sidekicks. When *The Ten Commandments* (1956) came to Groveton, our principal marched the entire grade school about a mile to the theater so that we could see the movie. When *Gone With the Wind* (1939) came to our theater, Mom and Dad did not allow their children to see it because it had *one* curse word in it!

I graduated from Groveton High School in 1965 on Friday night. On Sunday night, I left after worship services to go to Florida College where I worked through the summer at their woodwork shop (by going early, I would already have a job for the school year and not have to compete with several hundred others who also were looking for a job). Mom and Dad were not able to help pay my college expenses, although my brother, Cecil, helped raise some funds for my education. When children left home, they were expected to provide for themselves! And, they were expected to leave home upon graduation from high school! I don't think that any of the seven of us ever went to Mom and Dad and asked them to provide for us after we left home.

Did I grow up in Mayberry? No! I was reared in a culture where Christian values predominated. I relate this information to you, not to amuse you, but to announce to a generation that has never experienced any other culture than what we see today, that mankind does not have to live like we are with . . .

- Violence reported on the evening news nearly every day
- Divorce destroying half of our homes
- Families with absentee fathers
- Children conceiving children out of wedlock
- Various addictions controlling people: alcohol, drugs, pornography, sex
- Unemployed citizens living off government paychecks generation after generation
- Mothers and Dads uninvolved in their children's education

Let us acknowledge that every age has had its own share of sinners and one must not look back with such tinted glasses that he creates an idyllic age somewhere in the past. Solomon wrote, "Say not thou, What is the cause that the former days were better than these? For thou dost not enquire wisely concerning this" (Eccl. 7:10). The generation of the 1900-1950s had two world wars, witnessed the holocaust, dropped the first atomic bombs on Nagasaki and Hiroshima, fought urban battles over the illegal distribution of liquor during the Prohibition, and had its own share of other moral problems. We appreciate and applaud all of the advances in American culture that we experience on a daily basis, such as running water, flushing toilets, houses with central heat and air, automobiles that take us to our desired destinations in luxury, and the best medical care any generation of people have ever received.

Having acknowledged these blessings of our own age and the sins that have existed in every age prior to our own, however, one can accurately describe what occurred in the United States in the 1960s as a cultural revolution that began a systematic replacement of the Christian value system with that of secular humanism (also could be designated atheism or secularism). The precise dating of this change is impossible to fix, but here are some of the evidences of its occurrence: Homosexuals "came out of the closet,"[7]

---

[7] German lawyer Karl Heinrich Ulrichs (1825-1895) was perhaps the first activist

abortion rights were declared to be guaranteed by the Constitution (*Roe v. Wade*, 1973), the sexual liberation movement made living together outside the bonds of matrimony acceptable behavior, easy divorce and remarriage was granted through no-fault divorce laws, and court decisions declared pornography to be protected speech under the first amendment and that it was innocent and harmless. For years, American liberalism lived off the despised morality of Christian virtue,[8] but its incessant attacks have broken down many restraints that Christian teaching had on immoral behavior and thus American culture is showing signs of unmistakable degeneration. The increasing number of such incidents as mass shootings, increases in child abuse, efforts to legalize drugs, removing sodomy from the criminal code and treating it as an alternative lifestyle, the divorces which devastate the home (fatherless homes, more children being raised below the poverty level, etc.), all point to a society that is crumbling.

As one watches these changes in America, he is reminded of Paul's description of the decadent Roman empire in his own day. He wrote,

> For the wrath of God is revealed from heaven against all ungodliness and unrighteousness of men, who hold the truth in unrighteousness; Because that which may be known of God is manifest in them; for God hath shewed it unto them. For the invisible things of him from the creation of the world

---

for homosexual civil rights. He argued against Germany's adoption of Prussian law criminalizing sodomy (Paragraph 175). In a series of pamphlets published from 1864 to 1879, he argued that same-sex love was a congenital, hereditary condition, not a matter of immorality. Sigmund Freud argued that homosexuality was related to an Oedipus complex, an over attachment to one's mother. Clellan Ford's and Frank Beach's *Patterns of Sexual Behavior* (1951), relying on data from the Human Relations Area Files, found homosexuality to be common across cultures and to exist in almost all nonhuman species. Their work supported the notion that homosexuality was both natural and widespread (*http://www.aglp.org/gap/1_history/*, accessed April 2, 2013). In December, 1973 homosexual pressure groups succeeded in having homosexuality removed from the list of mental illnesses by the American Psychiatric Association. In the early 1970s homosexuals pushed for anti-discrimination laws. Particularly important was an anti-Anita Bryant campaign in Dade County, FL, after she spoke out against homosexuality. Bryant, a popular singer and beauty queen, fell out of favor with many in the media and celebrity circles when she spoke out. See *http://www.gvsu.edu/allies/a-brief-history-of-homosexuality-in-america-30.htm*, accessed on April 2, 2013.

[8] Robert H. Bork, *Slouching Towards Gomorrah*, 142.

are clearly seen, being understood by the things that are made, even his eternal power and Godhead; so that they are without excuse: Because that, when they knew God, they glorified him not as God, neither were thankful; but became vain in their imaginations, and their foolish heart was darkened. Professing themselves to be wise, they became fools, and changed the glory of the uncorruptible God into an image made like to corruptible man, and to birds, and fourfooted beasts, and creeping things. **Wherefore God also gave them up to uncleanness through the lusts of their own hearts,** to dishonour their own bodies between themselves: Who changed the truth of God into a lie, and worshipped and served the creature more than the Creator, who is blessed for ever. Amen. **For this cause God gave them up unto vile affections**: for even their women did change the natural use into that which is against nature: And likewise also the men, leaving the natural use of the woman, burned in their lust one toward another; men with men working that which is unseemly, and receiving in themselves that recompence of their error which was meet. And even as they did not like to retain God in their knowledge, **God gave them over to a reprobate mind**, to do those things which are not convenient; Being filled with all unrighteousness, fornication, wickedness, covetousness, maliciousness; full of envy, murder, debate, deceit, malignity; whisperers, backbiters, haters of God, despiteful, proud, boasters, inventors of evil things, disobedient to parents, without understanding, covenantbreakers, without natural affection, implacable, unmerciful: who knowing the judgment of God, that they which commit such things are worthy of death, not only do the same, but have pleasure in them that do them (Rom. 1:18-32).

I have highlighted these three times in which Paul said that "God gave them up. . ." as a judgment against their choice to remove God from their knowledge. Man has the freedom of will to choose what he wishes to do, but he cannot choose the consequences of having made that choice. Sin has the seed of its own destruction within itself. Unbridled sin destroys a society. We are witnessing within our own culture the effects of man's decision to cast aside the Christian beliefs and value system. As a consequence, the society in which my generation was reared in America is far different than the one in which my grandchildren are being reared.

Now It Is Different!

That the American family is unstable[9] is apparent from many statistical evidences: the divorce rate, the number of couples living together outside

---

[9] Of course, this is a generalization. Many Americans have good, stable homes and are passing down good family traditions to their children and grandchildren.

of wedlock, successive generations of adults who are unable to qualify for and hold a job, undisciplined children, failing schools, churches with no young families, and the list can be extended. Let's look at some details.

Divorce. Divorce has become so commonplace in our society that few families have escaped its blight. No-fault divorce laws have made it easier to tear apart the family. Consider these statistics showing how prominent divorce has become in twenty-first century American culture:

> Various studies on US rate of divorce show significant differences when a comparison is made in 1st, 2nd and 3rd marriage breakups in America. The marriage breakup rate in America for first marriage is 41% to 50%; the rate after second marriage is from 60% to 67% and the rate in America for 3rd marriage are from 73% to 74%. Reports also say that couples with children have a slightly lower rate of breakup as compared to couples without children. This is due to the fact that being childless is one of the prime causes behind divorce in America. Also, the children of divorced parents are prone to divorcing 4 times more than the children of couples who are not divorced.[10]

Recent trends toward lower divorce rates is not caused by a greater commitment to marriage, but by the increase in the number of people who are living together outside of marriage.

> Rates have been dropping during the last few decades. Data indicates that marriages have lasted longer in the 21st century as compared to the success rate of marriages in the 1990s. Also experts believe that the current rates trend might go down more in coming years as more and more couples prefer a live-in relationship. This is a type of relationship where couples live together like partners without marrying.[11]

Cohabiting Couples: Living Together Outside the Bonds of Marriage. Sharon Jayson wrote, "The number of unmarried couples living together increased tenfold from 1960 to 2000, the U.S. Census says; about 10 million people are living with a partner of the opposite sex. That's about 8% of U.S. coupled households. Data show that most unmarried partners who live together are 25 to 34."[12] In an article appearing in the April 5, 2013 issue

---

[10] *http://www.divorcestatistics.info/divorce-statistics-and-divorce-rate-in-the-usa.html*, accessed 2/19/2013.

[11] *Ibid.*

[12] "Cohabitation is Replacing Dating," *http://usatoday30.usatoday.com/life/lifestyle /2005-07-17-cohabitation_x.htm*, accessed 2/19/2013.

of *The Indianapolis Star*, Jayson reported on a survey of 12,279 women, ages 15-44, for the period of 2006 to 2010.

For almost half of women ages 15-44, their "first union" was cohabitation rather than marriage, according to a new study. . . .

Among the survey's findings:

- As a first union, 48 percent of women cohabited with their male partner, up from 43 percent in 2002 and 34 percent in 1995.

- 23 percent of first unions were marriages, down from 30 percent in 2002 and 39 percent in 1995. . . .

- 22 months is the median duration of first cohabitation, up from 20 months in 2002 and 13 months in 1995.

- 19 percent of women became pregnant and gave birth in the first year of a first premarital cohabitation.

- Within three years of cohabiting, 40 percent of women had transitioned to marriage; 32 percent remained living together; 27 percent had broken up.[13]

Jay Tolson posted "No Wedding? No Ring? No Problem" on the *U.S. News & World Report* site in which he said that "more than half of today's newlyweds live together before tying the knot." Quoting University of Michigan sociologist, Pamela J. Smock, Tolson reported, "About one half of previously married cohabitors and 35 percent of never-married cohabitors have children in the household."[14]

Redefining Family. The homosexual agenda is pressing hard to force their homosexual agenda on public institutions. They do not ask that everyone practice homosexuality, but do *demand* that those who speak their convictions that homosexuality is sinful and immoral behavior be fired from their jobs, put on administrative leave without pay, forced to go through diversity training, etc. Homosexuals came out of the closet in the early morning hours of June 28, 1969 at Stonewall Inn in the Greenwich Village neighborhood of New York City, but now have made themselves such a political force that they shape the dialogue in public media, newspapers,

---

[13] "Cohabitation Replacing Marriage?," The Indianapolis Star, April 5, 2013, p. A4.

[14] *http://www.usnews.com/usnews/culture/articles/000313/archive_021163.htm*, accessed 2/19/2013.

school districts, and business. A corporation whose CEO speaks out against homosexuality is certain to receive bad publicity; a successful person who announces his homosexuality is immediately a media hero. The homosexual agenda is a spiritual force to be reckoned with. Homosexuals demand the same legal standing for gay couples as is given to husbands and wives.

The effect of calling sodomy marriage is to legitimize it. If one acknowledges that homosexual relationships are "gay marriage," then one is taken down the civil rights trail. How can one treat "gay marriages" any differently than he treats heterosexual marriages? Even Christians are buying into the argument that gay couples should be granted equal civil rights. We then ask, what rights do bigamists have? Pedophiles? The very admission that sodomy is a marriage undermines Christian teaching and is a capitulation to humanist values. Homosexuality is sinful. It is uncleanness that dishonors one's body (Rom. 1:24); it is vile affections (Rom. 1:26); it is against nature, against the natural use of the body (Rom. 1:26); it is base lust (Rom. 1:27); it is unseemly (*aschēmonsunēn*, from the root word meaning "shame," Rom. 1:27); it manifests a reprobate mind (Rom. 1:28); it is improper conduct (Rom. 1:28); and, it causes one to receive "in themselves that recompense of their error which was meet" (Rom. 1:27). Clinton D. Hamilton explained the meaning of this judgment saying,

> It should be observed that vv. 24-28 state that when they rejected God and exchanged the glory and the truth that God is, there was then their acceptance of a lie. God "gave them up to uncleanness through the lusts of their own hearts, to dishonour their own bodies between themselves . . . unto vile affections," and accordingly, "receiving in themselves that recompense of their error which was meet." For their idolatry, God's judicial punishment or recompense was the dishonoring of themselves, and thus in themselves receiving the penalty for their rejection of him. Seen in this light, the first view[15] appears to be correct and in harmony with both the language and the larger context. It is also true secondarily that their bodies receive whatever dire consequences come from such acts as contradict the function and purpose for which they were created by the Creator.[16]

Children in Broken Homes. As of 2003, 43.7% of custodial mothers and 56.2% of custodial fathers were either separated or divorced. In 2002, 7.8

---

[15] Their sexual perversion is punishment for their exchanging the true God for a lie.

[16] Clinton D. Hamilton, *Truth Commentaries: Romans,* 93-94.

million Americans paid about $40 billion in child and/or spousal support.[17] Broken homes frequently result in absentee fathers, children whose fathers are not involved in their lives, or are less involved because of divorce or out of wedlock births. Paul R. Amato wrote, "Research clearly demonstrates that children growing up with two continuously married parents are less likely than other children to experience a wide range of cognitive, emotional, and social problems, not only during childhood, but also in adulthood."[18] Christine C. Kim, Policy Analyst in the Domestic Policy Studies Department of the Heritage Foundation, added,

> While numerous education reforms over the last quarter century have demonstrated little impact on overall student achievement, the research clearly shows that the intact family structure and strong parental involvement are significantly correlated with educational outcomes, from school readiness to college completion. Instead of favoring proven ineffective education policies, policy makers seeking effective education reform should consider policies that strengthen family structure in America and bolster parental involvement and choice in education.[19]

Despite the predominance of evidence verifying the obvious – that children living with their biological parents are more likely to be well adjusted than others – public policy is directed toward providing support for lifestyles than discourage this ideal. Easy divorce, aid for dependent children, food stamps, and other programs make possible the lifestyle choice of fathers to walk away from their wives and children. Government checks provide the financial support for mothers to divorce themselves from the father of their children (or never to marry him in the first place). An increasing number of homes are supported by government checks, not by the wages that the natural father provides for his wife and children.

---

[17] http://www.divorcestatistics.info/divorce-statistics-and-divorce-rate-in-the-usa.html, accessed 2/19/2013.

[18] "The Impact of Family Formation Change on the Cognitive, Social and Emotional Well-Being of the Next Generation," *The Future of Children*, 15:2 (Fall, 2005), p. 89.

[19] "Academic Success Begins at Home: How Children Can Succeed in School," posted September 22, 2008 at *http://www.heritage.org/research/reports/2008/09/academic-success-begins-at-home-how-children-can-succeed-in-school*, accessed 2/27/2013.

Reshaping the Family:
The Evolution of the Family on American TV Sitcoms

One of the primary influences on the change in American social trends is the television. It certainly has a significant impact on the family. In recent years, the "typical" American family, as portrayed on TV sitcoms, has changed drastically. In the 1950s, the TV programs that were based on the typical American family included such programs as *Leave It To Beaver* (1957-1963), *I Love Lucy* (1951-1957), *Father Knows Best* (1954-1960), *The Andy Griffin Show*[20] (1960-1968), *The Dick van Dyke Show* (1961-1966), *The Brady Bunch*[21] (1969-1974), *The Waltons* (1972-1981), and the Cunningham family on *Happy Days* (1974-84).

As the TV sitcom evolved, the role of the father was changed from the model displayed in *Father Knows Best* to shows where father was the least likely to know best, in such programs as Norman Lear's *All in the Family*[22] (1971-1979) and *The Cosby Show*[23] (1984-1992). *My Three Sons* (1960-1965) chronicled the life of a widower[24] raising his sons with the help of

---

[20] The family unit depicted in the Andy Griffin show was a father, son, and Aunt Bee filling the mother's traditional role.

[21] *The Brady Bunch's* real contribution as a game-changer was its emphasis on the blended family, at a time when divorce rates were on the rise. Mike Brady was a widower, but Carol was a divorcee – though it was never addressed outright on the show. Either way, it was one of the first sitcom families not completely related by blood, a blended family.

[22] The father, Archie Bunker, is presented as a working class bigot whose views are out of touch with reality. His character was used to lampoon the traditional position (more conservative politically and morally) so that the liberal position on various political and social issues looked more reasonable and attractive.

[23] Bill Huxtable, the father, is consistently shown to be less sensible than his wife, who shows the wisest leadership in the family. A major advancement in this series was that it featured a black family. Significantly, also, both the husband and the wife had careers.

[24] Deviations from the father, mother, and children pattern for the family was usually a result of a death in the family, rather than divorce which was eschewed in those days. *Maude* was the first to feature a divorced heroine who also had the first prime-time abortion. Shows like *One Day at a Time* and *Kate and Allie* featured divorced mothers. *Murphy Brown* took on single motherhood. Vice-President Dan Quayle delivered a speech on May 19, 1992 chiding the fictional character Murphy Brown for her decision to have a child outside of marriage. The

Uncle Charley, who effectively managed the household. Tom and Helen Willis on *The Jeffersons* (1975-1985), which premiered in 1975, was one of the early shows to feature interracial marriages.[25]

Shelby Taft observed these changes in the role of families as depicted in the 1980s, "The image of the family on television has now by the 1980's become more of an entertaining parody than a moralizing guideline for families in society."[26] *Who's the Boss?* (1984-1992) featured two single parents who lived together with reversed roles; he was the housekeeper and she was the breadwinner; and in *Kate and Allie* (1984-1989) two divorced mothers lived together, one taking the role of breadwinner and the other the homemaker.

As societal morés continued to shift, the "family" was depicted quite differently in *Three's Company* (1977-1984), *Married With Children*[27] (1987-1997), and *Roseanne*[28] (1988-1997).

Shows such as *Will and Grace*[29] (1998-2006) and *Friends* (1994-2004) presented changes in the depiction of family. In *Will and Grace*, a gay law-yer and a straight Jewish woman who owned an interior design firm decide to move in with each other. Both Will and Grace try to establish romantic relationships with others, while maintaining their reliance upon each other. In *Friends*, the lead characters are six unmarried young adults sharing apart-ments and being involved in various kinds of raucous behavior. The character Ross has one baby with a lesbian couple and another with a straight woman to whom he is not married. *Sister Wives* (2010-) features a polygamous family.

---

liberal news media attacked him mercilessly.

[25] Of course, interracial marriage is not a moral issue, but this program does show TV's influence in creating cultural change in American society.

[26] "The Evolution of the Family on Television," *http://voices.yahoo.com/the-evolution-family-television-1553487.html*, accessed 2/14/13.

[27] *Married With Children* was a mockery of the sitcom family. It was a pioneer in the parody of the traditional sitcom, opting for lessons in immorality as opposed to clichéd family values.

[28] The show dealt with nearly every sensitive topic always promoting the most liberal viewpoint in both societal moral issues and politics.

[29] According to *Wikipedia*, "The show was the highest-rated sitcom among adults 18–49, from 2001 and 2005. Throughout its eight-year run, *Will & Grace* earned 16 Emmy Awards and 83 nominations."

Linda White describes the TV sitcom family depicted in *Modern Family*: "Currently one of the highest-rated TV shows, it explores how one family can take on different forms through the stories of a gay couple and their adopted daughter, a straight couple and their three kids, and the father of the family, who has remarried a younger, Colombian woman with a son."[30]

Some people applaud the reshaping of the family through the use of the TV sitcom. Linda Jimenez wrote, "Let's hear it for the popular TV sitcom *Modern Family*, for its efforts to break down the stereotypes and perceptions of the nuclear family and include, embrace, and celebrate the diversity of our family evolution. This television show has opened the doors for us to include family structures in our diversity and inclusion discussions."[31]

Christians may minimize the influence that television has in shaping values in our country, but businesses do not agree with that assessment. Amber Lee wrote about the cost of commercials for the 2013 Super Bowl, "In 2013 the average 30-second spot costs upward of $4 million. That's roughly a 90 percent increase from a decade ago."[32] Why would a business be willing to spend $4 million to air a 30-second commercial? They are not trying to make a contribution to the network airing the Super Bowl. They believe that this 30-seconds of air time in front of an audience estimated to be 90 to 100 million (2012's Super Bowl audience set a record of 111.3 million viewers) will influence enough people to buy their product that they are willing to spend $4 million to advertise their product. That is a statement about the influence of television on the American population.[33]

Parents, and those of us who are preaching the gospel, must address

---

[30] "Evolution of the TV Family," *http://www.torontosun.com/life/2011/02/15/ 17282261.html,* accessed on 2/14/13.

[31] "The Diversity Evolution of Families," *Profiles in Diversity Journal*, April 21, 2012 (*http://www.diversityjournal.com/9733-the-diversity-evolution-of-families/,* accessed 02/14/13).

[32] *Http://bleacherreport.com/articles/1514409-super-bowl-commercials-2013- grading -the-best-worst-ads.*

[33] If 30-seconds of air time during a Super Bowl has that much influence, what do you think is the influence of continual presentations of sex, immodesty, violence, etc. on society? The television moguls do not want to accept responsibility for their role in the crime wave, saying that such programming does not influence people, but then turn around and charge $4 million for a 30-second ad during the Super Bowl because it will influence people!

television programing as a purveyor of moral teaching. Satan is using the movie and television industry to promote his values. We recognize the television evangelists as false teachers and sometimes address their preaching in Bible classes and the pulpit. These are blatant examples of false teachers – they are preachers, their doctrines are taught under the pretense of being Scripture, their presentations are in a worship service, etc. However, their influence is minimal compared to the influence of the twenty-four hours a day sitcoms, talk shows,[34] movies, news programming, etc. that spew out the secular mind set with its non-Biblical value system. We may have so disciplined ourselves that we have quit watching such programs and we may reassure ourselves that we are not being influenced by the programs we watch, but what influence are these programs having on our children, society, and churches?

Look within! How are we doing in passing down the faith of the Lord Jesus Christ to our children? How many are addicted to the popular music of our generation, use the language of the world, participate in sinful activities of the world (such as drinking, drugs, sex, etc.)? What church has not had to face the situation of a member who has sired or conceived a child out of wedlock? How many of our teenagers drop out of church when they are out on their own? The world is influencing us and our children. One of its main sources of spreading these influences is the ungodly influences of television. What are we doing to address this influence? Largely, we are ignoring it and trying to live as a sub-culture within the society. We have buried our heads in the sand, hoping this will all go away! In the meantime, secularism is rapidly eroding the last standing pillars of a Christian-based society in America, and television is changing American values, making divorce, homosexuality, and gay marriage more acceptable to the American population. Christianity seems much more likely to be persecuted in America's future than to be its most dominating force!

Effects of the Breakdown of the Family on the Nation
American schools. Many inner-city schools are so unsuccessful that the state is taking control of them because they are producing uneducated

---

[34] The influence of Oprah Winfrey's talk show on religion has generated several studies including *Oprah: The Gospel of An Icon* (Kathryn Lofton), *Where Has Oprah Taken Us? The Religious Influence of the World's Most Famous Woman* (Stephen Mansfield), *Oprah, Miracles, and the New Earth: A Critique* (Erwin W. Lutzer), *Oprah Theology: A Comparative Analysis of Oprah Winfrey's Worldview of Christianity and Biblical Christianity* (George B. Davis) and many others.

graduates – young people unprepared for college or trade school, and unable to provide for themselves. These inner-city schools have suffered because those who cared for the welfare of their children and had the funds to do so, fled to suburbia in search of safety and better schools. Add to this that private schools siphon out of public schools the most morally conservative children, whose parents frequently are the most involved in their children's lives. What is left in the public schools is fewer restraining moral forces. Some Christian teachers walk away from, or never enter, the public schools, despite the higher compensation offered, because they do not want to teach in the chaotic environment of the public school. Those who cannot afford to put their children in another district or a private school, and those who do not care, are what are left in the inner-city public schools.

The Centers for Disease Control and Prevention states that the birth rate outside of wedlock for all women is at 40.8%.[35] Breaking this down by race, 29% of whites, 72.5% of Blacks, and 53.4% of Hispanics give birth out of wedlock.[36] When school districts are predominately Black or Hispanics, the number of homes with absentee fathers rises exponentially; the number who depend upon government programs to provide for them is greater. Children who have both their parents heavily involved in their lives have the best opportunity to succeed in school. When the father is absent, and the mother is uninvolved in the schooling process, the child is much less likely to succeed. Teachers are forced to spend too much of their time filling the role of parent, rather than teacher. The schools feed children government subsidized meals, sometimes three meals a day, including during the summer! Sometimes children also have to be bathed, given clothes to wear, and disciplined because they are not getting these things at home. Throwing a few more billion dollars at these failing schools is not going to fix the problem, any more than did the preceding billions that were thrown there! Dollars cannot fix these problems in the schools when the problem is the breakdown of the family. These problems will not be corrected until the family unit is restored!

Violence to the Children and by the Children. Broken homes have led to violence in the home. America's cities have become "war zones" where hundreds are murdered every year, frequently children killing children.

---

[35] *http://www.cdc.gov/nchs/fastats/unmarry.htm*, accessed 2/19/2013.

[36] *http://www.cdc.gov/nchs/data/nvsr/nvsr61/nvsr61_01_tables.pdf#104*, accessed 2/19/2013.

Some schools have so much violence in them that neither the children nor the teachers feel safe. Armed guards are necessary to keep order in the halls. In advocating for abortion rights, America was told that abortion would greatly reduce child abuse, as if abortion itself were not child abuse! Since 1973, Americans have killed over 55,000,000 in our abortion clinics. But not surprisingly, incidents of child abuse continue to increase. The Childhelp organization reports,

> Every year 3.3 million reports of child abuse are made in the United States involving nearly 6 million children (a report can include multiple children). The United States has the worst record in the industrialized nations – losing five children every day due to abuse-related deaths.[37]

Approximately 80% of children who die of child abuse are under age 4.[38] Though the most likely one guilty of child abuse is the natural parent, live-in lovers frequently become involved in child abuse as well. Mackenzie Carpenter, writer for the *Post-Gazette*, quoted Walter Smith, director of Family Resources Inc., a local child-abuse prevention agency to say, ". . . it's very common, either because of a breakdown in attachment, or failure to create one" for live-in lovers to become involved. Carpenter continued:

> "They don't love the kid," said Martin Daly, author of a number of Canadian studies on the issue. "A lot of stepmothers and boyfriends regard the kid as undesired baggage who they wish had never been born. The child remains a resented nuisance at best."

> Daly is the co-author of a 1999 Canadian study that found that an American child living with one genetic parent and one step-parent or a live-in companion was 100 times as likely to suffer fatal abuse as a child living with two genetic parents.[39]

Abused children are more likely to perpetuate the cycle of violence than are those who have not been abused. "According to a National Institute of Justice study, abused and neglected children were 11 times more likely to be arrested for criminal behavior as a juvenile, 2.7 times more likely to be arrested for violent and criminal behavior as an adult, and 3.1 times more

---

[37] *http://www.childhelp.org/pages/statistics*, accessed 2/19/2013.

[38] *Ibid.*

[39] *http://old.post-gazette.com/regionstate/20010426boyfriend2.asp*, accessed 2/19/2013.

likely to be arrested for one of many forms of violent crime (juvenile or adult) (English, Widom, & Brandford, 2004)."[40]

Poverty. The breakdown of the family results in poverty and the most seriously affected is the divorced mother trying to rear her children. Divorce creates poverty because it takes more money to pay two house payments and two sets of utility bills; costs are doubled, but the incomes are not. Frequently, the wife gets the house and the kids (both of which mean a considerable financial burden to maintain, and no possibility for financial gain) and the husband is homeless, though more free of obligations (no mortgage payments, real estate taxes, child care, etc.). As a result one of the growing demographics of poverty is the divorced woman.[41] Poverty affects women almost twice as much as it does men. Here are some results taken from the reports from the United States Census:

- Children living with a parent who divorced in 2009 were more likely to live in a household headed by their mother (75 percent) than in a household headed by their father (25 percent). Additionally, children living with a parent who divorced in 2009 were more likely to be in a household below the poverty level (28 percent) compared with other children (19 percent), and they were more likely to live in a rented home (53 percent) compared with other children (36 percent).
- The economic well-being of those who experienced a recent marital event differed.
- Women who divorced in the past 12 months were more likely to receive public assistance than recently divorced men (23 percent and 15 percent).
- Women who divorced in the past 12 months reported less household income than recently divorced men. For example, 27 percent of women

---

[40] *https://www.childwelfare.gov/pubs/factsheets/long_term_consequences.cfm*, accessed 2/19/2013.

[41] Women's per capita family incomes decline about 30% after a divorce with the largest decline falling on middle-class women and women whose marriages have been of long duration. "Statistics for 1998 showed that in the United States, the median income was fifty-four thousand dollars for married couples, thirty-six thousand dollars for father-headed families, and twenty-two thousand dollars for mother-headed families. Thus, both mother- and father-headed single-parents households have an economic disadvantage compared with two-parent families" (Alison Clarke-Stewart and Cornelia Brentano, *Divorce: Causes and Consequences*, 68).

who divorced in the past 12 months had less than $25,000 in annual household income compared with 17 percent of recently divorced men.
- Similarly, women who divorced in the past 12 months were more likely than recently divorced men to be in poverty (22 percent compared with 11 percent).[42]

In summary, divorce creates poverty! And, unfortunately, the victims are the children and mostly the mother who is trying to rear her children without the husband's income. Admittedly, the father is not as well off as before the divorce (paying child support on top of his usual living expenses diminishes his standard of living), but he is usually better off than the wife and children.

Dependency of Adult Children. Recent studies indicate that a significant change has occurred in the United States culture in the number of adult children who are living at home. The National Endowment for Financial Education posted this information:

- 23% of U.S. adults aged 18-39 who are not students are currently living at home with their parents, significantly higher among men (27%) than women (19%).
- 29% of parents of adults aged 18-39 who are not students indicated that they have adult children who are not students living at home with them.[43]

About 75% of those adult children living at home contributed something toward their parents' increased expenses, and 42% provided some kind of non-financial assistance (cooking, cleaning, etc.).

So significant has this trend of adult children living at home become that there is a new age classification being used by psychologists to describe them: "emerging adults." "According to his theory, people in their 20s go through a time of development that's distinct from other stages of adult-

---

[42] "Divorce Rates Highest in the South, Lowest in the Northeast, Census Bureau Reports," *United States Census* release for August 25, 2011 (*http://www.census. gov/newsroom/releases/archives/marital_status_living_arrangements/cb11-144. html, accessed 2/19/2013*).

[43] *http://www.nefe.org/Portals/0/WhatWeProvide/PrimaryResearch/Consumer Polls /PDF/ParentsSupportingAdultChildren_ExecSumm.pdf*, accessed 2/12/2013. The sampling survey was of 683 U.S. adults ages 18-39 who are not students and 391 parents of children aged 18-39.

hood, and this developmental period explains some of the reluctance of adult children to leave the nest for good," said psychologist Jeffrey Arnett.[44] Sometimes this group is referred to as "boomerang" children. One thing that researchers noted is this:

> Researchers suggest that Generation Y has an inflated sense of self-esteem that clashes unpleasantly with the harsh realities of the modern world. Kids grow up believing that they're special, talented and can be anything they want to be, and when that doesn't always pan out, they easily fall into chronic disappointment and despair. In essence, the idea seems to be that if they cannot have exactly what they want, there is little point in trying; rather than working relentlessly toward their goals, these entitled youngsters simply give up.[45]

Parents who do not accept responsibility for training their children for independent living have failed in one very important goal as a parent. Just as the mother bird raises her young and pushes them out of the nest so that they will be forced to fly on their own, parents must also prepare their children to "fly on their own." There are some important character training values that some parents are neglecting. Consider these:

Responsibility: Children must be taught to accept responsibility for their own choices at an early age. It is better for a child to go through the anguish of not receiving an award for good grades as a fourth grader, because he did not do his homework, than to go through the anguish of punishment for manslaughter because he would not accept responsibility for his speeding and/or drinking and driving. Parents who "bail out" their children from the consequences of their poor choices only teach their children to expect them to bail them out of bigger and bigger problems. I remember a proverb that I have probably imprecisely stated (I could not find it on the internet), but it goes like this: "If you protect your children from the consequences of their foolish behavior, you raise fools!"

Work ethic. Sociologists used to write about the "Protestant work ethic" because it was so deeply engrained into American children. The concept is attributed to Max Weber's book, *Protestant Ethic and the Spirit of Capitalism.* Weber quoted John Wesley to say, "For religion must necessarily

---

[44] Alan Dunn, "Failure to Launch: Adult Children Moving Back Home," posted on Forbes.com (*http://www.forbes.com/sites/moneywisewomen/2012/06/06/failure -to-launch-adult-children-moving-back-home/*, accessed 2/21, 2013).

[45] *Ibid.*

produce both industry and frugality, and these cannot but produce riches" (175). This developed the sense that "people had a *religious duty* to labor selflessly, methodically, conscientiously in their callings in *this world* without undue preoccupations with personal pleasures, sensuous indulgences, and sportive play."[46] Biblical teaching about laziness (Prov. 6:6-11; 10:4, 26; 13:4; 19:15; 20:4, 13, 16; 24:30-34; 28:19), frugality (Prov. 6:11; 13:18; 21:17; 23:21), debt (Prov. 22:7; 17:18; Psa. 37:21), etc. certainly influenced this work ethic, whether or not Weber's was a balanced assessment of the Protestant work ethic. Sadly, however, many parents are failing to train their children to work. Lamentations 3:27 says, "It is good for a man to bear the yoke in his youth." Children should be taught to accept their part of work in enabling the family to survive. Cleaning one's room, making his bed, washing clothes, folding laundry, washing dishes, mowing the yard, washing the car, etc. develop responsibility.

I recall one of my Christmas presents as a youth was getting a red wagon, most probably a Radio Flyer. My father soon taught me how to use the red wagon – to bring in kindling for the fireplace. I was too young to chop wood or bring in the cut wood, but I could do my part by bringing in the kindling. As an elementary school child, I was expected to feed the chickens, gather the eggs, join other family members in pulling weeds from the garden, be part of the family as we planted corn, shelled beans and peas, shucked corn, etc. My family made us feel that work was a means of self-expression associated with one's self-esteem.[47] I was expected to make good grades in school, even if I did not like the teacher or the subject. Going to school was my job and, if one did not like that job, he dropped out of school and followed a hay baler picking up hay, picking cotton, hauling logs, or some other unskilled labor (a few hours of hauling hay in July and August in East Texas will help one learn that going to school to learn a skill that is less demanding on one's body is not all that bad!).

Allowing one's children to stay up all hours of the night, sleep till noon, watch TV or play video games all afternoon, run around with his friends all over town until the wee hours of the morning – and then repeat this day

---

[46] Benjamin Nelson, "Weber's Protestant Ethic: Its Origins, Wanderings, and Foreseeable Future," *Beyond the Classics?*, edited by Charles Y. Glock and Phillip E. Hammond [1973], 72.

[47] Do an internet search on job loss and self-esteem for further information on this topic.

after day – will not teach one's child self-discipline. And, for the sake of those who have not learned yet, being adept at playing a video game is not a job skill! Now add to this undisciplined lifestyle a sloven appearance, an arm full of tattoos, earrings, disrespectful speech, and an "attitude." The result is foreseeable and predictable: One can just about guarantee that a job interview is not going to go well for such a young adult! Soon he will become angry because of how unfairly the world is treating him.

Parents who fail in training their children to accept responsibility for their behavior, to learn a job skill, to manage their money, and such similar basic life skills will more than likely get an opportunity to try their hand at doing this again – they will be required to raise their grandchildren. Their irresponsible children will not likely accept responsibility for their own children and the grandparents will be required to step in to provide for the grandchildren. Not having learned a thing from what they did wrong in raising their children, they are now empowered to cripple a second generation!

America will never be able to rebuild the strength that our nation had in the past without strong families. Our nation was able to take on the strong and powerful enemies of freedom and liberty and of moral wickedness (as illustrated in the Holocaust, for example), fighting wars in two arenas (the Pacific and the Atlantic) at the same time, because of the moral fiber and character of the men and women who made up this great nation. A volunteer army of American soldiers sacrificed themselves and their families for the sake of our country. About 10,000 soldiers died in one day on the shores of Normandy! Over 400,000 American soldiers sacrificed their lives in World War II.

Those who survived that war came home as conquerors who built the most prosperous and one of the most peaceful nations in history. How many of us think that we have the moral fiber to do that again?

America entered World War II, after the December 7, 1941 bombing of Pearl Harbor, in which 2,402 Americans were killed and 1,282 were wounded. On September 11, 2001, America was again attacked, this time by Islamic terrorists, killing 2,753 people. America has lost 4,487 since the start of Operation Iraqi Freedom. Within a very short time, American newspapers and media were mounting an anti-war campaign that demonstrated to our enemy that America did not have the stomach for a prolonged war. The moral fiber of our nation does not appear to have the strength of will to sustain a war effort similar to World War II. And, more importantly for religious studies, American Christianity does not appear to have the doctrinal strength to sustain a life and death struggle with Islam, given its long term commitment to ecumenism. Robert Bork warned about the loss of will in his book, *Slouching Toward Gomorrah*. He said that a society may degenerate until it has a low morale.

> It displays loss of nerve, which means that it cannot summon the will to suppress public obscenity, punish crime, reform welfare, attach stigma to the bearing of illegitimate children, resist the demands of self-proclaimed victim groups for preferential treatment, or maintain standards of reason and scholarship. That is precisely and increasingly our situation today (11).

Effects of Breakdown of the Family on Churches

The breakdown of the family is affecting churches throughout America, as well as the national fabric of our nation. Here are some areas that are clearly evident:

Divorce and Remarriage. Divorce has become so common in the churches across America that little effort is made to enforce what Jesus said about divorce and remarriage. There have been many good studies of Jesus' teaching, but most of them end with a statement that allows one to hold fellowship in the denomination in spite of the fact that he is in a marriage that Jesus labeled as adultery.[48] *The 2008 Book of Discipline of the United Methodist Church* is fairly typical of the way denominations handle divorce and remarriage:

> C) *Divorce*—God's plan is for lifelong, faithful marriage. The church must be on the forefront of premarital, marital, and postmarital counseling in order to create and preserve strong marriages. However, when a married couple is estranged beyond reconciliation, even after thoughtful consideration and counsel, divorce is a regrettable alternative in the midst of brokenness. We grieve over the devastating emotional, spiritual, and economic consequences of divorce for all involved, understanding that women and especially children are disproportionately impacted by such burdens. As the church we are concerned about high divorce rates. It is recommended that methods of mediation be used to minimize the adversarial nature and faultfinding that are often part of our current judicial processes.
>
> Although divorce publicly declares that a marriage no longer exists, other covenantal relationships resulting from the marriage remain, such as the nurture and support of children and extended family ties. We urge respect-

---

[48] John Murray, *Divorce*, 111; William J. Heth and Gordon J. Wenham, *Jesus and Divorce*, 200.

ful negotiations in deciding the custody of minor children and support the consideration of either or both parents for this responsibility in that custody not be reduced to financial support, control, or manipulation and retaliation. The welfare of each child is the most important consideration.

Divorce does not preclude a new marriage. We encourage an intentional commitment of the Church and society to minister compassionately to those in the process of divorce, as well as members of divorced and remarried families, in a community of faith where God's grace is shared by all.[49]

Notice the statement that a "divorce does not preclude a new marriage." The result of this approach is that denominational churches receive into their fellowship those who have divorced for any and every reason and subsequently remarried.

The effect of living in a society in which the churches receive into their fellowship those who have disobeyed the Lord's teaching on divorce and remarriage is that those influences have spilled over into the Lord's church. The laws of most states have moved to no-fault divorce and condoned subsequent marriage, which has raised various issues within the church.[50]

---

[49] *The Book of Discipline of the United Methodist Church*, §161 (*http://www. nyac.com/pages/detail/1755*, accessed 2/25/2013). Similar "double-talk" is in the church's stance toward homosexuality: "The United Methodist Church does not condone the practice of homosexuality and consider this practice incompatible with Christian teaching. We affirm that God's grace is available to all. We will seek to live together in Christian community, welcoming, forgiving, and loving one another, as Christ has loved and accepted us. We implore families and churches not to reject or condemn lesbian and gay members and friends. We commit ourselves to be in ministry for and with all persons."

[50] Churches wrestle with issues such as whether or not the innocent party must initiate the civil filing for divorce for fornication to have the right of remarriage and whether or not the innocent party must obtain the divorce decree to have the right of remarriage. Brethren also wrestle with how to describe a divorce and remarriage that God does not condone: (a) it is an unscriptural divorce and/or marriage; (b) it is a divorce and/or marriage (they are divorced but still "bound"; they are married but not "bound"). Though it appears to me that both of these views come out in the same place, not all agree about that assessment believing that there are significant differences between the two views. With the advent of government defining marriage to include homosexual marriages, brethren are quite properly raising the question, "What role does government play in defining and controlling divorce and remarriage?" In my belief system, men are required to comply with the laws of the land (Rom. 13:1-7), but government has no God-

The problem of broken families has kept some from being converted (the individual was not willing to leave an unscriptural marriage to become a Christian, especially when there are churches just down the road that will welcome the unscripturally divorced and remarried); it has caused others to quit attending worship (the trauma of divorce was more than their faith could stand). Like the nation, American churches are suffering from the breakdown of the family.

Broken families lead to unfaithfulness. Those whose families are broken do not survive as well financially, educationally, emotionally, etc. Neither do they thrive as well spiritually. Broken families lead to children falling away from the faith. Families that stay together, but are not functioning as God taught families to function, also have trouble passing the faith down to their children. Most churches have seen a significant number of their teenagers depart from the faith when they become mature adults.

Christians' children seem to conceive and sire children out of wedlock at about the same percentages as non-Christians. (What church has not had a child conceived out of wedlock in the last five years?) Living with one another outside of wedlock has not been accepted in the churches of Christ, but there are plenty of evidences of premarital sexual activity. Children born out of wedlock put stresses on parents and grandparents. Do mom and dad get married? Are they able to provide for themselves and this new child? Will either husband or wife later feel like he is trapped in an unwanted marriage? These and other questions fill the heads of the expectant couple and their families.

Furthermore, parents who have not raised children prepared to provide for themselves when they become adults create problems for churches as well. If a man cannot demonstrate his ability to lead his family, he cannot qualify to be an elder or deacon in the Lord's church (1 Tim. 3:1-13). As these children who cannot provide for themselves age, they drain the assets of their parents who are not able to provide for two, three, or four dependent families. Adult children who are too irresponsible to hold a job are not likely to be responsible in their service to Christ. Families that do not function as God revealed are not likely to instruct their children about God's ideal for family living. The problem of dysfunctional families is then passed down to another generation.

---

given right to define marriage or bind and loose people in marriage; that is God's prerogative alone!

Broken families lead to their children falling into various sins. A church losing its youth leaves a church with a lot of grey heads and few babies. The church ages and its demise draws nearer and nearer every year. A church that loses more members due to death, apostasy, and moving away than it gains through baptisms, restorations, and new move-ins is destined to die.[51] Unfortunately, the effects of a growing secularism in our culture has diminished the number of people interested in learning about Christ, making church growth more difficult.

Conclusion

What this introduction has tried to demonstrate is that the reshaping of the family that we see occurring in contemporary culture is a result of a decided rejection of the Christian value system that is having a deleterious impact on the American family, churches, and our country. Neither churches nor the country can be strong without strong families!

Lee Wyatt, a Christian in the Panama City Beach church, explained to me his view of living in a society moving farther and farther away from God. What follows is my wording of what he expressed to me. Christians can most influence our society by controlling what is under one's power to control. I cannot have much impact at the national, state, or county level of government, but what I can do is be head of my house! I can teach my children about God's love for mankind as demonstrated by what He has done for my salvation in the Lord Jesus Christ's atoning death at Calvary. I can teach them God's laws for mankind and demonstrate before them the "beauty of holiness" (1 Chron. 16:29; 2 Chron. 20:21; Pss. 29:2; 96:9), so adorning the gospel (Tit. 2:10) that my children want to be Christians because they saw how their mom and I lived. I can help them develop their nascent faith, leading them to an ever growing spiritual maturity (1 Pet. 2:1-2). As my family lives in obedience to God's word, we will generate a little beam of light in the midst of a dark world (Matt. 5:13-16). I can use my opportunities to teach others the gospel, and spread its preservative influence in another home in our city, igniting another light in our city. These things I can do. If enough of us Christians successfully do this, we can be the righteous souls that preserve our nation from a destruction similar to how ten righteous souls could have delivered the

---

[51] The economy also contributes to the death of some churches (when there are no jobs in the area, young people have to go somewhere else for work). The young people moving away leaves an aging and numerically dying church, through no fault of their own.

ungodly cities at Sodom and Gomorrah (Gen. 19). The flood (Gen. 6-8), and the Assyrian and Babylonian captivities of Israel, occurred because wickedness permeated the societies. We see a similar development in our own society. We pray that there are enough righteous souls in our homeland to preserve our nation!

May God bless our efforts to build strong homes for the sake of our children, our churches, and our nation!

Sources Cited

Amato, Paul R. "The Impact of Family Formation Change on the Cognitive, Social and Emotional Well-Being of the Next Generation," *The Future of Children*, 15:2 (Fall, 2005), p. 89.

Bork, Robert H. *Slouching Toward Gomorrah*. New York: HarperCollins Publishers, Inc., 1996.

Carpenter, Mackenzie. *http://old.post-gazette.com/regionstate /20010426boyfriend2.asp*, accessed 2/ 19/2013.

Clarke-Stewart, Alison and Cornelia Brentano. *Divorce: Causes and Consequences*. New Haven, CT: Yale University Press, 2006.

Dunn, Alan. "Failure to Launch: Adult Children Moving Back Home," posted on Forbes.com (*http://www.forbes.com/sites/moneywisewomen/2012/06/06/failure-to-launch-adult-children-moving-back-home/*, accessed 2/21, 2013).

Gorner, Jeremy and Peter Nickeas, "Chicago Police Confirm 'Tragic Number' of 500 Homicides," December 28, 2012, *http://articles.chicagotribune.com/2012-12-28/news/chi-chicago-2012-homicide-toll-20121228_1_latest-homicide-500th-homicide-tragic-number*, accessed 2/19/2013.

Hamilton, Clinton D. *Truth Commentaries: Romans*. Edited by Mike Willis. Bowling Green: Guardian of Truth Foundation, 1998.

Heth ,William J. and Gordon J. Wenham, *Jesus and Divorce*. Nashville: Thomas Nelson Publishers, 1984.

Jayson, Sharon. "Cohabitation is Replacing Dating," *http://usatoday30.usatoday.com/life/life-style/2005-07-17-cohabitation_x.htm*, accessed 2/19/2013.

_____. "Cohabitation Replacing Marriage?," *The Indianapolis Star*, April 5, 2013, p. A4.

Jimenez, Linda. "The Diversity Evolution of Families," Profiles in Diversity Journal, April 21, 2012 (*http://www.diversityjournal.com/9733-the-diversity-evolution-of-families/*, accessed 02/14/13).

Johnson, Max Alan, "Tale of Two Cities: Homicides Plummet in New York, Leap in Chicago," *http://usnews.nbcnews.com/_news/2012/12/29/16218098-tale-of-two-cities-homicides-plummet-in-new-york-leap-in-chicago?lite*, accessed 2/29, 2013.

Kim, Christine C. "Academic Success Begins at Home: How Children Can Succeed in School," posted September 22, 2008 at *http://www.heritage.org/research/reports/2008/09/academic-success-begins-at-home-how-children-can-succeed-in-school*, accessed 2/27/2013.

Murray, John. *Divorce*. Phillipsburg, NJ: Presbyterian and Reformed Publishing Co., 1961.

Nelson, Benjamin. "Weber's Protestant Ethic: Its Origins, Wanderings, and Foreseeable Future," *Beyond the Classics?* Edited by Charles Y. Glock and Phillip E. Hammond. New York: Charles Scribner's Sons, 1973.

Rancinto, Ron, "Detroit Reports Highest Homicide Rate in 20 Years," *http://news.yahoo.com/detroit-reports-highest-homicide-rate-in-20-years-192557311.html*, accessed 2/19/2013.

Taft, Shelby. "The Evolution of the Family on Television," *http://voices.yahoo.com/the-evolution-family-television-1553487.html*, accessed 2/14/13.

Tolson, Jay. "No Wedding? No Ring? No Problem." *http://www.usnews.com/usnews/culture/articles/000313/archive_021163.htm*, accessed 2/19/2013.

White, Linda. "Evolution of the TV Family," *http://www.torontosun.com/life/2011/02/15/ 17282261.html*, accessed on 2/14/13.

The Home in America

The Broken Home in America

John Humphries

The devil wasted no time in attacking the home as far as the Bible record is concerned. No sooner had God arranged the home in the Garden of Eden, than Satan, in the form of the serpent, made his diabolical move to create havoc in God's creation (Gen. 3). Any assault against the home, therefore, is an assault against Almighty God who established the home.

Let us look briefly at God's creation and orderly arrangements that He put in place for the benefit of mankind and for our Creator's own ultimate glory.

When God created the world, the phrase, "And God saw that it was good," occurs over and over in Genesis 1 (vv. 10, 12, 18, 21, 25, cf. v. 31). God was pleased with His creation, but He wasn't finished yet. He "planted a garden eastward in Eden" and placed the man whom He had created there (Gen. 2:8). Even yet, He was not finished with His work of creation. He saw that it was not good for man to be alone and thus woman was created as a

---

John Humphries was born on December 30, 1937 in Lamar, South Carolina. He began preaching the gospel in the late 1950s. John did located preaching and/or teaching work in Annapolis, MD; Harrisburg, PA; Hopewell, VA; Poughkeepsie, NY; Louisville, KY; and at present, Montgomery, AL. John also began a long time effort of gospel work in India in 1976. He made annual trips of over six weeks of gospel work in India until recent years when he needed to remain at home in order to care for his faithful companion and wife of over fifty-one years, Elva, who passed from this life with ALS (Lou Gehreg's Disease) in 2012. John has done extensive radio and TV preaching over the years as well. He has authored a commentary on Jeremiah-Lamentations for the *Truth Commentary* series and a workbook for the *Bible Text Book* series as well (Jeremiah-Lamentations). As previously indicated, John now resides in Montgomery, AL with his new companion and help-meet, Edna, who had previously lost her husband of over fifty-one years to cancer. John and Edna are members of the Perry Hill Road church of Christ in Montgomery.

"helper comparable" to the man (v. 18). The Bible thus makes it abundantly clear concerning the origin of the family. The home or family (husband, wife, and children) is not the product of alleged human evolution. Nor is it the invention of any human ecclesiastical hierarchy. The human family was conceived in the omniscient mind of God and was established by His omnipotent hand (vv. 24-25). In the marriage arrangement when a man leaves his father and mother and becomes joined to his wife, it is God who has joined them or bound them together as one (Matt. 19:6). Furthermore, they are under a binding covenant with the Almighty God and with one another (Mal. 2:14). Husband and wife are thus divinely bound together and until death shall they part (Rom. 7:2).

God hates any and every assault against marriage and the home (Mal. 2:16) and woe unto any who would dare to put a marriage (their own or any other's) asunder (Matt. 19:6). When a marriage or a home is broken up, sin definitely is involved on the part of either the husband or the wife. In a divorce, someone is guilty of a sin or even multiple sins as one or both marriage partners have violated God's word in one or more instances and thus have caused this marriage to fail. In many cases both husband and wife are culpable when the breakup occurs, but at least someone has crossed the line at some point and has, therefore, angered the Lord by destroying the marriage. And if others (whoever they may be) are also involved in the destruction of a home, then they too will face the wrath of Almighty God (cf. Heb. 13:3; Mark 10:9). This includes those who counsel, teach, or preach false doctrine and thereby mislead people to enter into or remain in an adulterous relationship. Certainly, any third party who commits adultery with the husband or wife, or any and all busy-body in-laws who interfere with the marriage, or anyone who fosters or encourages, in any way, the violation of God's laws, as taught in the Bible, concerning marriage and the home will have blood on their hands (Matt. 12:36-37; James 3:1; Acts 20:26-27; Ezek. 3:16-21).

There are serious consequences (in time and for eternity) concerning the violation of God's teaching concerning sexual conduct (Prov. 6:32-35; Rom. 1:27; Gal. 5:19-21; Heb. 13:4). The only place or relationship where sexual expression may be exercised and be acceptable to God is in the marriage bond of a man and a woman joined together in holy matrimony for as long as they shall live upon God's earth. This is made clear by Jesus in Matthew 19:4-6 as He cites Genesis 1:27 and 2:24.

And He answered and said to them, "Have you not read that He who made *them* at the beginning *'made them male and female,'* and said, *'For this reason a man shall leave his father and mother and be joined to his wife, and the two shall become one flesh'*? So then, they are no longer two but one flesh. Therefore what God has joined together, let not man separate."

Satan sought to undermine God's authority with his deception of Eve (Gen. 3:1). This attack against the authority of God created tension in the home (cf. Gen. 3:12). Though we are not in the Garden of Eden and the Tree of the Knowledge of Good and Evil is not present (to my knowledge), Satan continues to attack the home and his assaults are relentless and cunningly deceptive with many, many casualties and wrecked lives to show for his diabolical work.

Satan uses at least three major allies in his assault against the home. First of all, he turns our own personal lust and unlawful desires against us.

> You have heard that it was said to those of old, "You shall not commit adultery." But I say to you that whoever looks at a woman to lust for her has already committed adultery with her in his heart (Matt. 5:27-28).

> But each one is tempted when he is drawn away by his own desires and enticed. Then, when desire has conceived, it gives birth to sin; and sin, when it is full-grown, brings forth death (James 1:14-15).

> Do not love the world or the things in the world. If anyone loves the world, the love of the Father is not in him. For all that is in the world—the lust of the flesh, the lust of the eyes, and the pride of life—is not of the Father but is of the world. And the world is passing away, and the lust of it; but he who does the will of God abides forever (1 John 2:15-17).

> Beloved, I beg you as sojourners and pilgrims, abstain from fleshly lusts which war against the soul, having your conduct honorable among the Gentiles, that when they speak against you as evildoers, they may, by your good works which they observe, glorify God in the day of visitation (1 Pet. 2:11-12).

Fleshly lust can lead to adultery which, in turn, is a powerful weapon that the devil uses to "war against" the home. Remember David and Bathsheba in 2 Samuel 11? "Fleshly lust" waged "war against (David's) soul" when he saw Bathsheba and he soon committed adultery with her. This led to the murder of Uriah, her husband, and thus that home was destroyed (2 Sam. 12:9-10).

The second tool that Satan uses are the false teachers and their doctrines concerning marriage and what constitutes marriage (including divorce and remarriage). In fact there are numerous sources of false teaching and unholy influences that surround us on every side. Family members, friends, fellow workers, as well as various forms of the media, etc. are some of these sources of error that will mislead us and influence us to do the wrong thing (cf. Rev. 2:20-22). What is especially distressing is that many of those who deceive and mislead us may even appear as "ministers of righteousness," but they are doing Satan's work when they teach doctrines that distort and pervert the Word of the Lord concerning marriage and the home.

> But what I do, I will also continue to do, that I may cut off the opportunity from those who desire an opportunity to be regarded just as we are in the things of which they boast. For such are false apostles, deceitful workers, transforming themselves into apostles of Christ. And no wonder! For Satan himself transforms himself into an angel of light. Therefore it is no great thing if his ministers also transform themselves into ministers of righteousness, whose end will be according to their works (2 Cor. 11:12-15).

To protect ourselves from being misled by error or anything false and contrary to God's will we must have the attitude of the noble Bereans of Acts 17:11. We need to compare all teaching and preaching with the Word of God and reject that which is contrary to the Scriptures.

> These were more fair-minded than those in Thessalonica, in that they received the word with all readiness, and searched the Scriptures daily to find out whether these things were so.

The third set of allies who are tools of Satan is the "spiritual host (army) of wickedness" (the devil and his angels) who are bound for perdition (Matt. 25:41). They are an unseen force (host) of immense evil in the land. The home is certainly one of their targets.

> For we do not wrestle against flesh and blood, but against principalities, against powers, against the rulers of the darkness of this age, against spiritual hosts of wickedness in the heavenly places (Eph. 6:12; cf. Rev. 12:9).

> Now the Spirit expressly says that in latter times some will depart from the faith, giving heed to deceiving spirits and doctrines of demons, speaking lies in hypocrisy, having their own conscience seared with a hot iron, forbidding to marry, and commanding to abstain from foods which God created to be received with thanksgiving by those who believe and know the truth (1 Tim. 4:1-3).

We will note some of the devices and schemes that Satan and his allies use in this relentless attack against the home and family as God would have it. These are truly serious challenges or problems that confront us on a daily basis. All of us without exception will be called upon to deal with these problems at one time or the other and at one level or the other. "There is no discharge in that war, and wickedness will not deliver those who are given to it" (Eccl. 8:8).

The Problem of Divorce

Obviously, one of the main causes of the existence of broken homes is the serious problem of divorce. Divorce displeases God and is certainly to be associated with the works of the flesh that will keep one out of heaven (Mal. 2:16; Gal. 5:19-21).

There is hardly a family anywhere that has not experienced the heart breaking news that some member of the family – some relative – has divorced his mate, or has been divorced by his mate. It is not our assignment in this lectureship to go into the issue of divorce and remarriage. We will simply suggest that the only adult man or woman who can scripturally marry is one who has never been married, one who has put away an adulterous mate, or one whose mate has died. But yet the land abounds with divorced and remarried couples who, we fear, are living in an adulterous relationship. Many continue on in "good standing" with local churches. Please be warned that the Word of God surely does not teach or condone the dozens of contradictory positions that are espoused and promulgated among us. We believe that there is truth on this vital issue and, sadly, that there is also a lot of error being taught and practiced. We also trust that none of us desires to have anyone's blood on his hands when he stands before the Lord in judgment. And stand before the Lord and give answer all of us surely will one day!

We need to remember that not only does divorce displease the Almighty God of heaven and earth, but it also seriously harms any of the innocent children that are the helpless victims in the breakup of the home.

We are informed by various sources that each year over 1 million American children suffer the divorce of their parents. Moreover, half of the children born this year to parents who are married will see their parents divorce before they turn eighteen. Mounting evidence presented in several social science journals maintain that the devastating physical, emotional, and financial effects that divorce is having on these children will last well into adulthood and affect future generations. Among these broad and damaging effects are the following:

• Children whose parents have divorced are increasingly the victims of abuse. They also exhibit more health, behavioral, and emotional problems and are involved more frequently in drug abuse as well as have higher rates of suicide.

- Children of divorced parents perform more poorly in reading, spelling, and math. They also are more likely to repeat a grade and to have higher dropout rates and lower rates of college graduation.

- Families with children who were not poor before the divorce see their income drop as much as 50 percent. Almost 50 percent of the parents with children who are going through a divorce move into poverty after the divorce.

- Religious worship, which has been linked to better health, longer marriages, and better family life, drops off after the parents divorce.

The divorce of parents, even if it is amicable, tears apart the fundamental unit of American society. According to the Federal Reserve Board's 1995 Survey of Consumer Finance, only 42 percent of children aged fourteen to eighteen live in a "first marriage" family – an intact two-parent married family. It should be no surprise to find that divorce is having such profound effects on society.

The emotional hurt is real and therefore not to be taken lightly by anyone contemplating divorce where there are children involved. Some children become painfully torn in their sense of loyalty as they are constantly paraded back and forth between feuding parents fighting over custody rights, where will they "go to church," where will they spend the holidays, vacation times, and on and on it goes. Many times the divorced parents will remarry and thus the situation for the children becomes even more complicated and emotionally disturbing.

Furthermore, God-fearing parents who deeply love the Lord and His truth are absolutely and totally devastated if and when any of their children or grandchildren divorces (or is divorced by) their mate. It is almost unbearable agony and distress. And the tears of their broken hearts continue to flow as the painful memories of the divorce linger on and on over the years. They never really get over the complete anguish of such an experience. It will haunt them to their graves. The hurt and regret, therefore, will never completely go away. God-fearing parents and grandparents truly hurt when their children and grandchildren hurt. And there is no deeper hurt or wound Satan can inflict upon loving parents and grandparents than the ugly, horrible, crushing news that a child or grandchild is "getting a divorce."

Time and space would fail us to deal with all of the worldly, ungodly media (movies, TV shows, novels, etc.) that promote (so-called) easy divorce and remarriage. And certainly not to be overlooked are the multiple marriages of the Hollywood stars that is also one of the effective propaganda tools that Satan uses to encourage widespread divorce in our land.

The Problem of the Absentee Father

Another serious challenge to the stability and wellbeing of the home is the problem of the absentee father. The consequences of fatherless homes are far reaching and seriously affect every aspect of our society. According to the *U.S. Census Bureau*, 24 million children in America live in biological father-absent homes. Consequently, there is an absentee father factor in nearly all of the social issues facing America today.

The National Fatherhood Initiative (NFI) provides the following data on absentee fathers. The data concerning absentee fathers indicates that the social, economical, emotional, physical well-being, and spiritual implications of this problem overlap.

Father Factor in Poverty

* Children in father-absent homes are almost four times more likely to be poor. In 2011, 12% of children in married-couple families were living in poverty, compared to 44% of children in mother-only families.[1]

* In 2008, American poverty rates were 13.2% for the whole population and 19% for children, compared to 28.7% for female-headed households.[2]

* From 1970-1996, there was a 5% increase in child poverty that was nearly all attributed to the rise in single-parent families, especially never-married mothers.[3]

* A study of nearly 5,000 children born to parents in twenty large U.S.

[1] U.S. Census Bureau, Children's Living Arrangements and Characteristics: March 2011, Table C8. Washington DC: 2011.

[2] K. Edin and R. J. Kissane (2010). "Poverty and the American family: a decade in review." *Journal of Marriage and Family*, 72, 460-479.

[3] I. V. Sawhill (2006). "Teenage sex, pregnancy, and nonmarital births." *Gender Issues*, 23, 48-59.

cities found that unmarried childbearing helped sustain high poverty rates due to multiple partner fertility and relationship instability.[4]

Father Factor in Emotional and Behavioral Problems

- Data from three waves of the Fragile Families Study (N= 2,111) was used to examine the prevalence and effects of mothers' relationship changes between birth and age three on their children's well being. Children born to single mothers show higher levels of aggressive behavior than children born to married mothers. Living in a single-mother household is equivalent to experiencing 5.25 partnership transitions.[5]

- A sample of 4,027 resident fathers and children from the Fragile Families and Child Well-Being Survey was used to investigate the effects of a biological father's multipartner fertility (having at least one child with more than one mother) on adolescent health. Resident fathers engaging in multipartner fertility were older, more likely to be White, and had lower education levels and income, compared to fathers with one partner. Results indicated children's externalizing behaviors were negatively affected directly and indirectly when their biological father had children with multiple partners.[6]

- A study of 1,977 children age three and older living with a residential father or father figure found that children living with married biological parents had significantly fewer externalizing and internalizing behavioral problems than children living with at least one nonbiological parent.[7]

Father Factor in Maternal and Child Health

- Infant mortality rates are 1.8 times higher for infants of unmarried mothers than for married mothers.[8]

---

[4] S. McLanahan (2009). "Fragile families and the reproduction of poverty." *Annals of the American Academy of Political and Social Science*, 621, 111-131.

[5] C. Osborne and S. McLanahan (2007). "Partnership instability and child well-being." *Journal of Marriage and Family*, 69, 1065-1083.

[6] J. Bronte-Tinkew, A. Horowitz, and M. E. Scott (2009). "Fathering with multiple partners: Links to children's well-being in early childhood." *Journal of Marriage and Family*, 71, 608–631.

[7] S. L. Hofferth (2006). "Residential father family type and child well-being: investment versus selection." *Demography*, 43, 53-78.

[8] T. J. Matthews, Sally C. Curtin, and Marian F. MacDorman. "Infant Mortality

- High-quality interaction by any type of father predicts better infant health.[9]

- Children living with their married biological or adoptive parents have better access to health care than children living in any other family type.[10]

- Premature infants who have increased visits from their fathers during hospitalization have improved weight gain and score higher on developmental tests.[11]

- When fathers are involved during the pregnancy, babies have fewer complications at birth.[12]

- Babies with a father's name on the birth certificate are four times more likely to live past one year of age.[13]

- Expectant fathers can play a powerful role as advocates of breastfeeding to their wives. Three-fourths of women whose partners attended a breastfeeding promotion class initiated breastfeeding.[14]

Statistics from the 1998 Period Linked Birth/Infant Death Data Set." *National Vital Statistics Reports*, Vol. 48, No. 12. Hyattsville, MD: National Center for Health Statistics, 2000.

[9] D. Carr and K. W. Springer (2010). "Advances in families and health research in the 21st century." *Journal of Marriage and Family,* 72, 743-761.

[10] B. G. Gorman and K. Braverman (2008). "Family structure differences in health care utilization among U.S. children." *Social Science and Medicine*, 67, 1766–1775.

[11] W. L. Coleman, C.F. Garfield, and the Committee on Psychosocial Aspects of Child and Family Health. "Fathers and Pediatricians: Enhancing Men's Roles in the Care and Development of their Children." American Academy of Pediatrics Policy Statement, *Pediatrics*, May, 2004.

[12] A. P. Alio, A. K. Mbah, J. L. Kornosky, P. J. Marty, and H. M. Salihu. "The Impact of Paternal Involvement on Feto-Infant Morbidity among Whites, Blacks, and Hispanics." *Matern Child Health Journal* 2010; 14(5): 735-41.

[13] A. P. Alio, A. K. Mbah, J. L Kornosky, P. J. Marty, and H. M. Salihu. "The Impact of Paternal Involvement on Feto-Infant Morbidity among Whites, Blacks, and Hispanics." *Matern Child Health Journal 2010;* 14(5): 735-41.

[14] Adam J. Wolfberg, *et al*. "Dads as breastfeeding advocates: results from a randomized controlled trial of an educational intervention." *American Journal of*

- Fathers' knowledge about breastfeeding increases the likelihood that a child will be breastfed. Children whose fathers knew more had a 1.76 higher chance of being breastfed at the end of the first month and 1.91 higher chance of receiving maternal milk at the end of the third month. [15]

- Twenty-three percent of unmarried mothers in large U.S. cities reported cigarette use during their pregnancy. Seventy-one percent were on Medicare.[16]

- A study of 2,921 mothers revealed that single mothers were twice as likely as married mothers to experience a bout of depression in the prior year. Single mothers also reported higher levels of stress, fewer contacts with family and friends, less involvement with church or social groups and less overall social support.[17]

- A study of 3,400 middle schoolers indicated that not living with both biological parents quadruples the risk of having an affective disorder.[18]

- Children who live apart from their fathers are more likely to be diagnosed with asthma and experience an asthma-related emergency even after taking into account demographic and socioeconomic conditions. Unmarried, cohabiting parents and unmarried parents living apart are 1.76 and 2.61 times, respectively, more likely to have their child diagnosed with asthma. Marital disruption after birth is associated with a six-fold increase in the likelihood a child will require an emergency

Obstetrics and Gynecology 191 (September, 2004): 708-712.

[15] Lurie Susin, R.O. "Does Parental Breastfeeding Knowledge Increase Breastfeeding Rates?" *Birth* 26 (September, 1999): 149-155.

[16] Sara McLanahan. "The Fragile Families and Child Well-being Study": Baseline National Report. Table 7. Princeton, NJ: *Center for Research on Child Wellbeing,* 2003: 16.

[17] John Cairney and Michael Boyle, *et al.* "Stress, Social Support and Depression in Single and Married Mothers." *Social Psychiatry and Psychiatric Epidemiology* 38 (August 2003): 442-449.

[18] Steven P. Cuffe, Robert E. McKeown, Cheryl L. Addy, and Carol Z. Garrison. "Family Psychosocial Risk Factors in a Longitudinal Epidemiological Study of Adolescents." *Journal of American Academic Child Adolescent Psychiatry* 44 (February, 2005): 121-129.

room visit and five-fold increase of an asthma-related emergency.[19]

Father Factor in Incarceration

- Even after allowing for income, youths in father-absent households still had significantly higher odds of incarceration than those in mother-father families. Youths who never had a father in the household experienced the highest odds.[20]

- A 2002 Department of Justice survey of 7,000 inmates revealed that 39% of jail inmates lived in mother-only households. Approximately 46% of jail inmates in 2002 had a previously incarcerated family member. One-fifth experienced a father in prison or jail.[21]

Father Factor in Crime

- A study of 109 juvenile offenders indicated that family structure significantly predicts delinquency.[22]

- A study of low-income minority adolescents aged 10-14 years found that higher social encounters and frequent communication with nonresident biological fathers decreased adolescent delinquency.[23]

- In a study using data from the National Longitudinal Study of Youth 1997, the researchers examined father-child relationship and father's parenting style as predictors of first delinquency and substance use among adolescents in intact families. The results indicated that a more

[19] Kristin Harknett. "Children's Elevated Risk of Asthma in Unmarried Families: Underlying Structural and Behavioral Mechanisms." Working Paper #2005-01-FF. Princeton, NJ: Center for Research on Child Well-being, 2005: 19-27.

[20] Cynthia C. Harper and Sara S. McLanahan. "Father Absence and Youth Incarceration." *Journal of Research on Adolescence* 14 (September, 2004): 369-397.

[21] Doris J. James. *Profile of Jail Inmates, 2002.* (NCJ 201932). Bureau of Justice Statistics Special Report, Department of Justice, Office of Justice Programs, July, 2004.

[22] Connee Bush, Ronald L. Mullis, and Ann K. Mullis. "Differences in Empathy Between Offender and Nonoffender Youth." *Journal of Youth and Adolescence* 29 (August, 2000): 467-478.

[23] R. L. Coley and B. L. Medeiros (2007). "Reciprocal longitudinal relations between nonresident father involvement and adolescent delinquency." *Child Development, 78, 132–147.*

positive father-child relationship predicts a reduced risk of engagement in multiple first risky behaviors. The positive influence of the father-child relationship on risk behaviors seemed to be stronger for male than for female adolescents.[24]

- A study using data from the National Longitudinal Study of Adolescent Health explored the relationship between family structure and risk of violent acts in neighborhoods. The results revealed that, if the number of fathers is low in a neighborhood, then there is an increase in acts of teen violence. The statistical data showed that a 1% increase in the proportion of single-parent families in a neighborhood is associated with a 3% increase in an adolescent's level of violence. In other words, adolescents who live in neighborhoods with lower proportions of single-parent families and who report higher levels of family integration commit less violence.[25]

- Adolescents, particularly boys, in single-parent families were at higher risk of status, property, and person delinquencies. Moreover, students attending schools with a high proportion of children of single parents are also at risk.[26]

- In a study of INTERPOL crime statistics of 39 countries, it was found that single parenthood ratios were strongly correlated with violent crimes. This was not true 18 years ago.[27]

Father Factor in Teen Pregnancy and Sexual Activity
- Being raised by a single mother raises the risk of teen pregnancy, marrying with less than a high school degree, and forming a marriage where both partners have less than a high school degree.[28]

---

[24] J. Bronte-Tinkew, K. M. Moore, and J. Carrano (2006). "The father-child relationship, parenting styles, and adolescent risk behaviors in intact families." *Journal of Family Issues,* 27, 850-881.

[25] C. Knoester and D. A. Hayne, (2005). "Community context, social integration into family, and youth violence." *Journal of Marriage and Family,* 67, 767-780.

[26] Amy L. Anderson. "Individual and contextual influences on delinquency: the role of the single-parent family." *Journal of Criminal Justice* 30 (November, 2002): 575-587.

[27] Nigel Barber. "Single Parenthood As a Predictor of Cross-National Variation in Violent Crime." *Cross-Cultural Research* 38 (November, 2004): 343-358.

[28] Jay D. Teachman, "The Childhood Living Arrangements of Children and the

• Separation or frequent changes increase a woman's risk of early menarche, sexual activity, and pregnancy. Women whose parents separated between birth and six years old experienced twice the risk of early menstruation, more than four times the risk of early sexual intercourse, and two and a half times higher risk of early pregnancy when compared to women in intact families. The longer a woman lived with both parents, the lower her risk of early reproductive development. Women who experienced three or more changes in her family environment exhibited similar risks but were five times more likely to have an early pregnancy.[29]

• A study using data from two studies of the National Longitudinal Study of Adolescent Health investigates the influence of the parent-child relationship on adolescent virginity status. The researchers examined how adolescents' perceptions of the quality of their parent-child relationships influence the likelihood of first sex among a sample of adolescent virgins living in biologically intact, two-parent families. The results indicate that girls with close father-child relationship were less likely to report first sex. The results did not indicate a direct relationship for boys or with the mother-child relationship.[30]

• A study using a sample of 1,409 rural southern adolescents (851 females and 558 males) aged eleven to eighteen years, investigated the correlation between father absence and self-reported sexual activity. The results revealed that adolescents in father-absent homes were more likely to report being sexually active compared to adolescents living with their fathers. The analysis indicates that father absence can have a detrimental effect on adolescents' lifestyle choices. This study also revealed a statistical significance between father absence and adolescent self-esteem.[31]

Characteristics of Their Marriages." *Journal of Family Issues* 25 (January, 2004): 86-111.

[29] Robert J. Quinlan. "Father absence, parental care, and female reproductive development." *Evolution and Human Behavior* 24 (November, 2003): 376-390.

[30] M. D. Regnerus and L. B. Luchies (2006). "The Parent-Child Relationship and Opportunities for Adolescents' First Sex." *Journal of Family Issues*, 27, 159-183.

[31] C. S. Hendricks, S. K. Cesario, C. Murdaugh, M. E. Gibbons, E. J. Servonsky, R. V. Bobadilla, D. L. Hendricks, B. Spencer-Morgan, and A. Tavakoli (2005). "The influence of father absence on the self-esteem and self-reported sexual

• A study assessing the risk and protective factors associated with early sexual intercourse among low-income adolescents revealed that variables such as, age, gender, race, two-parent households, separated households, households where the mother formed a union, transitioning into welfare, and delinquency increased the odds that adolescents were sexually active. The researchers found that maternal education and father involvement were the only protective factors for early sexual activity. In addition, the risk factors for early sexual contact were age, gender, race, two-parent households, separated households, and delinquency. Among all of the family processes, father involvement was the only factor that decreased the odds of engaging in sexual activity and none of the other family processes were found to be statistically significant.[32]

• In a study exploring the perspectives of daughters who experienced father absence during their childhood and/or adolescent years, the researchers interviewed sexually abused women aged 22-46. During the interviews, participants expressed difficulties forming healthy relationships with men and they associated these difficulties with their experiences of father absence. The interviewees also revealed a strong need for attention and affection from men which was also associated by the participants with the lack of affection received from their fathers. The desire for affection made these females more vulnerable to male attention which put them at higher risk of being exploited by any male who expressed any positive interest in them. Some of their poor relationship decisions were attributed to this vulnerability. One of the participants, when describing her first sexual relationship, stated that the sexual encounter with a friend's father occurred because of her desire for affection and attention from a father figure: "My first sexual encounter. . . . I felt that I had seduced a friend's father. . . . And I thought, no I'm not punishing my father by sleeping with someone else's father. Dad will never know this. Why did I do this?"[33]

---

activity of rural southern adolescents." *ABNF Journal*, 16, 124-131.

[32] T. Jordahl and B. J. Lohman (2009). "A bioecological analysis of risk and protective factors associated with early sexual intercourse of young adolescents." *Children and Youth Services Review* 31, 1272–1282.

[33] L. East, D. Jackson, and L. O'Brien (2007). "'I don't want to hate him forever': Understanding daughter's experiences of father absence." *Australian Journal of Advanced Nursing*, 24, 14-18.

- In a phenomenological study of adolescent mothers' experiences of having become sexually active, it was revealed that teen mothers' experiences of living without a strong father figure were an important factor for having become sexually active. Based on the study findings, the inability to bond in satisfactory ways with a father or father figure may result in earlier onset of sexual activity and the higher risk of teen pregnancy.[34]

- Adolescent girls who reported higher levels of relationship quality with their fathers were less likely to have sex before age sixteen, compared with adolescent girls who reported lower levels of father-daughter relationship quality.[35]

- Adolescent boys who had dinner with their family every day were less likely to have had sex before age sixteen, compared with those who report they eat dinner with their family less than five nights a week. 31% of teen boys who reported having dinner with their family every day were estimated to have had sex before age sixteen, compared with 37% of teen boys who reported that they had dinner with their family fewer than five days a week.[36]

- Researchers using a pool from both the U.S. and New Zealand found strong evidence that father absence has an effect on early sexual activity and teenage pregnancy. Teens without fathers were twice as likely to be involved in early sexual activity and seven times more likely to get pregnant as an adolescent.[37]

Father Factor in Child Abuse
- A study using data from the Fragile Families and Child Wellbeing

[34] V. E. Burn (2008). "Living without a strong father figure: A context for teen mothers' experience of having become sexually active." *Issues in Mental Health Nursing*, 29, 279–297.

[35] E. Ikramullah, J. Manlove, C. Cui, and K. A. Moore (2009). "Parents matter: The role of parents in teens' decisions about sex." Washington, DC: *Child Trends*.

[36] E. Ikramullah, J. Manlove, C. Cui, and K. A. Moore (2009). "Parents matter: The role of parents in teens' decisions about sex." Washington, DC: *Child Trends*.

[37] Bruce J. Ellis, John E. Bates, Kenneth A. Dodge, David M. Ferguson, L. John Horwood, Gregory S. Pettit, and Lianne Woodward. "Does Father Absence Place Daughters at Special Risk for Early Sexual Activity and Teenage Pregnancy?" *Child Development* 74 (May/June, 2003): 801-821.

Study revealed that in many cases the absence of a biological father contributes to increased risk of child maltreatment. The results suggest that Child Protective Services (CPS) agencies have some justification in viewing the presence of a social father as increasing children's risk of abuse and neglect. It is believed that in families with a non-biological (social) father figure, there is a higher risk of abuse and neglect to children, despite the social father living in the household or only dating the mother.[38]

- In a study examining father-related factors predicting maternal physical child abuse risk, researchers conducted interviews with mothers of three-year-old children. The results revealed that mothers who were married to fathers were at lower risk for maternal physical child abuse. Moreover, it was found that higher educational attainment and positive father involvement with their children were significant predictors of lower maternal physical child abuse risk.[39]

Father Factor in Drug and Alcohol Abuse

- Even after controlling for community context, there is significantly more drug use among children who do not live with their mother and father.[40]

- In a study of 6,500 children from the ADDHEALTH database, father closeness was negatively correlated with the number of a child's friends who smoke, drink, and smoke marijuana. Closeness was also correlated with a child's use of alcohol, cigarettes, and hard drugs and was connected to family structure. Intact families ranked higher on father closeness than single-parent families.[41]

- Youths are more at risk of first substance use without a highly involved father. Each unit increase in father involvement is associated with 1%

[38] "CPS Involvement in Families with Social Fathers." *Fragile Families Research Brief* No.46. Princeton, NJ and New York, NY: Bendheim-Thomas Center for Research on Child Wellbeing and Social Indicators Survey Center, 2010.

[39] N. B. Guterman, L. Yookyong, S. J. Lee, J. Waldfogel, and P. J. Rathouz (2009). "Fathers and maternal risk for physical child abuse." *Child Maltreatment*, 14, 277-290.

[40] John P. Hoffmann. "The Community Context of Family Structure and Adolescent Drug Use." *Journal of Marriage and Family* 64 (May, 2002): 314-330.

[41] *National Fatherhood Initiative.* "Family Structure, Father Closeness, and Drug Abuse." Gaithersburg, MD: National Fatherhood Initiative, 2004: 20-22.

reduction in substance use. Living in an intact family also decreases the risk of first substance use.[42]

- Using data from the National Longitudinal Study of Adolescent Health, researchers examined the relationship between parent-child involvement, such as shared communication, shared activity participation, and emotional closeness and three adolescent alcohol outcomes, including alcohol use, alcohol related problems, and risky behavior co-occurring with alcohol use. This study investigated both paternal and maternal involvement in understanding adolescent alcohol outcomes. The results indicate that shared communication with fathers and emotional closeness to fathers, but not shared activity participation, had a unique impact on each alcohol outcome and were not related to maternal involvement.[43]

- A study with 441 college students revealed that a poor parental bond with one's father was highly predictive of depression, a well-known predictor of alcohol abuse and related problems for both females and males. These findings suggest evidence for parental influences on pathways to alcohol abuse through depression.[44]

- A study of 296 at-risk adolescents whose fathers were drug abusers revealed that paternal smoking and drug use led to strained father-child relationships. This weakened relationship led to greater adolescent maladjustment with family and friends and a higher risk for adolescent drug use and smoking. Fathers who smoke cigarettes were less likely to enforce antismoking rules for their children and had weaker bonds in terms of adolescent admiration and emulation.[45]

---

[42] Jacinta Bronte-Tinkew, Kristin A. Moore, Randolph C. Capps, and Jonathan Zaff. "The influence of father involvement on youth risk behaviors among adolescents: A comparison of native-born and immigrant families." Article in Press. *Social Science Research,* December, 2004.

[43] E. A. Goncya and M. H. van Dulmena (2010). "Fathers do make a difference: Parental involvement and adolescent alcohol use." *Fathering,* 8, 93–108.

[44] J. A. Patock-Peckham and A. A. Morgan-Lopez (2007). "College drinking behaviors: Mediational links between parenting styles, parental bonds, depression, and alcohol problems." *Psychology of Addictive Behaviors,* 21, 297–306.

[45] D. W. Brook, J. S. Brook, E. Rubenstone, C. Zhang, and C. Gerochi (2006). "Cigarette smoking in the adolescent children of drug-abusing fathers." *Pediatrics,* 117, 1339-1347.

- In a study using a sample of 86 African American adolescents, the researchers assessed the effects of father's absence on adolescent drug use. The results revealed that boys from father-absent homes were more likely than those from father-present homes to use drugs. Interestingly, the results didn't reveal any difference between father-present and father-absent girls' self-reported drug usage. For girls, friends' drug use was the main predictor of drug use, while father absence was for boys. African American boys from father-absent homes might be at increased risk for drug use problems.[46]

- Even after controlling for community context, there is significantly more drug use among children who do not live with their mother and father.[47]

Father Factor in Childhood Obesity

- The National Longitudinal Survey of Youth found that obese children are more likely to live in father-absent homes than are non-obese children.[48]

- In a study using a sample of 2,537 boys and 2,446 girls, researchers investigated the relationship between Body Mass Index (BMI) status at ages four to five years and mothers' and fathers' parenting involvement and parenting styles. The results showed that only fathers' parenting behaviors and styles were associated with increased risks of child overweight and obesity. Mothers' parenting behaviors and styles were not associated with a higher likelihood of children being in a higher BMI category. In the case of fathers, however, higher father control scores were correlated with lower chances of the child being in a higher BMI category. Moreover, children of fathers with permissive and disengaged parenting styles had higher odds of being in a higher BMI category.[49]

- A study that looked at family lifestyle and parent's Body Mass Index

[46] J. Mandara, and C. B. Murray (2006). "Father's absence and African American adolescent drug use." *Journal of Divorce and Remarriage*, 46, 1-12.

[47] John P. Hoffmann, "The Community Context of Family Structure and Adolescent Drug Use." *Journal of Marriage and Family* 64 (May, 2002): 314-330.

[48] *National Longitudinal Survey of Youth.*

[49] M. Wake, J. M. Nicholson, P. Hardy, and K. Smith (2007). "Preschooler obesity and parenting styles of mothers and fathers: Australian national population study," *Pediatrics*, 12, 1520-1527.

(BMI) over a nine year period found: A fathers' body mass index (a measurement of the relative composition of fat and muscle mass in the human body) is directly related to a child's activity level. In a study of 259 toddlers, more active children were more likely to have a father with a lower BMI than less active children.

- ° Father's Body Mass Index (BMI) predicts son's and daughter's BMI independent of offspring's alcohol intake, smoking, physical fitness, and father's education

- ° Furthermore, BMI in sons and daughters consistently higher when fathers were overweight or obese

- ° Physical fitness of daughters negatively related to their father's obesity

- ° Obesity of fathers associated with a four-fold increase in the risk of obesity of sons and daughters at age eighteen.[50]

- Children who lived with single mothers were significantly more likely to become obese by a six-year follow-up, as were black children, children with nonworking parents, children with nonprofessional parents, and children whose mothers did not complete high school.[51]

Father Factor in Education
- Father involvement in schools is associated with the higher likelihood of a student getting mostly A's. This was true for fathers in biological parent families, for stepfathers, and for fathers heading single-parent families.[52]

---

[50] V. Burke, L. J. Beilin, and D. Dunbar. "Family lifestyle and parental body mass index as predictors of body mass index in Australian children: a longitudinal study." Department of Medicine, Royal Perth Hospital, University of Western Australia, and the Western Australian Heart Research Institute; Perth, Australia.

[51] R. S. Strauss and J. Knight. "Influence of the home environment on the development of obesity in children." Division of Pediatric Gastroenterology and Nutrition, University of Medicine and Dentistry of New Jersey, Robert Wood Johnson School of Medicine, New Brunswick, NJ.

[52] Christine Winquist Nord and Jerry West. Fathers' and Mothers' Involvement in Their Children's Schools by Family Type and Resident Status (NCES 2001-032). Washington, DC: U.S. Department of Education, National Center for Education Statistics, 2001.

- A study assessing 4,109 two-parent families examined the effects of early maternal and paternal depression on child expressive language at age twenty-four months and the role that parent-to-child reading may play in child's language development. The results revealed that for mothers and fathers, depressive symptoms were negatively associated with parent-to-child reading. Only for fathers, however, was earlier depression associated with later reading to child and related child expressive vocabulary development. The less the fathers read to their infants, the worse their toddler scored on a standard measure of expressive vocabulary at age two. Parents' depression has more impact on how often fathers read to their child compared to mothers, which in turn influences the child's language development.[53]

- A study revealed that youth who have experienced divorce, separation, or a nonunion birth have significantly higher levels of behavioral problems in school than do youth who have always lived with both biological parents. In contrast to previous GPA findings, youth living in stepfamilies or single-parent families are both more susceptible to school-related behavioral problems than youth who have always lived with both biological parents.[54]

- Students living in father-absent homes are twice as likely to repeat a grade in school; 10% of children living with both parents have ever repeated a grade, compared to 20% of children in stepfather families and 18 percent in mother-only families.[55]

- Students in single-parent families or stepfamilies are significantly less likely than students living in intact families to have parents involved in their schools. About half of students living in single-parent families or stepfamilies have parents who are highly involved, while 62% of

---

[53] J. F. Paulson, H. A. Keefe, and J. A. Leiferman (2009). "Early parental depression and child language development." *Journal of Child Psychology and Psychiatry*, 50, 254–262.

[54] K. H. Tillman (2007). "Family structure pathways and academic disadvantage among adolescents in stepfamilies." *Sociological Inquiry,* 77, 383-424.

[55] Christine Winquist Nord and Jerry West. Fathers' and Mothers' Involvement in Their Children's Schools by Family Type and Resident Status (NCES 2001-032). Washington, DC: U.S. Department of Education, National Center for Education Statistics, 2001.

students living with both their parents have parents who are highly involved in their schools.[56]

- In 2001, 61 percent of 3- to 5-year olds living with two parents were read aloud to everyday by a family member, compared to 48% of children living in single- or no-parent families.[57]

- Kindergarteners who live with single-parents are over-represented in those lagging in health, social and emotional, and cognitive outcomes. Thirty-three percent of children who were behind in all three areas were living with single parents while only 22% were not lagging behind.[58]

- In two-parent families, children under the age of 13 spend an average of 1.77 hours engaged in activities with their fathers and 2.35 hours doing so with their mothers on a daily basis in 1997. Children in single parent families spent on .42 hours with their fathers and 1.26 hours with their mothers on daily basis.[59]

- A study of 1330 children from the PSID showed that fathers who are involved on a personal level with their child's schooling increases the likelihood of their child's achievement. When fathers assume a positive role in their child's education, students feel a positive impact.[60]

A national two-generation longitudinal survey revealed that children who

---

[56] Christine Winquist Nord and Jerry West. Fathers' and Mothers' Involvement in Their Children's Schools by Family Type and Resident Status (NCES 2001-032). Washington, DC: U.S. Department of Education, National Center for Education Statistics, 2001.

[57] Federal Interagency Forum on Child and Family Statistics. America's Children: Key National Indicators of Well-Being, 2002. Table ED1. Washington, DC: U.S. Government Printing Office, 2003.

[58] Richard Wertheimer and Tara Croan, et al. "Attending Kindergarten and Already Behind: A Statistical Portrait of Vulnerable Young Children." *Child Trends Research Brief. Publication* #2003-20. Washington, DC: Child Trends, 2003.

[59] Laura Lippman, et al. Indicators of Child, Family, and Community Connections. Office of the Assistant Secretary for Planning and Evaluation. Washington, DC: U.S. Department of Health and Human Services, 2004.

[60] Brent A. McBride, Sarah K. Schoppe-Sullivan, and Moon-Ho Ho. "The mediating role of fathers' school involvement on student achievement." *Applied Developmental Psychology* 26 (2005): 201-216.

experienced multiple family transitions were more at risk for developmental problems than children who lived in stable, two-parent families.[61]

It is clear that God knows what is best for His creation. He set forth from the beginning that there is to be a father and a mother present together in the home and actively, jointly involved in the proper rearing of children and preparing them to go forth into the world.

Out of Wedlock Children

Closely related to this issue of the absentee father would be the children born out of wedlock where the father is not only absent but perhaps never there at any point except when the fornication took place. The "experts" are all over the place in explaining the tremendous increase in out of wedlock births in this country. In this presentation, we will not go into that area of discussion. We will simply observe that it is obvious to the Bible believer that men and women, boys and girls, are rebellious against God's authority and His Word concerning marriage. They are blatantly ignoring God's strong warnings against fornication and adultery. This rejection of God's authority, as expressed in and through His Word, and open, defiant rebellion against the Lord has become a way of life for many. God's severe judgment faces those guilty of all forms of sexual misconduct unless they repent and turn to the Lord.

> Marriage is honorable among all, and the bed undefiled; but fornicators and adulterers God will judge (Heb. 13:4).

The Problem of Abusive Parents

Child abuse is far more than bruises and broken bones. Physical abuse might be the most visible but there are other types of abuse, such as emotional abuse and neglect. These also leave deep, lasting scars that can affect a child for the rest of his life. Marital discord, domestic violence or abuse, unemployment or poverty, and social isolation are all factors that can precipitate abuse of children.

It is also a fact that neglect of the child's spiritual welfare by not training and guiding him or her in the Word of God is a serious form of abuse with present and eternal consequences. Parents must set the proper example of spiritual living before their children. To cause a child to stumble through spiritual neglect or by setting a poor example of what a Christian ought to

---

[61] P. Fomby and A. J. Cherlin (2007). "Family instability and child well-being." *American Sociological Review*, 72, 181-204.

be is seriously frowned upon by the Lord (Matt. 18:1-6). There are far too many "millstone" parents in the church and they need to repent and get on with the serious business of raising their children in the fear of the Lord. To do otherwise is but to heap spiritual abuse upon their children. They will face the wrath of God in judgment and suffer the eternal consequences of His rejection!

> At that time the disciples came to Jesus, saying, "Who then is greatest in the kingdom of heaven?" Then Jesus called a little child to Him, set him in the midst of them, and said, "Assuredly, I say to you, unless you are converted and become as little children, you will by no means enter the kingdom of heaven. Therefore whoever humbles himself as this little child is the greatest in the kingdom of heaven. Whoever receives one little child like this in My name receives Me. Whoever causes one of these little ones who believe in Me to sin, it would be better for him if a millstone were hung around his neck, and he were drowned in the depth of the sea."

Wise and truly loving parents will constantly speak of (and consistently reflect in their lives) the Scriptures in the home and engage in regular Bible study with their children (Deut. 6:4-9).

> Hear, O Israel: The LORD OUR GOD, THE LORD is one! You shall love the LORD YOUR GOD WITH ALL YOUR HEART, WITH ALL YOUR SOUL, AND WITH ALL YOUR STRENGTH. And these words which I command you today shall be in your heart. You shall teach them diligently to your children, and shall talk of them when you sit in your house, when you walk by the way, when you lie down, and when you rise up. You shall bind them as a sign on your hand, and they shall be as frontlets between your eyes. You shall write them on the doorposts of your house and on your gates.

In homes where people love God and one another, the problem of child abuse does not exist. Furthermore, where the Word of God is respected and implemented with unfeigned love and genuine faith, abusive parenting is unknown (Eph. 6:1-4). But the plaintive pleading of Reuben to his ruthless brothers concerning their mistreatment of Joseph is a refrain that needs to be heeded in far too many homes across the land – "do not sin against the child" (Gen. 42:22).

The Problem of Spouse Abuse

The problem of spouse abuse is another destructive tool of the devil in his attacks against the home. Spousal abuse, whether it is physical or emotional, is nothing to be taken lightly. The National Institute of Justice states that each year approximately 1.3 million women as well as 835,000 men are victims of domestic abuse in the U.S. In many instances spousal abuse easily and quickly escalates into violent behavior. The immediate consequences include being arrested and possibly doing jail time, having children bear witness to assault, and, in some of the extreme cases, even the death of a mother or a father. The ultimate consequence is to face the judgment of God and the loss of eternal life – unless sincere repentance takes place. We think of the news reports that we hear, or read in the newspaper, and fail to realize that there are even instances of this ungodly behavior taking place in the homes of those professing to be Christians – yes, even among members of the Lord's church. Ephesians 5:25-33 needs to be heeded, or else trouble lies ahead for a marriage.

> Husbands, love your wives, just as Christ also loved the church and gave Himself for her, that He might sanctify and cleanse her with the washing of water by the word, that He might present her to Himself a glorious church, not having spot or wrinkle or any such thing, but that she should be holy and without blemish. So husbands ought to love their own wives as their own bodies; he who loves his wife loves himself. For no one ever hated his own flesh, but nourishes and cherishes it, just as the Lord does the church. For we are members of His body, of His flesh and of His bones. "For this reason a man shall leave his father and mother and be joined to his wife, and the two shall become one flesh." This is a great mystery, but I speak concerning Christ and the church. Nevertheless let each one of you in particular so love his own wife as himself, and let the wife see that she respects her husband.

> Wives, likewise, be submissive to your own husbands, that even if some do not obey the word, they, without a word, may be won by the conduct of their wives, when they observe your chaste conduct accompanied by fear. Do not let your adornment be merely outward—arranging the hair, wearing gold, or putting on fine apparel – rather let it be the hidden person of the heart, with the incorruptible beauty of a gentle and quiet spirit, which is very precious in the sight of God. For in this manner, in former times, the holy women who trusted in God also adorned themselves, being submissive to their own husbands, as Sarah obeyed Abraham, calling him lord, whose daughters you are if you do good and are not afraid with any terror. Husbands, likewise, dwell with them with understanding, giving honor to the wife, as to the weaker vessel, and as being heirs together of the grace of life, that your prayers may not be hindered (1 Pet. 3:1-7).

The Problem of Homosexual Marriages

The challenge of homosexual marriages plaguing our nation is becoming a major device of Satan in his attack against the home. We have pointed out earlier that the Word of God is clear concerning the marriage relationship as ordained by God from the beginning. Consider the words of Jesus again as He reviews the actions and words of the heavenly Father (Mark 10:6-9).

> But from the beginning of the creation, God *"made them male and female. For this reason a man shall leave his father and mother and be joined to his wife, and the two shall become one flesh"*; so then they are no longer two, but one flesh. Therefore what God has joined together, let not man separate.

The language and implications of what is said in the text are clear. Only one man and one woman are to be joined together in a marriage. Only these two are allowed to become "one flesh" which includes the intimate union of husband and wife. This union of husband and wife is not to be separated by the actions of any man as only the Lord God has the authority for such an action to be undertaken – and at the same time be acceptable or scriptural. We have already mentioned the exceptions, specified by God's authority, namely, adultery or the death of one's spouse (Matt. 19:9; Rom. 7:1-2). Any other intimate union besides a husband and wife "joined together" is therefore outside the bounds of what God has authorized and is therefore unlawful and constitutes sin (1 Cor. 6:9-10, 18). This lawful union of a man and a woman thus excludes two men or two women cohabiting together and claiming to be a union or "marriage" acceptable to God. God destroyed the "cities of the plain" for corrupting this sacred relationship of one man and one woman "joined together" in holy matrimony (Gen. 18:20; 19:25; Jude 7). Paul also makes crystal clear God's attitude towards this perversion of the proper sexual relationship between men and women (Rom. 1:24-32).

> Therefore God also gave them up to uncleanness, in the lusts of their hearts, to dishonor their bodies among themselves, who exchanged the truth of God for the lie, and worshiped and served the creature rather than the Creator, who is blessed forever. Amen. For this reason God gave them up to vile passions. For even their women exchanged the natural use for what is against nature. Likewise also the men, leaving the natural use of the woman, burned in their lust for one another, men with men committing what is shameful, and receiving in themselves the penalty of their error which was due. And even as they did not like to retain God in their knowledge, God gave them over to a debased mind, to do those things which are not fitting; being filled with all unrighteousness, sexual immorality, wickedness, covetousness, maliciousness; full of envy, murder, strife, deceit, evil-mindedness; they are whisperers, backbiters, haters of God, violent, proud, boasters, inventors of evil things, disobedient to parents,

undiscerning, untrustworthy, unloving, unforgiving, unmerciful; who, knowing the righteous judgment of God, that those who practice such things are deserving of death, not only do the same but also approve of those who practice them.

The word of God makes it clear that God turns away in disgust and anger from those who rebel against his laws and will judicially give "them up" and hold them "deserving of death" unless they repent of their sin. Repentance and regeneration will provide access to the grace to God and the only hope for those guilty of sin, including the sin of homosexuality (1 Cor. 6:9-11).

> Do you not know that the unrighteous will not inherit the kingdom of God? Do not be deceived. Neither fornicators, nor idolaters, nor adulterers, nor homosexuals, nor sodomites, nor thieves, nor covetous, nor drunkards, nor revilers, nor extortioners will inherit the kingdom of God. And such were some of you. But you were washed, but you were sanctified, but you were justified in the name of the Lord Jesus and by the Spirit of our God.

But the ungodly world ignores and rejects God and continues to rush on and on further and further away from God, all the while spreading more and more of this moral filth into every nook and cranny of our beloved nation. The homosexual movement has gotten political and judicial clout in our society. Laws have been passed to not only protect homosexuals from violence but also to force all of us to give way to the homosexual in our businesses, our rental and sales properties, etc., etc. It perhaps will not be too long before one will hear of a church being sued for withdrawal from a practicing homosexual.

Homosexuals wall the halls of congress, sit in the chairs of college professors, teach in our public schools, occupy judicial benches in the land, preach from pulpits in many churches, marry one another, openly live together, parade up and down our streets, make movies and appear on TV shows, deny or pervert the Bible to seek to justify themselves, and on and on. We are quickly becoming a Sodom and Gomorrah all over again (if not so already) – and don't think for one minute that the Almighty God of heaven and earth is not fully aware of it, and will one day bring us down in judgment!

Homosexuality is all around us and manifests itself as a devastatingly destructive tool of Satan in his unholy war against marriage as ordained by God.

The Problem of Materialism

We must not overlook the problem of materialism as one of the devil's very effective tools in the destruction of the home. There are many, many causalities in this terrible war of materialism, which is actually the battle against covetousness. Covetousness in the Bible is the unholy desire for more and more of this world's goods which is a form of idolatry as we neglect God in the pursuit of the material things of this life.

> If then you were raised with Christ, seek those things which are above, where Christ is, sitting at the right hand of God. Set your mind on things above, not on things on the earth. For you died, and your life is hidden with Christ in God. When Christ who is our life appears, then you also will appear with Him in glory. Therefore put to death your members which are on the earth: fornication, uncleanness, passion, evil desire, and covetousness, which is idolatry (Col. 3:1-5).

> And He said to them, "Take heed and beware of covetousness, for one's life does not consist in the abundance of the things he possesses." Then He spoke a parable to them, saying: "The ground of a certain rich man yielded plentifully. And he thought within himself, saying, 'What shall I do, since I have no room to store my crops?' So he said, 'I will do this: I will pull down my barns and build greater, and there I will store all my crops and my goods. And I will say to my soul, "Soul, you have many goods laid up for many years; take your ease; eat, drink, and be merry."' But God said to him, "Fool! This night your soul will be required of you; then whose will those things be which you have provided?" So is he who lays up treasure for himself, and is not rich toward God (Luke 12:15-21).

> Now as He was going out on the road, one came running, knelt before Him, and asked Him, "Good Teacher, what shall I do that I may inherit eternal life?" So Jesus said to him, "Why do you call Me good? No one is good but One, that is, God. You know the commandments: 'Do not commit adultery,' 'Do not murder,' 'Do not steal,' 'Do not bear false witness,' 'Do not defraud,' 'Honor your father and your mother.'" And he answered and said to Him, "Teacher, all these things I have kept from my youth." Then Jesus, looking at him, loved him, and said to him, "One thing you lack: Go your way, sell whatever you have and give to the poor, and you will have treasure in heaven; and come, take up the cross, and follow Me." But he was sad at this word, and went away sorrowful, for he had great possessions. Then Jesus looked around and said to His disciples, "How hard it is for those who have riches to enter the kingdom of God!" And the disciples were astonished at His words. But Jesus answered again and said to them, "Children, how hard it is for those who trust in riches to enter the kingdom of God! It is easier for a camel to go

through the eye of a needle than for a rich man to enter the kingdom of God" (Mark 10:17-25).

One of the serious problems of materialism or covetousness is that there is never a feeling of sufficiency. The flesh always wants more and more.

Hell and Destruction are never full;
So the eyes of man are never satisfied (Prov. 27:20).

The leech has two daughters—
Give and Give!
There are three things that are never satisfied,
Four never say, "Enough!"
The grave,
The barren womb,
The earth that is not satisfied with water—
And the fire never says, "Enough" (Prov. 30:15-16)!

The covetous eye and the materialistic heart could be added to this list as they are never, never satisfied. They will eventually lead to the spiritual ruination and destruction of homes.

Now godliness with contentment is great gain. For we brought nothing into this world, and it is certain we can carry nothing out. And having food and clothing, with these we shall be content. But those who desire to be rich fall into temptation and a snare, and into many foolish and harmful lusts which drown men in destruction and perdition. For the love of money is a root of all kinds of evil, for which some have strayed from the faith in their greediness, and pierced themselves through with many sorrows (1 Tim. 6:6-10).

There are many such warnings in the Bible concerning the problem of materialism. The listing of Scriptures could go on and on. Many homes are destroyed over this problem of people wanting more and more of this world's good. The husband will get more and more "overtime" or even a second job in order to have more income for more and more material things – far beyond the real needs of the family. The wife and mother of small children will leave home to work simply because the family wants a bigger, fancier house, a bigger TV, or a more luxurious car, and many other play things to take up more and more of their time that ought to be used in personally teaching and training their children to love the Lord more and more (Tit. 2:4-5; cf. 1 Tim. 5:14-15). It is tragic that, because the father and the mother are so busy with the pursuit of more and more income, the children (and the adults as well) gradually love the Lord less and less and love the world more and more (cf. Luke 8:14; 1 John 2:15-17). This internal, spiritual weakening of the family members more often than not will eventually lead to the overt destruction of the home. As goes the home, so goes the church and the nation as well.

The obvious need is to put the Lord and His kingdom first in our lives and cease bowing to the altar of materialism.

> Do not lay up for yourselves treasures on earth, where moth and rust destroy and where thieves break in and steal; but lay up for yourselves treasures in heaven, where neither moth nor rust destroys and where thieves do not break in and steal. For where your treasure is, there your heart will be also. The lamp of the body is the eye. If therefore your eye is good, your whole body will be full of light. But if your eye is bad, your whole body will be full of darkness. If therefore the light that is in you is darkness, how great is that darkness! No one can serve two masters; for either he will hate the one and love the other, or else he will be loyal to the one and despise the other. You cannot serve God and mammon. Therefore I say to you, do not worry about your life, what you will eat or what you will drink; nor about your body, what you will put on. Is not life more than food and the body more than clothing? Look at the birds of the air, for they neither sow nor reap nor gather into barns; yet your heavenly Father feeds them. Are you not of more value than they? Which of you by worrying can add one cubit to his stature? So why do you worry about clothing? Consider the lilies of the field, how they grow: they neither toil nor spin; and yet I say to you that even Solomon in all his glory was not arrayed like one of these. Now if God so clothes the grass of the field, which today is, and tomorrow is thrown into the oven, will He not much more clothe you, O you of little faith? Therefore do not worry, saying, "What shall we eat?" or "What shall we drink?" or "What shall we wear?" For after all these things the Gentiles seek. For your heavenly Father knows that you need all these things. But seek first the kingdom of God and His righteousness, and all these things shall be added to you. Therefore do not worry about tomorrow, for tomorrow will worry about its own things. Sufficient for the day is its own trouble (Matt. 6:19-34).

There are many other factors that could be discussed in this book.

Home
Home is the place your heart resides
Home is the place that you decide
Home is the womb that holds the soul
Home is the place where one is whole

Home is the glow you hold in your eye
Home is the emotion that makes you cry
Home is safe and a place of peace
Home is where all strivings cease

Home is protective against the others
Home is full of sisters and brothers
Home is where you find your rest
Home is where you feel your best

Home is a memory that follows your being
Home is a dream for those agreeing
Home is the place where reserves fall
Home is the place you yearn to call

Home is where the family meets
Home is a place of restful retreats
Home is the place you know you'll be heard
Home is the pace where nothing blurs

Home is all these wonderful things
Home is the place you develop wings
Home is the place that you'll find one day
Home is the place where your heart will stay

– Aisha Patterson

Redefining Marriage:
A Historical Perspective

Kyle Pope

In September 1996, in response to growing moves by the state of Hawaii to recognize homosexual marriages, the United States congress passed into law "The Defense of Marriage Act" (DOMA). This law mandated that no state shall be required to accept as binding, the actions of another state to recognize ceremonies between those of the same sex as "marriage." DOMA explicitly declared that "the word 'marriage' means only a legal union between one man and one woman as husband and wife, and the word 'spouse' refers only to a person of the opposite sex who is a husband and or a wife" (§ 7). Since that time, nine states and the District of Columbia have now legalized marriages between those of the same sex: Connecticut, Iowa,

---

Kyle M. Pope (1963-) has preached the gospel since 1987 for churches in Missouri, Arkansas, Alabama, Kansas, and Texas. He currently serves as an elder for the Olsen Park church of Christ, in Amarillo, Texas where he preaches and conducts a two-year preacher training program. In 1982 he and his wife, Toni, were married. They have been blessed with three children, Torhi, Caleb, and Nathan, who are all faithful Christians. Kyle earned his B. A. from the University of Alabama (1997) in Humanities and M. A. from the University of Kansas (2000) in Greek and Latin.

He taught Greek, Latin, and Classical mythology while at the University of Kansas. He has formally studied Greek, Hebrew, Latin, German, and Coptic, and has informally studied other ancient languages. Kyle has written a number of books, including the Matthew commentary in the *Truth Commentary* series, *Biblical Guidance Through the Stages of Life, The Hardening of Pharaoh's Heart, Harmony of 2 Samuel, Kings & Chronicles, How Does the Holy Spirit Work in a Christian?, How We Got the Bible* and *Romans* in the *Bible Text Book* series published by the Guardian of Truth Foundation. Kyle also maintains a study website known as *Ancient Road Publications* that features material dealing with biblical studies as well as ancient language and archaeology.

Massachusetts, Maine, Maryland, New Hampshire, New York, Vermont, and Washington. Four other states, Delaware, Hawaii, Illinois, and Rhode Island, now recognize so-called "civil unions" between those of the same sex. As of November, 2012 twenty-seven states had instituted constitutional amendments banning "same-sex" marriage and a number of other states have bounced back and forth between the courts and the legislatures banning or approving the practice.[1]

For Christians, this is a shocking development, but it is important for us to understand that such attempts to redefine marriage are not new. In fact, from the very beginning of God's institution of marriage there have been constant attempts to reshape and redefine the beautiful relationship God created for man's happiness and companionship. In this study we will survey the biblical and historical record to illustrate that the challenges of our day are merely the latest in an ongoing effort that man has made to challenge God's original design. We will see that, while some things are not what we wish they might be, we by no means live in a time with the worst challenges to God's design for marriage. The objective of this is not just an exploration in history. It is my hope that this will encourage Christians to recognize, "That which has been is what will be, that which is done is what will be done, and there is nothing new under the sun" (Ecc. 1:9, NKJV). In this recognition my prayer is that it will help and motivate us to be the salt and light the Lord would have us to be (Matt. 5:13-16), so that we, like the forbearers of faith who came before us, might "shine as lights"—"in the midst of a crooked and perverse generation" (Phil. 2:15).

I. The Biblical Definition of Marriage.

When we speak of *redefining* something, we infer that there is an original *definition*. This is absolutely true when it comes to marriage. It is not, as many feminists assert that marriage was an institution created by men to dominate women—marriage is an institution created by God. In the creation of woman, God set down three elements that constitute the nature and participants in marriage. In a text that is sometimes called the "Marriage Constitution," God declared, "Therefore a man shall leave his father and mother, and be joined to his wife, and they shall become one flesh" (Gen. 2:24). The importance of this text is demonstrated by the fact that Jesus and Paul both quote it when teaching New Covenant law on the permanence of

---

[1] "Timeline: Gay Marriage Chronology." *Los Angeles Times.* [online] *http://graphics.latimes.com/usmap-gay-marriage-chronology/.*

marriage (Matt. 19:5; Mark 10:7) and the organization of the home (Eph. 5:31). We see three elements articulated that constitute marriage.

The Marriage Constitution.

1. Leaving Father and Mother. Adam and Eve had no earthly father or mother, but all of their posterity from that point on were commanded to recognize in the marriage relationship the establishment of a new and distinct family unit. This didn't mean families could not live together. Isaac took Rebekah into "his mother Sarah's tent" when "she became his wife" (Gen. 2:67). Jacob lived with his father-in-law Laban after he was married (Gen. 30:25-26). The idea is that the relationship between a husband and wife is independent and autonomous in nature. A married couple must honor their parents, but they are no longer under their authority in the same way. Many problems in marriage have come from a failure on the part of parents or newly-weds to recognize this element of the definition of marriage.

2. Being Joined to a Wife. God commanded that in marriage a man is to "be joined to his wife" (Gen. 2:24b). The very wording of the command specifies the parties involved in this relationship. It is "a man *('îš)*" who is to be joined to "his wife *('îš^etô)*." It is not a man joined to *his man* or a woman joined to *her woman*. The Hebew word *'îš* always refers to a male and the Hebrew word *'iššâh* always refers to a female. This is the same word used in the two previous verses when recording the creation of woman from the man's rib (Gen. 2:22) and the name given to her—"woman *('iššâh)*" (Gen. 2:23). The word translated "joined" is the Hebrew word *dāḇaq* meaning "*cling* or *adhere*; figuratively to *catch* by pursuit: abide, fast, cleave (fast together)" (Strong, Heb. 1692). This word has been variously translated into English "schal cleue to" (Wycliffe), "and cleve vnto" (Tyndale), "shalbe ioyned with" (Bishops), "shall cleave unto" (KJV, ASV), "be joined to" (NKJV, NASU), "be united to" (NIV), or "hold fast to" (ESV). This is not merely cohabitation or "living together" (cf. John 4:18), but some recognized affirmation that a permanent union has taken place. Scripture has not outlined a particular procedure for carrying out this *joining* under the Patriarchal, Mosaic, or New Covenants. It appears to be whatever a given culture recognizes as the method of determining who is and who is not married. In some cultures, it may be jumping over a broom. In others it might involve declaring the couple's intentions before the village elders. In our own culture, it involves securing a marriage license and speaking vows before witnesses.

3. Becoming One Flesh. Finally, we see that within the relationship of marriage the Lord commands "they shall become one flesh" (Gen. 2:24c).

When Jesus and Paul quote this text they both put it "the two shall become one flesh" (Matt. 19:5; Mark 10:8; 1 Cor. 6:16; Eph. 5:31)). This is either a paraphrase or evidence of a textual variant. Both the Samaritan Pentateuch and the Greek translation, made before New Testament times, read—"the two shall become one flesh." The Hebrew Masoretic text (on which most English translations are based) puts it "they shall become one flesh," but here again, the parties involved are specified—"a man" and "his wife." It does not say a man and *his wives* or a woman and *her husbands*. Paul's use of this text in 1 Corinthians makes it clear that the "one flesh" union is referring to sexual conduct. The sin of fornication takes a relationship that is to be reserved for one's mate and allows one to become "one flesh" with a harlot (1 Cor. 6:16). That does not mean that sexual contact *constitutes* marriage. Under Mosaic Law a man who violated a betrothed woman was to be put to death but he was not considered the husband of the woman, even though he was the first to have sexual contact with her (Deut. 22:25). If a man violated a virgin who was not betrothed he could marry her with the father's permission but was not automatically considered her husband because of sexual contact (Exod. 22:16-17). Instead, it indicates that only within the marriage relationship do human beings have the right to this most intimate type of contact.

"Wife by Covenant"

While Genesis 2:24 sets down the essential constitution of marriage, it is not the only text that establishes the biblical definition of marriage. In Malachi, when God rebuked the Israelites for mistreating their mates, He proclaimed:

> . . .The LORD has been witness between you and the wife of your youth, with whom you have dealt treacherously; yet she is your companion and your wife by covenant. But did He not make them one, having a remnant of the Spirit? And why one? He seeks godly offspring. Therefore take heed to your spirit, and let none deal treacherously with the wife of his youth (Mal. 2:14-15).

Whenever I study with a couple who would like for me to perform a wedding ceremony, it is my custom to first ask them a question—"on the most basic level *what is marriage?*" Answers vary depending upon the maturity of the couple involved, but I use this as a way to demonstrate from Malachi's words that at its most basic level marriage is a "covenant." It is a contract or agreement between two parties. Marriage is not *chemistry* (although there will be some of that). Many arranged marriages had no

chemistry when they began, but blossomed over time into loving, affectionate relationships (e.g. Isaac and Rebekah, Gen. 24:64-65; 26:8). Marriage
is not a *magical connection* (although couples should work to keep things
"magical"). Marriage is a promise. This is clear from the Lord's teaching
in the Sermon on the Mount. Jesus' condemnation of divorce (Matt. 5:31-
32) comes immediately after warning against *adultery in the heart* (Matt.
5:27-30) and before His teaching on honesty (Matt. 5:33-37). Marriage is
a promise to fulfill a role to one's mate that no other soul on earth has the
right to. The Lord declares that a woman becomes a "wife by covenant,"
but states even further that He acts as "witness between you and the wife of
your youth" (Mal. 2:14). Much like a notary public in our day witnesses a
transaction and documents that it has taken place, God is involved in every
lawful marriage covenant as "witness." This makes it clear that marriage
is not a purely human activity—God is *the* "witness" and God is the one
who "made them one" (Mal. 2:15). Jesus reaffirms this in commanding
"what God has joined together, let not man separate" (Matt. 19:6). God
not only defines marriage, but God is the One who ultimately joins a man
and a woman together in marriage.

II. Redefinitions throughout History.

In spite of these clear biblical teachings defining the nature and constitution of marriage, in both the biblical and secular record human history
demonstrates a long and repeated effort to twist and reshape this institution
according to man's desires and imagination.

A. Polygamy.
Ancient Polygamy and Concubinage

One of the first efforts to redefine marriage is recorded only two chapters after its institution. Lamech, the great-great-grandson of Cain, is the
first recorded bigamist in history. He married two wives: Adah and Zillah
(Gen. 4:19). Scripture does not record a divine comment on God's view of
this redefinition. It merely records it as a detail of the lineage from Cain. If
we are correct in understanding the statement of Genesis 6:1 that "sons of
God" refers to descendants of Adam's son Seth and "sons of men" refers
to descendants of Cain, it may suggest that this digression from the divine
pattern came from the more worldly-minded family of Cain, rather than
the more spiritually-minded family of Seth.

The next recorded example comes centuries later, after the flood in the
account of Abraham. When Abram's wife Sarai was unable to conceive,
she followed what had become customary during her time—she took her

servant Hagar and "gave her to her husband to be his wife" (Gen. 16:3), so that she could bear children for her husband. The same custom was followed by Abraham's grandson, Jacob. He was tricked into marrying two wives: Leah and Rachel, when he only wanted to marry Rachel (Gen. 29:15-30). When Rachel could not conceive she gave her servant Bilhah to Jacob "as wife" (Gen. 30:4, 7), and later, Leah also gave her servant Zilpah to him "as wife," when she thought she could no longer conceive (Gen. 30:9, 12).

Concubine Surrogacy

Although there is a large gap between the record of the polygamy of La-mech and the family of Abraham, this doesn't mean that it was not practiced. There is substantial evidence that polygamy and child-bearing through a concubine were common in ancient times. The 18th century B.C. Babylonian Code of Hammurabi allowed a husband to divorce a wife who had born him no children (138). To avoid this, the wife could give her husband a slave-girl to bear children to him, and if she did he could not take another woman as concubine (144). If she did not give him a slave-girl he could take a concubine to bear children but the concubine did not hold the same rank as a wife (145). A slave-girl who bore children could not aspire to the full rank of a wife. If she did, although her owner could not sell her, she could be reduced back to the rank of a common slave-girl (146). Hurrian tablets from Nuzi, near the Iraqi city of Kirkuk, dated from the 14th -15th century B.C. also record the custom of giving a slave-girl to a husband, if a wife could not conceive. One surviving text reads: "If Gilimninu [the bride] will not bear children, Gilimninu will take a woman of N/Lullu-land [whence the choicest slaves were obtained] as a wife for Shennima [the bridegroom]" (HSS 5 67:19-21, Gordon). As in the Code of Hammurabi, not only could a slave-girl be offered to a husband, but barrenness was also used as an excuse to take a second wife in the Nuzi texts (HSS 5 80:1-23; HSS 19 78; 84). God never commanded such customs, but it is clear that the family of Abraham followed the manmade customs of the people around them.

In the biblical account of Jacob, we noted that Bilhah was given to Jacob "to wife $(l^e\check{s}\check{s}\hat{a}h)$" (Gen. 30:4, KJV), but latter she is also called a "concubine $(pilege\check{s})$" (Gen. 35:22).[2] After Sarah's death, Abraham married another wife,

---

[2] There is no clear etymology for the word *pilegeš*. It is not believed to be Semitic, leading some to conjecture that it is of Indo-European origin. The Greek *pallax* (or *pallakis*) and Latin *pellex* both meant "youth" or "girl," from the source *plgs* meaning "marriageable" (Engelken, 549). Mansfield claims that in Athens the *pallakē* held "a kind of middle rank between a wife and a harlot (*hetaira*)" (349).

Keturah (Gen. 25:1), but he is also said to have had "concubines" (Gen. 25:6), as did his brother, Nahor (Gen. 22:23-24). As foreign as it is to our thinking, and the Law of Christ, we should not think of Patriarchal concubinage in the same way that in modern times we might speak of someone's "mistress" or one with whom a man might "have an affair." Concubines were viewed as legal wives of secondary rank. Mosaic Law made provisions regarding concubinage (Lev. 19:20), but it did not prohibit it. We should probably understand this as an allowance on the part of God, not an endorsement (cf. Matt. 19:8). Concubines held a different rank in matters of inheritance, and the children born to them generally did not receive allotments equal to those born by wives of a primary rank (cf. Gen. 25:5-6).

The Bible says more about polygamy than it does about concubinage, yet the line between the two was not always clear. After Sarah's death Keturah was Abraham's "wife (*'iššâh*)" (Gen. 25:1) but she is also called his "concubine (*pilegeš*)" (1 Chron. 1:32). Mosaic Law made more provision for polygamy than for concubinage, but it is clear that neither were prohibited. The Law taught that if a man took a wife from foreign slaves he could not diminish her status "if he takes another wife" (Exod. 21:7-11). Regulation is made to prevent the right of firstborn inheritance from being denied to a child born to a wife that was unloved "if a man has two wives" (Deut. 21:15-17). Even levirate marriage, by which a brother was to marry the widow of a brother who died with no children, made no exclusion for prior marriages (Deut. 25:5-10). As with concubinage, we should understand this as an allowance on the part of God, not an endorsement. As we shall see below in the case of divorce, there were some practices that were already going on which Mosaic law was intended to restrain and curtail. In many ways Mosaic law, when compared to the laws of other nations, protected

---

Mansfield cites the Greek writer Demosthenes, who wrote, "we keep mistresses (*hetairas*) for the sake of pleasure, concubines (*pallakas*) for the daily care of our persons, but wives (*gunaikas*) to bear us legitimate children and to be faithful guardians of our household" (*Against Neaera* 59.122). While this was certainly the Greco-Roman view, it may be that the sexual exploitation of the Greek and Roman "concubine" does not exactly parallel the Near Eastern form of this institution. It is pure speculation on my part, but another possible etymology might be the early Greek *pelix*, represented in the Mycenaean word *pelikes* (pe-ri-ke) referring to a small vessel (Ventris, 404). At least in early times the "concubine (*pilegeš*)" seems to have played more the role of a "surrogate-*vessel*" (so to speak) for the seed of the husband of the concubine's mistress, rather than that of a sexual paramour.

women even when it allowed redefinitions that had not been intended "from the beginning" (cf. Matt. 19:8). Some practices, on the other hand, such as adultery or homosexuality, were behaviors for which the Lord made no provision. Under Christ, a restatement and clarification of God's original design for marriage has now been fully implemented.

The Bible records that many faithful servants of God were polygamists. Gideon had "many wives" (Judg. 8:30) and a concubine (Judg. 8:31). Samuel's father had "two wives" (1 Sam. 1:1-2). Even the faithful priest Jehoiadah had "two wives" (2 Chron. 24:3). In spite of Mosaic warnings that a king should not "multiply wives for himself" (Deut. 17:17), many of the kings of Israel and Judah did so. Solomon is perhaps the supreme example of one given over to this redefinition. He is recorded as having 700 wives and 300 concubines, and Scripture specifically indicates that his unfaithfulness to the Lord was heavily influenced by these marriages (1 Kings 11:3). Under Christ's law, the general principle is that marriage to another while a mate still lives is considered adultery (Matt. 5:32; 19:9; Mark 10:11-12; Luke 16:18; Rom. 7:3; 1 Cor. 7:39). A Christian cannot be a polygamist! As the New Testament period approached, some Jews were beginning to reject the propriety of polygamy, just as Christ did. A Qumran text known as the *Damascus Document* described polygamists as being "caught twice in fornication (*znwt*)" having taken two wives in opposition to the "principle of creation" which it goes on to quote as taught in Genesis 1:27—"male and female he created them" (CD 4.20-21). In spite of this, polygamy continued to be practiced among the Jews into the second century and beyond (Justin, *Dialogue with Trypho* 134, 141). Polygamy is still practiced in Muslim countries, and concubinage is occasionally found in some Asian countries.

Polygamy in More Recent History

In the early 19th century a rebirth of this ancient redefinition came when Joseph Smith, the founder of the Mormon Church, claimed to have received a revelation regarding what Mormons call "plural marriage." Their false text known as *The Book of Mormon* had already been circulated, which declared plainly "Behold, David and Solomon truly had many wives and concubines, which thing was abominable before me, saith the Lord" (Jacob 2:24). As we noted above, the Bible never said that—God made allowance for it, although He did not endorse it. Even so, in his so-called "revelation" Smith claimed to have been told:

David also received many wives and concubines, and also Solomon and

Moses my servants, as also many others of my servants, from the beginning of creation until this time; and in nothing did they sin save in those things which they received not of me (*Doctrine and Covenants* 132:38).

In this Smith plainly contradicted his own texts, revealing beyond any question the manmade nature of this false religion. Unfortunately, Smith's claim to have received this revelation affected the practice of the Mormon Church for the remainder of that century, and has had a dramatic impact on laws and political events in the United States up to the present time.

The full text of Smith's supposed revelation is recorded in section 132 of the Mormon book known as *Doctrine and Covenants*. It begins by claiming to answer Smith's own questions about the polygamy practiced by Old Testament figures (132:1-2). The supposed answer, involved a redefinition of the terms of marriage. It claimed, while all "covenants, contracts, bonds, obligations, oaths" and "vows" not "made and entered into and sealed by the Holy Spirit of promise" and Mormon leaders "for time and for all eternity" end at death (132:7), a supposed new type of marriage covenant is introduced that can be "sealed by the Holy Spirit" and Mormon leaders that "in time, and through all eternity" he claims "shall be in full force when they are out of this world" (132:19). The text ends with a personal message to Smith's wife, Emma, charging her to accept this practice (132:51-54), even if Smith should take "ten virgins" (132:62). With this, Smith not only contradicted his own false *Book of Mormon,* but contradicted the teaching of Jesus that "those who are counted worthy to attain that age, and the resurrection from the dead, neither marry nor are given in marriage" (Luke 20:35, NKJV). In spite of these blatant contradictions many Mormons began to practice polygamy.

When the Mormons migrated to what would become Utah Territory, it was their desire to be admitted to the union of States as their own independent "State of *Deseret,*" a name taken from the *Book of Mormon* supposedly meaning "honeybee" (*Ether* 2.3). The primary obstacle to statehood was the practice of polygamy. Six failed attempts were made in 1849, 1856, 1862, 1872, 1882, and 1887, all denied because of the issue of polygamy. To the frustration of the Mormons, rather than granting statehood, the federal government established and governed "Utah Territory." In these years, what allowed the Mormons to continue polygamy was a political doctrine known as "popular sovereignty." Historians recognize that this doctrine delayed the Civil War from beginning earlier, because it allowed territories to decide their own position on matters such as slavery and polygamy. As Mormon polygamy became increasingly more intertwined in the growing conflict over states rights, it caused some advocates of popular sovereignty to renounce it. In 1856 the newly formed Republican Party, in their party platform asserted that it was, "the right and the imperative duty of Congress to prohibit in the Territories those twin relics of barbarism—Polygamy, and Slavery" (Third Resolution).

The United States Government's War on Polygamy

Many students of American history don't realize that before the Civil War another war was nearly fought over the issue of polygamy. During the Buchanan administration from May of 1857 to July of 1858, federal troops were poised for war with Mormon citizens and militia in Utah Territory. War was only avoided through negotiation and compromise. When Abraham Lincoln became president, in July of 1862 the Republican congress began to act on their party's platform, passing the "Morrill Anti-Bigamy Act." This law demanded a $500.00 fine and five years in prison for "every person having a husband or wife living, who shall marry any other person, whether married or single, in a Territory of the United States" (501). Although Abraham Lincoln signed the Act into law, with the rise of the Civil War, and fears that the Mormons might side with the Confederacy, Lincoln did not enforce the law, When Mormon leader Brigham Young sent T. B. H. Stenhouse, assistant editor of the Mormon *Deseret News,* to determine Lincoln's plans Lincoln told Stenhouse that the dilemma was like a fallen tree that he sometimes encountered as a young boy that. . .

> . . .was too hard to split, too wet to burn, and too heavy to move, so we plowed around it. That's what I intend to do with the Mormons. You go back and tell Brigham Young that if he will let me alone I will let him alone (Nibley, 369).

This inactive posture towards Mormon polygamy did not last for long. After the Civil War, in 1882, the "Edmunds Anti-Polygamy Act" was passed making polygamy a felony and demanding that polygamists lose the right to vote, hold political office, or serve on a jury. Under this law 1300 Mormon men were imprisoned. In 1885 *Murphy vs. Ramsey*, 114 U.S. 15 (1885), was brought before the U.S. Supreme Court arguing that this law prosecuted something after the fact (*ex post facto*), but the court did not agree, upholding the anti-polygamy laws. In 1887 the "Edmunds-Tucker Anti-Polygamy Act" was passed which further criminalized polygamy and required a marriage license for all marriages in Utah Territory. The act also moved to seize property over a certain value held by the Mormon Church, finally pressuring Wilford Woodruff, the president of the Mormon Church, to issue in 1890 what is known as "The Manifesto." Woodruff declared:

> Inasmuch as laws have been enacted by Congress forbidding plural mar-
> riages, which laws have been pronounced constitutional by the court of
> last resort, I hereby declare my intention to submit to those laws, and to
> use my influence with the members of the Church over which I preside
> to have them do likewise (*Doctrine and Covenants*, p. 257).

This officially ended polygamy as an accepted practice of the Mormon Church. "The Manifesto" is now included in the Mormon text *Doctrine and Covenants*. Six years after Woodruff's proclamation, in 1896 Utah was granted statehood. While officially the Mormon Church now discourages polygamy in the United States, recent history has shown that the practice has not ended. This program features a polygamist family associated with the Apostolic United Brethren, an offshoot of the Fundamentalist Mormon Church. The husband, Cody Brown, has only one "legal" wife, but three others he calls "spiritual wives." In 2012, Warren Jeffs, president of the Fundamentalist Mormon Church, was convicted of two felony counts of child sexual assault in connection with his ongoing practice of polygamy (Wagner). The irony of this is that while our modern culture rightly condemns polygamy (especially with minors), it moved long ago to accept unscriptural divorce and remarriage, which according to the teaching of Christ establishes millions of people in what are properly culturally sanctioned polygamous relationships.[3] The cable network TLC (The Learning Channel) has featured for the last few years a program called *Sister Wives*.

B. Homosexuality.

The next redefinition recorded in Scripture came in the account of Abraham's nephew Lot. When the Lord determined to destroy Sodom and Gomorrah, God sent angels to the city to bring Lot out. After the angels entered Lot's house the men of the city came to the house and demanded, "Where are the men who came to you tonight? Bring them out to us, that we may know them" (Gen. 19:5, ESV). The New King James adds in italics "know them *carnally*" (NKJV). The New American Standard puts it, "have relations with them" (NASB), and less literal translations paraphrase it "have sex them" (NIV, NLT). It is clear that the men wanted to have homosexual relations with the angels, thinking they were mere "men." When

---

[3] See my study, "Culturally Sanctioned Polygamy." *Biblical Insights* 8.6 (June 2008) 18 [online] *http://www.ancientroadpublications.com/Studies/ BiblicalStudies/SanctionedPolygamy.html*.

it comes to the redefinition of homosexuality there is clear indication that under Patriarchal Law this was considered sinful. Lot begged the men not to act "so wickedly" (NKJV). We might ask how such homosexuality sought to redefine marriage—they were not seeking to *marry* the angels. That is true, but in this behavior they sought to expand the "one flesh" relationship beyond the bounds of marriage, not to mention the fact that they were seeking to change the subjects engaged in the "one flesh" relationship from a "man" and "his wife" to those of the same sex.

Scripture leaves no question about God's attitude towards this behavior. Mosaic Law declared explicitly, "You shall not lie with a male as with a woman. It is an abomination" (Lev. 18:22). "If a man lies with a male as he lies with a woman, both of them have committed an abomination. They shall surely be put to death. Their blood shall be upon them" (Lev. 20:13). In the period of the Judges, men of Benjamin, described contemptibly as "sons of Belial" (KJV), acted as the men of Sodom had toward a Levite traveling through their city (Judg. 19:22). The events surrounding this incident led to a civil war among Israelite tribes and nearly exterminated the tribe of Benjamin (Judg. 20:1-21:25).

Male Cultic Prostitution

Beyond isolated instances of homosexuality, it is also evident that the pagan culture which surrounded the Israelites engaged in a more institutionalized form of this redefinition of the marriage relationship. Mosaic Law commanded:

> There shall be no ritual harlot (*qᵉdēšâh*) of the daughters of Israel, or a perverted one (*qādēš*) of the sons of Israel. You shall not bring the wages of a harlot or the price of a dog to the house of the LORD your God for any vowed offering, for both of these are an abomination to the LORD your God" (Deut. 23:17-18).

There was to be no female "ritual harlot (*qᵉdēšâh*)" in Israel (23:17a) . . . ➡	. . . and they were not to accept "the wages of a harlot" (23:18a).
There was to be no male "perverted one (*qādēš*)" in Israel (23:17b) . . . ➡	. . . and they were not to accept the "price of a dog" (23:18b).

As foreign as it may seem to our way of thinking, the nouns *qᵉdēšâh* (fem.) and *qādēš* (masc.) come from the root *qdš* meaning "to consecrate" or "make holy." In much of the ancient world cultic prostitution was associated with idolatry. Shrine prostitutes were considered by much of the pagan world as "holy." It is clear that at least some cultic prostitution involved male homosexual prostitutes. In the text above the two prohibitions of these verses form a parallel construction with each other:

Some modern scholars and homosexual activists question whether there is sufficient evidence to conclude that *q^edēšâh* and *qādēš* refer to prostitution. Ringren, for example writes, "Although the two terms are generally associated with cultic prostitution, none of the passages offers any unequivocal evidence of such" (542).[4] It is clear, however, that *q^edēšâh* referred to a female prostitute. This is the word twice applied to Tamar when she dressed as a prostitute in order to seduce Judah (Gen. 38:21-22). In the text above, the parallel association of *qādēš* (23:17b) and "dog" (23:18b) clearly (and graphically) demonstrates a reference to male homosexual prostitution (cf. Rev. 22:15). There is clear evidence that prostitution was associated with pagan fertility cults in much of the ancient world. The apocryphal book of Second Maccabees records that when the Greeks controlled Jerusalem in the period between the Old and New Testament, they carried on prostitution in

---

[4] This argument ignores the clear evidence of homosexual cultic prostitution throughout the ancient world preserved in both artifacts and literature that has survived. For example, in Assyria, male cult prostitutes of the fertility goddess Ishtar were called *assinnu*. An Akkadian omen tablet in the British Museum, thought to date to the 7th century B.C. claimed, "If a man copulates with an *assinnu*, a hard destiny will leave him" (Gadd, Tablet 104, Plate 45, line 32, Trans. Nissinen, 27). Oppenheim indicates that *assinnu* could be written with the Sumerian logograms LÚ.UR.SAL (341), which combine the words "man" + "dog" + a word for a woman's private parts. This clearly referred to homosexual conduct. In a similar way, Lucian describes Syrian priests who castrated themselves while engaged in "orgies" (*On the Syrian Goddess* 51). After their castration they wore women's cloths and performed, what he calls, "works of women (*erga gunaikōn*)" (*Ibid.*, 27). *The Greek Anthology* preserves an ancient epigram that uses the exact same phrase of bisexuals who "suffer the works of women" describing them as "men to women and women to men" (4.272). Greek had a verb, *gunaikazō* meaning "to play the woman," which was often used in the same way, of homosexual behavior (Cassius Dio, *History of Rome* 50.27.6; 59.26.8; 80:14, 16). The Latin phrase *muliebria puti* expressed the same idea (Sallust, *Conspiracy of Catiline* 13.3; Tacitus, *Annals* 11.36.5; Petronius, *Satyricon* 9.6). The *qādēš* in Israel, who received "the price of a dog" behaved just like these pagans did.

the temple (6.4). This may have included homosexual prostitution because it claims they consorted "with harlots (*hetairōn*)" and also "with women (*gunaixi*)." Eusebius records that up to the time of Constantine, male temple prostitution was practiced in a temple of Venus on Mount Lebanon until Constantine destroyed the temple and ended this practice by the threat of punishment (*Life of Constantine* 3.55).

If *qādēš* can be understood to include male homosexual prostitutes, the biblical record says a great deal about God's contempt for this behavior, and the Israelites all too common return to practice this type of redefinition of marriage. In the days of Rehoboam, Solomon's son, the Scripture tells us: "And there were also perverted persons (*qādēš*) in the land. They did according to all the abominations of the nations which the LORD had cast out before the children of Israel" (1 Kings 14:24). During the reign of Jehoshaphat he was said to have removed from the land of, "the rest of the perverted persons (*qādēš*), who remained in the days of his father Asa" (1 Kings 22:46). In both passages the singular is used in the male form. There is little doubt this refers to male cultic prostitutes because of its connection with the "abominations" of the nations cast out (cf. 18:3, 22). Asa was said to have "banished the perverted persons *(qᵉdēšîm)* from the land and removed all of the idols that his fathers had made" (1 Kings 15:12). Later, during the reforms of Josiah, "he tore down the ritual booths of the perverted persons *(qᵉdēšîm)* that were in the house of the Lord, where the women wove hangings for the wooden image *('ăšērâh)*" (2 Kings 23:7). In both of these passages the plural is used, which means that it could include both male and female qᵉdēšîm, but the connection with the "wooden image *('ăšērâh)*"—"Asherah" (ASV, NASB)—a Near Eastern fertility goddess—makes it likely that male and female cult prostitutes are being described. How shocking it is to consider that Israel and Judah went so far in their redefinition of marriage that they allowed homosexual prostitution to take place in the very courts of the temple!

Homosexuality in the World of the New Testament
The apostle Paul wrote some of the most specific condemnations of homosexual behavior in Scripture. In 1 Timothy 1:10 Paul describes the behavior of fornicators and sodomites as that which "is contrary to sound doctrine." In Romans 1:24-27 Paul traces the thinking which leads to such behavior describing it as "vile,"—"against nature" (1:26), and "shameful" (1:27). In this text Paul lists not only male homosexual behavior—"men with men" (1:27), but also female homosexuality (1:28). Although less common, it is

clear that this redefinition of the marriage relationship was also practiced in ancient times. The island of Lesbos, from which the modern name for this sin comes, was known for this conduct among women (Lucian, *Dialogues of the Courtesans* 5). In 1 Corinthians 6:9-10 Paul includes "homosexuals (*malakoi*)," meaning literally "soft"—"effeminate" (KJV) and "sodomites (*arsenokoitai*)" meaning literally "to lie with a man"—"abusers of themselves with men" (ASV), in a list of those who "will not inherit the kingdom of God." Here Paul used terms that refer to both passive and active roles to describe what God condemns. In the ancient pagan mind, the latter was acceptable, while the former was for slaves and young boys. As distasteful as it is to Christians, and even our modern world, in ancient times many thought it was perfectly acceptable for an older man to have a young boy to satisfy his sexual needs. In turn the older man educated and supported the boy. In Plato's *Symposium* one of the guests named Pausanius, during a discussion on love, argues. . .

> It is our settled tradition that when a man freely devotes his service to another in the belief that his friend will make him better in point of wisdom, it may be, or in any of the other parts of virtue, this willing bondage also is no sort of baseness or flattery (184c)

> Thus by all means it is right to bestow this favor for the sake of virtue. This is the Love that belongs to the Heavenly Goddess, heavenly itself and precious to both public and private life: for this compels lover and beloved alike to feel a zealous concern for their own virtue (185b-c).

It is important for Christians to realize that the world that surrounded the men and women of the Bible was a much different place than anything we have ever known. In many cases homosexual behavior was considered commonplace. Homosexual rape was considered acceptable punishment for trespassing (*Priapea* 52, 56). Slaves were often considered to be obligated to submit to sexual assault (Petronius, *Satyricon* 75). Yet it was into this cesspool of wickedness that the gospel was born—souls were converted—sin was forsaken, and Paul could say to those who abandoned such wickedness, "such were some of you. But you were washed, but you were sanctified, but you were justified in the name of the Lord Jesus and by the Spirit of our God" (1 Cor. 6:11).

Homosexual Marriage in Ancient Times

While Scripture records instances of promiscuous homosexual relationships in ancient history, it does not record any type of permanent relationships between those of the same sex. It is clear, however, that such things were practiced in ancient times. Annius Scapula, who rebelled against Caesar's forces in the Spanish Wars, had a male concubine (Julius Caesar, *Spanish Wars* 33). Tacitus records that Nero played the bride, in a public marriage to a man named Pythagoras, wearing a veil, and calling for witnesses with "all the forms of regular marriage (*in modum solemnium coniugiorum*)" (*Annals* 15.37.4). Suetonius tells us that Nero went through another public marriage ceremony with a boy named Sporus whom he had castrated. Sporus was provided a dowry, wore a veil, and was led to their house by a wedding procession (*Nero* 28.1). According to Dio Cassius, Nero chose to marry Sporus, even though he was already married to Pythagoras, because Sporus looked like Sabina (*Epitome* 62.28).[5] Poppaea Sabina was Nero's wife who had died after they got in a fight after coming home late from the races. Nero kicked her in the stomach even though she was pregnant with his child, leading to her death (Suetonius, *Nero* 35.3). Nero dressed Sporus like an empress, had him carried through the city on a litter, and even kissed him publicly (*Ibid.*, 28.2). When Nero was killed, Nymphidius Sabinus, the prefect of the Praetorian Guard who conspired in Nero's death, took Sporus as his own lover, calling him "Poppaea" (Plutarch, *Galba* 9.3).

The Roman poet Martial around 101 A.D. wrote a poem that was likely intended to criticize the fact that marriages between men produced no offspring. Describing the ceremony between a bearded man name Callistratus, who wore a bridal veil and a man named Afer, he describes all the elements of a Roman wedding "in the usual form in which a virgin marries a husband." Wedding torches, a wedding song, and even a dowry were involved, finally asking sarcastically, "Are you still not satisfied, O Rome? Are you waiting for him to give birth?" (*Epigrammata* 12.42). A few years later, around 117 A.D. Juvenal wrote a moral satire mocking a similar marriage between a man named Gracchus (a name that was honorable because of the leader in the early Roman Republic of the same name) who married a trumpet player (*Satire* 1.2.117-142). Once again, he describes all the trappings of a Roman wedding, including the signing of the "contract (*tabulae*)" (119), but Juvenal calls it a "sacrilege (*nefas*)" (127), even bemoaning the day "if we live long enough, it will happen openly, and they will want it reported

---

[5] Both Suetonius and Dio Cassius record that Nero's marriage to Sporus led to the saying common among Romans regarding Nero's father, Domitius, "It would have been well for the world if Domitius had such a wife!"—a back-handed way of wishing Nero had never been born (Suetonius, *Nero* 28.1; Dio Cassius, *Epitome* 62.28).

in the city record" (135-136). It is unclear, however, if Juvenal considered it "sacrilege" because it was a man with a man, or because it was "a man of high birth and wealth (*viro clarus genere atque opibus*)" (129) who married a man of the lower classes. Juvenal rejoiced that nature prevents such unions from reproducing (139-142).

After the emperor Constantine came to believe in Jesus, Roman law would no longer tolerate this. In 342 A.D. Constantine's sons, Constans and Constantius II passed a law prohibiting homosexual marriage and requiring the execution of those who violated this law. The law declared:

> Emperors Constantius and Constans to the people: When a male gives himself in marriage to a "woman" [i.e. an effeminate man], and what he wants is that the "woman" play the male role, where sex has lost its place, where the crime is such that it is better not to know it, where feminine beauty is changed into a different shape, where love is sought but not found, we order laws to arise, justice to be armed with an avenging sword, so that the disgraced persons who are now or who in the future shall be guilty, may be subjected to the most severe penalties (*Theodosian Code* C.Th. 9.7.3).

C. Sex Outside of Marriage.

The next redefinitions of marriage recorded in Scripture concern sex outside of marriage. We might not think of these as attempts to redefine marriage, but properly that is exactly how any attempt to move sexual behavior outside of the bounds of marriage must be understood. While God established the "one flesh" union of sexual contact within the covenant of marriage (Gen. 2:24), whether we are talking about pre-marital sex, a mate having sexual contact with the someone else, or the attitude that would engage in sexual conduct in any manner outside the marriage covenant, it changes marriage into something God never intended for it to be. We will note four examples that date to the earliest stage of biblical history: incest, pre-marital sex, adultery, and prostitution.

1. Incest. We have already noted the polygamy of Lamech (Gen. 4:19) and the homosexuality of the men of Sodom (Gen. 19:5-7), which would certainly qualify as types of sexual conduct outside of God's original design for marriage. However, the first example that is not a type of marital covenant, or involving partners of the same sex, concerns the behavior of Lot's daughters. After leaving Sodom, they committed fornication with their father (after they got him drunk) and conceived children, from whom the Moabite and Ammonite nations would descend (Gen. 19:31-38). We would call this *incest,* from the Latin word *castus* meaning "clean, pure"—from which our word *caste* comes—and the prefix *in-* meaning "un-." It technically means "unclean" or "impure" but has come to refer to sexual relations between those of the same family. The Patriarchal record records this incident with the assumed inference that it was condemned, but we are not told specifically what God's law on this subject (as revealed to the patriarchs) was at that time. Some fairly close relationships were allowed. The children of Adam and Eve would have had to marry each other in order to populate the earth, as would the descendants of Noah after the flood. Sarah was Abraham's half sister (Gen. 20:12). Rebekah was Isaac's first cousin, once removed (Gen. 22:23). Rachel and Leah were Jacob's first cousins (Gen. 29:10). Under Mosaic Law it was revealed, "none of you shall approach anyone who is near of kin to him to uncover his nakedness" (Lev. 18:6), followed by a detailed list of relationships that were forbidden (Lev. 18:7-16). If Abraham and Jacob had lived under Mosaic Law Abraham's marriage to Sarah would have been sinful (Lev. 18:9) and Jacob's marriage to sisters would have been sinful (Lev. 18:18). Now, the Law of Christ, in condemning "fornication" (and probably "uncleanness") echoes Mosaic sexual prohibitions (Matt. 15:19; 2 Cor. 12:21; Gal. 5:19; Eph. 5:3; Col. 3:5, et. al.). This makes it clear that all incest is condemned under Christ.

Before listing improper sexual relations in the Mosaic Law, the Lord declared that the Israelites were not to follow the practices of "the land of Egypt where you dwelt" or "the land of Canaan where I am bringing you" (Lev. 18:3). While we may find it distasteful to even read the detailed prohibitions of such relationships it is important for us to understand that these things were practiced as acceptable among the nations. For example, Hittite laws considered it acceptable for a man to have intercourse with slaves who were sisters and their mother, or for a father and son to have intercourse with the same slave (Held, 131-132). These are some of the very practices Mosaic Law specifically condemned (Lev. 18:17-18).[6] While western culture has never publicly approved of incestuous behavior, history is littered with examples of children being sexually abused by the very family members to whom they should have been able to depend for the most trust and protection. Particularly when such behavior is committed by those who put

---

[6] One of the clearest examples of this is seen in Hittite Laws regarding bestiality. While Mosaic Law condemned and required the death penalty for all such offenses (Lev. 18:23; 20:15-16), Hittite law permitted this with some animals, while condemning it with others (Held, 131-132).

on a show of religious piety, such wicked behavior can damage all chance some souls ever have of faith in God and trust in others. God will judge this wickedness and those who perpetrate it will answer for it in the Judgment!

2. Pre-marital Sex. God established the bond of marriage as the sole relationship in which the "one flesh" relationship is to be enjoyed. Yet, in our own day, as in most of human history, man has refused to honor God's design and chosen to engage in sexual behavior before marriage. The first recorded instance of this concerns the daughter of Jacob—Dinah. Although this is sometimes referred to as the "rape of Dinah" that may not necessarily be the case. Jacob had purchased some land from Hamor, the father of a young man named Shechem (Gen. 33:19). When Shechem saw Jacob's daughter, Scripture says, "he took her and lay with her, and violated her" (Gen. 34:2). Even after this we are told that he "loved the young woman and spoke kindly to her" (Gen. 34:3), but even so the Holy Spirit expresses the divine attitude towards his action—"he had done a disgraceful thing in Israel by lying with Jacob's daughter, a thing which ought not to be done" (Gen. 34:7). Just because love is involved does not make something that is wrong right. The final result was that Dinah's brother's Simeon and Levi ultimately killed Shechem and his family (Gen. 34:11-29).

When the Law of Moses was binding upon the Jews, pre-marital sex was also condemned. In Deuteronomy 22:13-29 several relevant laws were spelled out:

1. If it was discovered that a women was not a virgin when she was married she was to be stoned—"because she has done a disgraceful thing in Israel" (22:21).

2. If a betrothed women had sex with another man in the city, both the man and the woman were to be stoned (22:23-24).

3. If a man had sex with a betrothed woman in the countryside he alone was to be stoned, because although she may have cried for help no one could hear her (22:25-27).

4. If a man took a virgin who was not betrothed and had sex with her, he had to pay the girl's father fifty shekels of silver, and he was never allowed to divorce her (22:28-29).

We should clarify, at this point in our study some points about the word "fornication." In modern usage, man sometimes speaks of "fornication" when talking about premarital sex, and "adultery" when talking about sex outside of marriage. The Greek word *porneia* refers to "illicit sexual intercourse in general" (Thayer). All types of sexual immorality are "fornication." So while pre-marital sex is fornication, so is adultery or homosexuality. The New Testament, in its condemnation of "fornication" echoed the Old Law's condemnation of such things (Matt. 5:32; 15:20; 19:9; Mark 7:21; 1 Cor. 6:13, 18; 2 Cor. 12:21; Eph. 5:5; Col. 3:5; 1 Thess. 4:3). Paul reasserts God's original place for sexual contact, commanding, "because of sexual immorality, let each man have his own wife, and let each woman have her own husband" (1 Cor. 7:2).

Sadly, pre-marital sex has been a problem throughout all of human history. The drive for sexual contact is very strong, but it can be controlled. In our culture the "sexual explosion" of 1960s has certainly made this much more open and accepted than it was in times past. Our great-great-grandparents would never have dreamed there would come a time when contraceptives would be distributed in schools! Even so, we shouldn't see this as a new problem. Boys and girls have always been attracted to each other. That attraction is part of the mechanism God has designed to drawn people to one another, and ultimately to marriage. We must understand, however, that refusing to wait until marriage cheapens the "one flesh" union, and alters the definition God has established for marriage.

3. Adultery. In the same way that we noticed above that homosexuality and pre-marital sex are behaviors that seek to redefine marriage, we must properly understand adultery as an additional redefinition. Adultery adds a third party into the "one flesh" relationship that was never authorized by God.

The first example of this redefinition overlaps the first issue we have already considered—polygamy. As we remember, Rachel gave her servant Bilhah to Jacob "as wife" (Gen. 30:4). So Bilhah was Jacob's legal wife in spite of the fact that concubinage itself was a redefinition of marriage. Scripture tells us that Jacob's oldest son, Reuben, "went in and lay with Bilhah, his father's concubine" (Gen. 35:22). There is no question this was considered sinful under Patriarchal Law. Jacob later cursed Reuben because he "defiled" his father's bed (Gen. 49:4). This is equally clear when it does not involve concubinage. When Joseph would be tempted by the wife of his master Potiphar to commit adultery, he responded, "How then can I do this great wickedness, and sin against God?" (Gen. 39:9). Joseph recognized that such a sin would not only be a sin against his master, but against God! That makes it clear that God had revealed this prohibition during the

Patriarchal Age. In the Law of Moses, adultery was prohibited under the Ten Commandments (Exod. 20:14; Deut. 5:18) and the death penalty was commanded for its violation (Lev. 20:10). Mosaic Law commanded the same for the man who had intercourse with his father's wife (Lev. 20:11), so if Reuben had lived under the Mosaic Law he should have been put to death. When David took the wife of Uriah, he rightly deserved death (2 Sam. 11:1-27). He was only spared because of the direct pardon granted to him by the Lord, in response to his humble repentance (2 Sam. 12:13-15; cf. Psa. 51:1-19).

The Law of Christ equally condemns adultery, including it among things that disqualify one from inheriting the kingdom of heaven (1 Cor. 6:9-10; Gal. 5:19-20; Heb. 13:4). Although the Law of Christ does not specifically command the death penalty for those who commit adultery, neither does it specify the death penalty for murder. The responsibility for punishment of crime rests with the civil authority (cf. Rom. 13:4). Church discipline is commanded for the adulterer who is unrepentant. In a case reminiscent of Reuben's sin with Bilhah, a man in the church in Corinth had his father's wife (1 Cor. 5:1). The church was commanded to withdraw from this unrepentant adulterer (1 Cor. 5:5). Jesus, extends the definition of adultery beyond its Old Testament sense to include remarriage after unscriptural divorce and remarriage. Anyone who marries a "put away" mate "commits adultery" and anyone who "puts away" a mate for a cause other than sexual immorality and marries another "commits adultery" (Matt. 5:32; 19:9; Mark 10:11-12; Luke 16:18). Thus, in Jesus' teaching, adultery is not only possible while a marriage covenant is in place, but can occur even after a covenant has been unlawfully broken.

Human history is a torrid and twisted tragedy of lives broken by this heart-breaking corruption of the marriage bed. In many cases man has allowed himself a double standard in this area. Adultery on the part of a husband has been tolerated (or even expected), but viewed as shameful and intolerable on the part of the wife. This can be seen as far back as Homer's epic *The Odyssey.* This work, believed to have been written around 735 B.C. became a virtual bible for the Greco-Roman world for centuries. It praised the feats of the legendary figure Odysseus during his ten years of wanderings following the Trojan War. It proudly records without scorn, the exploits and numerous adulteries of "godly (*dios*) Odysseus," (1.196ff.)—the standard epithet for Odysseus. But the real hero (in my opinion) ought to be his wife, Penelope. She doesn't know where he is or whether he is alive or dead. She has dozens of suitors pursuing her for marriage but she resists. While his adulteries are treated as if they are almost expected, her faithfulness to him is equally expected. She is "wise Penelope" or "constant (*echephrōn*) Penelope" (4.111ff).

G. W. Peterman has documented how this double standard was the common view in much of the ancient world. In studying marriage contracts from this period often the woman was not to "be with (*suneinai*) another man," but for the man "the restriction is not against being with (*suneinai*), but against having (*echein*)" another woman (166). Sadly, this changed little in more modern times. Some slave owners in Colonial and pre-Civil War America granted themselves liberty to use female slaves for their own sexual exploitation. After DNA testing was done in 1998, it is now generally accepted that Thomas Jefferson fathered six children by Sally Hemings, a slave at Monticello ("Thomas Jefferson and Sally Hemings: A Brief Account"). It is commonly believed that Bill Gates, founder of Microsoft, had a clause written into a prenuptial agreement before he married allowing him to take a two-week vacation each year with a mistress! In an interview with CBS new, Gates denied that there was a prenuptial agreement, but such an arrangement would not be surprising given modern attitudes (Kohn, "Behind the Gates"). In January of 2012, in the midst of the presidential primary process, it was revealed that former speaker of the house Newt Gingrich (a presidential candidate at the time) told his second wife Marianne in 1999 that he either wanted a divorce or an "open marriage." In an interview with the *Washington Post*, Marriane Gingrich said, "He said the problem with me was I wanted him all to myself." Speaker Gingrich said the report was false but is currently married to the woman he was having an affair with at the time (Grimaldi). Whether it is the man or the woman, adultery is sin! God demands and expects a husband and a wife to keep the covenant they make with one another for life (Rom. 7:2-3; 1 Cor. 7:39).

4. Prostitution. The final redefinition we shall consider involving a type of sexual behavior outside of marriage is prostitution. The first scriptural reference to this practice comes in the words of Jacob's sons, Simeon and Levi, when they defended their actions in killing Shechem for defiling Dinah. They asked their father, "should he treat our sister like a harlot?" (Gen. 34:31). Although this is the first scriptural reference it infers to us that the practice was already going on—Jacob understood their words, and they were probably cursed later for their impulsive action (Gen. 49:5-7). There is great irony in Simeon and Levi's words! Dinah's brothers were outraged at what

Shechem did to their sister, but their younger brother Judah seemed to have no reservation treating someone else's daughter or sister *like a harlot!* When Judah's two sons sinned and were struck dead by the Lord, Judah promised his third son, Shelah, to Tamar, the wife of his firstborn in order to raise up children. But Judah didn't honor his word, forcing Tamar to return to live with her father (Gen. 38:1-11). Judah's wife Shua died, and, while traveling, Judah committed fornication with a prostitute, not knowing the prostitute was Tamar, who had dressed this way to deceive him because he had not honored his word (Gen. 38:12-23). Judah's own words reveal that under Patriarchal Law this was considered sinful—when he was told that she was "with child by harlotry" he commanded her to "be burned" (Gen. 39:24). How hypocritical! *He* would fornicate with a harlot, but then turn around and be ready to *burn* his daughter-in-law for "harlotry." Tamar exposed Judah's hypocrisy and she was spared, because Judah had not honored his word to her (Gen. 38:27-30). This shows how important it was in ancient times to a woman's very identity and security to be able to bear children.

Under Mosaic Law Israelites were forbidden to allow their daughters to be a harlot (Lev. 19:29a), especially a "ritual prostitute (*qᵉdēšâh*)" (Lev. 23:17), describing this as causing the land to "become full of wickedness" (Lev. 19:29b). Even so, harlotry continued in Israel. Jephthah was the "son of a harlot" (Judg. 11:1) and the wise man warned young men that they could be "reduced to a crust of bread"—"by means of a harlot" (Prov. 6:26). Non-Israelite cities were filled with harlotry. The house of a harlot would occasionally be a place Israelites could hide during times of war (cf. Josh. 2:1; Judg. 16:1). The New Testament has little to say about harlotry. Contrary to the common claim, there is nothing in Scripture to indicate Mary Magdalene was a harlot. Harlotry is also condemned in the condemnation of "fornication" (Matt. 5:32; 15:20; 19:9; Mark 7:21; 1 Cor. 6:13, 18; 2 Cor. 12:21; Eph. 5:5; Col. 3:5; 1 Thess. 4:3). In fact, the verb form of the word *porneia*, translated "fornication," is *porneuō* meaning "to play the harlot" (1 Cor. 6:18; 10:8; Rev. 2:14, 20; 17:2; 18:3, 9).

In our own day we are certainly surrounded by many who dress in "the attire of a harlot" (Prov. 7:10), but with the exception of isolated places like Las Vegas, prostitution is something Americans would have to pursue, not something that surrounds us in respectable society. It is important for us to understand that this was not the environment of the ancient world, especially when Jews and Christians were dispersed into the Gentile world. We noted above that prostitution was deeply rooted within pagan religion.

The phrase to "play the harlot with their gods," used frequently in the Old Testament (Exod. 34:15-16; Deut. 31:16; Judg. 2:17; 8:33; 1 Chron. 5:25; Ezek. 6:9), likely had a figurative and literal application when describing those who turned to idolatry. Strabo claimed that the temple of Aphrodite in Corinth at one point in history had 1000 shrine prostitutes (*Geography* 13.6.20). Corinth was so known for its wickedness that the Greek playwright Aristophanes preserves the use of the verb *korinthiazomai*, meaning to "to act like a Corinthian," i.e. to commit fornication (*Fragments* 370). It is little wonder that to the church in this city Paul warned, "Do you not know that your bodies are members of Christ? Shall I then take the members of Christ and make them members of a harlot? Certainly not!" (1 Cor. 6:15). Herodotus records that in Babylon the law required every woman of the land to serve as a temple prostitute at least once in her lifetime (*Histories* 1.199). Even though I believe John used the phrase figuratively of Rome, it is little wonder that he would speak of "Babylon the Great, the Mother of Harlots" (Rev. 17:5) as a way of describing Rome's wickedness. In the same text that speaks of Babylon, Herodotus says the same thing about some parts of Cyprus, the home of Barnabas (Acts 4:36; cf. 15:39). Lucian describes similar requirements in Byblos (*On the Syrian Goddess* 6). Herodotus tells us that in Lydia young women were expected to serve as prostitutes in order to earn their dowries before they could get married (*Histories* 1.93.4).

Not all prostitution was religious. In the second century Justin described the perverse dependence that had developed between the prostitution industry and the barbaric custom of "exposing babies" (i.e. abandoning them in a public place). Both boys and girls who were exposed were regularly collected in order to be raised up as prostitutes (*First Apology* 27). While the rise of pornographic uses of the internet has made accessible some things that were once relegated only to the seedy back allies of the worst parts of town, nothing in our modern culture has yet come close to the dark and depraved world into which the gospel was born.

D. Divorce and Remarriage.

The final redefinition we shall consider that is addressed in the biblical record is divorce. Divorce is also a redefinition of marriage because it changes the God-ordained terms of the marriage covenant. When this is compounded by unscriptural remarriage, it creates relationships that are defined by Jesus as adulterous. The first instance of divorce recorded in Scripture, once again concerns the family of Abraham. When Sarah became concerned that Ishmael, Abraham's son by her servant Hagar, might receive the inheritance that belonged to Isaac she urged Abraham to "cast out the bondwoman" (Gen. 21:10). After God promised to make a nation of Ishmael also (Gen. 21:13), Scripture tells us, "So Abraham rose early in the morning, and took bread and a skin of water; and putting it on her shoulder, he gave it and the boy to Hagar, and sent her away. Then she departed and wandered in the Wilderness of Beersheba" (Gen. 21:14). The Hebrew verb *šilleḥāh*, translated "sent [her] away" is the same word used in the Mosaic Law's ordinance on divorce (Deut. 24:1-4) and in God's later declaration that He "hates putting away" (Mal. 2:16).

Mosaic Law on Divorce

As we saw in the case of polygamy, while this is the first recorded instance of "putting away" it was not the first instance of its practice. The Babylonian Code of Hammurabi (ca. 1700 B.C.) required that, if a woman wanted to leave her husband, he has to give his consent, saying to her, "I have put her away," she could go and he did not have to pay her a dowry. If he said, "I have not put her away" he could take another wife, and the woman who tried to leave had to become a servant in his house (141). Mosaic Law has often been misunderstood as divine approval of divorce. A better way to understand it is that it was an allowance aimed at curbing a practice that was already going on "because of the hardness" of men's hearts (Matt. 19:8a). Jesus taught that it was not intended "from the beginning" (Matt. 19:8b). Mosaic Law demanded that a man give a wife a "certificate of divorce" and "send her from his house" if his wife no longer "found favor in his eyes" because he found in her some "uncleanness" (Deut. 24:1). This "uncleanness" likely referred to some type of indecency short of adultery, since adultery would require the death penalty (Lev. 20:10).

There was much debate about this law among the Jews. The Babylonian Talmud records three distinct views taught by respected teachers. Before the time of Jesus, Shammai taught that the "uncleanness" in this passage concerned sexual misconduct. His opponent, Hillel taught that an "unseemly thing in her" could be something as minor as a wife spilling her husband's food. In New Testament times, the Jewish teacher Akiba taught that the phrase "no favor in his eyes" meant that a man could divorce his wife even if he just became attracted to another woman (*Gittin* 90a). The Law of Christ makes it clear that God intends marriage to last for life. The only terms under which one may "put away" a wife and remarry without it being considered adultery is when the "putting away" is because of fornication (Matt. 5:32; 19:9). All remarriage on the part of one "put away" is defined as "adultery" (cf. Mark 10:11-12; Luke 16:18). Since God makes them one (Mal. 2:15), Jesus teaches "what God has joined together, let no man separate" (Matt. 19:6).

Divorce in the Ancient World

This teaching was as revolutionary and life-altering when it was first taught as it is today. The world of the New Testament was plagued by divorce. The Romans claimed that Romulus, the legendary founder of Rome, established marriage laws which allowed a man to put away his wife only for poisoning the children, counterfeiting the keys to the house, and adultery (Plutarch, *Romulus,*22), but by the first century such laws were disregarded. Caesar Augustus pushed through legislation intended to strengthen marriage and limit divorce, yet mostly these laws concerned financial penalties for unjustly divorcing a wife (Seutonius, *Augustus,*34). Sadly, the dowry women brought into marriage was the only thing that preserved many ancient marriages. The Roman poet Seneca, Nero's tutor, bemoaned the fact that in his day, "some noble ladies reckon the years of their lives, not by the number of the consuls, but by that of their husbands, now that they leave their homes in order to marry others, and marry only in order to be divorced" (*On Benefits* 3.16.2).

In the Greek world divorce was allowed for many reasons. In Athens while a woman seeking a divorce had to go before the Archon, a man could simply send a wife from his house (Plutarch, *Alcibiades* 8). Among the Spartans it was believed that a barren woman should be put away. (Herodotus, 5.39). Not all ancient people were so tolerant of divorce. Tacitus claimed that the Germans maintained very strict marriage codes. Adultery was severely punished and a woman was said to take "one husband, just as she has one body for life" (*Germania* 18-19).[7]

Ancient Divorce Procedures

Divorce in ancient times was a much simpler thing than in our time. Mosaic Law taught that a husband simply gave a "certificate of divorce" to the wife. God would use this procedure in describing either His sustained faithfulness to Israel—He had not given her a certificate of divorce (Isa.

---

[7] For more on ancient attitudes toward divorce see my study "Divorce and Remarriage in the Pagan World," *Christianity Magazine* 15.7 (July 1998) 16. Reprinted as "Divorce and Remarriage in Ancient Times," *Truth Magazine* 50.2 (Jan. 19, 2006) 21 [online] *http://www.ancientroadpublications.com/Studies/ BiblicalStudies/ AncientDivorce.html.*

50:1)—or as proof that His covenant with them was broken—He had put Israel away and "given her a certificate of divorce" (Jer. 3:8). The Babylonian Talmud, records the custom that a Jewish man could put away his wife (or betrothed wife) merely with two witnesses present (*Gittin* 5b). In Roman divorce, typically the nuptial tablets were broken, and the husband said to the wife *tuas res tibi habeto,* "you keep your things" (cf. Plautus, *Amphitryon* 3.2.47). A similar formula was used among the Greeks. Justin tells us of a Christian woman in the second century who submitted a *repudium* because of her husband's fornication (*Second Apology* 2.6). This was a Latin term used for a particular type of divorce procedure. Under the *Lex Julia,* enacted by Augustus, a *repudium* was required to take place in the presence of seven witnesses of full age who were Roman citizens (*Digest* 24.2.9). Under Antoninus Pius and Marcus Aurelius the Roman jurist Gaius records that a *repudium* declared the words "have your things for yourself (*tuas res tibi habeto*)," or "conduct your own affairs (*tuas res tibi agito*)" (*Digest* 24.2.2).

Modern Divorce

In ancient times divorce was not really government affair. As we shall see below, just as marriage was a contract between families or the man and woman, the ending of that covenant was generally also a private matter. Civil government only played a role if there was some irregularity in the contract or some failure to abide by the terms the parties had agreed upon. This changed in the early 20th century when states adopted policies of marriage licensing. From that point on just as government essentially *granted* marriages, it also put itself in a position to *grant* divorces. Each state set its own terms. Some, following New Testament patterns, only granted divorce for "adultery," but others allowed other causes. In 1970 the National Conference of Commissioners on Uniform State Laws, a national conference of appointees sent by state governors drafted "The Uniform Marriage and Divorce Act (UMDA)." This proposal attempted to move state legislatures to apply common standards and laws concerning divorce. UMDA introduced the principle of "irreconcilable differences" as the only grounds needed to obtain divorce. Only the states of Arizona, Colorado, Illinois, Kentucky, Minnesota, Missouri, Montana, and Washington fully adopted it, but this was very influential on state laws across the country in that it moved towards the elimination of so-called "fault divorces" and removed some of the defenses in divorce cases that had historically been applied.

These changes have created tremendous challenges for Christians. We are to obey civil authorities (Rom. 13:1-7) and the laws they enact (1 Pet. 2:13-17), but what about times when civil authority assists in the violation of what God commands? In cases where civil law commands the violation of divine ordinance we clearly must "obey God rather than men" (Acts 5:29). Yet, the very teaching of Jesus against divorce and remarriage acknowledges conditions in which human beings "put away" a mate "and marry another" contrary to divine law (cf. Mark 10:11-12). Whether civil authority grants this or not, it is contrary to God's command. In modern times, when is it that a mate is actually "put away"? We have seen that, through most of human history, this was not something that the civil government determined, but now it has presumed that right. We cannot just ignore our obligation to submit to civil authority. The Bible doesn't teach a so-called "mental divorce," but neither can we yield to wicked schemes of men to manipulate or ignore divine law in order to satisfy their own desires. I have heard about situations in Latin American countries where the influence of the Roman Catholic Church is so intertwined with the government that citizens with the scriptural right to "put away" a mate can only do so at the cost of a fee equal to the average yearly salary, even though the same is not demanded of Catholics! As with a marriage covenant, something actually happens when two people marry. It is not just living together, or a feeling in the heart. Something must actually happen that properly determines when one has been "put away." At the same time, we must be careful as Christians never to make excuses that would allow us to violate God's laws, or misjudge the sincere efforts of those trying to balance obedience to the Law of Christ and submission to a civil government disinterested in what Scripture teaches.

E. Human Control over Marriage.

The final redefinition that we will consider concerns efforts that man has often made to assume the role that rightly belongs only to God. We noted earlier that the reference to *being joined* in Genesis 2:24 refers to what is understood within a particular culture to identify who is and who is not married. This does not mean that man has the right to *define* marriage. The very dilemma our country now faces demonstrates this. No matter what government may say "same-sex" marriage is not marriage, as God designed it. It is clear that Christians are to obey civil authorities (Rom. 13:1-7) and the laws which they enact (1 Pet. 2:13-17). Even so, there have been times throughout history when the dominance of apostate religion or the ungodly imaginations of secular government have led man to presume a control over the divine institution of marriage that he was never given. Martin Luther said it well, "The joining together of a man and a woman is a divine law and is binding, however it may conflict with the laws of men; the laws of men must give way before it without hesitation" ("Babylonian Captivity," 263).

God and Man's Roles in the Marriage Covenant

From Malachi, it becomes clear that being joined has both a divine and a human element. It is God who acts as "witness" to the pledge made between a man and a woman who are free to marry, and so it is God who makes "them one" when this covenant is made (Mal. 2:14-15; cf. Matt. 19:6). It is, however, the man and woman who make the covenant. Something has to take place to identify them as married. In the account of Jesus talking with the woman at the well, He told her she previously had five husbands "and the one whom you now have is not your husband" (John 4:18). Simply living with the man did not make him her husband—they had not made a covenant. John Calvin was correct that "the curse of God lies on every man and woman cohabiting without marriage" (*Institutes* 2.8.41). While some covenant is made when two people marry, it is possible for men to make covenants that God does not approve. It is not that He does not *see* that a covenant has taken place—He sees it as an unlawful covenant. The Israelites were forbidden to make some covenants (Exod. 23:32; Deut. 7:2), but Ahab made an unlawful covenant with Ben-Hadad, the king of Syria (2 Kings 20:34). God knew that He made the covenant, but He did not approve of it (2 Kings 20:42).

The Marriage Contract

When a covenant is made, man does something to indicate that an agreement has been reached. From the earliest times marriages did not involve a license but a contract. The Sumerian law code known as the Laws of Ur-Nammu speak of the necessity of a "marriage contract" (Col. 2, 250-255). Between the Old and New Testament, the apocryphal book of Tobit described a father and mother giving their daughter in marriage and writing and sealing for her "an instrument of covenants" (7:14). Among the Romans *tabulae* contracts were signed by witnesses and the couple (Tacitus, *Annals* 11.27; Juvenal, *Satires* 2.119) and literally broken if a marriage was dissolved (*Ibid.,* 9.75-76). In the time of Tiberius (42 B.C. to A.D. 16), Tacitus records that an old ceremony once practiced to transfer a woman from the authority of her father to the authority of her husband was only rarely practiced (*Annals* 4.16), but contracts were still signed. For most of human history marriage was understood to be a private contract between families or between the bride and groom that was not dependent upon either the church or the government to recognize the covenant.

Fortunately many examples of such marriage contracts have survived that help us understand what they involved. Hunt and Edgar translate two notable papyri believed to date the first century B.C. *P.Teb.* 104 (90 B.C.) describes the arrangement between a man named Philiscus and a woman named Apollonia. Philiscus agrees in the contract to provide Apollonia with clothes and necessities "in proportion to their means" and not to "bring in another wife"—"have a concubine or boy"—"have children by another woman," nor "to eject or insult or ill-treat her." Apollonia agrees "to obey him as a wife should," and not "to consort with another man," or bring him shame or dishonor (5-9, from Peterman, 164-165). Another contract, *BGU* 1053 (13 B.C.) is made between a man named Apollonius and a woman named Thermion. It is almost identical to the first, but adds the condition that Apollonius will forfeit the dowry "increased by half" if he ever should "ill-treat her"—"cast her out"—"insult her" or "bring in another woman" (10-11, *Ibid.,* 166-167). Milligan translates P. Oxy. 905 (A.D. 170) which records not only that the husband and wife were present, but also documents the fact that his mother, "being present assents to the wedding" (87). Roman law set twelve as the lowest marriageable age for a young girl and fourteen for a boy (Justinian, *Institutes* 1.22). Perhaps this was a young couple, so the mother's assent is noted. This contract also lists the value of the dowry and ends by stating that "the contract is valid, being written in duplicate that each party may have one" (*Ibid.*). Instone-Brewer offers some Jewish marriage contracts dated to the 2nd century A.D. Notable in the introductory portion of *P. Yadin* 18 (A.D. 128), is the fact that the bride is said to be "a virgin" (226). The contract ends with signatures from both parties, two witnesses, and the scribe who wrote the contract (227). *P. Yadin* 10 specifies that the parties will live "according to the Law of Moses and the Judeans" promising that the wife can live in the husband's home if he should go to his "eternal home before" the wife (231). The husband agrees to replace the contract for the wife at any time upon request (*ibid.*). All of these are formal declarations of terms. Both parties are expected to honor the terms. In each of these examples it is clear that it is the parties involved who are transacting the agreement. Any involvement by the government would simply be to enforce the terms agreed upon. This stands in stark contrast to the modern marriage license which essentially allows the parties to enter into their covenant (after the waiting period specified). This differs also from modern vows, in which couples say words of pledge to one another, but often don't consider them as binding as they might a business contract.

Church Control of Marriage

The steps that led from government having limited involvement in marriage to our present condition in which the state has presumed for itself the authority to *define* marriage can be traced through history. It begins with challenges faced by Christians in the first years after the New Testament. In turning to Christ Gentile Christians could not continue in any practices that involved idolatry (cf. 1 Cor. 10:28-29). Tertullian claimed that one reason Christians did not marry pagan wives was because of the idolatry that was involved in the manner in which pagan marriages were initiated (*On the Crown* 13). So how were Christians to enter into the marriage covenant? One of the earliest apostasies of church history was the appointment of a single man from among an eldership who was appointed as "bishop" over a church, then a city, and ultimately a region. An early writer named Ignatius (ca. 30-107), who had already bowed to such apostasy, offered some advice that would set the stage for an apostasy that affected marriage. Ignatius taught, "it becomes both men and women who marry, to form their union with the approval of the bishop that their marriage may be according to God, and not after their own lust" (*The Epistle of Ignatius to Polycarp* 5). Ignatius was probably just advising a way to help strengthen marriage. Tertullian, in a similar way, argued that marriages must be "first professed in presence of the Church" in order to avoid any appearance that the union between the couple was fornication (*On Chastity* 4.4). Such notions of seeking the *"approval of the bishop"* and involving the church to avoid the appearance of wrongdoing, would expand quickly into a concept that marriage was a "sacrament" only truly administered by church officials.

Development of the Sacramental Concept of Marriage

In classical usage the Latin word *sacramentum* referred to a sum that was deposited by parties in a dispute then used for religious purposes by the losing party. Over time this meaning expanded to refer to oaths, secrets, and even to things held to be sacred (*Lewis and Short Latin Dictionary*). In Roman Catholic theology a "sacrament" is: 1) a religious rite, 2) that is a sign of inner sanctification, 3) it confers divine grace, and 4) this grace is bestowed through the rite (Lehmkuhl, "Sacrament of Marriage"). Catholics believe there are seven sacraments: Baptism, Confirmation, the Eucharist, Penance, Extreme Unction (or last rites), Order (of church officials), and Matrimony. Thomas Aquinas (A.D. 1225-1274) would express it, "Matrimony, then, in that it consists in the union of a husband and wife purposing to generate and educate offspring for the worship of God, is a sacrament of the Church; hence, also, a certain blessing on those marrying is given by the ministers of the Church" (*Contra Gentiles* 4.78.2).

In truth this view of marriage did not fully develop for some time. Catholic scholar Augustinus Lehmkuhl, in his entry on the "Sacrament of Matrimony" in the *Catholic Encyclopedia* acknowledges, "The name *sacrament* cannot be cited as satisfactory evidence, since it did not acquire until a late period the exclusively technical meaning it has today; both in pre-Christian times and in the first centuries of the Christian Era it had a much broader and more indefinite signification" (Lehmkuhl). In spite of this, he cites early evidence to defend this false doctrine. The early use of the word *sacramentum* in biblical translation undoubtedly contributed to a growing misapplication of its meaning. After Paul's quote of Genesis 2:24 in Ephesians 5:33, the Latin Vulgate (ca. 4th century) translated the Greek word *mustērion,* rendered "mystery" in most English translations, with the Latin word *sacramentum.* Augustine (354-430), commenting on this text wrote, "This the apostle applies to the case of Christ and of the Church, and calls it then 'a great sacrament.' What, then, in Christ and in the Church is great, in the instances of each married pair it is but very small, but even then it is the sacrament of an inseparable union" (*On Marriage and Concupiscence* 1.23).

These moves led church leaders to presume the right to define marriage, but there were also political factors that influenced this. After Constantine there was more of an effort by emperors to promote religious objectives through the arm of the state. The emperor Justinian I (ca. 482-565), for example, in an effort to end false claims "that men and women living with each other had called each other husband and wife, and in this manner invent marriages that in fact were never contracted" (*Novellae* 74.4.preface), made laws which served to further establish the concept that the Catholic Church defined marriage. Justinian ordered that, if those of high rank wished to be married without "wedding documents (*nuptialia documenta*)," they had to go to a "house of prayer (*orationis domum*)" and before at least three witnesses of the church declare their intention to be married and have them sign "letters (*litteris*)" signifying this (*Ibid.,* 4.1). This certification was to be filed in the "archives of the church of the Most Holy" (*Ibid.,* 4.2). Common people who did not "contract in writing (*non scripto convenire*)" also had the same opportunity (*Ibid.,* 4.3). It would be sufficient to make an oath "touching the Holy Scriptures in a house of prayer" (*Ibid.,* 5.1). In spite of what motivated these changes, they reinforced the notion that marriage was only valid if it was endorsed by the Catholic Church.

Church *and* State: The Protestant Response

The Protestant Reformation brought a dramatic change in western culture's view of marriage. The Protestants rejected the idea that marriage was a "sacrament" administered only by the Catholic Church. Martin Luther argued, "marriage is an outward, bodily thing, like any other worldly undertaking" ("Estate of Marriage," 25). John Calvin called it a "good and holy ordinance of God" but added that "agriculture, architecture, shoemaking, and shaving are lawful ordinances of God; but they are not sacraments" (*Institutes* 4.19.34). Luther and Calvin both rejected the Vulgate's rendering of *mustērion* and affirmed that it referred to a secret once unknown and not to marriage as a "great *sacrament*" ("Babylonian Captivity," 257-258; *Institutes* 4.19.35-36). Luther wrote, "we read nowhere that the man who marries a wife receives any grace of God," going on further to conclude, "since marriage existed from the beginning of the world and is still found among unbelievers, it cannot possibly be called a sacrament of the New Law and the exclusive possession of the Church" ("Babylonian Captivity," 257). John Witte, Jr. in his book *From Sacrament to Contract: Marriage, Religion, and Law in the Western Tradition,* describes how this change of attitude influenced Protestant politics in the sixteenth century in Geneva, which was setup to be a model of Reformed Protestant thinking. According to Witte, *The Marriage Ordinance of Geneva* drafted by Calvin in 1545 set in place "the dual requirements of state registration and a church wedding to constitute marriage" (182).

In response to Protestant opposition to marriage as a sacrament administered by the church, the 24th Session of the Council of Trent in 1563 declared, "If any one saith, that matrimony is not truly and properly one of the seven sacraments of the evangelic law, (a sacrament) instituted by Christ the Lord; but that it has been invented by men in the Church; and that it does not confer grace; let him be anathema" (*On the Sacrament of Matrimony,* Canon 1). They also further affirmed their position that Catholic Church determined the validity of marriage, claiming, "Whosoever contracts marriage, otherwise than in the presence of the Parish Priest and of two or three witnesses, contracts it invalidly" (*Decree on the Reformation of Marriage,* Ch. 1). This view has continued since then. In 1898 pope Leo XIII declared, "No marriage can be considered firmly ratified unless it is joined according to Church law and discipline" (*Encyclical on Civil Marriage Law*).

Marriage Licensing in the United States

Historically immigrants to the British colonies in North America, and to the United States after its establishment have been predominately Protestant rather than Catholic. Principles of freedom of speech and the free exercise of religion influenced a political atmosphere in this country that was unwilling to shape political action in submission to any particular religious organization, let alone the Roman Catholic Church. That is not to say that religion has not affected political action. Opposition to polygamy was essentially motivated by religious values. We noticed above that the requirement of a marriage license was used in the federal government's effort to end Mormon polygamy. A cultural distrust of religious power, but a desire to regulate Protestant values moved political leaders in the twentieth century to an increased reliance on the power of the state. Marriage licensing became a tool to accomplish other political objectives as well. In 1911 the Conference of Commissioners of Uniform State Laws, composed of appointees sent from the various state governors, submitted a proposed draft for marriage licensing procedures throughout the states. This draft, known as "American Uniform Marriage and Marriage License Act" was aimed, at least in part, at ending the practice of "common law" marriages. It specified, "No person shall be joined in marriage within this state until a license shall have been obtained for that purpose" (§ 2). In the years that followed its draft every state adopted some form of marriage licensing similar to the proposal. Sadly, history shows that marriage licensing during this period was also used as a mechanism to prevent so-called *miscegenation,* or racial intermarriage. Peggy Pascoe explains:

> During the first three decades of the twentieth century, eugenicists, vital statisticians, and white supremacist threw themselves into the development of marriage license procedures, from somewhat different perspectives but with remarkably similar results. Displaying considerable faith in the administrative state, they assigned marriage license officials the task of sorting applicants into a wide, and increasing, number of categories, some racial, others physical or mental (Pascoe, 138).

Under this approach, various state governments presumed the right to deny the right of marriage to couples of different races. The United States Supreme court, in *Loving vs. Virginia,* 388 U.S. 1 (1967) ruled it unconstitutional to restrict marriage on racial grounds. Marriage licensing, however, continues to be a statistical tool for determining taxation and administering certain government benefits. Our modern battles over "same-sex" marriage mostly stem from issues concerning taxation and benefits. Had it not been for the government's move from simply recording marriages to determining who and when people could get married, we would not find ourselves in a position of waiting with nervous anticipation to see what the state *defines*.

Marriage licensing is the standard practice in the United States, but there are political and religious movements that continue to oppose it. The Libertarian Party argues that marriage licensing violates Article One, Section 10, of the U.S. Constitution, prohibiting any state from passing laws "impairing the obligation of contracts." Its 2012 platform asserted, "Government does not have the authority to define, license or restrict personal relationships" (1.3 *Personal Relationships*). "The American Uniform Marriage and Marriage License Act" when first drafted proposed that provision be made for ceremonies such as those practiced by Quakers, in which there is no officiating officer, but may be satisfied "by declaring in the presence of at least two competent witnesses, that they take each other as husband and wife" (§ 1.2). Some states recognize "Quaker Marriage." Today some Protestant fundamentalists argue that the very concept of *licensing* infers that the state holds authority to permit marriage which it was never given (Deschesne). Advocates of this view secure a simple "Marriage Certificate" signed by witnesses and a preacher, that can be submitted to a local courthouse without a marriage license. Couples who take this approach face a number of difficulties regarding their married status for taxation, Social Security, and other types of identification and licensing. I would advise any Christians considering such an approach to seek legal advice regarding this, as it may or may not be considered valid in their particular jurisdiction. I do not see marriage licensing as it now stands to be sinful, but we must continue to be watchful that it does not become sinful. The same presumption of power that restricted marriage along racial lines might one day try to control marriage along religious and moral lines! Once again, as Christians we must submit to the laws of the land (Rom. 13:13:1-7; 1 Pet. 2:13-17), but in doing so we must never surrender to civil authority rights that properly belong only to God.

III. Perspective on the Present.
We have considered many efforts that man has made to redefine marriage, but there are many others we could also have considered. Living together without marriage, pornography, efforts to change roles in the home, improper attitudes towards childrearing, spousal abuse and neglect, false religious doctrines that sex even in marriage, is sinful, or expanding the authority of the husband over divine law are all redefinitions of God's original design. For now we must limit our study to the issues that we have considered.

Where Things Now Stand

The fact that man has constantly sought to redefine marriage throughout the biblical and historical record should comfort Christians in the knowledge that things are not "worse than they have ever been"—it is not that "everything is falling apart"—the gospel was born in a world far more given to skewed definitions of marriage than our own. We must stand for truth, but truth will survive. At the same time, the knowledge of the struggles of the past does not take away the challenges of the present. In the presidential election of the last year, something happened for the first time in American history—the president of the United States came out publicly in support of "same-sex" marriage. In an interview with ABC News reporter, Robin Roberts, President Obama announced:

> I've been going through an evolution on this issue. . . .I had hesitated on gay marriage—in part, because I thought civil unions would be sufficient. . . .And—I was sensitive to the fact that—for a lot of people, you know, the—the word marriage was something that evokes very powerful traditions, religious beliefs, and so forth. . . .At a certain point, I've just concluded that—for me personally, it is important for me to go ahead and affirm that—I think same-sex couples should be able to get married (Obama, May 9, 2012).

How things have changed! From a government that once saw the redefinition marriage in the form of polygamy as barbaric, the Chief Executive of our Republic has now moved to support a practice that would have fit right in with the pagan wickedness of Nero's Rome! On February 28, 2013 the Obama administration filed a "friend-of-the-court" (*amicus curiae*) brief with the United States Supreme Court appealing to the court to overturn California's Proposition 8, which passed in 2008 adding a provision to the state constitution overturning the State Supreme Court's previous ruling legalizing same-sex marriage. The U.S. Supreme Court is expected to rule on this question near the time this lecture is published.

It is not the role of the church to promote political action. The church is a spiritual kingdom that permeates the hearts and souls of its subjects (Luke 17:21). It is the responsibility of the church and Christians as individuals to teach the truth. Whether the world around us moves away from biblical definitions of marriage or returns to the pattern recorded in Scripture members of the Lord's church must maintain our role as "the pillar and ground of the truth" (1 Tim. 3:15). When we fulfill this role, it will not be by political action or military conquest, but through persuasion of the mind and conversion of the soul that we will pull "down strongholds" and cast "down arguments" and "every high thing that exalts itself against the knowledge of God, bringing every thought into captivity to the obedience of Christ" (2 Cor. 10:5). May God help us to do this.

Works Cited

American Uniform Marriage and Marriage License Act. Commissioners on Uniform State Laws in National Conference (Nov. 1, 1911). Williamsport, PA: Railway Printing Co., 1911.

Aristophanes, *Fragments.* Vol. 5. Trans. Jeffery Henderson. Cambridge: Harvard University Press, 2007.

"Defense of Marriage Act." (P.L. 104-199), *United States Statutes at Large.* Vol. 110 (Act of Sept. 21, 1996) 2419-2420.

Deschesne, David. "Did you marry the god of the state?" *Fort Farfield Journal* [online] *http://www.mainemediaresources.com/mpl_marriage.htm.*

The Doctrine and Covenants of the Church of Jesus Christ of Latter Day Saints. Salt Lake City: Church of Jesus Christ of Latter Day Saints, 1973.

"Edmunds Anti-Polygamy Act." *United States Statutes at Large.* Vol. 22 (Act of March 22, 1882), 30-32.

"Edmunds-Tucker Anti-Polygamy Act" *United States Statutes at Large.* Vol. 24 (Act of March 3, 1887), 635-641.

Engelken, Karen. "*Pilegeš.*" *Theological Dictionary of the Old Testament.* Vol. 11. Ed. G. Johannes Botterweck, Helmer Ringgren, and Heinz-Josef-Fabry. Grand Rapids: Wm. B. Eerdmans Pub. Co., 2001.

Gadd, C. J. *Cuneiform Texts from Babylonian Tablets in the British Museum.* Part 39. London: Oxford University Press, 1926.

Gordon, Cyrus H. "Biblical Customs and the Nuzu [Nuzi] Tablets." *The Biblical Archaeologist* 3.1 (Feb. 1940) 1-12.

Grimaldi, James. "Marianne Gingrich, Newt's ex-wife, says he wanted 'open marriage.'" *The Washington Post.* Jan. 19, 2012 [online] *http://articles.washingtonpost.com/2012-01-19/politics/35439086_1_callista-bisek-marianne-gingrich-newt-gingrich.*

The Greek Anthology. Vol. 4. Trans. W. R. Patton. New York: G.P. Putnam's Sons, 1926.

Held, Warren H. Jr., William R. Schmalstieg, and Janet E. Gertz. *Beginning Hittite*. Columbus, OH: Slavica Publishers Inc., 1987.

Hunt, A. S. and C. C. Edgar. *Select Papyri I: Non-Literary Papyri, Private Affairs*. Cambridge: Harvard University Press, 1988.

Instone-Brewer, David. "1 Corinthians 7 in the Light of Jewish Greek and Aramaic Marriage and Divorce Papyri." *Tyndale Bulletin* 52.2 (2001) 225-243.

Kohn, David, producer."Behind the Gates." *CBS News* Feb. 11, 2009 [online] *http://www.cbsnews.com/ 2100-500164_162-69630.html.*

Lehmkuhl, Augustinus. "Sacrament of Marriage." *The Catholic Encyclopedia*. Vol. 9. New York: Robert Appleton Company, 1910. [online] *http://www.newadvent.org/cathen/09707a.htm.*

Libertarian Party Platform 2012. [online] *https://www.lp.org/files/LP%20 Platform%202012.pdf.*

Luther, Martin. "The Babylonian Captivity of the Church (1520)." Trans. A.T.W. Steinhaeuser. *Works of Martin Luther*. Vol. 2. Philadelphia: A.J. Holman Co. and the Castle Press, 1915. 257-273.

Luther, Martin. "The Estate of Marriage (1522)." Trans. Walther I. Brandt. *Works of Martin Luther*. Vol. 45. Philadelphia: Muhlenberg Press, 1962. 11-49.

Mansfield, John Smith. *"Concubina: Greek."* *The Dictionary of Greek and Roman Antiquities*. 2nd Edition. Ed. William Smith. Boston: Charles C. Little and James Brown. 1854.

Milligan, George. *Selections from Greek Papyri*. Cambridge: University Press, 1910.

"Morrill Anti-Bigamy Act." *United States Statutes at Large*. Vol. 12 (Act of July 1, 1862), 501-502.

Nissinen, Martti and Kirsi Stjerna. *Homoeroticism in the Biblical World: A Historical Perspective*. Minneapolis: Augsburg Fortress, 1998.

Nibley, Preston. *Brigham Young: The Man and His Work*. Salt Lake City: Deseret News Press, 1936.

Obama, Barack. Interview with Robin Roberts. *ABC News*. May 9, 2012 [online] *http://abcnews.go.com/ Politics/transcript-robin-roberts-abc-news-*

interview-president-obama/story?id=16316043& singlePage=true.

Oppenheim, H. Leo. *"Assinnu." The Assyrian Dictionary.* Vol. 1, Part 2. Chicago: The Oriental Institute, 2004. 341-342.

Pascoe, Peggy. *What Comes Naturally: Miscegenation Law and the Making of Race in America.* New York: Oxford University Press, 2009.

Peterman, G.W. "Marriage and Sexual Fidelity in the Papyri, Plutarch, and Paul." *Tyndale Bulletin* 50.2 (1999), 163-172.

Pope, Kyle. "Culturally Sanctioned Polygamy." *Biblical Insights* 8.6 (June 2008) 18 [online] *http://www.ancientroadpublications.com/Studies/ biblicalStudies/SanctionedPolygamy.html.*

Pope, Kyle. "Divorce and Remarriage in the Pagan World." *Christianity Magazine* 15.7 (July 1998) 16. Reprinted as "Divorce and Remarriage in Ancient Times." *Truth Magazine* 50.2 (Jan. 19, 2006) 21 [online] *http://www.ancientroadpublications.com/Studies/BiblicalStudies/An-cientDivorce.html.*

Ringren, Helmer. *"Qādēš, qᵉdēšâh." Theological Dictionary of the Old Testament.* Vol. 12. Eds. G. Johannes Botterweck, Helmer Ringren, and Heinz-Josef Fabry. Grand Rapids: William B. Eerdmans Pub. Co., 2003. 543-543.

"Timeline: Gay Marriage Chronology." *Los Angeles Times.* [online] *http:// graphics.latimes.com/usmap-gay-marriage-chronology/.*

"Thomas Jefferson and Sally Hemings: A Brief Account." *Thomas Jefferson's Monticello.* The Thomas Jefferson Foundation Inc., 2012 [online] *http://www.monticello.org/site/plantation-and-slavery/ thomas-jefferson-and-sally-hemings-brief-account.*

Ventris, Michael and John Chadwick. *Documents in Mycenaean Greek.* Cambridge: University Press, 1956.

Wagner, Dennis (February 24, 2011). "Jailed sect leader retakes legal control of church." *USA Today.* [online] *http://www.usatoday.com/news/ nation/2011-02-24-jeffs-church_N.htm.*

Witte, John Jr. *From Sacrament to Contract: Marriage, Religion, and Law in the Western Tradition.* Second Ed. Louisville: Westminster John Knox Press, 2012.

The Blessing and Threat of Civil Government

Mark Hudson

It is a common practice when we pray to include thanksgiving to God for the country we live in and for the freedoms we enjoy that allow us to worship Him without fear of harm from authorities or outside forces. This is proper and good to do. But it is important to remember that the freedoms that allow us to worship God without fear are that same that allow the atheist to be critical of God and religion, that allow individuals to believe and do

Mark Hudson is a Deputy Attorney General with the Tennessee Attorney General's Office where he has practiced law for 26 years. He heads the Civil Rights and Claims Division which defends all departments and agencies of state government in tort and workers' compensation actions. The division also defends state employees of various departments sued in civil rights actions. The division is also responsible for handling cases involving judicial review of agency decisions and declaratory judgment actions. Mark regularly appears before state and federal courts in Tennessee and has tried many jury cases. During his tenure in the division, Mark was lead counsel in successful defenses of several challenges to the constitutionality of Tennessee's death penalty in state and federal court. He has spoken at legal seminars on such topics as legal issues in corrections and end-stage capital litigation.

Mark is a 1980 graduate of Florida College. He earned his Bachelor of Science degree from Tennessee State University in 1983. He received his juris doctor degree from the University of Tennessee College of Law in 1986.

Mark has been a member of the Westvue Church of Christ in Murfreesboro since 2000. Before that, Mark was a member of the Broadmoor Church of Christ in Nashville where his father, Leroy, served as an elder. Mark is an army brat and considers himself fortunate to have been stationed with his family in Germany on three different occasions for ten years. He now lives in Murfreesboro, with his wife Rhonda (Hester) and sons Samuel (7), Benjamin (5), and Luke (3).

things that are contrary to God's will. And it is the civil government that upholds these freedoms for all men.

When considering the ways in which we are blessed by civil government as well as the threats it can pose, it must first be recognized that civil government has a divine origin. It did not originate in the mind of man. It is not merely a human institution. Its divine source is unequivocally stated in the Bible (Rom. 13:1-7; 1 Pet. 2:13-17). Men are the instruments through which God carries out His purposes in civil government, but civil government has its conception with God. It is important to understand what God had in mind when He ordained civil government.

There is a need for government. Government has to do with people being governed, being restricted, or controlled. Anarchy is contrary to God's design and destructive to human society. Where there is no government, or where the government is so weak that it cannot enforce its laws, there is anarchy. In the days of Noah, just before the flood, wickedness ruled the earth and God was sorry He made mankind. So, He flooded the earth, destroying all humanity—except for the righteous family of Noah (Gen. 6:5–7:24). The principle is simple: where there is no government, sinful people make up their own morality; and when those moralities come into conflict, as they inevitably will, then the majority or the most powerful will oppress the minority and weak, eventually leading to the destruction of civilization. If there is no governmental authority to restrict and control, then disorder will reign.

Since the idea of government has a divine origin, we should consider biblical examples of how man has been governed. God, as the creator of all things is sovereign over all. From the very beginning God ordained laws that established order and restricted and controlled man's conduct (Gen. 2:16-17; 4:4-5; 9:6). God also punished violations of His law (Gen. 3; 4:10-12). As time progressed, kingdoms ruled by men were established. Yet men such as Enoch, Noah, Abraham, Isaac, and Jacob were directed by God and acknowledged Him as Lord. When God delivered the children of Israel out of Egyptian bondage and gave them His law at Mount Sinai, Moses led the people, but it was recognized that he was being guided and governed by God.

In Deuteronomy 17:18-20, anticipating the time when Israel would demand a monarchial form of government, God decreed that kings of Israel would not be absolute sovereigns but would be simply administrators of

God's law, and would, in fact, be subject to God's law themselves. From the way Israel's monarchy was founded we can infer that human monarchy was not God's first choice for the governance of Israel. His first choice was the Kingship of God, who, because He did not speak to the people directly, used a prophet to transmit His words to the people. In this form of rule, exemplified by Moses and Samuel, God employs the prophet to communicate not only generalities to the people but also specific legal judgments.

The key to Israel's success and prosperity was its adherence to the law of God. The law of God was the true blessing to Israel. "And now, Israel, what doth Jehovah thy God require of thee, but to fear Jehovah thy God, to walk in all his ways, and to love him, and to serve Jehovah thy God with all thy heart and with all thy soul, to keep the commandments of Jehovah, and his statutes, which I command thee this day for thy good?" (Deut. 10:12-13). "This book of the law shall not depart out of thy mouth, but thou shalt meditate thereon day and night, that thou mayest observe to do according to all that is written therein: for then thou shalt make thy way prosperous, and then thou shalt have good success" (Josh. 1:8). A government is a blessing to its citizens when it upholds and enforces laws that are consistent with the laws of God.

Conversely, a government can be a threat to its citizens when it fails to uphold the law. In 1 Samuel 8:1-3, the sons of Samuel became judges in Israel but instead of upholding the law they "turned aside after lucre, and took bribes, and perverted justice." Even more threatening to its citizens is a government that rejects the basic principles of God's law and establishes laws based on human wisdom and desires. When God's laws are altered or substituted, failure and destruction are sure to follow. It is no different from when the law of God is substituted for commandments of men: our worship to God is vain (Matt. 15:9).

God's law is a supreme law in that man cannot improve upon it. Moses told the Israelites that they are neither to add to nor subtract from God's commandments (Deut. 4:2). Throughout Scripture, we find that God is concerned that men obey His will as He has given it. "Do not add to his words, lest he rebuke you and you be found a liar" (Prov. 30:6). The danger of changing God's law is seen in the example of Jeroboam in 1 Kings 12:26-33:

> And Jeroboam said in his heart, Now will the kingdom return to the house of David: if this people go up to offer sacrifices in the house of Jehovah at Jerusalem, then will the heart of this people turn again unto their lord, even unto Rehoboam king of Judah; and they will kill me, and return to Rehoboam king of Judah. Whereupon the king took counsel, and made

two calves of gold; and he said unto them, It is too much for you to go up to Jerusalem: behold thy gods, O Israel, which brought thee up out of the land of Egypt. And he set the one in Beth-el, and the other put he in Dan. And this thing became a sin; for the people went to worship before the one, even unto Dan. And he made houses of high places, and made priests from among all the people, that were not of the sons of Levi.

And Jeroboam ordained a feast in the eighth month, on the fifteenth day of the month, like unto the feast that is in Judah, and he went up unto the altar; so did he in Beth-el, sacrificing unto the calves that he had made: and he placed in Beth-el the priests of the high places that he had made. And he went up unto the altar which he had made in Beth-el on the fifteenth day in the eighth month, even in the month which he had devised of his own heart: and he ordained a feast for the children of Israel, and went up unto the altar, to burn incense.

The sin of Jeroboam in departing from God's law was repeated by successive kings of Israel until the nation was carried away into captivity by the Assyrians as punishment (1 Kings 17:22-23).

The same principles that determined the efficacy of civil governments in the Bible are applicable to civil governments in existence today: Does the government uphold the law and are the laws consistent with the law of God? It is important to note that no particular form of government is ordained by God, nor is the government of one society ordained by God while governments in other societies are not sanctioned by God. As a general principle, the authority that government has, whether it be a dictatorship, a monarchy, or a democracy, comes from God.

Our nation was formed as a republic, in a constitutional form of government. As a republic, we have what is known as a *representative* form of government. That is, the people elect persons to represent them in the formation of the laws by which the nation will be governed. While the ideal is that we are "one nation under God," the reality is that special interests politics dominates the political landscape. Each special group of individuals in society has a desire to see its competitive interests represented in public policy. As a result, interest-group politics often predominate over the just and moral action that should be taken. Moreover, those elected to represent the interests of their constituents are often swayed by the power and prestige of the elected position. As a result, their focus is not on what is best for their constituents or for the people at large, but what is best for getting reelected and maintaining political power. A recent example can be seen following the 2012 elections when many Republican Party politicians changed their formerly hard-line stance regarding immigration reform and adopted a less stringent approach to the issue. The intent is to appeal to Hispanics in an effort to win their votes for Republicans in the next election. When we as a nation become more concerned about politics rather than policy, about satisfying public interests rather that what is just and right, the resulting government will be far from being the blessing God intended it to be.

Civil Government as a Blessing

"Every good gift and every perfect gift is from above" (James 1:17). It follows that civil government, as ordained by God, is good. God, through the Scriptures explain why government is good. In general, law itself exists to curb the conduct of those who are not inclined to curb their own conduct. "But we know that the law is good, if a man use it lawfully, as knowing this, that law is not made for a righteous man, but for the lawless and unruly, for the ungodly and sinners, for the unholy and profane, for murderers of fathers and murderers of mothers, for manslayers, for fornicators, for abusers of themselves with men, for menstealers, for liars, for false swearers, and if there be any other thing contrary to the sound doctrine" (1 Tim. 1:9-10). The primary purpose of civil government is to restrain injustice and crime, so that people can live without fear.

A proper understanding of Romans 13:1-7 is essential to a proper understanding of civil government.

> Let every soul be in subjection to the higher powers: for there is no power but of God; and the powers that be are ordained of God. Therefore he that resisteth the power, withstandeth the ordinance of God: and they that withstand shall receive to themselves judgment. For rulers are not a terror to the good work, but to the evil. And wouldest thou have no fear of the power? Do that which is good, and thou shalt have praise from the same: for he is a minister of God to thee for good. But if thou do that which is evil, be afraid; for he beareth not the sword in vain: for he is a minister of God, an avenger for wrath to him that doeth evil. Wherefore ye must needs be in subjection, not only because of the wrath, but also for con-science' sake. For this cause ye pay tribute also; for they are ministers of God's service, attending continually upon this very thing. Render to all their dues: tribute to whom tribute is due; custom to whom custom; fear to whom fear; honor to whom honor.

Every individual under heaven is subject to "higher powers" (Rom. 13:1). The "higher powers" under consideration are civil authorities (national, state, and local governments) under which one lives. Paul explains why a Christian should be in subjection to these "higher powers." There is no power but of God. God has given the right and the means for every governing institution to reign upon this earth today. Only by God's permission, by His appointment, or by the arrangements of His providence, has any governing body been established upon the face of the earth. It is also important to note that while one must submit to the governing powers, verse 1 does not mean that the sinful deeds of evil rulers are ever approved of God.

If one refuses to submit to these powers, he is resisting the very ordinance of God (Rom. 13:2). When one thinks of resistance against authorities, violent opposition and sedition usually come to mind. Resistance, however, is not limited to these means. Resistance is inclusive of all forms of opposition and disobedience. To defy and undermine the government is resistance and rebellion and would bring reproach upon the gospel of Christ. The means by which we can serve in the greatest way does not come by protest or by violence, even when it comes to the cause of righteousness. The way that we go about living our godly life is important, it is essential. We are not to be subversive to the government by overtly undermining it. We are not to be subversive to the government by wishing or seeking harm against the government. We are not to be subversive by malice and disrespect toward government leaders. Judgment is coming for those who would rebel against these "higher powers" established by God. They are violating not only civil law but the law of God.

It should also be understood that suffering persecution at the hands of government because of our faith is a real possibility. Persecution should be an expectation of a Christian (2 Tim. 3:12). History teaches us this is so. Shadrach, Meshach, Abed-nego, and Daniel were subjected to punishment had the hands of the governing authority because of their devotion to God (Daniel 3; 6). Stephen died at the hands of Jewish authorities because he preached Jesus, leading to the persecution of Christians in Jerusalem and elsewhere (Acts 6-8). Historians record many instances of religious persecution by governing authorities. Christians were blamed by Nero for a fire that burned a great portion of Rome, resulting in a great persecution against them. Domitian persecuted Christians because of their refusal to worship him as a god. Adherents to non-Catholic religions suffered as "heretics" during the Inquisition. Many Puritans fled England and came to America to escape religious persecution from the ruling Anglican church. China is well known for its brutal persecution of religious groups not sanctioned by the government.

But when a government operates as intended by God, there is no terror for them that live righteously (Rom. 13:3). A person who does not break the law and obeys the civil authorities will not have to suffer the fear and worry of getting caught and punished. Rulers in power are not appointed to punish the good. Their appointment is not to inspire terror in those who are virtuous and peaceable citizens. The government, if it is functioning properly, will approve, commend, protect, and encourage those who do right. If you obey the civil laws you have nothing to fear from the rulers but if you violate them you will be held to account.

God has given higher powers the right to exist for the primary purposes of protecting and encouraging good (Rom. 13:3) and restraining and punishing wickedness (Rom. 13:4). If one participates in evil activity, there is adequate cause to fear the "higher powers" given of God. When one transgresses the civil laws, one is subject to the wrath of the civil government. Civil power has been ordained of God to have the power of enforcement of its laws. When a government fulfills its responsibility upon those who are evil, it "does not bear the sword in vain."

Echoing Paul, Peter wrote, "Be subject to every ordinance of man for the Lord's sake: whether to the king, as supreme; or unto governors, as sent by him for vengeance on evil-doers and for praise to them that do well" (1 Pet. 2:13-14). The civil officer functions as a minister or servant of God in the execution of governmental law and order. He possesses this God-given power with the expectation that he will execute wrath upon evildoers. Paul clearly recognized the governing authority's power to execute wrath on its citizens. As Paul stood accused of wrong-doing before Festus and Caesar's judgment-seat he stated, "If then I am a wrong-doer, and have committed anything worthy of death, I refuse not to die; but if none of those things is true whereof these accuse me, no man can give me up unto them. I appeal unto Caesar" (Acts 5:11). Paul knew there were things worthy of death, but yet he claimed innocence from those things. Higher powers have the right and the duty to execute wrath upon those that do evil.

Two reasons are given to be subject to the higher powers (Rom. 13:5). The first is for the sake of wrath. In other words, obedience allows one to escape punishment from the civil power. The second reason given is conscience. God requires that His people maintain a pure conscience. To do so requires that we live up to what we know or believe to be right. To violate one's conscience is to do wrong (Rom. 14:23). Thus, to have God's continuing approval, Christians must follow God's will – from the heart. In doing this, he will keep himself well within the requirements of civil law.

For a citizen to be subject to the higher powers, it is his responsibility to pay tribute, or taxes, to the higher powers (Rom. 13:6). Taxes are necessary for a government to function properly. There is no question about the payment of imposed taxation regardless of how unpopular it may be. This is not optional; it is obligatory. In Romans 13:7 Paul continues his thoughts of the preceding verses. "Tribute," "custom," "fear," and "honor" were due to those who were deserving of receiving these; the office of government deserves all of these.

The government's duty is not only to punish the wicked but to praise the righteous. Peter's command to submit to civil authorities does not include a promise that we will always be praised by earthly authorities for the good things we have done. He does, however, infer that praise is certain for the Christian. We are not to live righteously primarily to obtain the praise of men. We are to live righteously in order to bring praise to God and to await His praise. Thus, Peter instructs us to submit ourselves "for the Lord's sake" (1 Pet. 2:13). Submission is to be "as to the Lord" (Eph. 5:22), "in the Lord" (Eph. 6:1), and "for the Lord's sake" (1 Pet. 2:13). Our submission to civil authorities should be carried out as obedience to our Lord. If we submit in this way, we will receive praise from Him whom we serve, to whom we are ultimately in submission.

When civil government functions as God intended, what is the result? It results in a society that provides for the safety and security of its citizens (1 Tim. 2:2). It results in a stable society that will provide an effective opportunity for evangelism (1 Tim. 2:4). It results in the creation of society wherein its citizens may live peacefully, mind their own affairs, and work with their own hands, doing what is right for themselves, their families and their neighbors (1 Thess. 4:11; 1 Tim. 5:8; Rom. 13:1-10). It results in a society that punishes those whose actions are harmful and detrimental to the divinely ordained function of society.

It was noted above that the government "does not bear the sword in vain" (Rom. 13: 4). This is a clear allusion to the administration of capital punishment. Capital punishment reminds us of the seriousness of spilling the blood of a creature made in the image of God. It reminds us of God our Creator. "Whoso sheddeth man's blood, by man shall his blood be shed: For in the image of God made he man" (Gen. 9:6). Anytime a culture abandons capital punishment it is simultaneously abandoning God and the value He places on human beings. Increasingly, our culture is losing the value of human life because more and more of us are rejecting the biblical view that God created all of us in His image. As a result, we care more for the pain and suffering of the murderer and less for the victims.

Capital punishment can deter crime when it is carried out consistently and in a timely fashion. If civil government does not fulfill its duty to restrain criminals in accordance with Biblical guidelines then crime will flourish. Ecclesiastes 8:11 says, "Because sentence against an evil work is not executed speedily, therefore the heart of the sons of men is fully set in them to do evil." Certainly capital punishment will not deter all crime. Psychotic and deranged killers, members of organized crime, and street gangs will no doubt kill whether capital punishment is implemented or not. A person who is irrational or wants to commit a murder will do so whether capital punishment exists or not. But social statistics as well as logic suggest that rational people will be deterred from murder because capital punishment is part of the criminal law. Swift execution of God's justice is necessary to keep a culture of crime from growing in a nation. When, as a society, we do not set up capital consequences for capital crimes, we can expect a growth of cynicism, mockery of the law, and violent lawlessness.

Civil Government as a Threat

Though governments are ordained of God and are intended as instruments for good, there are occasions when governments act in ways that are contrary to God's law and sanction sinful conduct by its citizen. Rulers are ordained by God for the purpose of doing justice and righteousness. When they abandon this responsibility, the people and the nations go astray. The same was said of Judah: "My people have been lost sheep: their shepherds have caused them to go astray; they have turned them away on the mountains; they have gone from mountain to hill; they have forgotten their resting-place" (Jer. 50:6). Such is the case when leaders of governments abandon the wisdom of God and take it upon themselves to direct the steps of a people according to human wisdom. What follows is a consideration of governmental involvement in issues that threaten biblical principles.

Political Correctness

For some in Congress, it's not enough to put someone in jail for harming another, but if they have "hate" or a prejudice in their heart they should be incarcerated even longer and be subject to federal prosecution. The Local Law Enforcement Hate Crimes Prevention Act of 2009 identifies crimes which may have been perpetrated due to potential prejudice as federal criminal offenses, with the possibility of life imprisonment. According to the legislation, crimes motivated by the "actual or perceived race, color, religion, national origin, gender, sexual orientation, gender identity, or disability of any person" will be prosecuted at the federal level.

Legally, legislation like this is unnecessary. Under the 14th Amendment all citizens are treated equally under the law. If one is assaulted, it legally makes no difference whether the perpetrator was motivated by animosity, prejudice, or abject hatred. And ideally it makes no difference what color, sex, or sexual orientation the victim is.

Since this legislation is not legally necessary, the most likely motive behind it is the enforcement of political correctness. Political correctness is perhaps the greatest culprit leading to a degeneration of our culture and diluting our freedom of speech. It has advanced to an illogical extreme and elevates those protected by the political correctness protocol to a level disallowed for the population at large. Such extremism can lead to the restriction of preaching publicly against homosexuality using verses from the Bible. It has been suggested that the legislation could be used against individuals and churches who speak out on issues such as defending marriage and religious liberty. The implication is that in any future efforts to legalize same sex marriage, any individual or organization, including churches, supporting traditional marriage could be prosecuted under broad interpretation of the statute.

Political correctness describes language, ideas, policies, and behavior seen as seeking to minimize social and institutional offense in occupational, gender, racial, cultural, sexual orientation, religious belief, disability, and age-related contexts. The key word here is "offense." No individual or group is to be offended in the politically correct world. Certainly, as Christians, we are not to go out of our way to offend anyone personally, but the truth is that Christianity itself is offensive. Jesus said that "men loved darkness rather than light, because their deeds were evil" (John 3:19). Political correctness is frequently an attempt to justify sin. "Woe unto them that call evil good, and good evil; that put darkness for light, and light for darkness; that put bitter for sweet, and sweet for bitter!" (Isa. 5:20). Proponents of political correctness—increasingly in charge of our society—feel a sense of guilt when confronted with the truths of the Bible. To relieve this guilt, they turn against others who teach a way of life that has always brought peace and stability throughout any society to the degree that it has been sincerely practiced. "He that justifieth the wicked, and he that condemneth the righteous, Both of them alike are an abomination to Jehovah" (Prov. 17:15). When Christians today explain that fornication, adultery, drunkenness, homosexual practices and abortion are absolutely wrong, the world takes great offense. In fact, they often try to persecute those who hold such views. But that is to be expected. "All that would live godly in Christ Jesus shall suffer persecution" (2 Tim. 3:12).

Political correctness is based on the idea that there is no such thing as "absolute truth." Thus, what is politically correct today may be politically incorrect tomorrow. The barometer of the political correctness tends to be what gratifies one person or one particular group of people. It can be determined by the manners, customs, beliefs, and traditions of its adherents. It can also be the product of the propaganda machinery of a ruling regime used to mobilize the population to support its agenda. For example, in Nazi Germany propaganda campaigns portraying Jews and gypsies, and other non-Aryans as subhuman created an environment where it was viewed as politically correct to discriminate against and persecute such groups. Likewise, in the former Soviet Union, propaganda was used to arouse and condone violent political emotions against the regime's enemies including religious groups and intellectuals. More recently, amid a growing crackdown on religious freedom, Iranian police have been rounding up Muslims they suspect have converted to Christianity. Though they are protected under the Iranian constitution and have a long history within the country, Christians are not given the same freedoms as other citizens in Iran. They cannot worship freely or hold public office, and they can be arrested for even speaking to Muslims about Christianity. By accusing converts to Christianity of "apostasy," the regime seeks to indoctrinate its citizens to view non-Muslims with suspicion if not contempt, and to perpetuate the regime's theocratic ideology.

While "tolerance" is a favorite buzzword of the politically correct, political correctness actually creates its own intolerance that often quickly shouts down alternative viewpoints. For example, in 2011 Vanderbilt University adopted a new nondiscrimination policy that prohibited a student organization from requiring its members and even its leadership to adhere to a statement of faith. The policy was adopted after Beta Upsilon Chi, a Christian fraternity, removed one of its leaders because he disagreed with the fraternity's official stand on homosexuality. Following a public meeting in January 2012, Vanderbilt required Christian student organizations to rewrite their constitutions and remove leadership statement of faith requirements. Organizations that failed to comply with the new policy would forfeit their status as an official student organization and thus lose their right to use school facilities, advertise meetings at school events, and apply for student fee funding. In essence, the Christian organizations had to comply by compromising their beliefs or leave campus. Vanderbilt's actions are part of a larger trend in our society. Christian beliefs are now considered discriminatory and must yield to the state or to society at large.

Paul's description of man's condition without God paints a picture of the end result of the "politically correct" road (Rom. 1:18-32). Christians have no obligation before God to be politically correct. Rather, we have a divine obligation to be biblically correct. If we are biblically correct, people's lives will change and we will positively impact society.

Divorce

In Matthew 19 the Pharisees asked Jesus if it was *lawful* for a man to put away his wife for any cause. God set forth laws that governed the practice of divorce. The Pharisees had many reasons to "put away" their wives, but Jesus stated there was but one reason for a man to "put away" his wife and be married to another, i.e., adultery.

Today in this nation there are many reasons given for one putting away his or her spouse, but this was not always the case. Many American states enacted divorce legislation soon after Independence, in the 1780s and 1790s. Connecticut was the most liberal, permitting divorce for ". . . adultery, fraudulent contract, desertion for three years, or prolonged absence with a presumption of death."[1] In 1843, the state added two additional grounds for divorce: habitual drunkenness and intolerable cruelty. The Connecticut state legislature also dissolved marriages on other grounds by legislative action. In 1849, the courts were given sole responsibility for divorce, and grounds were extended to include "life imprisonment, any infamous crime involving a violation of the conjugal duty, and – most important – 'any such misconduct as permanently destroys the happiness of the petitioner and defeats the purpose of the marriage relation.'"[2]

Divorce laws were generally more liberal in the West than in the rest of the country.

---

[1] Roderick Phillips, *Putting Asunder; A History of Divorce in Western Society*, Cambridge University Press, 1988, p. 440.

[2] Phillips, p. 442.

California's first divorce law, in 1851, contained the following grounds for divorce: impotence, adultery, extreme cruelty, desertion or neglect, habitual intemperance, fraud, and conviction for a felony. In practice, the courts extended the definitions of these terms. Historian Carey McWilliams writes that California's divorce rate was the highest in the world during the gold rush, and that "divorces were naturally looked upon with favor and were freely granted."[3]

American states broadened the grounds for divorce throughout the 19th century, encompassing more and more matrimonial conditions. By 1900, most states had adopted four major elements of divorce law: fault-based grounds, one party's guilt, the continuation of gender-based marital responsibilities after divorce, and the linkage of financial awards to findings of fault.[4]

Divorce rates in the United States and in other Western countries have been climbing steadily since 1860. There was a large jump in the U.S. rate after World War II, a period of stability in the 1950s, an increase from 2.1 per 1000 people in 1958 to 2.9 in 1968, and a peak of 5.3 in 1979, followed by a decline to a recent rate of 4.5 per 1000.[5]

The 1970s was a decade of major change in divorce laws, a period widely referred to as the "divorce revolution." Foremost of these changes was the introduction of *unilateral divorce*.

Between 1968 and 1977 the majority of states passed such laws, moving from a regime in which the dissolution of marriage required the mutual consent of both spouses, to one in which spouses could unilaterally file for divorce. If one spouse wants the marriage to continue, and is willing to work to keep it alive, that does not matter. The law favors the person who wants to end the marriage, not the person who wants to work at keeping it together. In addition to changing the right to divorce, the law also established that no assignment of fault was required, nor did fault play any role in divorce settlements.

---

[3] Carey McWilliams, *California, The Great Exception*, A. A. Wyn, New York, 1940, p. 82.

[4] Lenore Weitzman, *The Divorce Revolution*, The Free Press, 1985, p. 7.

[5] Ira Mark Ellman and Sharon Lohr, "Marriage as Contract, Opportunistic Violence, And Other Bad Arguments For Fault Divorce," *University of Illinois Law Review*, 1997, 719.

Divorce detrimentally impacts individuals, families, and society in numerous ways. When parents divorce another sort of divorce occurs between the parents and their children. An effect of divorce (and of the parental conflict that precedes the divorce) is a decline in the relationship between parent and child.[6] Children in divorced families receive less emotional support, financial assistance, and practical help from their parents.[7] Divorced homes show a decrease in language stimulation, pride, affection, stimulation of academic behavior, encouragement of social maturity, and warmth directed towards the children.[8]

Children of divorced or separated parents exhibit increased behavioral problems, and the marital conflict that accompanies parents' divorce places the child's social competence at risk.[9] When parents divorce, their children's attitudes about sexual behavior change. Children's approval of premarital sex, cohabitation, and divorce rises dramatically, while their endorsement of marriage and childbearing falls.[10] Children from divorced families are also more likely to believe that marriage is not important prior to having children and are more likely to have a child out of wedlock.[11]

Compared with children of always married parents, children of divorced

---

[6] Elizabeth Meneghan and Toby L. Parcel, "Social Sources of Change in Children's Home Environments: The Effects of Parental Occupational Experiences and Family Conditions," *Journal of Marriage and Family* 57 (1995): 69-84.

[7] Paul R. Amato and Alan Booth, *A Generation at Risk* (Cambridge, MA: Harvard University Press, 1997), 69.

[8] Carol E. MacKinnon, Gene H. Brody, and Zolinda Stoneman, "The Effects of Divorce and Maternal Employment on the Home Environments of Preschool Children," *Child Development* 53 (1982): 1392-1399.

[9] Donna Ruane Morrison and Mary Jo Coiro, "Parental Conflict and Marital Disruption: Do Children Benefit When High-Conflict Marriages Are Dissolved?" *Journal of Marriage and the Family* 61 (1999): 626.

[10] William G. Axinn and Arland Thornton, "The Influence of Parents' Marital Dissolutions on Children's Attitudes toward Family Formation," *Demography* 33 (1996): 66-81.

[11] William H. Jeynes, "The Effects of Recent Parental Divorce on Their Children's Sexual Attitudes and Behavior," *Journal of Divorce and Remarriage* 35 (2001): 125.

parents have more positive attitudes towards divorce[12] and less favorable attitudes towards marriage.[13] Specifically, "adolescents who have experienced their parents' divorces and remarriages may feel that marriage is unpredictable and unstable."[14] People raised in divorced families are less likely than those from intact families to believe that marriage is enduring and permanent,[15] are less likely to insist upon a lifelong marital commitment,[16] and are less likely to think positively of themselves as parents.[17]

Most significantly, following a divorce, children are more likely to abandon their faith,[18] and they may be less traditional themselves, with a parental model differing from a lifelong commitment to marriage.[19] Furthermore, abandoning religious practice deprives children of its beneficial effects in a host of areas: marital stability, sexual restraint, education, income, crime,

---

[12] Paul R. Amato and Alan Booth, "The Consequences of Divorce for Attitudes toward Divorce and Gender Roles," *Journal of Family Issues* 12 (1991): 306-322.

[13] A. Marlene Jennings, Connie J. Salts, and Thomas A. Smith, Jr., "Attitudes Toward Marriage: Effects of Parental Conflict, Family Structure, and Gender," *Journal of Divorce and Remarriage* 17 (1992): 67-78.

[14] Sharon C. Risch, Kathleen M. Jodl, and Jacquelynne S. Eccles, "Role of the Father-Adolescent Relationship in Shaping Adolescents' Attitudes Toward Divorce," *Journal of Marriage and the Family* 66 (2004): 55.

[15] Daniel J. Weigel, "Parental Divorce and the Types of Commitment-Related Messages People Gain from Their Families of Origin," *Journal of Divorce and Remarriage* 47 (2007): 23.

[16] Kristen A. Moore and Thomas M. Stief, "Changes in Marriage and Fertility Behavior: Behavior versus Attitudes of Young Adults" (Child Trends, Inc., July 1989).

[17] Jennifer Langhinrichsen-Rohling and Colleen Dostal, "Retrospective Reports of Family-of-Origin Divorce and Abuse and College Students' Pre-parenthood Cognitions," *Journal of Family Violence* 11 (1996): 331-348.

[18] Sociologists at Nassau Community College in New York developed a profile of former believers who stopped practicing their religious beliefs: William Feigelman, Bernard S. Gorman, and Joseph A. Varacalli, "Americans Who Give Up Religion," *Sociology and Social Research* 76 (1992): 138-143.

[19] Paul R. Amato and Alan Booth, "Consequences of divorce for attitudes toward divorce," *Journal of Family Issues* 12 (1991): 306-322. As cited in Alan Booth and Paul R. Amato, "Parental Pre-Divorce Relations and Offspring Postdivorce Well-Being," *Journal of Marriage and the Family* 63 (2001): 207.

addictions, physical and mental health, and general happiness.[20]

The laws of the land have accommodated society's desire to be able to divorce easily and for any reason. Society has suffered as a result as shown above. All men and women everywhere need to be reminded that marriage is a covenant between a man, his wife, and God. Some men in the days of Malachi had been unjust to their wives. The prophet reminded them that "the Lord has been a witness between you and the wife of your youth, with whom you have dealt treacherously; yet she is your companion and your wife by covenant" (Mal. 2:14). The immoral woman of Proverbs 2:17 had forsaken her husband and forgot the "covenant of her God." There are many obligations in the marriage covenant. The husband is to love his wife "as Christ also loved the church" (Eph. 5:25). He is also to provide for his family (1 Tim. 5:8). The wife must be in submission to her own husband "just as the church is subject to Christ" (Eph. 5:24). They are both required to render the "affection" due the other (1 Cor. 7:3). In addition, they are "bound by the law" to their spouse as long as they live (Rom. 7:1-4). This is obviously the law of God, and not the law of man.

Abortion
Abortion did not burst upon the American scene with *Roe v. Wade*. For nearly all of our country's existence, taking the life of a baby in the womb was prohibited. In the years prior to and immediately after the American Revolution, colonists and citizens followed the rule of law brought by British settlers, the "common law." Rather than being a code of statutes passed by a legislature, the common law was a set of legal standards established in England through court decisions and legal custom. According to Sir William Blackstone, the renowned 18th century English jurist, under common law, the abortion of a "quickened" fetus was a very heinous crime, the penalty for which could be; loss of a limb, confiscation of property, or life in prison ("Quickening" was then determined by when a pregnant woman first felt her child move – generally in the fourth month).

The first U.S. law against abortion, adopted by Connecticut in 1821, criminalized the administration of poison or of any "destructive substance"

---

[20] Patrick F. Fagan, "Why Religion Matters: The Impact of Religious Practice on Social Stability," *Backgrounder* 1064 (Washington, D.C.: The Heritage Foundation, 25 January 1996). Patrick F. Fagan, "Why Religion Matters Even More: The Impact of Religious Practice on Social Stability," *Backgrounder* 1992 (Washington, D.C.: The Heritage Foundation, 18 December 2006).

to induce a miscarriage. It applied only to cases where the baby had "quick-ened." In 1840, however, Maine became the first state to pass a law that expressly protected all babies, "quick or not." The abandonment of the "quickening" requirement coincided with the 19th century discovery of how conception takes place.

In the mid-19th century, the newly formed American Medical Association undertook to organize physicians and medical societies in support of laws against abortion. An 1859 AMA committee investigating abortion issued a report which stated:

> the frightful extent of [abortion in the US] is found in the grave defects of our laws, both common and statute, as regards the independent and actual existence of the child before birth, as a living being. These errors, which are sufficient in most instances to prevent conviction, are based, and only based, upon mistaken and exploded medical dogmas.

In the twenty years following this AMA report, aided by lobbying from the medical profession, thirty-one states passed or amended their laws on abortion to protect pre-term infants at all stages of gestation. By 1910, every state except Kentucky had passed an anti-abortion law (and Kentucky's courts had declared abortion at any stage of gestation to be illegal). By 1967, not much had changed. In forty-nine states, abortion was a felony; in New Jersey, it was a high misdemeanor.

In 1967, though, state abortion laws began to change, but only after years of organized campaigns by pro-abortion forces. The American Law Institute (ALI) proposed, in its 1959 model criminal code for all the states, a "reform" abortion law. The model bill, approved by ALI in 1962, declared that abortion should be permitted for the physical or mental health of the mother, for fetal abnormality, and for rape or incest. Also in 1967, the American Medical Association voted to change its long-standing opposi-tion to abortion. With a new resolution, the AMA now condoned abortion for the life or health of the mother, for a baby's "incapacitating" physical deformity or mental deficiency, or for cases of rape or incest.

That same year, Colorado, North Carolina, and California became the first states to adopt versions of the ALI "reform" abortion law. By 1970, though, four states – New York, Alaska, Hawaii and Washington – passed laws that basically allowed abortion on demand. Of those four, New York's was the only law without a residency requirement and the state quickly became the nation's abortion capital.

The pro-abortion onslaught was beginning to face opposition, as pro-life proponents organized. In 1972, the New York legislature voted to repeal the state's liberal abortion law, but Governor Nelson Rockafeller vetoed the repeal. Ballot questions in Michigan and North Dakota that same year attempted to decriminalize abortion; the measures were defeated.

Just as pro-life proponents were beginning to turn the tide however, the Supreme Court handed down *Roe v. Wade* in January, 1973. With one judicial stroke, over 200 years of legal protection for the unborn was rendered null and void. For the first time in American history, abortion was the "law of the land." *Roe* ruled (7-2) that though states did have an interest in protecting fetal life, such interest was not "compelling" until the fetus was viable (placing viability at the start of the third trimester). Thus, all state abortion laws that forbade abortion during the first six months of pregnancy were thereby invalidated. Third trimester abortions were declared to be legal only if the pregnancy threatened the life or health of the mother. But the decision in *Doe v. Bolton*, issued with *Roe*, defined "health of the mother" in such broad terms, that any prohibitions to third trimester abortions were essentially eliminated.

In 1976, abortion again made its way to the Supreme Court, in *Planned Parenthood v. Danforth*, where all state laws requiring spousal or parental consent were thrown out. *Thornburg v. American College of Obstetricians and Gynecologists*, a 1986 case that was split 5-4, struck down all manner of abortion restrictions including the requirement to inform women about abortion alternatives, the requirement to educate women about prenatal development, the requirement to inform women of the potential risks of abortion, the requirement to keep records of abortion, and the requirement that third trimester abortions be performed in such a way as to spare the life of the viable child. All these were argued to be violations of a woman's right to privacy.

In 1989, however, the decision in *Webster v. Reproductive Health Services*, dealt *Roe* a serious blow. The court, in a 5-4 opinion, let stand a Missouri statute stating that human life begins at conception, and declared that the state does have a "compelling" interest in fetal life *throughout* pregnancy. The trimester/viability framework of *Roe* was basically thrown out, but Justice Sandra Day O'Connor, despite arguing for essentially the same thing in prior case law, withheld her endorsement from the portion of the *Webster* opinion which would have actually overturned *Roe*.

In 1992, *Planned Parenthood v. Casey* reached the Supreme Court. The right to legal abortion was upheld, but a 24-hour waiting period was put in place, as well as an informed consent requirement, a parental consent provision, and a record keeping mandate. States were also given more discretion as to when viability begins. The last abortion-related case to reach the Supreme Court was *Gonzales v. Carhart*, which was decided in 2007 by a 5-4 vote. It upheld a 2003 congressional ban on the abortion procedure known as intact dilation and evacuation – also known as dilation and extraction (D&X) or partial-birth abortion. The Partial-Birth Abortion Ban Act of 2003 came in response to the Supreme Court's ruling in *Stenberg v. Carhart* (2000) that Nebraska's partial-birth abortion ban violated the Federal Constitution as interpreted by *Roe* and *Casey*.

Our society, reflected in our laws, considers abortion to be a mother's choice since it is her body, and the unborn child is not considered a living human. Yet, God sees the unborn as human beings at conception. "Before I formed thee in the belly I knew thee; and before thou camest forth out of the womb I sanctified thee, and I ordained thee a prophet unto the nations" (Jer. 1:5). *Roe v. Wade* stemmed from a rejection of the biblical world view and has contributed significantly to the erosion of objective morality in our culture. It is perhaps the foremost factor in the lack of respect for human life. What can we do as children of God to try to stem and ultimately stop the terrible tide of legalized abortion? First and foremost we must uphold and defend the fundamental truth that life in the womb is formed by God in his image (Psa. 139:13-16). And, though the Supreme Court may call it legal, men need to be made to understand that destroying life for the sake of convenience is not merely "exercising choice." It is practicing wickedness.

Homosexuality and Same Sex Marriage

The Bible teaches homosexuality is a sin. Many today do not accept this. In fact, they teach the Bible accepts homosexuals as they are with no change required in their life. However, they do this in contradiction to the word of God. From the beginning, God made it clear that sexual relations and intimate companionship is to be between a man and a woman. He made a woman for the man (Gen. 2:18-23). He did not make another man for Adam. He also said the man is to leave father and mother and be joined to his wife, not his husband (Gen. 2:24).

The account of Sodom and Gomorrah serves as an everlasting example of God's attitude toward homosexuality (Jude 7; 2 Pet. 2:6). When the messengers visited Lot, the men of the city demanded sex with them (Gen.

19:4, 5). God destroyed the cities and surrounding area because of their gross immorality. In Leviticus, God gave laws concerning Israel including laws governing sexual relations. In Leviticus 20:13 sexual relations between men is condemned. Under the Mosaic Law, it was punishable by death. The New Testament expresses the same condemnation about homosexual acts. The Holy Spirit reveals that homosexuals and sodomites will not inherit the kingdom of God (1 Cor. 6:9, 10). To be sure, so will other sinners. It is not that homosexuality is the only sin condemned, but it is a sin and must be forsaken.

Paul also writes about the ancient Gentiles and their depraved condition. He stated that their homosexuality was "vile," "against nature," "shameful," and "error" (Rom. 1:26, 27 NKJV). He wraps up the condemnation of this and other sins by saying, "who, knowing the righteous judgment of God, that those who practice such things are deserving of death, not only do the same but also approve of those who practice them" (Rom. 1:32). Homosexuality is a sin; no matter what our modern culture says to the contrary.

Today we can see that legislative attempts to enact anti-bias laws protecting homosexuals have occurred at the federal, state, and local level. Opposition to such laws, particularly from conservative religious groups, has often been strong, and opponents of homosexual rights measures have frequently gained their repeal. In 1992, Colorado became the first state to nullify existing civil rights protection for homosexuals by amending its constitution; the provision was stuck down by the U.S. Supreme Court in 1996. By means of a statewide public referendum in 1998, Maine became the first state to repeal its gay-rights statute.

In 1993 the Defense Department, at the order of President Bill Clinton, changed the ban on homosexuals in the military to a ban on homosexual activity. The much discussed policy, known as "don't ask, don't tell," was presented as a way to allow homosexuals in the military to serve without fear of discharge or other penalty as long as they did not reveal their sexual orientation. This policy was repealed in 2010.

Beginning in the mid-1990s, many states began explicitly banning same sex marriages; more than four-fifths of the states now do so. The Vermont Supreme Court declared in 1999 that the state must grant homosexual couples the same rights and protections that married heterosexuals have, and in 2000 the state legislature backed "civil unions" for same sex couples that offer many benefits similar to those of heterosexual marriage. Legislation permitting homosexual marriage was passed in Vermont in 2009. Massachusetts' highest court ruled in 2003 that homosexual couples have the constitutional right to marry, and the state began issuing licenses for same sex marriages in 2004. At the same time, however, eleven states passed voter approved state constitutional amendments restricting marriage to a man and a woman and in some cases also banning same sex civil unions. More than half of the states now have such amendments. After New Jersey's supreme court ruled in 2006 that the state must extend equal rights to same sex couples, the state enacted civil-union legislation. The supreme courts in California and Connecticut overturned those states' bans on same sex marriage in 2008, as did the court in Iowa in 2009. Voters in California subsequently passed a constitutional amendment banning it, but that was overturned in federal court in 2010. Same sex marriage was legalized in 2009 in Maine (subsequently overturned by referendum) and New Hampshire, in 2010 in the District of Columbia, in 2011 by New York, and in 2012 by Washington state and Maryland. Several other states recognize same sex civil unions or domestic partnerships, which offer fewer rights than civil unions.

In 1996, to help defend one man, one woman marriage from efforts to redefine it, the U.S. Congress overwhelmingly passed – and President Bill Clinton signed – the "Defense of Marriage Act" (DOMA). It defined "marriage" in federal law as a legal union between one man and one woman as husband and wife, and the word "spouse" as a person of the opposite sex who is a husband or a wife. DOMA also enabled states – even in the face of claims made pursuant to the Full Faith and Credit Clause – to decline to recognize same sex marriages from other states.

On December 7, 2012, the Supreme Court of the United States announced that it would hear two cases challenging laws that define the institution of marriage as it has traditionally been understood: as a union between one man and one woman. In *United States v. Windsor*, the Court will review the decision by the U.S. Court of Appeals for the Second Circuit holding that Section 3 of DOMA, which defined marriage as one man and one woman for purposes of federal law, is unconstitutional. In *Hollingsworth v. Perry*, the Court will review the U.S. Court of Appeals for the Ninth Circuit's decision striking down Proposition 8, which California voters adopted in 2008 to reestablish the definition of marriage as the union of a man and a woman in that state after judicial action had redefined it to include same sex couples. The plaintiffs in both cases argue that the government's refusal to recognize same sex marriage violates their Due Process and Equal Protection rights.

In February 2011, President Obama instructed the Justice Department to stop defending the constitutionality of the Defense of Marriage Act. The Constitution requires the president to "take care that the laws be faithfully executed," which historically has included defending them in court. But President Obama believes that Section 3 "is unconstitutional" in that it violates the Due Process Clause of the Fifth Amendment (including its equal protection component). President Obama advised that the Executive Branch of the government will continue to enforce Section 3 consistent with the Executive's obligation to take care that the laws be faithfully executed, unless and until Congress repeals Section 3 or the judicial branch renders a definitive verdict against the law's constitutionality.

Before the modern effort to redefine marriage gained momentum, there was never a suggestion that the male-female relationship that produces the children who will carry society into the future could not be given special status under law. It has been this way in the United States for over 200 years and repeatedly recognized as such by the courts. The potential to produce children naturally is unique to opposite-sex relationships. It is not the law that "discriminates" based on "sexual orientation" – it is nature as created by God.

All citizens, including governmental leaders, should do their part to uphold the institution of marriage, because it provides the best environment for raising children, who are the future of our society. Strengthening marriage creates a stronger foundation for the family, the basic social building block, and produces a stronger nation that benefits many future generations. Unfortunately, marriage has been badly weakened by decades of divorce, out-of-wedlock childbearing, and cohabitation. We need to work to restore a culture of marriage in which monogamous, life-long marriages are the norm, and marriage between a man and a woman is treasured as the safest and best haven for children. We do our part when we faithfully preach and teach God's plan for marriage and live it out in our lives.

Conclusion

Many people, even some Christians, want civil government to have a far greater role than what the New Testament outlines. There are many who look to our government to provide for people's health care, welfare, education, financial security, etc. There is much disagreement about the value of government involving itself in these things. But if government has been given a role in these areas, it was not by God's design, but by man's. Whether or not we agree with the human wisdom behind the additional, man-ordained works of civil government, we should all agree that God expects certain things of our leaders and those things should take precedence over all others. God is our ruler. Christ is our King. We obey the civil authorities only so far as the God's word allows us. We should remember not to put our trust in civil government but in God. Christians would do well not to forget these things. "But seek ye first his kingdom, and his righteousness; and all these things shall be added unto you" (Matt. 6:33).

Putting God First in the Home

Norm Webb, Jr.

"Everyone who hears these words of Mine and does not act on them, will be like a foolish man who built his house on the sand" (Matt. 7:27).

The picture that Jesus paints in this phrase is completely ridiculous. Had the point of the metaphor not been so eternal-life altering serious, it could have easily been the beginning of a stand-up comedic scenario. What person would build his house in a wadi? Who would jeopardize such an investment of money and labor, and possibly his own life, by building the dwelling for him and his family upon a foundation so obviously unreliable? That is exactly the point that Jesus wants to drive home to His listeners. No one, with any sense, would do this, yet is this not what so many people do with their lives and families? When lives and homes are built upon worldly wisdom, popular trends, humanistic philosophy, and evolution-based psychology, temporal and eternal devastation is certain to follow. These foundations cannot handle the wail of life's beatings and sin's temptations without crumbling failure. One only needs to observe the failing experiment of 21st century America in order to conclude that any foundation composed of

Norm Webb currently resides in Athens, AL with his lovely wife, Barbara Jo (Britnell) and their three daughters: Emily, Kara, and Sabrina. He currently serves as the Vice-President of Athens Bible School, overseeing fundraising, public relations, Information Technology, and facility operations, and teaches a daily Bible class to sophomores. From 2001 to 2011, he served as the evangelist for the Jones Road church of Christ in Athens, AL and, prior to that, served six years as the evangelist for the Congdon Avenue church of Christ in Elgin, IL. He graduated from Florida College in 1993 and continued another year in Biblical studies. He has also worked with churches in China and Mexico. He enjoys coaching soccer for the Athens Bible School men's team and spending his free time with his family.

current postmodern thinking is insufficient. Is there any statistic or societal trend that suggests our country is better off than it was sixty years ago? Is there any evidence that is convincing enough to demonstrate that more single parent homes, higher teenage sexual activity, and increasing homosexual rights are making for a better world or a better country? While the success of God's wisdom is not first and foremost measured by the temporal status of humanity, following that wisdom has proven to be nothing but positive for the finite race. Jesus' assurance is that those who build upon the rock of God's word will not be disappointed.

Jesus' warning to build upon the rock of His words is applicable to every aspect of the Christian's life. From one's treatment of others, to his finances, to his character, to his giving, and to his religion, his life should be dictated by the inspired Scriptures. This includes his marriage and his family.

Building homes is God's business. He is an expert at it. I don't ask my accountant to wire my house and I don't ask my doctor to install the plumbing. They are not experts in those fields. So why do we believe that we can build families better than God? The psalmist warns that building a home on your own is a work of vanity.

> "Unless the LORD builds the house, they labor in vain who build it" (Psa. 127:1).

Building a family is not for the faint of heart. While it is one of the most rewarding endeavors (Psa.127:3-5), it is also one of the most challenging, most emotionally draining, and most exhausting work in which a person may engage. God gives a warning: "If you are not going to build on my foundation you are wasting your time and you are destined to fail." Listen to His words: "It is vain for you to rise up early, to retire late, to eat the bread of painful labors" (Psa.127:2). Every parent can relate to this; from the early morning feedings of an infant to anxiously waiting up late for the teenager to come home, God says that all of the effort, all of the time, all the money, all of the love is futile if He is not the one building the home. However, in the same passage, God gives a promise to His children, "For He gives to His beloved sleep." The family that builds on the Lord's foundation is assured that sleep will come with relative ease, because they can be confident in the Lord's building plan.

Building a family by any plan other than God's plan is much like a chemical experiment with no lab procedure booklet. We begin to mix chemicals together hoping we don't blow up ourselves and those around us. God constantly assures us, that by following His building plan, we will have a home that not only brings joy to our lives, but also brings glory to Him and light to the world. This requires that we trust and obey His plan. It requires that He takes first place in our families. It requires an unwavering commitment to God's word and God's ways. Putting God first is the only reliable foundation.

"Seek first the kingdom of God and His righteousness and all of these things will be added unto you" (Matt. 6:33).

So often, God links His promises to success-driven conditions. The promise of "all these things" (what the Gentiles seek) "shall be added unto you" requires kingdom-first priorities. God inextricably ties eternal success to an undivided loyalty and obedience to His eternal rule and righteousness. "For bodily discipline is only of little profit, but godliness is profitable for all things, since it holds promise for the present life and also for the life to come" (1 Tim. 4:8).

This principle applies to the family as well. Heaven-driven and earthly-healthy families are only possible when they are devoted to kingdom priorities. God speaks to His people (then and now) and delivers the formula that will equate to God-centered, heaven-reaching families. In Deuteronomy 6:4-14, God tells us that He and His word are to dominate the family's conversation all the time – morning, noon and night – and in every setting – in your house, when you walk, when you go to bed, when you get up. He tells us that His commands and His wisdom are to be written (figuratively or literally?) on the doorposts (plural) of our house. His commands are to be on the frontals of our foreheads – literally between our eyes. In other words, there is to be no room in the home where God is not seen, no vision of life not filtered through God's commands.

Why? Because if God and His word do not have this priority in my home, my family and I will forget Him and follow other gods (Deut. 6:12; 8:14). The children of Israel proved this immutable principle. Over and over God testifies of why they became unfaithful to Him and why their nation ended in ruin (Judg. 8:34; Psa. 106:21; Hos. 8:14). Israel is a case study for why nations collapse. Every identifying factor of a crumbling nation is magnified in Israel's history. Look at the history of any nation or any church that has come to ruin and you will discover one common factor – spiritually and morally dilapidated homes – homes that put gods over God, that prioritized earthly baubles over eternal riches. This should not be surprising to Bible readers. God said it would happen, "It shall come about if you ever forget the LORD your God and go after other gods . . . you will surely perish" (Deut. 8:19).

Challengers to God's First Place Position

Proverbs 22:6 states, "Train up a child in the way he should go, even when he is old he will not depart from it." The implication in this passage is that there is a "way" a child should go. God provides a path upon which the family should walk, yet the world offers an endless number of roads from which to choose. Consider three alluring, deluding, Devil-designed paths that are broad and lead to destruction.

1. Busyness in Good Things. I don't believe there is any argument against the Christian being engaged in a productive life. We need to be doing things that are upright and acceptable to God. Unfortunately, so many of us are filling our lives with so many activities that God is being choked out. Work, school, sports, hobbies, friends, and entertainment can all have a rightful place in the life and home of the Christian, but we have become so enamored with life on earth that we forget the heaven to which we are to be looking. In Matthew 13:22, Jesus warns in the Parable of the Sower of the danger of over-crowded hearts and over-crowded lives, when He describes the growing sapling, sprouting from the heart that hears God's word, but is choked out by the thorns that invade its root system and drains the soil of its nutrients. He identifies these thorns as the worries of the world, the deceitfulness of riches, the pleasures of this life and the desire for other things (Mark 4:19; Luke 8:14).

With lives constantly on the go, we fail to make time for God to have His rightful forefront position in our schedules and our minds. We are engaging in enriching activities, but none that feed our spiritual relationship with our spouses, our children, our brethren, the lost, and, most importantly, our Lord.

As one who works for a school that promotes wholesome activities fitting for Christian participation, I readily admonish our families that too much of a good thing can be harmful. The constant engagement in upright, but earth bound affairs provides no time for the private spiritual devotion and nourishment required for growth in the Lord. We must beware of this subtle delusion that constant busyness is always a good thing. We must protect times of spiritual devotion. While at one time in our nation there seemed to still exist a respect for Sundays and even Wednesday evenings as times in which most people attended a worship assembly, today very few areas of the country exempt Sundays as a time free from ball games and other activities. The godly family can not rely upon the world to protect times of worship and spiritual devotion. If Christ is to be sanctified in our hearts (1 Pet. 3:15), He must be sanctified in our schedules, so that the family, and the individuals of the family, may grow up together in the Lord.

2. The God of Social Media and Technology. Never in the world's history has such a phenomena of technological and communicational advancement been seen than in the last 10 years. The individuals on planet earth have never been more in touch with each other than what they are right now. That is not necessarily a bad thing.

Never has there been a greater opportunity to reach people with the gospel and to edify distant brethren. Never has the human race been able to exchange information at such a high rate of speed, enabling a growth in knowledge at an exponential rate. Nevertheless, the use of such outlets as Facebook, Twitter, MySpace, YouTube, Face Time, texting, email, online searches and games, and the host of other social media requires the highest amount of self-discipline. Who hasn't observed the modern family all sitting in the same room, yet totally disconnected from one another because they are completely connected to a personal, technological, hand held device? We are addicted to technology, yet unaware or unwilling to admit it. We crave it, rely on it and want to believe that we are helpless without it.

Do not misunderstand; it is part of the world we live in. One hundred years ago, we could have been critical about our increasing reliance on automobiles or kitchen gadgets. The answer is not to toss away the cell phone or the computer, or disconnect permanently from the internet. The answer is found in Paul's words regarding the secret to his own spiritual success: "I discipline my body and make it my slave, so that after I have preached to others, I myself will not be disqualified" (1 Cor. 9:27). We need to be keenly sensitive to what our eyes see, our minds absorb, and how our time is spent, lest these beneficial advancements destroy our marriages and our families. To protect our hearts and minds and those of our families, we need to place guards and filters on not only our computers, but also on the time we spend on these devices. We need days of family fasting from technology, if for no other reason, but to help us expose any dangerous dependency on it. We need to ask, has the Lord become second place in our hearts to technology? Have we fooled ourselves to believe we need our mobile devices more than we need God and His word? Or, are we learning to effectively use technology to serve the Lord?

3. Belittlement of God's Design of the Family. While the above challengers to the God designed family come from within, this challenger is external.

A dramatic shift of thought has taken place in the last fifty years regarding the characteristics of the ideal family. In 1960, 70% of American adults were married. That number today is around 50%. A 2010 Pew and *Time Magazine* survey indicated that 39% of people in the U.S. now believe that marriage is becoming obsolete, which is up 11% from 1978. A 2006 survey indicated that, for the first time in history, homes with traditional marriages at their core are now below 50%. Eight times as many children are born out of wedlock today, than in 1960. The fact is, how society thinks about the God-designed family has significantly changed. This is reflected in the popular TV shows, as we have gone from *Family Ties* and *The Cosby Show,* which portrayed nuclear families, to *Modern Family*, which portrays a marriage between homosexuals who have an adopted child.

Does God's design of the family, with a husband and wife who are married, raising children, really matter anymore? In 1934, J.D. Unwin, a British anthropologist, released the results of his research in a study entitled, *Sex and Culture*. In that study he researched sixteen civilized and eighty uncivilized cultures over 5000 years of human history. Of his many findings, he concluded that strong sexual ethics, which restrained sex to the exclusive relationship of legal marriage, was directly related to the health and prosperity of a given civilization. He also concluded that cultures that allowed sexual freedom did not display endeavors toward the betterment of their society. What J. D. Unwin discovered in 1934, God has been saying since the beginning of time. His original design of the family is important and is what is best for us!

As the cultural norms of our nation continue to drift from God's design of the family, so will there be a shift within the church. The continual saturation of godlessness will become a major threat to the Christian family who does not actively battle against this trend. If the value of marriage and the family is to be protected, then God's people must espouse in their families the value and benefit of God's design. Marriages between Christians must do more than survive, they must thrive, and children must be raised to love God over everything else (Matt. 22:37; Deut. 6:1-15).

Foundational Cracks: The Illusion of God Being First
While the internal and external factors mentioned above challenge the

reign of God being placed first in the family, there is also a threat that is even more subtle, yet equally dangerous. One of the most subtle threats is the illusion that God is first in the family, when in reality we have only exalted an external religion. We must be careful that our devotion to God does not just hold to a "form of godliness," but rather is characterized by obedience to God drawn from a sincere trust in and love of the One who gave all to save us.

While faithful attendance to the Bible classes and worship assemblies of the church helps to promote the growth of knowledge and understanding, they are only a supplement to the spiritual and biblical teaching and guiding that takes place in the home. Having rules in the home that promote good morals and ethics is helpful, but they will carry no weight with maturing teenagers if they are not built and explained on the eternal principles of God's word and taught to carry eternal consequences. A private education from a biblical worldview in a Christian environment will have very little impact on children if the example of godly parents, devoted prayer and biblical instruction are not taking place in the home. After twelve years of teaching Bible at a private educational institution, at which some students attend for thirteen years, it is not difficult to ascertain which students are being taught at home and which ones are only being taught at school and church assemblies. Nothing replaces the influence of parents on children or the influence between spouses. When Junior High and High School students are asked who the number one influence is in their lives, the dominant answer is, "My parents." The dangerous illusion is to think that we are building our homes on a foundation that looks like God is first, but in reality is nothing more than an institutional raising and an external religion. This foundation will not sustain the home when the storms of doubt, affliction, or temptation threaten it (Matt. 7:27). Great will be its fall.

Characteristics of a God-First Home

The story of Noah is one of the most well-known stories in the world. We are often astounded by the magnitude of the flood waters, the size of the ark, the length of time Noah and his family were on it, and the rainbow that was God's sign of a promise. However, in a world in which the people thought evil continually, Noah got his boys on the ark. That is impressive; especially when one considers that Shem was yet to be born when Noah received the command to build the ark (see Gen. 5:32; 11:10). Noah raised his sons to believe and obey God and take wives who would do the same in a world that would have been equally corrupt as our own, if not worse.

Like Noah, we have the ability and the resources to build our homes on solid ground. God's word provides us that help and assurance. Consider some general biblical principles that characterize a God-first home.

God's word is read and shared regularly (Deut. 6:1-14). Nothing can replace God's communication to His creation. If spouses want to have the wisdom for a strong, happy marriage, the commands and principles of God's word must be read and discussed. If we want our children to know God and what God has said, God's word must be read. As parents do this for their children, and as they grow, with their children, then the children will see the love that their parents have for what God has to say. There is no substitute for this. Not the most eloquent and powerful preacher has the influence that a mother and father have who relate God's word to their children. If young people are going to grow up and develop a faith of their own, they must be equipped with God's armor and that starts with knowing and understanding God's word.

Truth is valued (Prov. 23:23). In a world that "suppresses the truth" (Rom. 1:18) and discards it, it is essential that the standards of God's word be regarded as immutable and immoveable. While we must not possess the truth arrogantly, we must help our children and spouses to understand that without it there is no salvation (John 8:31-32). While attempting to dilute the truth may appease our desires for the moment, such thoughts will reap no eternal benefit.

Husbands and wives must fulfill their roles (Eph. 5:21-33). In a world turned upside down, where fathers are portrayed as baboons and homosexual rights are promoted and the nuclear family is now a minority, it is all the more important that a husband fulfill his role of leading and providing for the home and loving his wife like his own flesh. A wife needs to manage her home, while respecting and submitting to her husband. They both need to understand their spouses needs and serve those needs as they would serve no one else. They need to be faithful to one another. If children are to grow up to be godly husbands and wives, they must see it in their parents.

Moms and Dads must be living Christ-like examples (1 John 2:6; Eph. 5:1-2). Nothing replaces the example that parents provide for their children. Children emulate first and foremost what they see from their parents. What does honesty, respect, love, self-control, and faith look like? Mom and Dad will be the primary source for that answer. What do you do when making the right choice is hard? Mom and Dad's example will be the answer. Just like everyone else, children need to see Christ in their parents.

Make service a priority in the home (Phil. 2:1-8; Gal. 6:9-10). We live in a world filled with selfish people. To raise servants, we must be servants, first and foremost, to one another in the family. Children should see Mom and Dad being a servant to one another. Mom and Dad should expect their children to be servants to them and to their siblings. Create opportunities to serve strangers, Christians, and non-Christians.

Create boundaries for the family (Eph. 6:1-4). This is not just for children. There needs to be boundaries regarding how much the adults work, how much T.V. the family watches, how long any member of the family spends with technology, and how much time will be dedicated to sports and hobbies. There needs to be rules and everyone needs to know those rules, and what the consequences are for breaking them, and the rewards for following them. Those boundaries need to be rooted in God's word and backed by biblical commands, precedents, and principles. Everyone needs to realize that there is accountability to those rules both temporal and eternal.

The Gospel needs to be shared (Matt. 28:19). This starts in the home. The words Jesus, Christ, love, sin, salvation, redemption, faith, repentance, confession, baptism, and faithfulness should not be words that are strange or awkwardly used. The members of the family have to help one another get to heaven. When the gospel is shared in the family, then family members become equipped to share it with others. God-first families should be a forced to be reckoned with in this world.

Be devoted to prayer (Rom. 12:12). Where did you learn to pray? For many Christians, their answer is, "In the worship assembly." While prayers in the assembly can be helpful, it will be the prayers in the home that will have the most impact. Husbands and wives need to pray together. Parents need to pray with and for their children and pray often. This communication with God is essential for developing a deep, meaningful relationship with God.

Building on the Rock, Set on a Hill
"Everyone who hears these words of Mine and acts on them, may be compared to a wise man who built his house on the rock" (Matt. 7:24).

There is only one foundation that can stand the storms of this life and endure unto eternity. That foundation is Christ and the truth He has revealed through His word. If we are going to take on the challenge of building a home, let's build it on that which we know will stand. Let us build our marriages by God's design, for then they will last. Let us raise our children using God's design, for then they will be prepared. When we do this, we will be building on a rock that is set on a hill, which will provide a light for God to the world around us. A God-first family is a family full of light that becomes a beacon in a dark world (Matt. 5:14-16). A God-first family is a family that glorifies God and a family whom God will glorify.

Sex Is Limited to Marriage

Phillip E. Stuckey

And the LORD God caused a deep sleep to fall upon Adam, and he slept: and he took one of his ribs, and closed up the flesh instead thereof; And the rib, which the LORD God had taken from man, made he a woman, and brought her unto the man. And Adam said, This is now bone of my bones, and flesh of my flesh: she shall be called Woman, because she was taken out of Man. Therefore shall a man leave his father and his mother, and shall cleave unto his wife: and they shall be one flesh. And they were both naked, the man and his wife, and were not ashamed (Gen. 2:21-25, KJV).

The Bible reveals that God is the giver of all good things in this world. James wrote by inspiration, "Every good gift and every perfect gift is from above, and cometh down from the Father of lights, with whom is no variableness, neither shadow of turning" (Jas. 1:17). Most of us would agree that marriage is one of those good gifts (Gen. 2:24; Matt. 19:4-5). If one accepts this to be true, then one must also accept that sex is among those good things that God has given us. "Marriage is honourable in all, and the bed undefiled: but whoremongers and adulterers God will judge" (Heb. 13:4).

Like many of God's gifts to mankind, sex has been abused and perverted to mankind's own twisted desires. Truly, "God hath made man upright; but

---

Phillip E. Stuckey was born in Americus, GA on August 21, 1975. He grew up in the small town of Oglethorpe, GA and has lived in Central Georgia most of his life. It was there that he first heard and obeyed the gospel and where he began preaching. He now lives in Warner Robins, GA with his wife of sixteen years, Elizabeth, and their three children (Ian, Zoe, and Aidan). He labors with the Bonaire church of Christ in Bonaire, GA. He began working with the brethren there in 2003. He attended the preacher training program in Ellettsville, IN in 2010. He also works for the Macon County Board of Education as a Technology Specialist. He received his B.S. in Information Technology from Macon State College.

they have sought out many inventions" (Eccl. 7:29). While the scourge of sexual sin in our nation is nothing new, it certainly continues to make itself felt in our society. According to a brief from Guttmacher Institute:

- 13% of teens have had sex by the age of 15.
- 7 in 10 female and male teens have had sex by their 19th birthday.
- On the average, most young people have sex for the first time by age 17, but do not marry until their mid-20s.
- Each year, it is estimated 750,000 women aged 15-19 become pregnant.

In 2011, 15% of high school students reported having four or more sexual partners (National Campaign to Prevent Teen and Unplanned Pregnancy). A report examining trends in premarital sex from 1954-2003 found that by the age of 20, 77% of their survey's respondents had had sex with 75% having had premarital sex (Finer). One of the conclusions from the survey was, "Almost all Americans have sex before marrying" (Finer). The CDC reported in 2004 that of 6.39 million pregnancies, 1.22 million ended in abortion (Ventura, Abma, and *et al*). Is this the role God intended for sex? Is this the picture that God had in mind when He created man and woman? Did God really intend for each man and woman to enjoy sex whenever and with whomever they want or did God intend for sex to be limited to marriage? For the Bible believer the answer to the question is self-evident. God has limited sex to marriage (Heb. 13:4) and, like all of God's commandments, this is for our benefit (1 John 5:3). Why, however, is sex limited to mar-riage? Is it really sinful when it occurs outside of marriage? Is sex outside of marriage truly detrimental to the home and society?

Sex Is Limited to Marriage

Nevertheless, to avoid fornication, let every man have his own wife, and let every woman have her own husband. Let the husband render unto the wife due benevolence: and likewise also the wife unto the husband (1 Cor. 7:2-3, KJV).

To understand why sex is limited to marriage and why sex outside of marriage is sinful one must go back to the beginning, back to when God created man and woman. The Bible teaches that in the beginning God made man and woman in His image (Gen. 1:26-27). This is significant when we understand its meaning. One aspect of being created in the image of God is that men and women are not just physical beings but also spiritual beings. They have not only a mortal nature but also an immortal nature. When this life is over, each person's soul will live on in eternity (John 5:28-29). Each will spend eternity with God in heaven or without God in hell. God's plan for each one is to glorify Him in doing the good works He has purposed (Eph. 2:10).

Sin causes God's plan and purpose for each soul to be undone (Isa. 59:1-2). Thus when sex is taken outside of marriage it brings condemnation; that is not what God made our body for (1 Cor. 6:13; Heb. 13:4). Understanding this one fundamental fact is essential to understanding why sex is limited to marriage and why failing to respect God's will on the role sex is to play in our lives is so harmful.

God did not purpose for mankind to explore sexual relationships outside of marriage. This is evident since God clearly purposed marriage to be for a man and a woman to live together in a lifelong relationship (Gen. 2:24; Matt. 19:4-6). The Bible teaches that God created marriage. Marriage, therefore, was a part of creation; it originated by God's design and not man's. Since God purposed for man and woman to be united in marriage for a lifetime, we know that marriage is important and significant. In creating marriage, God planned for the sexual relationship between a man and a woman. The Bible reveals that God intended for sexual relations to play a part in marriage (Gen. 2:24; 1 Cor. 6:16). Evidently, this relationship between a husband and wife is important to God. But why is the sexual relationship important in marriage? What did God intend for it to accomplish?

An examination of the Scriptures reveals that God has several purposes for the sexual relationship in marriage. One of the most obvious is procreation (Gen. 1:28). The conception and rearing of children was planned by God to occur within the confines of marriage. It is noteworthy that both the first blessing and the first command recorded in Genesis to Adam and Eve was related to sexuality: "be fruitful and multiply" (Gen. 1:28). Not only is marriage the ideal environment for raising godly offspring (Prov. 22:16; Eph. 6:4), but the birth and the rearing of children that come from this union also tend to draw a husband and wife closer to one another, increasing the strength of their relationship even after the children are grown (Psa. 127:3-5).

Another purpose for the sexual relationship in marriage is the affirmation of love and affection between a husband and wife. God said it wasn't good for Adam to be alone (Gen. 2:18). He needed a companion, one that would complement him in every way. God made woman; Adam understood that she was the perfect companion for him (Gen. 2:21-25). In the Garden of Eden after Adam and Eve had sinned, God told the woman that even though her pain in childbearing would be multiplied, still she would desire her husband (Gen. 3:16). God's design for two becoming one flesh involves not only the physical union of a man and woman, but also their emotional, mental, and spiritual union. It is the giving of oneself to another that binds two hearts together in love and affection (1 Cor.7:3-4).

The sexual relationship also provides pleasure; this too is by God's design. The Bible speaks to this in several places (Prov. 5:15-19). Some say this is merely a by-product or consequence of the other purposes God has ordained for sex. This is true to some degree. Consider, though, that God has created in man various physical appetites such as hunger and thirst. In turn, He has provided the lawful means to exercise and satisfy these desires. The desire for sexual pleasure is satisfied in marriage, another aspect that strengthens and binds married couples together.

The sexual relationship in marriage also has the purpose of protecting men and women from sexual sin (Prov. 5-7). God is fully aware of the desires of mankind and, as stated previously, has made provision for those that are lawful, needful, and beneficial. Thus the wise man said, "Drink water from thy own cistern" (Prov. 5:15). The apostle Paul spoke explicitly about marriage and the sexual relationship therein as a means to "avoid fornication" (1 Cor. 7:1-5). Men and women need not corrupt themselves with sexual immorality in any form since God has provided a proper and beneficial means of satisfying the sexual needs of every person.

Thus God intended and purposed for the sexual relationship to be limited to marriage where it would provide for the procreation of the race, draw the man and woman into deeper union, and protect them from temptation. Sex in marriage is honorable and right in God's sight, but outside of marriage it is unlawful, it is an abomination (Heb. 13:4). Impressing upon someone the purpose of sex is vital to his understanding of why sex is limited to marriage, why it is sinful outside of marriage, and why the home is devastated when we fail to use sex as God has purposed.

Sex Outside of Marriage Is Sinful

Marriage is honourable in all, and the bed undefiled: but whoremongers and adulterers God will judge (Heb. 13:4, KJV).

Sex outside of marriage can be either premarital or extramarital; the difference being the former describes sex before marriage and the latter describes sexual relations outside of one's marriage. The Bible speaks of fornication and adultery which encompass both of these concepts. *Merriam-Webster's Dictionary* defines "fornication" as "consensual sexual intercourse between two persons not married to each other." The Greek word *porneia* translated "fornication" is defined as "1) illicit sexual intercourse, 1a) adultery, fornication, homosexuality, lesbianism, intercourse with animals, etc., 1b) sexual intercourse with close relatives; Lev. 18, 1c) sexual intercourse with a divorced man or woman; Mk. 10:11, 12); 2) metaphorically the worship of idols, 2a) of the defilement of idolatry, as incurred by eating the sacrifices offered to idols" (Thayer, 531-532). From the above definitions it should be evident that fornication is a very broad term that includes any and all sexual relations outside of marriage. Any and all sexual contact with anyone other than one's spouse is fornication.

Adultery is a more specific sexual sin that involves at least one married person. *Merriam-Webster's Dictionary* defines "adultery" as "voluntary sexual intercourse between a married man and someone other than his wife or between a married woman and someone other than her husband." The Greek word *moichao* which is translated "adultery" is defined as "to have unlawful intercourse with another's wife, to commit adultery with" (Thayer 417). Adultery is a form of fornication though it is sometimes differentiated from it. Any sexual relations with someone other than one's spouse or with someone who is someone else's spouse is adultery.

Society's views of these sexual sins are conflicting and contradictory. Many are unsure of the meanings of "fornication" and "adultery" and what acts constitute them. Some broad definitions include even a lustful thought, while some are so narrow in their definition that some forms of homosexuality would be excluded. While most people in society would probably still agree that adultery is wrong, many consider that fornication for unmarried people is not negative, but rather an inevitable, if not desirable occurrence. One writer boldly stated, ". . .having sex before marriage is the best choice for nearly everyone." She declared, "It turns out that feminist values – not 'traditional' ones – lead to the most stable marriages. And feminist views plus later marriage typically equals premarital sex" (Filipovic). Such talk is reminiscent of the days of Isaiah when many called good evil and evil good (Isa. 5:20)! Despite these attitudes God has not changed His mind. Indeed, "Marriage is honourable in all, and the bed undefiled: but whoremongers and adulterers God will judge" (Heb. 13:4). Let us make no mistake about it – fornication and adultery are sinful!

Contrast what God has said in His word with what the world says concerning fornication. It is the only scriptural exception allowing for divorce and remarriage (Matt. 5:32; 19:9), even though God hates divorce (Mal.

2:16). Jesus said that fornication proceeds from one's heart and defiles a person (Matt. 15:19-20; Mark 7:21-22). Yet the world tells us that it is only natural and is even beneficial. God said it is not to be indulged in, but instead to be abstained from (Acts 15:20, 29; 21:25; 1 Thess. 4:3). The world says it makes one acceptable and happy, but the Scripture reveals it was the cause of the brethren withdrawing fellowship from a brother at the church at Corinth (1 Cor. 5). Today the world sees fornication as a rite of passage but Paul said it keeps one from inheriting the kingdom of God (1 Cor. 6:9). In other words, it will condemn one to hell!

Fornication is contrary to God's purpose for the body (1 Cor. 6:13). God made us to glorify Him in our bodies and not to shame Him or one another. Thus He enjoins every soul to flee from and avoid fornication (1 Cor. 6:18; 7:2). It is a work of the flesh that is not even to be named among the saints (Gal. 5:19; Eph. 5:3). Those who have committed fornication must repent (2 Cor. 12:21) and strive to put to death the desire to fornicate (Col. 3:5). Adultery is sinful for these same reasons as it is a type of fornication.

It should be beyond dispute that these things are wrong and ought not to be committed by any soul but, as with so many other sins, many fall into temptation. Today, even among so-called evangelicals, fornication is at epidemic proportions. The National Association of Evangelicals reported that 80% of young evangelicals have engaged in premarital sex (Banks). How can this be when they have been taught not to? The response of one of these young people is revealing: "The Bible says not to do it, but I think, for most people, they need more than that. . . .We want to know why. And most of the time folks aren't prepared to answer the question why" (Banks). The question is a fair question and deserves an answer. That God said not to settles it. But some consideration about what God has revealed about mankind and His desires for each of us explains to us in large degree why sex outside of marriage is wrong. At the heart of it is, I believe, the fact that God did not create mankind to sin, certainly not for fornication (1 Cor. 6:13).

As stated before, God created man in His image (Gen. 1:26-27) and for His purposes: to do His will and glorify Him in our bodies (1 Cor. 6:19-20), to be filled with the fullness of God (Eph. 3:19; 4:13), and to be busy doing good works (Eph. 2:10). Thus we were made to be pure, not impure (1 Tim. 5:22). We were made to love God with all our heart, mind, body and soul and to look on, and love one another with the love of God (Matt. 22:37-38). Since God didn't make us to be instruments of unrighteousness but instead instruments of righteousness, to look on and use another human being to satisfy our sexual appetites outside of God's chosen and created arrangement is not a loving act, but is in fact an unloving and hateful act. It desecrates a being God has made for purity and holiness. Sex outside of marriage is a sin against the Creator who made us, against another person, and against our own selves and all for what? A passing pleasure that brings nothing but destructive and devastating consequences on every soul that gives in to its enticement (Heb. 11:24).

Sex Outside of Marriage Is Destructive
Can a man take fire in his bosom, and his clothes not be burned? Can one go upon hot coals, and his feet not be burned? (Prov. 6:27-28, KJV).

The wise man compared the one who would commit adultery to the one who would take fire into his bosom or walk on hot coals; obviously one cannot do so without getting hurt. Truly, no one can commit adultery or any sexual sin without suffering serious consequences. When people engage in sex outside of marriage, they bring physical, emotional, and spiritual consequences upon themselves and also upon others. These can have long-term catastrophic effects on the home.

The Old Testament reveals some of the horrific physical consequences that sexual sin can have on the home. The sexual sins of the men of Sodom and Gomorrah caused the death of all those in the cities of the plain and the destruction of Lot's family (Gen. 19). Balaam's counsel to entice the Israelites to sin through fornication led to the death of 23,000 people (Num. 22-25; 1 Cor. 10:8). The record of Shechem violating Dinah is another example that is instructive (Gen. 34:1-3). They were not married to one another and regardless of whether one considers it rape or seduction we can see several damaging consequences that resulted from their sexual union. Dinah was ashamed and her father Jacob was upset (Gen. 34:5). Her brothers who felt she had been treated as a prostitute were exceedingly angry (Gen. 34:7, 31), so much so that they deceived Shechem and his father into having all the males in their city circumcised and in their rage killed them all (Gen. 34:24-25). This deed ultimately led to Dinah's entire family having to relocate (Gen. 34:30; 35:1).

The sexual sin here led to many emotional consequences, such as stress, grief, and rage. That rage led to the killing of many innocent people and the destruction of many homes. What do you think became of those homes? What were the effects on the women and children who survived? While some may consider this an extreme example, the fact remains that these sins often incite anger and violence in the participants and the families of those involved. Fornication and adultery always victimize both parties (whether they realize it or not) and their families. In the case of adultery the wise man noted, "But whoso committeth adultery with a woman lacketh understanding: he that doeth it destroyeth his own soul. A wound and dishonour shall he get; and his reproach shall not be wiped away. For jealousy is the rage of a man: therefore he will not spare in the day of vengeance. He will not regard any ransom; neither will he rest content, though thou givest many gifts" (Prov. 6:32-35). When these acts of violence occur, homes are often left without the financial resources and parental guidance needed to provide a healthy, happy, and godly home. Loved ones are often killed, disabled, or imprisoned. Families are estranged and impoverished. The legacy of this sin is long-lasting and far-reaching.

The physical consequences from sexual relations outside of marriage are obvious and well documented. Today there are few among us who haven't heard of the epidemic of sexually transmitted diseases that plagues the world. While some of these diseases result in mild and temporary shame and limited physical discomfort, others can lead to great physical suffering and even death. Not only do those who engage in fornication and adultery personally contract these diseases and suffer their effects, but they often pass them on to their unsuspecting spouse or friends and family through non-sexual contact. Even the children who are conceived and born to such individuals sometimes contract these diseases and suffer health issues long after birth. Surely those who engage in sin and contract these diseases would concur with the warnings of Proverbs: "And thou mourn at the last, when thy flesh and thy body are consumed" (Prov. 5:11).

Another physical consequence that often results from sexual promiscuity is unplanned and unwanted pregnancy, as in the case of David and Bathsheba (2 Sam. 11:5) and Judah and Tamar (Gen. 38:18). What becomes of children born of fornication and adultery today? A quick look at the statistics will reveal that many of them are aborted. According to the CDC, out of 6.6 million pregnancies in 2008, 1.2 million were aborted, 84% by unmarried women (Ventura, Curtin, *et al*). Babies that aren't aborted are very often born into damaged, broken, dysfunctional homes without one or both of their biological parents, leading to physical and emotional scars that follow them into adulthood and are even passed on to the next generation. Those who are responsible are like the adulterers of Malachi's day whom the Lord said, "covereth violence with his garment" (Mal. 2:16).

Those who are married and commit adultery betray a sacred trust with their spouse and with God. This betrayal of trust often leads to another physical consequence – divorce. Though God grants the innocent party the right to put away the adulterer and remarry (Matt. 19:9), the sundering of a marriage always leaves a lasting legacy. Not only will the lives of the husband and wife be forever changed, but their children, grandchildren, and their own parents and extended family will also have their lives forever changed. Is such destruction worth the passing pleasures of sin (Heb. 11:24)?

These physical consequences inevitably give way to emotional consequences. Many who have been promiscuous prior to marriage or entangled in adultery during marriage become paralyzed by guilt for what they have done. This guilt often leads to depression which can have disastrous consequences on one's spouse and children in various ways. Therapists and sociologists have found that children suffer when their parents commit adultery, even if their parents keep the affair secret (Brooks). Young children whose parents are involved in affairs often exhibit "anxiety symptoms" such as, "clinging, bed-wetting, thumb-sucking, fire-setting, temper tantrums, night terrors – in fact, anything that seems an appropriate response to the fear that their family is about to be wiped out" (Brooks). Older children may feel anger and betrayal and may act out their feelings (Brooks). Often these parental affairs become "the training ground for a child's adult behavior." These studies have revealed that children of those who engage in adultery are more prone to have affairs when they marry (Brooks).

Consider the Old Testament account of David's adultery with Bathsheba and murder of Uriah, her husband, to cover up his sin. One can only speculate as to what emotional effect David's affair with Bathsheba had on his own children. Perhaps David's guilt kept him from seeking to restrain and punish Amnon for his fornication with his sister Tamar (2 Sam. 11-12; 13:1-21)! Amnon's sexual sin prompted David's other son, Absalom, to kill Amnon. Absalom later rebelled and tried to take the kingdom from David. During the rebellion Absalom committed fornication with his father's concubines (2 Sam. 16:21-22). All of this eventually ended with Absalom's death. David's sexual sin had devastating emotional consequences that led to the physical and emotional destruction of his family and home. The same is true for many today.

No doubt many parents today who were promiscuous at one time are now reluctant to restrain their own children due to their lingering guilt for their own indiscretions. Like David, they are unable to forgive themselves for all the harm they have done to themselves and to others by their promiscuity (Psa. 32:3-4; Prov. 5:12-13). May this not be said of any of us. If we have done wrong we must repent and resolve to make things right. We must seek to restrain ourselves and teach and admonish all who are within our influence to abstain from fornication and adultery. Regardless of what we may have once done, we cannot afford to be paralyzed by guilt and depression and to let others fall without warning (Gal. 6:1-2; Jude 22-23).

Guilt is not the only emotional damage done by sex outside of marriage. Promiscuity can cause people to be unable to recognize the difference between lust and love. As young people bounce from person to person they inevitably separate love and intimacy from sexual relations. Over time, their consciences becomes seared (1 Tim. 4:2) and they wax worse and worse (2 Tim. 3:13). For them, sexual relations are almost a game, even a conquest: the more people they can have sexual relations with, the better they feel. The pure desire for the love and intimacy of marriage is replaced by the aim to satisfy their physical lust. One recent news story reported a group of high school students who drafted young, often unsuspecting ladies in to a "fantasy slut league" where they would earn points for documenting their sexual encounters (Martinez). Like Amnon, they find their love replaced by hatred and disgust once their sexual appetites have been satisfied (2 Sam. 13:15; Ezek. 23:17).

Once love and intimacy have been separated from sexual relations, it is often difficult to reunite them. When they finally marry, they are often so wounded that they are unable to have a productive and proper emotional relationship with their spouse. They are unable to see thier spouse as another person who has feelings and needs. If this has not been resolved, depression, dysfunction, and eventually the destruction of the marriage will follow. Sadly, this is the case with far too many today. Spouses don't view one another as human beings with precious souls but as objects for their sexual gratification. When one does marry, having had multiple sexual partners can lead to doubts about sexual fulfillment. Their spouses may wonder if they are being compared to previous partners and indeed the once promiscuous mate may struggle with this. These doubts inevitably lead to greater dysfunction and can lead to a complete breakdown of the marriage, often incurring even more sexual sin.

Mutual distrust results whenever people who have been promiscuous before marriage decide to commit to one another. When there is infidelity, the anger, frustration, and violation of trust by an adulterer can lead to feelings of jealousy as well as a desire for vengeance that can consume and destroy the marriage and home (Prov. 6:29-35). The injured spouse is suspicious of the adulterer and jealous of the former lover. This often leads to a failure to forgive as God does. Adulterers often struggle, projecting their guilt onto their spouse, even sometimes blaming the spouse for their own adultery. They may even assume their spouse is also adulterous and become suspicious, jealous, and angry. It is a vicious cycle that perpetuates destruction as long as it continues unchecked.

While the physical and emotional consequences are very real to us and are the ones that most visibly affect our homes, there is another consequence that has a much more long-term effect on our homes – the spiritual consequence. We have already established that both fornication and adultery are sinful (Heb. 13:4). Sex was created by God to be confined to the marriage relationship. When we engage in sex outside of marriage we violate God's law and are cut off from His love and His fellowship (Gen. 2:24; Isa. 59:1-2). One need only refer to the record of Potiphar's wife when she tried to entice Joseph to commit adultery. He refused because he knew it was a great wickedness against God Almighty (Gen. 39:9). Not only does it offend God, but it is a sin against the other party who joins one in sexual relations outside of marriage. The one who commits these evil deeds is like Amnon who violated his sister Tamar (2 Sam. 13:14). Though some cry out that their liaisons were consensual, it makes no difference. There is no love between two persons who would engage in such, only hate as they use one another for shameful gratification. The Scripture says, "Love worketh no ill to his neighbor" (Rom. 13:10), but those who engage in adultery and fornication are not seeking the best interest of one another. The two persons in effect become stumbling blocks for one another, a grievous offence (Matt. 18:6). These sins are most assuredly personal in nature because Paul said one who commits fornication "sinneth against his own body" (1 Cor. 6:18). When anyone commits fornication he sins against himself and destroys his own soul. If one doesn't repent of sex outside of marriage there is no hope of redemption, only an assurance of condemnation (Prov. 6:23; 1 Cor. 6:9; Heb. 13:4).

There Is Hope After Fornication and Adultery
And such were some of you: but ye are washed, but ye are sanctified, but ye are justified in the name of the Lord Jesus, and by the Spirit of our God (1 Cor. 6:11).

Perhaps you or someone you know has fallen prey to these sins, has suffered the terrible consequences and is unsure of what to do to repair the hurt and the wounds that have been suffered. The good news is that there is hope for those who recognize they have sinned against God and desire to make things right. Like all sin, fornication and adultery can be forgiven. The Corinthians whom Paul said were guilty of fornication, adultery and even homosexuality repented and were forgiven by God (1 Cor. 6:9-11). They were able to turn things around and have a right relationship with God. This is true for everyone who has succumbed to this temptation. If you have done so, repent and "sin no more" (John 8:11).

However, it would be wrong to conclude that resolving the spiritual consequence removes and repairs all the physical and emotional consequences that come from sin. Some of them never can be repaired, but thanks be to God, many can in time be overcome through God's grace and love, vigilant prayer, study, and personal application of His word. Physical consequences such as disease can be dealt with by coming to grips with the disease and accepting the consequences, praying to God for healing, and learning to cope with the effects. Remember the lesson the apostle Paul learned: "strength is made perfect in weakness" (2 Cor. 12:9). Perhaps you have become pregnant. Don't compound your sin by seeking an abortion. Don't abandon your child either, whether you are the father or the mother. Instead seek to do as God has decreed and raise your child. Strive to follow Paul's instructions to fathers to bring children up in the "nurture and admonition of the Lord" (Eph. 6:4).

Perhaps you are an adulterer or an injured spouse. If you are contemplating divorce consider why you are doing it (2 Cor. 13:5) and if you have the right (Matt. 19:9). Have you considered the consequences divorce will have on your children and both you and your spouse's families? Though God grants an exception to the innocent spouse, it may not always be the most expedient choice. It has been said facetiously that *divorce is the gift that keeps on giving*; this is so true. Long after you have moved on, the effects of the divorce will remain. Are your motives selfish? There are some who are only concerned about themselves and their well-being. Some are only interested in ensuring that they will have the right to have sexual relations with someone other than their current spouse. God forbid! Are you willing to forgive your spouse? Though the guilty party must be penitent, the willingness to forgive is essential if we desire forgiveness (Matt. 6:14-15; Luke 17:3).

Are you willing to work things out? Some are not willing to listen, to talk, or do anything to try to save their marriage; they just want out. Are you trying to bring your adulterous spouse to repentance? Perhaps the thought of facing the remainder of their lives celibate may bring the adulterer to his or her senses. Are you seeking to hurt your spouse because of the pain and suffering inflicted on you? Remember, vengeance belongs to the Lord (Rom. 12:19). What are your motives in considering divorce? Only you know the answer. David wasn't afraid to say, "Examine me, O LORD, and prove me; try my reins and my heart" (Psa. 26:2). Are your motives pure enough to say the same thing? The emotional pain and consequences of sexual sin can be overcome in time with faith, hope, and perseverance in the Lord (Phil. 4:13). Guilt and depression can be dealt with by repentance and prayer for forgiveness. Family dysfunction can be overcome with counseling and study with elders and older faithful brethren. Consider the cost before you end your marriage.

Perhaps you are a young person and are struggling because you don't know how to be a godly husband or wife or how to have a godly marriage. Seek out the wisdom of the Lord in His word and seek the advice of faithful older brethren. Brethren, we need more teaching on the home and more worthy examples for one another to emulate. Learning to love our spouses as our own bodies and considering one another's needs will go a long way in overcoming many of these emotional issues (Eph. 5:25, 28; 1 Cor. 7:2-3). Too many of us have overlooked that God has commanded us to love our spouses and our children (Eph. 5:25; Tit. 2:4). That means it is not optional. That means we can do it if we have the mind to. Too many of us are consumed with ourselves. Let us follow the Lord in serving one another instead of ourselves (Phil. 2:3-4).

Ultimately, in order to avoid sex outside of marriage each of us must cultivate a renewed mind, a guarded heart, and a protected body. Thus we have to desire and nurture the love of God and our neighbor in our hearts, desiring to do all that is pleasing to God and seeking the best interest of our fellowman (Matt. 22:37-39). This will lead us to learn, appreciate, and remember that God's will for us is not fornication and adultery but is to use our bodies as instruments of righteousness to glorify Him. We must strive to possess our own bodies as a "vessel in honor" and not give them away for a trifle, as Esau who gave away his birthright for a meal (1 Thess. 4:3-8; Heb. 12:16). Each of us is worth far more than that. We must not let it ever leave our minds that each man, woman, boy, and girl has an immortal soul that will spend eternity with God in Heaven or without Him in Hell (Gen.

1:26-27). Our love for God and for one another and our mutual desire to be in Heaven with Him should lead us to guard our hearts and minds. We should not look on one another with selfish desires to satisfy our own lusts. We should flee fornication and adultery and give no opportunity to engage in it (Gen. 39:9-12; Prov. 5:1-23; 6:23-25; 7:1-27; Rom. 13:13-14).

We must learn to protect our hearts and our minds from ungodly lust. Following the example of Job in Job 31:1, we should make a covenant with our eyes to focus on things that are "pure, lovely and good" as the apostle Paul said in Philippians 4:8 and to "set no worthless thing before our eyes" as David said in Psalm 101:3. We should exercise our senses to be wary of things that stir up lust in ourselves or others (Heb. 5:12-14; Gal. 5:19-21). This involves being honest with ourselves about whom we spend time with, where we go, and what we watch, read, and listen to. We must have a mind that abhors fornication and adultery if we hope to resist it. We should desire to abstain from sexual relations until we are in a lawful marriage with a suitable spouse and thereby avoid fornication and enjoy the blessing of sex in a way that is right and honorable before God (1 Cor. 7:1-5; Heb. 13:4; 1 Cor. 7:6-9). Remember, if you plan to marry, the person you will marry is most likely alive right now and hopefully preparing to meet you. Do you want this person to prepare for you and preserve his or her body for you? If so, do the same. We must labor to draw on the strength God provides to nurture our marriages and home and resist temptation (Rom. 6:2; Col. 3:5-7).

The apostle Paul penned, "For this is the will of God, your sanctification; that is, that you abstain from sexual immorality; that each of you know how to possess his own vessel in sanctification and honor, not in lustful passion, like the Gentiles who do not know God" (1 Thess. 4:3-5 NASB). Though the world around us is ungodly and promotes promiscuity, the child of God must ever "abstain from fornication" and "flee" from it (1 Thess. 4:3; 1 Cor. 6:18). God is the giver of all good things. He has given mankind the gifts of sex and marriage. The two belong together and not apart. This is what God had in mind when He created man and woman and this is what God intends for every man and woman who would enjoy these gifts today. God has limited sex to marriage (Heb. 13:4) and like all of God's commandments, this is for our good (1 John 5:3). God did not make any of us to profane our bodies and our homes through fornication and adultery. Whenever sex occurs outside marriage it is detrimental to every soul and every home. It destroys the mind, body, and soul of every person engaged in it. It destroys the lives of innocent children and families. It is nothing more than the pursuit of selfish desires. Let every saint strive to keep the sexual relationship where it belongs – in a godly marriage – and every home intact and strong.

Works Cited

"Adultery." Merriam-Webster.com. Merriam-Webster, 2012. Web. 15 October, 2012.

Banks, Adelle M. "With High Premarital Sex And Abortions Rates, Evangelicals Say It's Time To Talk About Sex." *Huffington Post*. 23 April, 2012: n. page. Web. 11 Dec. 2012. <*http://www.huffingtonpost.com/2012/04/23/evangelicals-sex-frank-talk_n_1443062.html*>.

Brooks, Andree. "HEALTH: Psychology; Experts Find Extramarital Affairs Have a Profound Impact on Children." *New York Times* [New York] 09 March, 1989, n. pag. Web. 12 Dec. 2012. <*http://www.nytimes.com/1989/03/09/us/health-psychology-experts-find-extramarital-affairs-have-profound-impact.html*>.

Filipovic, Jill. "The Moral Case For Sex Before Marriage." *Guardian*. 24 2012: n. page. Web. 11 December, 2012. <*http://www.guardian.co.uk/commentisfree/2012/sep/24/moral-case-for-sex-before-marriage*>.

Finer, Lawrence B. "Trends in Premarital Sex in the United States, 1954¬2003." Public Health Reports. 122. New York: 2007.

"Fornication." Merriam-Webster.com. Merriam-Webster, 2012. Web. 15 October, 2012.

Guttmacher Institute. Facts on American Teens' Sexual and Reproductive Health, In Brief. New York: Guttmacher, 2012. < *http://www.guttmacher.org/pubs/FB-ATSRH.html* >, 10/15/12.

Martinez, Michael. "Principal reports high schoolers' 'Fantasy Slut League,'" CNN. CNN, 23 2012. Web. 24 October, 2012. <*http://www.cnn.com/2012/10/23/us/california-fantasy-slut-league-school/index.html?hpt=hp_t3*>.

Thayer, Joseph Henry. *Greek-English Lexicon of the New Testament*. Grand Rapids: Zondervan, 1977. Print.

The National Campaign to Prevent Teen and Unplanned Pregnancy (2012). Fast Facts: Teen Sexual Behavior and Contraceptive Use: Data from the Youth Risk Behavior Survey, 2011. [Online]. 15 October, 2012. <*http://www.thenationalcampaign.org/resources/pdf/FastFacts_YRBS2011.*

pdf>. Washington: Author.

Ventura, Stephanie, Joyce Abma, *et al*. United States. CDC. National Vital Statistics Reports; Vol. 56, No. 15. Hyattsville, MD: National Center for Health Statistics, 2008. Print.

Ventura, Stephanie, Sally Curtin, *et al*. United States. CDC. National Vital Statistics Reports; vol 60 no 7. Hyattsville, MD: National Center for Health Statistics, 2012. Print.

The Threat of Being Too Busy

Colby Junkin

The mundane lifestyle where life passes slowly and everything is done in an orderly manner is all but extinct in 21st century America. The ordinary day of an average family is spent either at practice, games, recitals, school functions, etc., leaving no time for anything else, which often causes God to be pushed out of their routines. The amount of activities planned in any one day causes the parents to seek additional help in keeping their schedules straight. The introduction of smart phones and the wonderful world of apps offer us hundreds of different avenues to keep a schedule open, but packed. The apps do not have a limit when to tell a person he is too busy. Instead the apps will continue to organize and press each item

Benjamon C. Junkin was born March 30, 1985 in Birmingham, Alabama. When Colby was three years old, his family (including older brother, Scott) moved to Cullman, Alabama, where Colby graduated from Good Hope High School in 2003. Colby enlisted in the Army National Guard in October 2002 and was honorably discharged in 2008. Colby met his wife Melissa, daughter of Alton and Diana Bailey, in 2004 and they were married on April 16, 2005. Colby and Melissa are blessed with two sons, Ben (4 years old) and Luke (9 months old at time of writing). Colby attained a B.S. degree (Social Science) from Athens State University in Athens, Alabama in the Spring of 2010.

Colby was not raised in the church but as a Southern Baptist. His father was a Southern Baptist pastor for seventeen years. His brother, Scott, was the first one introduced to the truth through his future wife, Magan, and was baptized into Christ. Colby was influenced by Scott, Magan, and Melissa, and was baptized on January 5, 2005. Colby continued to try and study with his family, but nothing changed until August, 2007. In the span of three weeks, his little sister (Katie), father (Tim), mother (Rene), and little brother (John) were all baptized into Christ. Colby did appointment preaching during the years of 2006-2007. He began a part-time work with the Hillside Chapel church of Christ (Albertville, AL) from August, 2007 to December, 2009. Colby currently lives in Decatur, Alabama and works with the Piney Chapel church of Christ (Hillsboro, Alabama) from January 2010-present.

into an already busy schedule. What if the apps did have a limit and said, "You are too busy!" What if our phones told us to stop using them and start spending time with our children? We live in a society that must have information at a moment's notice, and we will sacrifice whatever to ensure those notifications in our lives.

As our lives become more crowded with the hundreds of things to accomplish, how easy does it become for God to be pushed out? The symptoms of busyness are catastrophic not only for the individual but more importantly for their families. A child is left wondering whether or not his mother/father loves him, because he is always told to "Be quiet," or "Leave me alone, I'm working." Charles Swindoll graphically depicts this problem with busyness:

> Busyness rapes relationships. It substitutes shallow frenzy for deep friendship. It promises satisfying dreams, but delivers hollow nightmares. It feeds the ego, but starves the inner man. *It fills the calendar, but fractures the family.* It cultivates a program, but plows under priorities (emphasis mine, bcj).[1]

The problems that evolve from a parent's busyness lead to a cancer that will erode the ties of a family bond and will produce an environment of complete strangers. The only family time spent together is no longer at the dinner table, or on family night, but rather at some particular activity.

The 21st century has dawned and has brought with it great technological advances and opportunities to excel in time-management, but it also has brought a culture that idolizes individualism and has forgotten the strength of a united family. The nuclear families of the past are almost extinct in a society that is primed for single-motherhood and alimony fathers. The influence of television and Hollywood has produced a generation that believes families are supposed to be separated and divorced. No longer is *family* defined by God as husband and wife, but is now considered by our world to be two fathers, or two mothers (Gen. 2:24). The perpetual effect of busyness only aides the ideology of broken homes further. Because of their schedules, husbands and wives have become like ghosts that only pass in the night. They never have time to speak, listen, or enjoy one another's presence, because that time has been lost to add another hour of practice or work.

When a person is driving his car toward a cliff, he will encounter many

---

[1] Charles R. Swindoll. *Killing Giants, Pulling Thrones.* Portland, Oregon: Multnomah Press (1978), 79.

warning signs of his impending doom. The logical person will generally take his foot off the gas and apply the brake and glide safely to a stop prior to the edge. It seems that many homes today are completely ignoring the warning signs of being too busy and are falling to their eventual ruin in a world prepared for their demise. Homes are falling apart from within and it comes with such a shock when it is your friends, neighbors, or maybe even ourselves. We must be vigilant, learning from the past, and guarding our future, because this environment does not mature overnight, but is cultivated by days, months, and years of allowing busyness to drive our lives instead of the Word of God.

Examples of Busyness

The threat of busyness is never mentioned in the Bible. There is no "Thou shalt not be too busy" command, but the effect of busyness and its ramifications can be found throughout the Old Testament. Numerous times we witness the crumbling of strong families, because they had taken their eyes off God and had placed them upon things of this world. Busyness is a plague that has always caused grief and anguish, and without properly seeing its warning signs we too can be susceptible to its horrific end.

The failure of Eli is evident within Scripture (1 Sam. 2:12-17).[2] He had raised sons who did not know the Lord, nor did they honor Him with their lives. His sons were eventually given over to complete debauchery and their father's honor was stripped because of their sinfulness (1 Sam. 2:22-36). How could this happen to Eli? He was a godly man and a good high priest, but he had raised two completely worthless boys. Is it possible that Eli had neglected his duties as a father and had not taught his sons to respect and fear God? Eli must have been a very busy man with daily offerings and caring for the nation of Israel, but did that leave him with no time to spend instructing his sons to faithfully obey God's will?

Another great man plagued with sinful offspring was David. David, king of Israel, built the Israelite nation into a great power and extended its boundaries on every side (2 Sam. 7:8-9). David had learned humility through his own trials and errors and had remained a man given over to the Lord's will (Ps. 23; 51). He was courageous and kind, and is a wonderful example of love and devotion for our lives as Christians, but something plagued David.

---

[2] Unless otherwise indicated, all Scripture quotations are from the NASB Bible (*New American Standard Bible) 1995 Update*. LaHabra, CA: The Lockman Foundation, 1995.

He was plagued with sons who did not honor their father but rather brought great grief and anguish upon him. Amnon was completely given over to his sinful lust when he raped his own sister, Tamar (2 Sam. 13:14). After two years, Absalom saw no apparent discipline against Amnon. In anger, Absalom arranged Amnon's death by the hands of his servants (2 Sam. 13:28). Absalom did not stop after killing Amnon, but later conspired against his own father, took Jerusalem, and lay with all of David's concubines in the sight of Israel (2 Sam. 16:15-22). How could these things happen to such a man of God? Had David forgotten to teach his sons the fifth commandment, "Honor your father and mother" (Exod. 20:12)? Is it possible that David, in his kingly duties, had allowed time to escape him often enough that his sons were not raised to honor God as their Father?

King Hezekiah is another great example of the threat of busyness. Hezekiah ruled in Judah during tumultuous times. He battled against the Philistines and rebelled against the king of Assyria (2 Kings 18:7-8). Hezekiah's strength was not from within himself, but as he "clung to the Lord" (2 Kings 18:6). We find in Hezekiah a strong leader and one of the few good kings during the divided kingdom. He stood against Sennacherib and trusted in God for victory (2 Kings 19). In all of his victories, however, he lost the battle of raising his son, Manasseh. Manasseh became the next king in Judah and was extremely wicked. He is noted as being an idolater, a practicer of witchcraft, user of divination, and a killer who shed the blood of the innocent (2 Kings 21). How could Manasseh follow the reign of Hezekiah with such sinfulness and disregard for God? What failures were made by Hezekiah that produced such a son? Did Hezekiah allow the time needed to rule the nation to become more important than spending time and raising a faithful son? He may have saved Israel from Sennacherib, but he delivered them into the hands of Manasseh.

Busyness is not a plague just for those in great power or high offices, but it is a mistake that can be made by poor and rich alike. Joshua's generation provides the greatest of all examples of the failure to raise their children to know God (Judg. 2:10). This generation led by Joshua had witnessed many of the great miracles both in Egypt and in the conquest of the land. They stood against all of their enemies and valiantly drove them from the land of Canaan. If any generation was ever given the easiest route to teach their children concerning God, it had to have been this generation. Upon their arrival in the land of Canaan – through the dry ground of the Jordan River swollen in the days of harvest, the Israelites placed twelve stones from the midst of the river upon the Jordan's banks:

> He said to the sons of Israel, "When your children ask their fathers in time to come, saying, 'What are these stones?' then you shall inform your children, saying, 'Israel crossed this Jordan on dry ground.' For the Lord your God dried up the waters of the Jordan before you until you had crossed, just as the Lord your God had done to the Red Sea, which He dried up before us until we had crossed; that all the peoples of the earth may know that the hand of the Lord is mighty, so that you may fear the Lord your God forever" (Josh. 4:21-24).

Can you imagine the stories that could have been told to their children concerning these twelve stones? The fathers could have spent days declaring the glory of God to their son(s), but they failed to complete this simple task. Why?

God had prepared the Israelites countless times for the coming glory of the promised land, but He also forewarned them to not forget the One who delivered the land into their hands (Deut. 8:11-20). The Israelites constantly promised to uphold God's law, but they failed miserably. This generation was given everything essential to ensure their sons and daughters would know and fear God, but they failed to teach and train, so their children became unfaithful idolaters of the Canaanite's gods (Judg. 2:11-13). Why did the next generation of Israel fall away from God and provoke His wrath? Could it possibly be that their parents were too busy to teach them about the Law of the Lord?

We need to recognize within each of these examples the warning signs for impending doom. The fathers and mothers had apparently allowed other things to become more important than raising their children as faithful followers of God's will. As we have witnessed, we cannot attribute all of these mistakes to one specific sin; many different causes led to generations of weak and sinful Israelites. The problem that remains is their failures are becoming ours also (Rom. 15:4; 1 Cor. 10:11). We are not learning from their mistakes, but we are dooming ourselves to repeat them. Why? Is it possible that in our prosperity we have forgotten who God is? Is it possible that in our busy lives, God has been given a backseat to whatever activity is in season? We must be careful that we do not raise another generation that will not know the Lord or adhere to His commands.

The Effects of Being Too Busy. . .

The modern American family has evolved into a collection of fast paced lives that have no regard to cohesiveness or truly meaningful relationships. Familial relationships are no longer growing deep roots in nurtured soil but are being grown in shallow soil ripe for anger and division instead of love and devotion. One of the greatest effects of being too busy is the strained relationships between the husband and wife, between parents and their children. It is required of Christians to love their neighbors, and the closest of all neighbors is our family (Matt. 22:39). This love is not described within the pages of the Bible by word only but by deeds (1 John 3:18). The parable of the "Good Samaritan" is a display of love by action and not by just mere words (Luke 10:29-37). The problem in our homes, beset by busyness, is our relationships are not given the proper time and attention to cultivate true love for one another.

The love shared between husbands and wives is to imitate the love shown to man through Jesus Christ (Eph. 5:22, 25). If our children were polled concerning the love shown toward our spouses, how would they describe it? We are all well acquainted with the description of love in 1 Corinthians 13. We devote time to reading those verses on our wedding day, but why do we neglect the verses' message after a few years of marriage? The love to be shown toward our wives and children must resemble the love described, or we will be guilty of raising a new generation that will not know how to properly love one another.

A second effect of busyness upon the family relationship is a lack of communication. If the husband is working all the time or the wife is carrying the children to different activities all the time, when do they have time for themselves? We need to understand that busyness can muzzle the communication between husband and wife. Before long, he comes home to a house that is not spotless, and she comes home to a yard not manicured. Therefore, a brewing resentment can begin to grow toward one another. Then a calm conversation can turn into an argument about what the other is not doing. This type of atmosphere will destroy a marriage and damage the parent's influence on their children.

Communication lines must always be open between the husband and wife. A husband needs assurance from his wife that he provides according to her needs and a wife needs to be praised for her work in the home. The thoughts of man and woman are different, and when communication within marriage ceases those differences only widens the gap. Therefore, husbands and wives must strive to discuss daily their feelings, opinions, and activities. The wife needs to be given time to discuss adult issues without the interruption of children. A husband needs to inform his wife concerning his situation at work and whether a change or move might be within their future. As preachers, we need to ask and respect our spouses' opinions concerning moving to a new congregation or getting a full-time job in the secular world. Closed communication lines only spell out problems for the future. We must guard against the silence that prevails in so many homes, by always taking time for each other to communicate our thoughts and feelings concerning our lives.

A third effect of busyness in our families and stemming from the lack of communication is the development of dishonesty and mistrust that easily thrives in a unsuspecting family. A husband must have complete trust in his wife and vice versa, but if lies are told to paint pretty pictures, one day those canvases will be destroyed. A household needs to be built on the firm foundation of a love that unites one another in trust. The lack of honesty in our homes only allows the devil an opportunity to create damage (Eph. 4:25, 27). Husbands and wives must be able to confide in each other, because mistrust and division will only lead to adultery, fornication, drunkenness, etc. A home should always be a place of trust and honesty between all inhabitants. Honesty may hurt at times, but it is a necessity to prevent sorrow, hurt, and separation.

Steps to Guard Against Busyness
We must guard our lives against the influence and effects of busyness. The first step that we can take is to work for the Lord and our family (Col. 3:23). The American dream is to make a lot of money, buy a big home, and drive nice cars, but we must evaluate what we will lose in the meantime. If buying a bigger home causes you to spend twenty percent more time away from your family, is it worth it? If driving a nice car means picking up a second job on the weekends, does that constitute missing that time with our wives and children? Husbands must take care of their families both physically and spiritually, the problem is which of these become more important (1 Tim. 5:8)? Every father's aspiration is to do more for his children than his father was able, but what is worth the time forfeited to ensure they have more worldly possessions? Jesus asked a similar question, "For what will it profit a man if he gains the whole and forfeits his soul" (Matt. 16:26)? Any person facing a terminal illness can tell you how much the big house and car are worth when their lives hang in the balance – nothing!

Our society insists that it is mandatory for both husbands and wives to work to ensure the family's societal influence and economic security. Paul said the responsibility is laid upon the fathers, and the wives were to be workers at home (1 Tim. 5:8; Titus 2:5). Surely, in the 21st century, this can add stress to the father, but a godly wife will live modestly and below their means to ensure her husband's providence. Husbands, as the providers for our families, we must take advantage of each moment we work to ensure adequate time will be spent with our children. As we go to work, our time needs to be spent completing the job, not engaged in "water-cooler" conversations, Facebook, or day dreaming. The result of good time management is more time can be spent with our families at home. As Thomas Edison once said:

> Being busy does not always mean real work. The object of all work is production of accomplishment and to either of these ends there must be forethought, system, planning, intelligence, and honest purpose, as well as perspiration. Seeming to do is not doing.

We may need also to make special arrangements to ensure family time is not forfeited. If we have the opportunity to go into work earlier and leave early, we need to take these steps to spend more time with our families. These steps are taken to ensure that we are not devoting ourselves to more than our forty-hours-a-week jobs, but to the Lord and our families.

Our duty as Christians is to develop the quality of self-control. Time management will only exist when a person has self-control and the ability to say "no" to excessive demands upon his time. Paul places special attention upon self-control as being a part of the fruit of the Spirit (Gal. 5:23). Peter, in his list of seven graces, says that self-control must be added to our character (2 Pet. 1:6). What we should take away from these verses and others is that self-control must be administered on the job to ensure that we are not decreasing the precious time that can be spent with our families.

Preaching is a special profession in which the schedules are not always dictated by a 9-5 routine. Even though we may find ourselves generally spending more than the average forty-hours a week, we must be very careful in our studies to not allow time to be taken away from our families. As a young preacher, the advice most often given to me is not to lose my family. Our task as evangelists is to preach the gospel and try to save every person we meet, but what does that amount to if we have lost our children, or even our spouse? Our obligations may be different timewise, but we will be held to the same responsibilities of any father. We are commanded to raise our children in the "discipline and instruction of the Lord" (Eph. 6:4).

We need to always appropriately align our priorities in our work for the Lord. We are first Christians. Therefore, we look to our own spiritual condition and ensure its strength, because how else can we instruct others, while the plank is in our own eye (Matt. 7:4)? As husbands, our wives deserve our attention and devotion away from the job. We do not need to neglect them, because it is their love and honesty that can help motivate us to keep straight. As fathers, we must put our children and family above others, because that is where our first priorities lie. Lastly, we are preachers. If we will keep these priorities in line, we can better ensure our families' physical and spiritual health, as well as those that are lost in the world. Jesus established these priorities in Matthew 6:33, "But seek first His kingdom and His righteousness, and all these things will be added to you."

A second step taken to ensure our families from becoming too busy is adapting our schedules around God. It is too easy as a family to adopt schedules without God, than to adapt their schedules around God. If every decision made within a home is based upon time spent together and with God as their focus, what type of activities can be eliminated immediately? Anything that has a continual interference with services or Bible studies must be avoided altogether. Nothing is more frightening than witnessing hundreds of children playing softball, soccer, or any other leisure activity on Sunday morning at ball fields rather than being in church. When God is completely stripped from any facet of a child's life, it will be hard to ever reach him with the gospel of Jesus Christ. What message is being sent to the children of those families who regularly miss services due to busyness? Those children are extremely preceptive and will understand that God comes first, but only when nothing else is interfering. They are learning that they do not need to adapt their schedules around God, but God needs to adapt around their schedules.

Within our daily activities we need to give time to prayer, study, and thinking about God. If our family takes a trip to the zoo, perhaps we need to take a few minutes out of the schedule to talk to our children about God's creation. Or maybe read a Psalm devoted to praising God for His creation and handiwork (Pss. 8, 19, 29, 33, 65, 104). We need to teach our children that God created the world in six days and on the seventh day He rested (Gen. 1). We may be able to encourage our children to participate in activities that will promote Bible study and family togetherness. The Boy Scouts is a wonderful activity that enables fathers and their sons to enjoy this type of atmosphere together. It is one of many different avenues that can be taken to promote good citizenship and faithfulness to God.

An intimate family is able to overcome the tremendous stresses placed upon them. As Tim Kimmel wrote:

> Intimacy is the strength that runs through each link of the family chain. With it, a family can endure anything. Without it, we are at the mercy of our hurried lifestyles. Intimacy provides the immune system for the soul. It battles the psychological infections of discouragement, rejection, inadequacy, insignificance, and insecurity. Being assured of acceptance gives us confidence. Confidence gives us the ability to endure. Rushed schedules rob us of time needed to develop personal relationships. Too many people are duped into thinking that a little bit of "quality" time compensates for the lack of "quantity" time.[3]

We must be careful not to allow our excuse to be "quality over quantity." Family time is absolutely essential for our family strength. We must be willing to always take the necessary steps to ensure our family's safety both physically and spiritually.

Within the daily "grind" and busy schedules there also needs to be time set aside for family studies. These can be conducted in a backyard, in a van traveling, or prior to bedtime, but there needs to be time given to devotion and praise of God within every family. It is always hard trying to introduce new routines in a already busy schedule, but if we will instill within our children the importance of God and His providence within our lives, we may truly begin training "up a child in the way he should go" (Prov. 22:6). At meals, we need to give thanks to God for His provision (Matt. 6:11; 1 Tim. 4:4-5). We need to pray with our children concerning our needs and cares as a family (Phil. 4:6). The old saying remains true, "The family that prays together, stays together." Probably the greatest thing that can be done in the 21st century family is turning off our televisions and engaging one another in conversation and the reading of God's Word.

Finally, a third step to guard against busyness within our homes is to keep the ordinary, ordinary. This may seem a little redundant or simple, but it is the simple things that build the strongest families. Sunday mornings, in so many of our homes can be filled with total chaos, but if we would just play some gospel music on the radio and sing as we prepare for services, what type of spirit will we have when we enter our worship? This is not some profound step, but it is a simple ordinary one that can ensure our desire to

---

[3] Tim Kimmel. *Little House on the Freeway.* Portland: Multnomah Press, (1987), 29.

worship God. We need always to have in the back of our minds that, "This is the day the Lord has made; We will rejoice and be glad in it" (Ps. 118:24).

The problem with having busy lives is that even the days of ordinary tasks can become frenzied with obligations. As parents it would be a good idea to devote a day each month to nothing more than to pay special attention to our children. This does not have to be anything more than giving our full attention to them and spending a day caring for their needs. We must recognize that each ordinary day spent teaching our children, getting to know our neighbors better, having a date night with our wives, is a day used in the service of God. God has so richly blessed us with family; we need to take advantage of these opportunities and not allow the busyness of schedules to interfere.

Conclusion
One day the amount of baseball training, piano lessons, or time spent on the job will be meaningless. The day is coming when the only thing necessary in life will finally be weighed against us and we will either be found wanting or approved. Distractions will no longer keep us from maintaining the date. We will not be able to blame school, work, taxes, politics, or anything else for the deeds that we have done, but only ourselves. We will then have to answer for our busy lifestyles. What is the most important goal for your family? We tend to focus upon individual achievements, but what about the family goal? What is your family manifesto? May our goal be to join one another in heaven and to spend eternity praising God. The route to get there may be difficult or even seem impossible in the busyness of our lives, but with God's grace, everything is possible for a family who is willing to assist and encourage each other (Matthew 19:26; Philippians 4:13)!

Man in the Home

The Father as a Provider

Tommy Hagewood

One of the greatest joys in life is the joy of being a father. One of the greatest responsibilities in life is the responsibility of being a father. Both joy and responsibility are mingled together into one of the greatest blessings God ever provided. The truly godly father faces his task as provider for his family with joyful and vigilant fear and trembling. He understands that how his children view their Father in heaven may very well depend on how they view their father on earth.

Any normal male can father a child but it takes a real man to be a godly father to a child. The problem is that godly fathers in our time are an endangered species. The breakdown of the home is ample evidence of the absence of godly fathers. The entitlement mentality so prevalent in our society has added fuel to the fires that are destroying our homes. Too many children are growing up without fathers at home. Children are being neglected and abused in alarming numbers. We can blame the world for its ungodly influence on the young but the world has always been ungodly. What accounts

Thomas Aubrey Hagewood was born in Nashville, TN on April 9, 1946 to William Preston and Annie Aubrey (Dickerson) Hagewood. He and his wife of nearly 47 years, Ruby (Light), have three children: Mark, who lives in Seminole, FL; Jennifer (Jack) Byars, who live in Rock Spring, GA; and Michael (Lisa), who live in Temple Terrace, FL. They have four grandsons: Jackson, Preston, Nathaniel, and Zachary Byars. Tommy preached his first sermon at age fifteen at the Riverside Dr. church in Nashville, TN. He continued preaching during his time in high school and at Florida College and began full-time preaching work in 1967. He has served churches in Kingston Springs, TN (1967-70); Crestwood, IL (1970-78); Mt. Pleasant, TN (1978-2003); Nashville, TN (2003-2012); and is presently working with the Beverly Shores church in Leesburg, FL. He has preached in gospel meetings in sixteen states. His articles have appeared in various publications.

for the breakdown of Christian homes? Again, where are the godly fathers, fathers who provide the leadership and example so desperately needed in our time by our children and our grandchildren? Will the real godly father please stand up?!

We Begin By Submitting to God Through Jesus Christ.

Submission has become a bugaboo word despised by the world and shunned by many Christians. The common thought is that of a person enslaved to another. It is often thought that, when one submits to another, he or she becomes nothing more than a doormat to be trampled on at the whims of another. Ironically, when people learn what the Scriptures truly teach about submission they are repulsed even more than they are by their misconception! Truly Jesus' teachings constitute *hard sayings* that the world simply will not accept. However to the Christian, Jesus alone has the words of eternal life (cf. John 6:60-69).

Let me give you a simple definition of "submission." Submission is acting on behalf of another for his benefit at your expense. And just why should I be willing to do that? The answer is because that is all that Jesus ever did. According to Philippians 2:5-8, Christ Jesus emptied Himself and left heaven to come to the earth to live as a slave and to die as a criminal on a cross! His entire life on earth and death on the cross exemplify submission. He submitted to His Father's will by submitting to the needs of mankind. In His life, and His alone, we see perfect selfless dedication to His Father's will and to the needs of others. All of this was planned by the Father, the Son, and the Holy Spirit in the counsels of eternity before the world began (Eph. 1:1-14). We can all praise God for the final outcome of Jesus' total submission: "though He was a Son, yet He learned obedience by the things which He suffered. And having been perfected, He became the author of eternal salvation to all who obey Him" (Heb. 5:8-9, NKJV).

With the cross heavily on the mind of our Lord and with His disciples arguing about who would be the greatest in the kingdom, Jesus stooped down and washed the disciples' dirty feet! (John 13:1-17). Again, submission means acting on behalf of others for their benefit at your expense.

None of us are totally selfless as was our Lord Jesus Christ. He always did what pleased His Father (John 8:29). As we strive to walk in the steps of Jesus we can never lose sight of our need for God's grace and mercy (cf. 2 Tim. 1:16-18).

Fathers must learn to submit to God to meet the needs of their families. Submitting is often thought of as what wives are to be in relation to their husbands. The truth is every Christian is to submit to every other Christian. Note the passage: "submitting to one another in the fear of God" (Eph. 5:21, NKJV). In the next verse wives are told to submit to their husbands. Wives submit to their husbands by respectful obedience and husbands submit to their wives by lovingly meeting their needs even as Christ lovingly met and continues to meet the needs of His bride, the church (Eph. 5:21-33). Fathers submit to their children by meeting their needs. Children submit to their parents by obeying them (Eph. 6:1-4). Again, submission means acting on behalf of others for their benefit at your expense.

For the Christian, all submission to God is through Jesus Christ. Wives are to submit to their husbands *as to the Lord* (Eph. 5:22), children are to obey their parents *in the Lord* (Eph. 6:1), bondservants are to submit to their masters *as to Christ* and masters are to treat their slaves justly and fairly knowing they have a Master in heaven (Eph. 5:22; 6:1, 5, 7; Col. 3:18-4:1).

In submitting to God to meet the needs of their families, fathers need to be cautioned against provoking their children. In Ephesians 6:4 Paul warns fathers against provoking their children to anger. In Colossians 3:21 he warns fathers against provoking them to discouragement. Fathers need to seek wisdom from God to avoid being overbearing to their children. Children may rebel or may cower like a whipped pup as they react to a provoking father. Fathers also need to be admonished against being subservient to their children. Children need a father – not a buddy. They need loving instructive discipline. They need caring correction when they are wrong. Fathers do a great disservice to their children when they never correct them. Children are growing up thinking more highly of themselves than they ought to think or going to the opposite extreme and having little or no self-esteem. Where are the fathers and grandfathers who are acting on behalf of their children for their benefit at the fathers' expense?

In both Ephesians and Colossians Paul gives the instructions to fathers rather than to mothers. Mothers play an indispensable role in the upbringing of children but the father is to take the lead. There are far too many absentee fathers in our time and our homes are suffering the terrible consequences. We make a lot of mistakes in the raising of children and our children can overlook them if they are persuaded as adults that we had their best interest at heart and truly loved them. But children have an extremely difficult time overcoming neglect, hypocrisy, or abuse.

We Continue with Fathers Providing
According to the Lord's Instructions

Just what are fathers to provide their children? What are their needs? Who decides what those needs are? Again, the Lord Jesus Christ has the right and the ability to decide what provisions a father should make for his family. Personally, I like to use Jesus' own development from a child to adulthood as a framework from which to work. Luke 2:52 tells us: "And Jesus increased in wisdom and stature, and in favor with God and men." *Wisdom* relates to mental development, *stature* to physical development, *in favor with God* to spiritual development and *in favor with men* to social development. Mental, physical, spiritual, and social are the areas of development for every person. A father is responsible before God to provide to the best of his ability all of these needs. Let's consider each one separately.

Mental development is a need no one would dismiss. We want our children to get the best education possible. There's nothing wrong with that per se but why do we want them to develop mentally? Think about this and we'll come back to it in a moment.

Physical development is also extremely important. Godly fathers strive to provide the best environment for their children to grow up healthy and strong. Again no one would deny the importance of physical development.

Spiritual development is of utmost importance. Fathers need to raise their children, teaching them to respect their authority so that when they are grown they will respect the authority of their heavenly Father. Fathers who neglect or abandon the spiritual development of their children are almost certainly dooming their children to a lifetime and an eternity apart from God. If their children ever do obey the Lord as adults, they'll do so in spite of their upbringing and not because of it!

Social development is the fourth thing mentioned in the Lord's development from childhood to adulthood. The Lord had a social life. His first miracle was turning water into wine at a wedding feast in Cana of Galilee (John 2:1-11). Jesus had a social life and intends for us to have one too. He wants us to be in the world but not of the world (John 17:15-18).

So what happens when any one of these four things is neglected or abandoned? What happens is that a person becomes distorted in his personality. Lacking wisdom certainly handicaps one to live in a competitive society. Lacking physical strength disqualifies one from most any productive behavior. One who is mentally and physically strong but spiritually weak is a spiritual dwarf!

How do many fathers approach the marriage of their grown children? Too many fathers focus on the physical to the neglect of the spiritual. Statements are made such as, "He's marrying a beautiful girl." Or, "She's marrying a great looking guy." Or, "She's marrying a man who has a great job and makes a lot of money." The fact that the child is not marrying a Christian seems to be of little concern for the excited father!

What about the couple getting married in the above illustrations? If their focus is on the physical with little or none on the spiritual, what kind of future do they have together? If they enter the marriage with little regard for God's will in their lives, what kind of home will they have apart from God and what kind of security do they have that their home will stay intact when tough times come?

Consider the children of such a marriage. Do you really think they will grow up any different from their parents? If the children grow up in a home where God and His word are not respected or obeyed are they likely to serve the Lord in their lives? If they do it will be in spite of their upbringing and not because of it.

Before I proceed let me offer a disclaimer. I am not suggesting that every time a father and mother attempt to raise godly children that godly children will be the result. There are many godly parents who did their best to raise their children in the training and admonition of the Lord only to see their children depart from the faith in their adulthood. Such children turn away from the Lord in spite of their upbringing and not because of it. I certainly do not want to put a guilt trip on such parents. We shall be judged by whether or not we did our best to raise our children as instructed by the Lord and not by how they actually turn out. They will account for that. When our children are grown they have minds of their own and will act accordingly.

Jennifer Mann, a specialist in Talent Acquisition and Director of Client Services for Pinstripe, attended a Human Resources conference and shared some interesting employment trends with her dad a few years ago. From the conference, it was shared that the U.S. employment market would divide into three buckets:

- **Specialist Workforce** – These are workers who have attained the required education and specialized skills to maintain not only employment, but positions with growth potential.

- **Contingent Workforce** – This is the workforce who will be employed but will likely work as a temporary or contingent workforce. Why? With the downsizing and closures of so many manufacturing organizations (i.e., automobile industry) as well as the shift of positions overseas, the U.S. is experiencing a gap between positions which require higher education and candidates who possess these skills. As a result, individuals will be forced to consider contingent positions which lack the longer term stability and benefits of which this workforce was previously accustomed.

- **Perpetually Unemployed** – There is a third group who will consistently struggle remaining employed.

This is not a picture inspired by those who follow Biblical teaching. It is a picture all too often painted by those who are more persuaded by the world than by God's word.

Paul warned Christians in Romans 12:1-2 not to be conformed to this world but to be transformed by the renewing of our minds to the will of God. In other words Paul is emphasizing how we ought to think. John Maxwell, world famous authority on leadership, once said that the greatest determining factor in how one turns out in life is how he thinks. This is true not because Dr. Maxwell said it but because God's word teaches it. Keep your heart with all diligence, for out of it spring the issues of life (Prov. 4:23). We need to bring our thinking in line with God's word and not allow ourselves to be pushed into the world's mold regarding how we should think and act.

Perhaps the first concern we need to address is our work ethic. The Scriptures teach that one who will not provide for his own has denied the faith and is worse than an unbeliever (1 Tim. 4:8). Providing for one's own does not mean relinquishing one's parental responsibilities to the government or to grandparents. It means providing both the spiritual and the physical needs of the children. All too often I have seen grandparents bring their grandchildren to church services regularly because parents were either too lazy or too busy at other things they deemed more important than taking their children to worship God. Sadly, in far too many instances I have seen the children grow up and follow in the ungodly steps of their parents rather than in the godly steps of their grandparents.

The scriptures also teach that we are to provide honest labor for an honest wage. In Ephesians 4:28 Paul admonished the Christian to labor at what is honest so that he may have to give to him who is in need. Again this self-less, submissive concern for others is so lacking in our society. Surely it should not be lacking among God's people! What a shame when absentee or dead beat fathers fail to provide adequately for the needs of their children and for others they should rightfully support. It is not surprising that when those children are grown and the parents are in their declining years often they become the neglected ones as their adult children take little to no responsibility for their welfare. Two wrongs do not make a right. Jesus took a dim view of those who neglect their parents when the parents are in need (cf. Mark 7:1-13). He Himself saw that His mother would be provided for even as He was dying on the cross (John 19:25-27). We see in Jesus a sense of personal responsibility for those who depended on Him. We see this same sense of responsibility in those who truly follow Him.

"Don't ever claim responsibility" seems to be the spirit of our time. Too often people are living in la-la land with very few willing to accept responsibility for their actions. They had rather let the government or the grandparents provide for their children. Again the Scriptures are quite clear about our personal accountability before God. In Galatians 6:2 we are taught to bear one another's burdens. In verse 5 we are told that each one must bear his own burden (KJV). More modern translations use two different English words for the two different Greek words used in the verses. The first "burden" (*barē*) is a heavy load one needs help to bear. The second word (*phortion*) is a word that corresponds to a soldier's backpack. There are times in all of our lives when we need help as we struggle under the weight of a heavy load. However, each one must bear his own backpack – his own responsibility. Years ago, when my children were still at home, I experienced some car trouble as I was taking them to school. A brother in Christ happened by and offered his assistance. I asked him to take my children to school and to call for a tow truck and he graciously agreed to do so. I did not ask him to take my children and finish raising them. That was my backpack – not his.

Too often today fathers are asking the government or their parents to bear the God-given obligations they are responsible to bear while they indulge in their own selfish or sinful pursuits. Where is the ambition to succeed as a faithful child of God? Couple that lack of ambition with a lack of common sense and you have disaster for the home. Far too many spend more than they take in, max out credit cards for things they should have saved for first or not gotten at all and then asked their parents to help them pay their rent or utility bills! Fathers are often too carnal, too weak or too unwilling to take the responsibility for their families.

At the opposite extreme is the workaholic dad who is determined to provide his wife and children all the things in life all of his neighbors have, even if he has to have a second mortgage, a second job, and a second wind! The rich farmer of Luke 12:16-20 thought all his hard work had secured his future for many years. God called him a fool and told him that his soul would be required of him that very night. "Then whose will those things be which you have provided?" was Jesus' soul-penetrating question. Jesus ended the parable with the following words: "So is he who lays up treasure for himself, and is not rich toward God." It is interesting that Jesus preceded the parable with the following words in verse 15: "Take heed and beware of covetousness, for one's life does not consist in the abundance of the things he possesses."

Jesus' life and death not only provided the only way to salvation but they also turned the world's value system upside down. "Foxes have holes and birds of the air have nests," Jesus once said to an undiscerning would-be follower, "but the Son of Man has nowhere to lay His head" (Matt. 8:20). Jesus died penny-less on a cross while the soldiers gambled for His clothes. Shouldn't His example tell us all something about how we should prioritize our lives? Shouldn't it tell us to love people and use things rather than to love things and use people?

Another area of concern is that of grown children, often in their 30's, who are unable or unwilling to provide for themselves and who depend on their parents for a place to live. In Jesus' day the Jews had a saying that if a father did not teach his son a trade he was teaching him to steal. Jesus Himself was taught to be a carpenter (Mark 6:3). Paul, though highly educated, was taught to be a tent maker (Acts 18:3). Fathers have a responsibility to teach their children to work rather than to depend on others because of an entitlement mentality.

In his commentary, Pondering the Proverbs, Donald Hunt makes the following statement about Proverbs 22:6:

> A commandment with a promise. The commandment: train up a child in the way he should go; the promise: even when he is old he will not depart from it. Such training requires many things: knowledge, wisdom, time,

patience, determination and love. There are many failures in child-rearing because of lacking one or several of the above requirements. Child-training is something that is easy to neglect or try shortcuts with, but what a shame when the future of one's entire posterity is at stake! What is really more important? Ephesians 6:4 commands this type of training. Timothy had been taught the Scriptures from a child (2 Tim. 1:5); as a result the great faith that had dwelt in his mother and grandmother was in him also (2 Tim. 1:5). No wonder that as a young man he was well reported of by his home congregation (Lystra) and by other Christians in the area (Acts 16:1, 2). Other passages on child rearing: Prov. 1:8; 13:1; 19:18; 22:15; 23:13, 14; 29:15, 17 (Donald Hunt, *Bible Study Textbook: Pondering the Proverbs*, 289, 290).

The passages cited at the end of the previous quote speak of disciplining a child. Discipline should primarily be instructive but must also involve corrective discipline as well. This is but another area where the world is at odds with God's word. Proverbs 19:18 focuses on the stern reality of the need for corrective discipline with the following words: Chasten your son while there is hope, and do not set your heart on his destruction. Hunt again gives us poignant comments on this verse:

> Correction administered in time without which the child's mischief becomes meanness, and the character becomes set in wickedness. Other passages teaching parental correction: Prov. 13:24; 23:13, 14; 29:17. A German saying: 'It is better that the child weep than the father.' 'Clark': It is better that the child may be cause to cry, when the correction may be healthful to his soul, than that the parent should cry afterwards, when the child is grown to man's estate, and his evil habits are sealed for life.' Non-chastening parents finally give up on their children and seem content to await the inevitable (whatever may result in life for them, which in Old Testament days would have been death by stoning: Deut. 21:18-21). But this verse would condemn such parents (Donald Hunt, *Bible Study Textbook: Pondering the Proverbs*, 248).

Oh that parents could see the big picture of a failure to properly discipline their children! Without common sense discipline, children develop destructive habits of laziness, arrogance, disrespect for authority, and a disrespect for God and His will for their lives.

Years ago as I was teaching a Ladies' Bible Class an elderly lady began to criticize many of the young people of our time for being lazy and for not learning to work. "When I grew up on the farm," she said, "I had chores to do and had to work hard. Now the young people have nothing to do but watch television all day and are not learning to work!" I responded to her by asking her if she had anything at all to do with how and where she grew up. Obviously she said she did not. "Well the young people of our time have no more say about these things than you and I did," I replied. "If they are going to learn to work today, it's up to parents to teach them." The problem often is that too many fathers today are lazy and have poor work habits. It's hard to teach what you don't know or don't practice yourself.

Jesus condemned laziness in Matthew 25:26. The book of Proverbs uses almost three dozen verses to condemn laziness. It attributes too much sleep, too much idle talking, and no motivation as deterrents to work (cf. Prov. 6:9-11; 14:23; 19:15, 24; 26:14-15). Too often children are allowed to sleep half the day and play video games and text idle chatter on their cellphones the rest of the day. When they grow up and are too lazy to work, parents often blame the ungodly world for the problem they themselves created!

Fathers are instructed to be self-disciplined and motivated (Prov. 6:6-11; 16:26). We can teach our children by our own example of diligence in serving God and others and in providing the needs of our families. We can also instruct our children in the principles of God's word regarding work. Finally, we can give our children work to do or see to it that they learn to work in some productive manner. I'm thankful that my own father taught me in all these ways. We need to go back to teaching our children and grandchildren the lessons we learned as children ourselves, if we were so fortunate.

Years ago I heard the late Paul Harvey on the radio make the statement, "Many parents are so concerned about giving their children all the things that they never got that they often fail to give them the important things that they did get." How true that is! Have we forgotten that God's word always works?

We Conclude by Submitting to God Through Jesus Christ
Out of a Heart of Love

A person can do everything the Lord says in His word and it all will be for nought if the person is lacking in love (1 Cor. 13:1-3). A father can do all the Lord commands and his actions be nothing more than legalism, going through the motions of obedience without love. The apostle Paul once said that the love of Christ controlled him (2 Cor. 5:14). The love Christ has for us must be reciprocated in our love for Him.

In 1 John 4:9-11 we learn that God first loved us and that we ought to love one another also. God's love was primary or first and as a result we love

Him in return. Our love must be a selfless concern for others as expressed in 1 John 3:16-18: "By this we know love, because He laid down His life for us. And we also ought to lay down our lives for the brethren. But whoever has this world's goods, and sees his brother in need, and shuts up his heart from him, how does the love of God abide in him? My little children, let us not love in word or in tongue, but in deed and in truth."

Every parent knows this kind of selfless love for his or her child. Everything the child needs when he or she comes into the world must be supplied by the parent(s). A parent has to give up his or her own liberties to meet the needs of a child. Thankfully most parents do so willingly and joyfully. Sadly some parents never grow up and hardly do it at all. Sadder still is the fact that there are so few God-fearing fathers who surrender themselves fully to the Lord to accomplish His will in their homes. I recall to your mind Jesus Christ and His perfect life of selfless sacrifice on behalf of others – a submission and surrender to His Father's will that took Him all the way to the cross. In Galatians 2:20 Paul personalized the love and sacrifice of Christ on the cross and so can we personalize it. Jesus did it for you!

There are no perfect parents and no perfect children. We all sin and make mistakes and we all must rely on God's loving-kindness, mercy, and long-suffering as we journey through life in a humble, trusting manner. There is no greater joy in life than to hear that our children are walking in truth (3 John 4). This is especially true when our children in the faith are also our children in the flesh. Conversely, there is no greater heartache than when our children turn back and walk no more with Jesus.

So what can a father do to impact the lives of his children in a positive way for the Lord? Prayer comes to mind and I pray every day for my children and grandchildren. I first thank God for blessing them so abundantly. I then ask the Father to help me to be the kind of father and grandfather I ought to be to have a good influence in their lives. Then I take each child and each grandchild (and they are grand!) by name before the Father in heaven with the request that they may continue faithfully glorifying His name in the lives they live. I end by asking God again to help me seize the opportunities to be the kind of person I need to be in my home life.

Several years ago my wife, Ruby, and I took a college course entitled *The Seven Habits of Highly Effective People*. It was based on the book by that name by Stephen Covey. The most important thing I learned from the course is to schedule your time around people as much as you can instead of around things. What can I do today for my wife? What can I do today for my children and for my grandchildren? What can I do for my brethren? What can I do to reach the lost for Christ? When you prioritize your schedule this way it takes you out of yourself so much and puts you into the lives of other people for their benefit.

Submitting to God through Jesus Christ is where each of us must begin. We so desperately need fathers who unashamedly take a stand for Christ and who faithfully discharge their obligations before God as fathers. The greatest thing a father can do for his children is to love their mother. The throwaway spirit of our society has even infected the Lord's church with disposable marriages that will not stand the strains of everyday living. Couples are getting married with no greater promise than to abide together as long as they both shall love. The selfless, undefeatable goodwill love Christ commanded in Ephesians 5 and Titus 2 has been discarded for an emotional attachment with very little strength to hold it together. Too many marriages are like chewing gum that is sweet for a time but when the sweetness is gone it is time to discard it for another piece. When the marriage has lost its sweetness it is time to discard one's partner for another partner with no greater commitment than what was given to the first marriage. When a person reaches the point where his marriage does hold together, the same principles he applies to make it so would have held his first marriage together.

When children are involved in such family situations they suffer the most. Jesus warned against causing one of the little ones who believe in Him to sin. He said it would be better for that person to have a millstone hung around his neck and he was drowned in the depth of the sea (Matt.18:6).

Again, where are the fathers who stand on God's word and exemplify in their lives what it means to be a Christian? May our children and grandchildren see God as a loving heavenly Father as they mature because they first saw a loving, self-sacrificing father in us. When we leave this world it will matter little what material things we leave behind for our children. It will matter greatly that we leave behind an example that they can follow and get to heaven. Without this legacy we will leave them spiritual paupers regardless of how much we may leave them materially.

To provide for their families as God directs in His word, fathers need hearts of compassion, heads instructed in God's word, and hands ready to work.

On June 27, 1997 I received a phone call from a distressed mother whose 16-year-old son had just been killed in a terrible accident. He had left the school where his mother was working and was on his way home when his truck left the road and struck a tree. He died instantly. His mother asked me to meet her and the rest of the family at the hospital where his body had been taken. I tried as best as I could to console the family over this unspeakable tragedy.

A few days later I spoke at the boy's funeral. His name was John Lee Kennedy. I mentioned the fact that there had been another John Kennedy, John F. Kennedy, who also died a tragic death. John F. Kennedy, 35th president of the United States, had good looks, riches, popularity, and power – everything the world thinks one must have to be somebody and to be happy. Yet on November 22, 1963, in a moment of time, he lost it all as an assassin's bullet took his life.

John Lee Kennedy was a handsome young man but he had no material riches, no world-wide popularity and no political clout, and his death not announced in most every newspaper across the world. He had nothing the world says one must have to be somebody or to be happy but in a moment of time when he lost his life he gained it all because he was a Christian.

John F. Kennedy's body was laid to rest in Arlington National Cemetery in Arlington, Virginia; John Lee Kennedy's body was laid to rest in Arlington Cemetery on the south side of Mt. Pleasant, Tennessee.

Now let me tell you the rest of the story. Sometime after John's funeral I received a phone call from his dad asking me to meet him at the church building. As we met in my office, tears began to trickle down his cheeks as he choked out the words, "It's about time that I obey the gospel. My children have both become Christians and have set the example for me when I should have set the example for them." Joyfully I baptized Joel into Christ.

Fathers, wake up and man up spiritually to be the kind of fathers God expects you to be! May each of us who are fathers resolve to be totally dedicated to God, submitting to Him through the revelation of Jesus Christ and serving others as we journey through life.

Absentee Fathers

Don Miller

Few things can be done as an absentee in life, but voting is one of them. As a citizen in our country one can vote on an absentee ballot. During the 2012 fall election, record numbers chose this method to cast their vote in our area. Stockholders in corporations and organizations cast their vote by proxy, giving someone else the right to vote for them in their absence. In my banking career, I have seen countless numbers of people giving another person a power of attorney to act on their behalf in financial matters when either absent in body or mind.

One thing that can never be done as an absentee is being a father to one's children. Yet, the absentee father home has reached almost epidemic proportions in our country. According to the U.S. Census Bureau, in 2011, 24 million children in America, one out of three, live in biological father-absent homes. I inquired of one elementary teacher who taught in another state what percentage of her students had the father and mother of a child living under the same roof with them. She stated only 1 of 3 lived with their

---

Don Miller is fifty-seven years old. He is married to Brenda (Jackson) Miller. They have three sons, Matt, Brandon, and Seth, who along with their wives are faithful Christians and very active in the Lord's work in the local congregations they attend. They also

have seven grandchildren. Don and Brenda are natives of Limestone County and both graduated from Clements High School. They have resided in Florence since 1978. Don has been employed securlarly with the same local bank for the past thirty two years. He is currently serving in the role as Excecutive Vice President and Sr. Lender. Presently, he is a member of the River Bend congregation in Lauderdale County, Alabama since 1981 and has served as an elder at River Bend since May of 2005. He began preaching for this work in 1981 and continued until 1991 when the congregation was able to fully support a local evangelist. Since that time, he has preached on an as need basis and in gospel meetings for various congregations throughout North Alabama.

biological father. As a consequence, there is an "absentee father factor" in nearly all of the social issues facing our country today. Some of these issues are poverty, maternal and child health, incarceration, crime, teen pregnancy child abuse, drug and alcohol abuse, education, and childhood obesity. And the worst consequence of all is the lack of spiritual guidance and the likelihood that those precious souls will be lost for an eternity.

I believe that many of the social issues we face are a result of the neglect of fathers to adhere to the spiritual principles revealed in God's Word not only in parenting but in their attitude toward His instructions concerning marriage and the home. It might be more accurate to say that the problem comes from ignorance of His Word rather than neglect with the general population. It's alarming at the number of men who don't have a clue what being a father and head of a household are about. And what's even more alarming is that most of them could care less. But even so-called Christians are neglecting their duties within this realm.

As David was approaching his death in I Kings 2:1, 2, he charged his son Solomon to "shew thyself a man." There are many males today who father children, but not many men who are fathers of children as God intended. He went on to say in v. 3 in that same text to be a "man" involves "keeping the charge of the Lord thy God, to walk in his ways, to keep his statutes, and his commandments, and his judgments, and his testimonies." I realize he was referring to the Old Testament in this text, but the same principles are found in the New Testament instructing us how to become a "man" and what the duties and responsibilities of being a father are. If we are ever going to stem the tide of this epidemic of absentee fatherhood, we must do as Paul instructed Timothy in 2 Timothy 2:25 to "instruct those that oppose themselves." We must use every opportunity either by Scripture or example to drill these principles into men today to become the responsible fathers that God expects us to be.

There are basically four reasons for Absentee Fathers. They are as follows: (1) **Divorce,** (2) **Unmarried parents,** (3) **Incarceration,** (4) **Death.** There is nothing that can be done about the last one. Death can occur at any time in a person's life and there are many sad cases of an untimely death leaving a devastated widow to rear one or more children without a father. My mother had that happen to her at age 39. I had just left home and she had two children, my fifteen-year-old sister and my seven-year-old brother, to finish rearing on her own. By the grace of God and great determination and faith on her part, she was able to be like Timothy's grandmother, Lois, and mother, Eunice (2 Tim. 1:5). Just like Timothy's father, my father was not a Christian (Acts 16:1). He had been little or no help spiritually before he died. But he was a good father to us in every other way. It made Mother's task even more difficult when he died. Mother continued teaching my siblings well and they have become faithful Christians throughout their lives – without the aid of a father. It can be done with having an absentee father, but the task is much more difficult.

Divorce and unmarried parents are by far the most common cause of absentee fathers. The underlying cause is a sign of the times. The home as God prescribes in His Word is the bedrock of any society. It is breaking down if not already broken in this country. 40% of all marriages end in divorce. It is very common place now for couples to have children and not be married. What is the reason for this? A total disregard for God's law and instruction for the home. Why? *Ignorance of God's law.* Millions are no longer taught God's word. If you do teach what God says, people think you are crazy due to the perverted views on the home today. Another reason why is *indifference.* People just don't care what God has to say. And they don't want to know. And that leads to the underlying reason for the absentee father problem. *Selfishness.* In 2 Timothy 3:2-5, Paul describes those who are "lovers of themselves" and "lovers of pleasures more than lovers of God." Reading these verses from the first century perfectly describes what is occurring in the twenty-first century. Males who father children want the pleasure of the sexual act and selfishly shun the duties and responsibilities of being a father when that child is brought into this world.

The absentee father also realizes that it requires a lot of time, energy, effort, and money in rearing children. Selfishly, he does not want to sacrifice the time but rather, he wants to utilize it on things he desires. Nor does he want to devote the energy and effort, but rather he channels that on things that he loves to do. The expense of rearing children is something he avoids by shunning his responsibility to "provide for his own" (1 Tim. 5:8).

The consequences of absentee fathers on their children can be devastating. One of the effects on a child's behavior is the feeling of *abandonment.* A father has a direct impact on his child's well being. My wife and I have reared three sons. I remember that, early in their lives, it seemed all they wanted was their mother and that maybe I wasn't needed very much. When that first happened, it almost gave me a complex. But as time moved on, I began to see in their eyes the importance of dad being there at different milestones. I can't imagine having missed sharing things such as their school days, sports teams and events, spiritual development, or other things that were important to them.

When a father abandons the home, it leads the child to believe that they may be the cause. If a divorce has occurred, the children blame themselves. They think they have done something wrong to cause their father to disappear from their lives. This feeling of abandonment leads to additional problems in the child's development.

One of those problems is in the *emotional development* of that child. According to the Department of Human Services, 43% of the children who have absent fathers are less likely to get mostly A's in school. They go on to say that fathers nurture children in a different way than mothers and the balance of the two styles helps create a child's sense of confidence. I remember that was the case with my wife and me. She was the quiet, calming, compassionate one and I was the more stern, demanding, and disciplinarian type. I made more than my share of mistakes, but it seemed to work for us and for our sons, although they may strongly disagree.

When a child has a nurturing relationship with his father, it is believed he is more likely to develop better speech and decision making practices. When both parents are actively involved in the child's early years of development, the chances of that child being prepared mentally for schooling is greatly enhanced.

Another problem when the father is absent is in the area of *communication*. The child becomes withdrawn because he finds himself unable to communicate with his peers and other people. When the father is in the home and helps with the nurturing of the child, the child develops a sense of security. When that is not present, it creates much more stress in the life of that child. He or she then suffers socially and academically because of his/her inability to handle the additional stress levels and is overwhelmed more easily.

The previous problems lead to *behavioral* problems. Without a father in the home and helping nurture that child, he becomes more disruptive in his behavior. I remember being told growing up when a small child was misbehaving that it was only to get attention from one or both of his parents. Usually, that was the case. And when I did that I usually received attention alright. Only it wasn't exactly the attention I wanted. It was some form of discipline that got the attention of my backside.

The absence of fathers leads to antisocial and rebellious behavior. Study after study shows they are more prone to drug abuse, teen pregnancy and sexual activity, violent behavior, crime, and ultimately incarceration.

There may be little that can be done to help with those men who refuse to be a father and have left their homes or who never want to be a part of their children's lives in the first place. But, what about the women who are contemplating marriage and those who end up marrying a worthless deserter and shirker of his responsibilities as a father?

First and foremost, we must advise our young ladies who naturally want to marry and rear godly children to seek a man who wants the same. There is an old proverb that is quoted in Ezekiel 16:44, "As is the mother so is her daughter." I believe this applies to a father and his son as well. When looking at a prospect for a lifelong mate, look closely at the relationship the young man has in his home. If the young man's father is absent or abusive of his mother, chances are that the son will have the tendency to be the same way. When a young man comes from a broken home, chances increase dramatically that the same will happen with his marriage. Many a heartache can be avoided and the chances of a successful home increased when marrying the right person. This is one thing my wife and I stressed when our sons were growing up. We advised and encouraged them to marry a Christian. And not only a Christian, but to look at the homes they came from. Were the parents faithful to the Lord? How were they allowed to dress? And in which activities were they allowed to participate? Did they love spiritual matters? Or were they more concerned with worldly things? If the person you are dating doesn't care much for the right things now, what makes you think he will change suddenly just because you marry them?

Fortunately, all three of our sons married young ladies who are also faithful to the Lord. Together, they are working diligently to provide a godly home in which to rear our seven precious grandchildren. And with the Lord's guidance and helping one another, chances are they will be successful. Even then, it is a difficult task. That's why getting it right up front is so vitally important.

Unfortunately, there are many women who are or were married to an absentee father. The mother is a single parent trying her best to rear her children without the help of their father. Congregation after congregation of the Lord's people have those in their midst struggling with this. Unfortunately, this is a problem that is not going away, but in all likelihood, will become even more widespread. Is it a hopeless case when that mother is faced with that daunting task, or are there things she can do to compensate for an absent father?

I would have to go back to my mother and advise some things she did that really helped with all of us. First, make up your mind you are going to serve God regardless. Mother did that and it really made an impression on me when growing up. I saw how much it meant to her and remember thinking that I wanted to learn more about her faith and why it was so important. She took us to every service alone and today when I see a young mother struggling alone with her children during the services, I try to encourage her to keep it up for one day it will pay off. Another thing that Mother did was to make sure I was around men who were faithful to the Lord and good examples to follow. There were men such as Carl Alexander at the Oakland church in Limestone County who just spent time with me. He also taught me how to lead singing and encouraged me in becoming a Christian and remaining faithful. There are men in the Lord's church ready and willing to help in those same type situations today. It is perfectly scriptural to "mark them which walk so as ye have us for an example" (Phil. 3:17). I would also advise these single parents to provide as much contact with other young people whose parents are Christians when they are very young. Then, as they mature and reach the age of accountability, do your best to encourage them to spend time with other young Christians who love serving the Lord.

In my profession as a banker, I often see single mothers struggling just to make ends meet. Many times they either work long hours or more than one job. What can she do then to make it all work with her children if she is not there due to providing a living? When Dad died unexpectedly at age 41, Mother had to go to work to support my brother, age 7, and sister, age 15. She had to have help. Fortunately, she had good neighbors who stepped up and helped. And so did various family members, including myself. And everyone was glad to do so. There are people today who are looking for opportunities to provide a good influence for children in homes like that. So, bottom line, search for those who would be a good influence and don't be afraid to ask for help. The soul of your children may depend on it as well as your own.

I believe there are at least three different scenarios in which there are father absent homes. It is much like forsaking the assembly. You can forsake the assembly by never showing up at all, just showing up every now and then or only on Sunday morning, and you can forsake the assembly even when you're there. I believe it is the same with an absentee father. The *first* and most obvious is when the father deserts the home or never makes an effort to be a father to his children. The *second* is when he is still part of the family but is seldom there to be a father. And the *third* is he can be an absentee father even when he's there.

There may be little that can be done to help with those men who refuse to be a father and have left their homes or who never want to be a part of their children's lives in the first place. But, I believe we can perhaps make a difference with those who are still in the home. We can through example or teaching, instill a desire to be the kind of father to their children that pleases God. We can make the greatest impact and difference with those fathers who are still in the home. We can through example or teaching, instill a desire to be the kind of father to their children that pleases God.

The place to begin this process is with God's Word. We can find examples of fathers in the inspired pages of God's Word that should be good templates for us to follow in becoming good fathers. I want to begin with **Abraham** and what God says about him in Genesis 18:19 – *"for I know him, that he will command his children and his household after him, and they shall keep the way of the Lord, to do justice and judgment; that the Lord may bring upon Abraham that which he hath spoken of him"*

There are several things that stand out in looking at this statement from God that speaks volumes about Abraham and the type father he was. He was known as the father of the Jews, but it began long before that in his own home. Elders and other leaders of God's people would do well to study the way Abraham reared his family. In doing so, they would see before they could become effective in leading others, they must first begin with those under their own roof.

God began by saying, *"I know him."* God sees all and knows all. He made each one of us and knows what makes us tick. He knows what abilities we have in every facet of life and how we use those abilities. He knew what kind of father Abraham was to his children. The same holds true for each father today. He knows our hearts and minds and whether we are giving our all to rearing our children properly. But I also believe in this statement is the implication that Abraham also knew God. In James 2:23, Abraham is called the "friend of God." Think about it. In order for someone to be our friend, they have to know us pretty well, too. I believe Abraham knew God well. He had a good relationship with God first and foremost. In order to be a good father here, we must do the same, for our children will know. Abraham's children saw clearly that he had a relationship with God.

That is further emphasized by the next statement in Genesis 18:19. He stated, *"that he will command his children and his household after him."* This statement teaches us several things about Abraham. It teaches us that he gave them his **time**. You can't teach your children properly without it requiring a lot of time. I can imagine Abraham living out Deuteronomy 6:6, 7 – *"and these words, which I command thee this day, shall be in thine heart: and thou shalt teach them diligently unto thy children, and shalt talk of them when thou sittest in thine house, and when thou walkest by the way, and when thou liest down, and when thou risest up.*

At best, we only have our children for a few short years. One of the best gifts you can give your children is your time. A good father will be present in the lives of his children. And what better way to spend that time than to teach your children about God and what he wants for each of them? And yet today, so much of our time and the time of our children is spent on things that are temporal rather than spiritual. It amazes me now how much time is spent by fathers with their children in secular activities such as sports. There is a sports complex on the same road as the church building where we assemble and the activities are practically year round. It is nothing anymore for ball games to be held all day on Sunday now. When I was growing up, people still gave Sunday to the Lord. Even Wednesday night was taboo back then for such activities. It was due to authorities knowing that people would be attending worship services during those times. Enough respect was given to them and the Lord that those times were left alone. Now with travel ball, year round sports, and other recreational activities so prevalent, it has gobbled up any time to be spent with our children at any time, much less on Sundays.

In order to prevent us from becoming absentee fathers even while in the home, we must devote ourselves to giving our children our time for their spiritual development. It may mean they won't make the All-Star team or reduce the participation in some of their activities. But it may mean the ultimate saving of their soul.

Fathers are to be the spiritual leaders and instructors in the home. In Ephesians 6:4, *"Fathers, provoke not your children to wrath, but bring them up in the nurture and admonition of the Lord."* Your children will only learn about God when we begin at an early age to teach them who

God is and what He desires us to be in order to please Him. Fathers are given that charge and responsibility by God to make sure that command is carried out. Your children are learning something every day about something or someone. And chances are that in this world, they will have few opportunities to learn about God from anyone else outside the home. And that responsibility lies squarely at the feet of fathers. Abraham gladly accepted that role and taught his children about God and His Word. He did so every single day. We must do the same.

This spiritual development is a time process in and of itself. Love them. Don't just say it. Show them. It begins by taking an interest in each child's life. In every phase of life begin teaching the spiritual principles that apply to each. Work less, and play more with them. Turn off the TV. Help them with their school work and their Bible lessons. Lead them and teach them your role as a parent and theirs as children in family life according to God's plan. Make eye contact with them as they tell you about their day.

There was a father at the local McDonalds Play Place where we often take our grandchildren. One father caught my eye by what he did with his children. He was playing video games provided at McDonalds and several times one of his children would come up and ask him to play or just come and watch them. Each time he told them to go play on their own and they would walk away dejected. If we do that when they are young, how in the world can we expect them to listen to us when they are older? That may be why so many good people have lost their children to the world. They were just too busy when the greatest impact could have been made when the child was young.

When the statement in Genesis 18:19 is made that God knew Abraham would *"command his children and his household after him,"* I believe something else is implied – **Discipline**. Couple that with the following statement in that verse, *"that they will keep the way of the Lord, to do justice and judgment."* In order for someone to follow a command, they must respect the commander. Can you imagine Abraham's children talking back to him with a smart mouth and he not doing anything about it? Or refusing to handle a chore when asked to? Or worship God when called upon to do so? Do you think he was fond of using our modern day psychology in disciplining children by giving them "time outs"? Or think that rebellious attitudes were some cute stage they were going through? Or afraid he might destroy their self esteem by handing out harsh discipline when needed? Remember, he knew God and taught his children that God was a just God and one of judgment. He knew God rewards those who obey Him and punishes those who disobey. In Hebrews 12:6-11 we read:

> For whom the Lord loveth he chasteneth, and scourgeth every son whom he receiveth. If ye endure chastening, God dealeth with you as with sons; for what son is he whom the father chasteneth not? But if ye be without chastisement, whereof all are partakers, then are ye bastards, and not sons. Furthermore we have had fathers of our flesh which corrected us, and we gave them reverence: shall we not much rather be in subjection unto the Father of spirits, and live? For they verily for a few days chasteneth us after their own pleasure but he for our profit, that we might be partakers of his holiness. Now no chastening for the present seemeth to be joyous, but grievous: nevertheless afterward it yieldeth the peaceable fruit of righteousness unto them which are exercised thereby.

We find in this passage that, as God's children, we are disciplined or chastened by God. He disciplines us because He loves us and because discipline is for our benefit to make us suitable for service above. Notice in verse 11 that "afterward it yieldeth the peaceable fruit of righteousness" and verse 10 "we might be partakers of his holiness," and verse 9 when we subject ourselves to it we shall "live."

He illustrates God's discipline by the "fathers of our flesh" in verse 9. Discipline by our fathers in the flesh is motivated by "love" in verse 7. It produces "reverence" or respect in verse 9. This reverence causes us to have a respect for authority, which is sorely needed in our day and age. When the father in the home is teaching his children to have respect for authority, then that child will be no problem in school, with the law, and most especially in adhering to the authority of God through the Scriptures.

In verse 11, discipline is not "joyous" when it is administered, but rather "grievous," but afterwards it "yieldeth the peaceable fruit of righteousness." When discipline begins at an early age with our children, it will cause them to live a good life when older. But when children are not disciplined at an early age, the child grows up and causes a great deal of pain for themselves and their parents. It's almost like the old saying, "You can pay me now or pay me later." I used that saying on my youngest son after having to spank him one day when he did something wrong, only using the word "thank" rather than "pay." I sat him down and read these verses to him and told him one day he would thank me for doing this and said, "You can thank me now or thank me later." Through the tears and sobs he snapped his head up and said, "I will thank you later." I don't think at that particularly time he had much appreciation for what had been dealt out to him, but hopefully since he now has children of his own, he understands perfectly what I meant.

There are many passages, particularly in Proverbs, that deal with the importance of discipline with our children. In Proverbs 23:13, 14 we read, "Withhold not correction from the child: for if thou beatest him with the rod, he shall not die. Thou shalt beat him with the rod, and shalt deliver his soul from hell." These verses are not talking about a little pat, but it says to "beat" the child. This passage is not advocating child abuse and neither am I, but the discipline to be administered sometimes has to be harsh or hurt. My dad thought nothing of using a belt or a keen switch and I hated both. But I needed both and now am very appreciative he did that. It will deliver the child's soul.

Another Proverb along this line is 13:24, "He that spareth his rod hateth his son: but he that loveth him chasteneth him betimes." I remember my dad telling me he was whipping me because he loved me and I remember looking at him and thinking he was crazy. Now, after having reared three sons, I know exactly what he meant. The passage also says you have to use the rod a lot and promptly. But when used appropriately with love, remember that child's soul is being shaped and formed according to how God intended it to be.

Proverbs 22:15 says, "Foolishness is bound in the heart of a child; but the rod of correction shall drive it far from him." I was sitting around the kitchen table of brother Lindsay Allen of Florence many years ago. He was a faithful gospel preacher and retired educator and I cherished those opportunities to sit at his feet and study. My two oldest sons were there with my wife and me one night when they were very young. They were being a little rambunctious and we were looking at this passage. It probably prompted brother Allen to say in that stern voice of his, "Now, Don, children are like wild animals, and you have to tame them." He was right because God was right when He said it. Discipline works. And it does so by turning a child's rebellion and stubbornness into conviction if administered correctly.

We live in an age where this is unpopular at best. And yet another Proverb tells us "a child left to himself bringeth his mother to shame" (29:15). The failure of an earthly father to discipline his children brings a lifetime of heartache and shame. It damages society and ultimately leads to the destruction of precious souls.

I have no doubt Abraham disciplined his children as God intended when he *commanded his children and household.* I doubt he tried to be a buddy to his children as I see so many fathers doing so today. It's almost impossible to discipline children as needed when you try to be a buddy to them. I always told my sons that I was their father and not their buddy. I also told them that when they grew up we could then become buddies. And hopefully that has been the case.

One final thing I would like to point out in Genesis 18:19 that made Abraham such a good father is he "commanded his children and household *after him.*" This tells me that, not only did Abraham talk the talk, but he walked the walk. He lived a godly life before his children and family, a life in which he was not ashamed for them to do so, a life that cast a huge shadow of influence over his children. To me, this is the most sobering of all facts to face as a father in this life. Every single one of my sons did the exact same thing when they were very young. I would be sitting in the den and hear a sound coming up the hall. It was a faint clomp at first, but as they got closer to the den, the clomps got louder. Guess what they were wearing? Daddy's shoes. And they would look me in the eye and say, "Daddy, when I grow up, I want to be just like you." You think that won't get your attention. And they were right. Whether I like it or not, they did grow up a lot like me. And you know what? Your children will too. Remember the proverb in Ezekiel 16:44 that says, "As is the mother, so is her daughter"? There are exceptions to this, both good and bad, but in most cases, the children will indeed pattern their lives after the example of their parents before them.

Jesus said in Matthew 5:13-16 that we are the "salt of the earth" and "the light of the world." He uses salt and light to illustrate the tremendous power of influence, "that they may see your good works," that we have at our disposal through our example to others. In so doing we "glorify your Father which is in heaven." What better place to glorify God by others seeing your good works than in the home and before our children? You think Abraham's children noticed he built altars first everywhere he went to worship God? Or his great faith in seeing the unseen promises of God? His prayer life? His fairness in dealing with his nephew, Lot, and others? His love for his wife, Sarah?

Children observe closely everything we say and do. It's the only pattern they have to follow. Sometimes we forget this.

My children noticed everything I did, too. My oldest son can still recall when we had a couple of young men from the Mormon faith come to the house while he and I were working in the yard. He recalls I went inside to get my Bible to show them the passages about some differences, particularly how they didn't fit the qualifications of an elder. The younger, who I assume was the trainee, began to agree with the teaching of the Bible and stated he had never seen that. The older one, or the trainer, became very angry, and grabbed the other young man to leave hurriedly. As they were walking out our driveway, he began to loudly call me a "blasphemer." I politely told him, "Thanks for the compliment, for so did they with my Lord."

Hopefully, remembering this has helped him in life when he encounters those who differ with him spiritually by using God's Word and it only in answering (1 Pet. 3:15) and how to diffuse a potential hostile situation by speaking kindly when answering those who become angry with us. Did not the Proverb writer teach us that in Proverbs 15:1 when he said, "A soft answer turneth away wrath, but grievous words stir up anger"?

Recently, a lady at church told me she is teaching her children to put down the Bible passages where answers are found to questions in class material. She told her daughter that Mr. Don teaches that way and it helps her remember the passages when that particular subject is discussed in the future. Her daughter told her that my son, Seth, teaches their class the same way, and it helps her too. I didn't realize he was doing that until told. He is following the example that was set before him, which in this case, fortunately, is a good one.

These are a couple of things that were good for my sons to follow as examples. Unfortunately, there are also many I wish they did not have before them. Have you ever said something you really didn't want repeated and one of your children repeated it, causing you more than a little discomfort and embarrassment? Abraham was a good example as a father, but even he made mistakes with his children. Remember Abraham lying about his wife, Sarah, by telling only a half truth by saying she was his sister? It happened twice, first in Genesis 12 and then in Genesis 20. What did his son Isaac do later in Genesis 26 concerning Rebekah his wife? The same thing. Granted, Isaac was not yet on the scene when his father did that, but do you think maybe that story had been passed down to Isaac? People still recall things I did that I am ashamed of long before my children were born and they hear about them. And when they do, it causes concern that they may think since Dad did some of these things, then maybe it's OK for them too.

The power of influence in the home as a father. Abraham took full advantage of it in training his children and commanding them *"after him."* Did he make mistakes? Yes. Will we make mistakes? Yes. When you do, own up to them. Tell your children you are sorry when you are wrong. Let them see how you overcome those mistakes by living a life that is a godly example for them to follow. And follow they will.

In summarizing the things we learn from Abraham in being a good father, we must: **(1) Have a relationship with God. Know Him. (2) Give children our time. (3) Be the spiritual leader in our family. (4) Use discipline as God prescribes. (5) Be a godly example before our children.** If we follow the example of Abraham, there is no way we can be an absentee father in our homes.

There are many other good examples of fathers in the Bible. I would like to use a few in the time remaining and make just a couple of points about each.

Joshua was a good father to his children. In Joshua 24:15, he made the statement that is well known. It reads, "but as for me and my house we will serve the Lord." Not only was he the spiritual leader of his family by stating this, but we learn it requires making a *commitment*. But that commitment was made long before that in Joshua's life. Remember Joshua and Caleb being faithful in spite of the vast majority turning against them after spying out the land of Canaan? Being a faithful Christian today will mean no doubt we will be in the minority. Our children will observe how we react and how firmly we stand when faced with those same type situations. Four times in Joshua 1, God told Joshua, "Be strong and of good courage" (vv. 6, 7, 9, 18). It required *strength* and *courage* to honor that commitment. And so it will with us. Did Joshua honor that commitment? In verse 31 of Joshua 24, it reads, "And Israel served the Lord all the days of Joshua, and all the days of the elders that overlived Joshua." The commitment he made was kept due to his spiritual leadership and tremendous influence he had and displayed by honoring God in fulfilling that commitment. What a great example for us to follow as a father.

Noah was an example of a father who taught his children and family to serve God. He is described as a "just man, perfect in his generation, and Noah walked with God" (Gen. 6:9). He preached for a 120 years about the flood that would destroy the earth. No one else listened. But his children did. They saw his *persistence* in continuing with God's message, even though rejected by the vast majority. They witnessed his *patience* in dealing with rejection and in the long process of building an ark day by day for a 120 years exactly as God instructed. And they noticed his *preparation* through the faith he had in God's word and unfailing promises. *Persistence, patience, and preparation.* Three great lessons to learn from Noah in saving his children. It will require no less from us.

Job is described in Job 1:1 as follows: "that man was perfect and upright, and one that feared God, and eschewed evil." In verse 2 he had "seven sons and three daughters." He is described in verse three as a very wealthy man, yet that's not where his primary interest was according to verse 5. Job would rise up "early in the morning" and offer burnt offerings according to the number of his children. He was concerned about their spiritual welfare and the possibility they had sinned and cursed God in their hearts. The last statement in verse 5 teaches us a great lesson. "Thus Job did continually." These were grown children and what was Job doing? Every day, he was concerned about their spiritual condition. First and foremost, he wanted his children to be in good standing with God. What's the lesson for us? While we are not to offer burnt offerings for our children, there is something we can offer on behalf of our children early in the morning, daily, and continually. *Prayer.* We need to pray for ourselves to be good fathers. We need to pray for strength in being upright before them. We need to pray that we instill in them the principles from God's Word in how to live and be pleasing to Him. We need to pray that they will make good decisions based on those principles that they have been taught.

When Job's children were full grown and making their own decisions, his primary concern remained their spiritual condition before God. As our children become independent and start making lives of their own, the prayers on their behalf only intensify that they will remain faithful. And even more so when the grandchildren come on the scene.

The prayers begin before birth as did Samson's father Manoah in Judges 13:12 when he said, "How shall we order the child, and how shall we do unto him?" We realize from the first moment we hold those precious creatures that we will need a lot of help and guidance in rearing them and training them to be as God desires. And that help comes from the instruction manual called the Bible. The prayers continue the remainder of our days much like the Apostle Paul's prayer concerning Israel (Rom. 10:1). The record says, "My heart's desire and prayer to God for Israel is that they might be saved." If Paul could earnestly say that about his fellow Jews, then by all means we can say the same prayer for our children substituting their name in the place of Israel.

Learn from God's Word what will make you a better father. Look at the examples of godly men who we've studied about within that Word and pattern your role as a father after them. By designing the home as God did, He made the family the ideal vehicle to use in allowing the glorious light of the gospel to shine in a sin darkened world. The influence of a godly family is far reaching. It provides inroads to teaching the lost and being an example for others to follow. My favorite time of parenting was the twelve years from 1994 to 2006 when we had Bible studies for the area young people as each son was going through his teen years. Opportunity after opportunity was provided in reaching many young and tender hearts of that age group. My sons learned the value of spending time with others who were struggling with the same things in life. They received encouragement by finding others who loved to study and worship together. It provided opportunities for each to find a mate who would be a help meet in the Lord's Kingdom.

I always told my sons and the other young people who came to our home that my prayer was they would continue as they married and had their own families. Many of them have done just that. They are participants in having group studies and providing those same type opportunities for their children. I also hope that those who read this will do the same. It will help in glorifying God, strengthening your faith and the faith of your children, and providing many opportunities in furthering the cause of the Lord's Kingdom.

Unfaithful Husbands

Greg Chandler

The blinding camera flashes. A plethora of microphones fill the podium. A disheveled political leader steps forward to admit, after weeks of denial, that he has been involved with another woman. Another "gotcha" moment in American media brings on a host of talking heads who lament his demise, discuss what it means for his career, and wonder how his political party will deal with the fallout. Lost in the discussion is the fact that another American family has been assaulted. His political demise fails to compare with a grieving wife who has been publicly humiliated and betrayed by one who promised fidelity. Loss of future office in no way corresponds to his children, whether young or adult, who now must face the fact that their father has created a chasm within their family that perhaps cannot be crossed. Sadly, this scene has played out numerous times within modern American government. Men who failed to learn from others' failures make the same mistake and soon learn that they are not the ones who "will get away with it." Even sadder is the fact that the same event happens, less the lights and cameras, with numerous ordinary American men who fall to the sin of adultery.

Greg Chandler was born in Florence, Alabama and has lived in Athens, Alabama most of his life. He attended Florida College and graduated from the University of North Alabama with a Bachelor of Science degree in social science education. He later received a Master's degree in history education from the University of West Alabama. Over the past few years, he has preached primarily in rural Limestone County, Alabama. He also spent one year in evangelistic efforts in Sao Paulo, Brazil. Since 1990, he has been a full-time faculty member at Athens Bible School, where he teaches Bible, history, government, and economics. He also currently works with the church of Christ at Gooch Lane and Hughes Road in Madison, Alabama. Greg and his wife Pam have three sons, Adam, Ethan, and Isaiah.

God's Warnings to Ancient Israel Concerning Adultery

Adultery is a grievous sin that impacts numerous others besides the two involved in the act. The Lord clearly expressed His view of this sin when He codified its prohibition in simple terms within the Law of Moses: *"You shall not commit adultery"* (Exod. 20:14). He showed the serious nature of this sin to Israel when he mandated the death penalty for those involved. Any Israelite tempted to leave his wife for a relationship with another woman faced the sobering words of the Law: *"If a man commits adultery with the wife of his neighbor, both the adulterer and the adulteress shall surely be put to death"* (Lev. 20:10). It is no surprise that the wisest man of all times would tell his fellow countrymen *"He who commits adultery lacks sense; he who does it destroys himself"* (Prov. 6:32). He also spent a major portion of the first nine chapters of the book of Proverbs warning his sons to keep away from the adulterous woman. He knew the dangers that came from such a relationship and the temptations that would be faced by his sons to become involved in such a seductive relationship. Rather than listening to words from the *"smooth tongue of the adulterous"* (Prov. 6:24), he wanted his sons to *"keep their father's commandment, and forsake not their mother's teaching"* (6:20).

The prophets of God often used the example of adultery to illustrate how sinful the nation of Israel had become. In illustrating the hypocrisy of the people, Jeremiah asked, *"Will you steal, murder, commit adultery, swear falsely, make offerings to Baal, and go after other gods that you have not known, and then come and stand before me in this house, which is called by my name, and say, 'we are delivered!' – only to go on doing all these abominations?"* (Jer. 7:9-10). In also pointing out the glaring ungodliness of the false prophets, the Lord spoke through Jeremiah and stated: *"But in the prophets of Jerusalem I have seen a horrible thing: they commit adultery and walk in lies; they strengthen the hands of evildoers, so that no one turns from his evil"* (Jer. 23:14). Through the prophet Hosea, God illustrated how that Israel had become an adulterous nation by turning to other gods. The prophet was told to marry a wife from harlotry in order to experience firsthand the feelings God had toward His people. Through this, he could better understand what the Lord meant when He said things such as this: *"For the Lord has a controversy with the inhabitants of the land. There is no faithfulness or steadfast love, and no knowledge of God in the land; there is swearing, lying, murder, stealing, and committing adultery. . . .Therefore the land mourns"* (Hos. 4:1-3). These prophetic warnings show God's contempt for the sin of adultery and how that, ultimately, it was a way of seeing Israel's complete disregard for their marriage covenant and, most importantly, their covenant with God.

God's Warnings to New Testament Christians Concerning Adultery

Adultery was certainly not only a problem for the Jews, and they were not the only people warned about its consequences. Jesus Christ, in laying the foundation for Christianity, stated that not only should this sin be avoided, but also the very activities of the mind that would lead one to improper thoughts about another should be avoided. The religious elite of the day had minimized the sin of adultery. Though they were opposed to the physical act and would have believed it to be wrong, they failed in teaching the necessity of imprisoning the thoughts that could lead to this sin. As Christ razed the *"righteousness of the Pharisees"* that focused only on the outward, He illustrated that a commitment to holiness would prevent even the seed of thought from growing in one's mind. He stated *"but I say to you that everyone who looks at a woman with lustful intent has already committed adultery with her in his heart"* (Matt. 5:28). He follows by showing that even the most drastic measures must be taken to prevent one from becoming involved in this sin. Rather than falling prey to this sin, Jesus stated, *"If your right eye causes you to sin, tear it out and throw it away. For it is better that you lose one of your members than that your whole body be thrown into hell. And if your right hand causes you to sin, cut it off and throw it away. For it is better that you lose one of your members than that your whole body go into hell"* (Matt. 5:29-30). The sin of adultery is one that takes men off the road of holiness and places their soul in danger of eternal destruction.

Even the laws of marriage show the Lord's hatred of this sin. There is no doubt that, from the very beginning, the Lord wanted a man and woman committed to a faithful, monogamous, life-long relationship. This was established in the Garden of Eden when the Lord stated that *"a man shall leave his father and his mother and hold fast to his wife, and they shall become one flesh"* (Gen. 2:24). Jesus Christ fully endorsed this idea when, in Matthew 19, He recited the above verse to His Pharisee oppressors when questioned about marriage and divorce. His point was that marriage was designed for life and illustrated this by showing God's standards that were set at the creation of marriage.

In light of all the passages noted thus far concerning this sin, it becomes painfully obvious adultery is not a sin that "just happens." While many men have sought to explain away their transgression by reasons such as being in the wrong place at the wrong time, it ultimately comes down to a problem within the heart. The Lord said that *"out of the heart come evil thoughts, murder, adultery, sexual immorality, theft, false witness, slander. Those are what defile a person"* (Matt. 15:19-20). A man who does not keep his heart right with God will have a difficult time withstanding this sin that is so heinous in the eyes of the Lord.

With the Lord's strong words about this sin, why do men, generation after generation, continue to be involved in an activity that strikes against the home and wounds those to whom they have pledged the utmost fidelity? The answer to this question is the same answer given concerning many sins – lack of self-control and lack of forethought. As the Apostle Paul explained to the Galatians about the war for their souls, note that he listed sexual immorality as the first work of the flesh (Gal. 5:19). It is a sin of gratification; of giving the flesh what will physically satisfy without fully considering the ramifications to one's family and one's own soul. In this, twenty-first century American men are no different from first century Jews or ancient Israelites. It is succumbing to a temptation that will have temporary pleasure, yet have long lasting ramifications.

The Sexual Liberation Movement and Adultery

How widespread is this sin within modern culture? While attempts are made to determine this answer, it is notoriously difficult to pinpoint an accurate number since those involved have a vested interest in keeping their activities secret. A *Time* magazine study, pending its accuracy, gives a frightening and staggering statistic that 47% of men and 35% of women will get involved either emotionally or physically with someone other than their spouse.[1] Another study notes that, while only 8% of 1940's American women under 25 were involved in adultery, 24% of modern women in this age bracket are presently involved in adulterous relationships.[2] While adultery is not a new problem, it is definitely an American problem.

The premise of this presentation is to understand how the sexual liberation movement has impacted the home, especially the husband, and to

---

[1] L. Fitzpatrick (Friday, June 26, 2009). "Why Good People Cheat." *Time.com*. Retrieved from *http://www.time.com/time/nation/article/0,8599, 1907202,00. html*.

[2] S. Mintz (Saturday, December 22, 2012). "The Modern Family." *digitalhistory. uh.edu*. Retrieved from *http://www.digitalhistory.uh.edu/historyonline/modern-family.cfm*.

understand its correlation to the sin of adultery. Historically, there have been a number of sexual liberation movements. Whether it be the musings of ancient Greeks, writings of thinkers in the Age of Enlightenment, or the thoughts of Sigmund Freud, there have always been those seeking to end what they viewed as sexual repression. Perhaps no movement, however, has had the universal impact of the sexual revolution that had its origin in the 1960s subcultures of the United States. While, as noted earlier, adultery has always been a problem, the restraints that kept many from falling to this sin began to erode during this time. Many citizens of western nations dismissed what they deemed as puritanical and Victorian in relation to the concept of morality. Sadly, this dismissal was not simply the culture of a highly religious group or the mores of 19th century England, it was the standards that the Lord had placed upon mankind to keep them godly and holy.

One area of this movement and its monumental impact on American culture is highly evidenced from events in the presidential election of 2012. In the midst of huge economic problems and international uncertainty, one of the main issues to arise in this election was a woman's right to government financed birth control. One party highlighted this by inviting a young woman to speak as a part of their national convention. A few months earlier, this young woman had been the subject of a talk radio host who chose very unfortunate words to describe her and her campaign for tax-funded birth control. Seizing on the moment, her political party lauded her as an example of one who would lose her "right" to government-funded birth control if the other party were elected. It was a moment showing that one of the goals of the sexual revolution had come of age. Turning the clock back to the late 1950s would find a time when most Americans could hardly fathom the idea that birth control would, first, be spoken of openly and, second, that it would be one of the main debates in a presidential campaign. Yet, in less than a decade, easy and affordable birth control would be readily available. Known in vernacular as "the pill," this type of birth control would open the door to a very different view of sexual relations.

To say that the pill led to the sexual liberation movement would be a massive overstatement. To say that its misuse was one of the foundation stones in the sexual liberation movement would portray a more accurate picture. How, though, does this fit into a discussion of adultery? While relatively inexpensive and easily attainable birth control has been used in wholesome ways, it has also given rise to a much freer attitude toward sexual relations because it greatly decreases the chance of an out-of-wedlock child. While speculative, this would seem to draw the conclusion that men might be more willing to become involved in an adulterous affair since this part of the risk is minimized. It would perhaps also draw a conclusion that women might be more willing to partner in these affairs since their own risk of pregnancy is minimized. With the threat of a child seemingly out of the way, the secrecy of an extra-marital affair seems more achievable.

A second and more horrific aspect of birth control was nationally codified in 1973. The controversial issue of abortion has a long and sordid history in the United States. Abortion and abortion laws date to the earliest portions of the United States' colonial period. While the purpose of this material is not to review abortion's history, it should be noted that abortions increased dramatically in the 19th century. They were primarily performed on young women who had become prostitutes in order to meet the demand created by a new class of traveling businessmen in the United States.[3] This allowed men, no doubt many of whom were married, to engage in one-time affairs with these young women with no responsibility and allowed the young women to destroy the resulting baby. Throughout this time, there were those who stood in moral opposition and laws were passed to end the practice. In the 1960s, discussion of abortion turned to the danger that women were placed in as they tried to secure illegal abortions. As a result, states began legalizing abortion and, in the landmark case of *Roe v. Wade, 1973*, the United States Supreme Court made abortion legal in all fifty states. There was now a legal choice if contraception did not work. An unwanted child could be destroyed. Again, links between this decision and adultery are somewhat anecdotal, yet another "safety net" of sorts was given to men who were involved in affairs. Their partner could now end any pregnancy and the secrecy of their relationship could still seemingly be maintained.

Another aspect of the sexual liberation movement can be seen in the relaxing of moral standards in American society. The medium of television presents a clear picture of how far the United States has come in dismissing standards of morality. Most any modern program that has high ratings will deal with some issue of immorality. It may be an unmarried couple living together, a homosexual couple, a character involved in fornication, or a couple where one or both parties are involved in adultery. Contrast such programming with those programs popular in the early days of television.

---

[3] Unknown (Tuesday, June 26, 2012). "U.S. Abortion History." *abort73.com*. Retrieved from *http://www.abort73.com/abortion_facts/us_abortion_history/*.

Discussion of anything sexually related was taboo, with couples presented as happily married and their bedrooms complete with twin beds. As television "came of age," 1970s programming begin to challenge the censorship standards of the 1950s and early 1960s. Even a program as innocent (at least by modern standards) as *The Mary Tyler Moore Show* began exploring the idea of a young woman being freed by the sexual liberation movement. The program occasionally dealt with topics such as birth control, acceptance of fornication, and other issues that were transforming the moral code of the nation. From the 1970s forward, successful programming seemed by necessity to include a lighthearted view of sex, a plotline involving immorality, inappropriate joking, or other issues directly related to changing moral standards. The relaxed moral standards illustrated by American television programming unfortunately bespeak a public who has also relaxed such standards. Such an atmosphere can often dull spiritual senses and create an environment where falling to temptation becomes much easier. The "new normal" has led to an environment where adultery is sensationalized and even made to look attractive.

Combined with the medium of television is the somewhat new and ever changing Internet. While the Internet has provided wonderful opportunities, it has also provided new challenges, especially for men. The sexual liberation movement has perhaps reached its pinnacle with a medium where no stops are in place. A man looking for opportunities to fill his mind with sexual scenes is literally only one click away. Often, these images create a desire that will ultimately be fulfilled, not in virtual terms, but in the reality of an affair. *Facebook* and other social media outlets have allowed old romances to be rekindled more easily and a new wave of adulterous opportunities to come of age for a plugged-in generation. Divorce attorneys are finding that reasons for divorce now include a number relating to *Facebook*. This fact is illustrated in the following quote concerning attorneys who deal with divorce cases: "Maryland and D.C. divorce attorney Regina Demeo says at least 20 percent of her cases involve illicit relationships that began on Facebook. The stats don't lie – attorneys estimate that 80 percent of their cases now involve evidence that they are pulling off of Facebook pages for use in court."[4] Such activity has become so rampant that a website en-

---

[4] J. Donalen (Wednesday, May 16, 2012). "Facebook Adultery Trend Rising As People Find Long, Lost Flings." wjla.com. Retrieved from *http://www.wjla. com/articles/2012/05/facebook-adultery-trend-rising-as-people-find-long-lost-flings-76049.html.*

titled *facebookcheating.com* has been set up as a support group for victims who have seen their spouses connect with old acquaintances and become unfaithful.

One other aspect of the sexual liberation movement has been seen in the economic empowerment of women. While working women is not a new concept for the United States by any means, the increase of women in the work place alongside male workers has risen steadily and coincided with changing attitudes on the roles of men and women. This has given rise to work related affairs, where a man and woman are drawn together due to their close proximity in working conditions. Often such relationships begin with seeming innocence, but soon advance into forbidden territory as conversations progress into areas that should be reserved for husband and wife. Men who perhaps have difficulty at home find comfort and solace in these workplace relationships.

The sexual liberation movement has obviously enjoyed widespread success. It has challenged the role of men both in home and in society. It has created a misconception that sexual relations know no bounds. It has no doubt been responsible for implanting ideas that have destroyed many homes and brought a new generation to have little to no anchoring in Biblically moral beliefs that were once foundational in the United States and other western nations.

With all of this said, can the sexual liberation movement be blamed for the increased number of adulterous affairs? The answer to this is a resounding no. It is a weak and cowardly man who seeks to blame his lack of moral fortitude on the corruption around him. No matter what the time period, faithful men have always been surrounded by wickedness. Though unwise in his choice of settlement, consider what is said about Lot. In speaking of the Lord's ability to save, Peter writes, *"And if he rescued righteous Lot, greatly distressed by the sensual conduct of the wicked (for as that righteous man lived among them day after day, he was tormenting his righteous soul over their lawless deeds that he saw and heard)"* (2 Pet. 2:7-8). Men can be surrounded by wickedness and remain firm in their resolve to faithfully withstand the temptations placed in front of them. Like Job, they can make a covenant with their eyes not to look upon a virgin (Job 31:1). A man must, however, also realize the dulling nature of being constantly surrounded by immorality. While he cannot use society as an excuse, he must be ever aware of how a constant temptation can bring him to give up his moral footing. Samson was vexed daily by Delilah's temptations and eventually lowered his guard to his own demise. So, too, can modern man allow the endless flow of sexual perversion that entertains a modern world to pollute his mind and influence him to lower his own guard. He can also swallow the lie of "safe sex" to convince him that no lasting consequence will come of secret affairs. He can allow his close proximity to other women to tempt him into thinking he deserves a relationship with someone who appreciates him for who he is. The decision to fall into this sin will, however, be his own.

Adultery's Impact on the Family

The second premise of this material is to illustrate what adultery will do to a man's wife and children. When a man chooses to enter into marriage, he has to realize the great responsibility God places on him. The Apostle Paul told husbands to *"love your wives, as Christ loved the church and gave himself up for her, that he might sanctify her, having cleansed her by the washing of water with the word, so that he might present the church to himself in splendor without spot or wrinkle or any such thing, that she might be holy and without blemish. In the same way, husbands should love their wives as their own bodies. He who loves his wife loves himself"* (Eph. 5:25-28). He explains that husbands are to have the same sincere love and the same fidelity that Christ illustrates to His own bride. While this comparison is sobering, it is within the ability of every man to have this loving, monogamous relationship with his wife. What, though, happens when a man fails? What is the outcome for the woman who has placed her total trust in him?

First, a man must realize the injury to which he is subjecting a woman he has promised to love until death. A sad picture of this break in trust is presented within the writings of the prophet Malachi. As he explained how these men had profaned the Lord's covenant with Him, he stated that the Lord *"was witness between you and the wife of your youth, to whom you have been faithless, though she is your companion and your wife by covenant"* (Mal. 1:14). These men had shown complete disregard for their wives and, as a result, broken the covenant and broken their hearts. The hurt of a broken promise is painful, no matter the promise. The hurt of infidelity, however, goes much deeper since the closest relationship that two humans can experience has been violated. Husbands must realize that no amount of temporary pleasure can equate to the lifetime of hurt created by infidelity. They must also realize that the most fundamental way they are commanded to treat wives has been violated. Peter stated that husbands are to *"live with your wives in an understanding way, showing honor to the woman as the weaker vessel"* (1 Pet. 3:7). The basic makeup of emotion differs radically between men and women. Peter commands husbands to recognize this difference and to treat wives in a godly and acceptable way. The entire idea behind this verse is shattered when a man chooses to cheat on his wife. Far from treating her as a precious vessel, he shows contempt for the vows he has taken and shows no concern for her emotional wellbeing.

Second, and most important, a man must realize the spiritual danger in which he places his wife when he becomes involved in adultery. Peter completed his thoughts about how men should treat their wives by telling husbands to remember that their wives are *"heirs with you of the grace of life"* and that there is a responsibility to treat wives in a godly manner so that *"prayers may not be hindered"* (1 Pet. 3:7b). While his own soul is certainly in jeopardy of being lost, he may very well present a stumbling block over which his own wife may fall. Studies reveal that when a man has an affair, his wife may seek to retaliate by also being unfaithful. An article by Colleen Oakley reveals this thought. In interviewing women who had been subjected to unfaithful husbands, she found this sentiment expressed. The woman being interviewed stated: *"I was very angry, but I was also very hurt, because I felt like I wasn't enough for him – like there was something I wasn't doing for him as his wife, which is why he felt the need to go outside of our marriage," . . . . "I cheated on him – mostly for revenge, but in retrospect it was also because I wanted validation. I wanted to know that I was still desirable to other men."*[5] While revenge is never a justifiable act, a man must realize the cloud of emotion he introduces when he fails to honor his marriage vows. He may very well place his wife in a situation where she is tempted to commit the same ungodly act. Even for a wife who remains loyal to her cheating husband, her spiritual strength and vitality may be curtailed so that growth does not occur as it should. A man must realize the danger he is placing not only himself in, but also the danger in which he places his wife.

Ultimately, a man who sins against his wife through adultery must realize that he has treated her in a way totally unbefitting a husband and fellow-heir of salvation. The Apostle Paul stated, *"For the commandments, 'you shall not commit adultery, you shall not murder, you shall not steal, you*

---

[5] C. Oakley, C. (2012). "Why I Cheated On My Husband." Womansday.com. Retrieved from *http://www.womansday.com/sex-relationships/dating-marriage/why-i-cheated-on-my-husband-124536.*

shall not covet,' and any other commandment are summed up in the word: 'You shall love your neighbor as yourself'" (Rom. 13:9). A man involved in adultery has treated another in a way he would believe totally unacceptable in a reversed situation. He has violated the very heart of Christianity by first not loving God, but also not loving another as himself.

Children are also placed in great jeopardy by a philandering father. Just as with his wife, a man also has great responsibilities to his children. Again, the Apostle Paul explains this. He tells fathers not to *"provoke your children to anger, but bring them up in the discipline and instruction of the Lord"* (Eph. 6:4). The power of influence a parent has over a child is a sobering thought. In many ways, parents will train their children's thoughts about politics, worldviews, social customs, and basically every area of life. This is most definitely the case in spiritual matters as well. The father's role in this is essential. A 1994 Swiss survey bore out how important the father's influence plays in spiritual matters. The survey looked at what produced "church goers" and found the following: "If the father is non-practicing and mother regular, only 2 percent of children will become regular worshippers, and 37 percent will attend irregularly. Over 60 percent of their children will be lost completely to the church."[6] With this vast influence over the spirituality of children, consider the devastating impact an affair would have on the spiritual and moral development of children. The one who is responsible for guiding the home in spiritual growth illustrates contempt for his wife and for his God, while also setting a major obstacle in the path of his children's spiritual growth. Though the Lord's words may have been directed toward new Christians, the principle remains the same for impressionable children when He said, *"Whoever causes one of these little ones who believe in me to sin, it would be better for him if a great millstone were hung around his neck and he were thrown into the sea"* (Mark 9:42). Even a temporary transgression may very well have lasting impact on the young souls who are subjected to this blight. No amount of self-justification can ever account for the spiritual harm caused by adultery. While parents will make mistakes, this is one area where a father can take a stand and make sure that this sin against the Lord stays far from his home.

While the sin of adultery is grievous enough in a one-time affair, what

---

[6] R. Low (2012). "The Truth About Men And Church." *Touchstonemag.com.* Retrieved from *http://www.touchstonemag.com/archives/article.php?id=16-05-024-v#ixzz2Fhe5dEej).*

happens to a man's family when he makes his adulterous relationship permanent? The Lord stated that one who is unfaithful to his or her spouse and marries another commits adultery (Matt. 19:9). Current times consider divorce as a commonality. Few families have not been touched in some way by the pain of divorce. Sadly, a number of these divorces result in the breaking up of a home and the establishment of a new home where a man and "the other woman" now live in adultery. Children are thus subjected to having parents living in separate locations, with one parent in a relationship that is wrong by biblical standards. The father, in this situation, is not only failing to bring his children up in the discipline of the Lord, he is openly setting an example of ungodliness for the child. Besides the hurt of having a broken home, the child is also hurt by not having the godly standard he or she needs to see in a faithful father.

A man's relationship with his family is precious. In no way should he ever seek to jeopardize his marriage or his relationship with his children for the fleeting pleasures of the moment. His actions will have an eternal impact on those to whom he has vowed his complete loyalty and love. This relationship must never be minimized or endangered by the sin of adultery. In fact, a man must work every day to keep this temptation at bay. He never boastfully states that such a sin *"can never happen to me."* Instead, he lives in a way to keep himself under control so that this sin *will never* happen to him. Rather than looking for comfort in the arms of another woman, he daily reaffirms his vows to his wife and seeks solace with no one but her. The relationship begun with her on their wedding day is nourished and allowed to grow richer and fuller with every passing year. With his children, he also reaffirms his devotion to them and to the well-being of their home every day. Rather than having to explain why he committed such a transgression against them, his fidelity allows him to maintain a position of respect in the home. He instructs them on trust and faithfulness, just as Solomon instructed his own sons in the book of Proverbs. He warns them, he helps them to understand, but most importantly, he sets the worthy example of a man who has not gone to an adulterous woman as *"an ox goes to the slaughter, or as a stag caught fast"* (Prov. 7:22).

Conclusion

Is there ever a good reason for adultery? The answer to this question is an obvious no! No amount of self-deluding thought could ever justify this transgression. This idea is well summed up in the words of Marina Pearson. As a psychological professional, Pearson helps patients deal with the problems of adultery. She, however, chose to cheat on her own husband. In writing of this experience, she stated, *"I was still living in the illusive notion that happiness was something that I could acquire from an external source, so I bought into a fantasy. It's a fantasy that I see a lot of my clients buy into, which is that there is a fairy tale, one-sided man that exists to bring happiness up on a silver platter. . . .This of course wasn't true and to this day, still isn't. In fact, the whole ordeal stressed me out and exposed me to more confusion and unhappiness."*[7] Many men delude themselves in the same way. They believe that "the other woman" can satisfy their needs and make them feel young and alive. Such feelings are illusive and may very well destroy the reality of the true happiness that can be found in a home where the father leads his family spiritually upward. Any man tempted to be unfaithful must consider the cost of his decision. While it is a grievous sin against his family, he must also know that it is a grievous sin against God. It illustrates that the foundation of his faith is weak and that his soul is in great danger. He must take the drastic actions that the Lord speaks of in figuratively plucking out eyes and cutting off hands to remove a temptation that may very well bring his soul, and possibly the souls of his family, into an eternally wrong relationship with the Lord. An honest look at his relationship with God and his love and responsibility for his family will quickly drive the fleeting, pleasure filled thoughts of adultery away. He will be the better man for it.

---

[7] M. Pearson (November 30, 2012). "Confession: Why I Cheated On My Husband." *Magazine.foxnews.com*. Retrieved from *http://magazine.foxnews.com /love/confession-why-i-cheated-my-husband*.

The Father:
Spiritual Leader of the Home

Justin McCorkle

Thousands of people assembled and awaited words from this great leader. In a time before microphones or sound systems, voices were hushed so that all would hear the last great delivery of this now aged commander. Raising his eyes to the crowd, Joshua knows that these people had put their trust in him. Years ago they had been homeless and wandering through the wilderness. Now they had a land to call their own. Blood had been spilled. Loved ones had been lost along the way. But, at the end of his life, Joshua is still looking forward.

Opening his mouth, Joshua begins, "Thus says the Lord, the God of Israel" (Josh. 24:2). He recounts their shared victories and remembers that every one is a blessing from God. Joshua then challenges the people to live for the God who has done so much for them. This speech continues to echo throughout the ages. How many of us can quote Joshua's words, "Choose for yourselves today whom you will serve . . . but as for me and my house, we will serve the Lord" (Josh. 24:15)? Truly, Joshua was a great leader of

Justin McCorkle was born September 24, 1984 and raised in Splendora, TX. He attended Stephen F. Austin State University in Nacogdoches, TX where he finished a Bachelor's degree in Communications in 2007, with a double-minor in History and Business. He married the love of his life, Kelly Moulder, in 2006 and with her has a son, Jackson McCorkle, and a daughter, Avy McCorkle. He preached his first sermon in 2002 and began working with the Maple Street church of Christ in Liberty, TX in 2005. From 2006 until 2012 he worked with the West Austin Street congregation in Nacogdoches, TX and is currently an evangelist with the Mauriceville church of Christ in Mauriceville, TX. Justin has also made multiple trips preaching the gospel to El Salvador, Central America.

the nation, but these words reveal more about Joshua than that he knew how to lead a nation; he also knew how to lead a family.

In this study we are seeking to reflect upon the role of the Father as the spiritual leader of the home. So often we hear lessons and do studies on the issues of marriage, marital roles, and the role of the father, but the issue of family leadership is often neglected.

Just as a person can have the title of Manager in some business and yet be an ineffectual leader, so can we be husbands and fathers and yet fail to lead our families in a godly manner. Our goal as servants of God should be, first and foremost, to excel in our spiritual walk for the glory of our Master. As the role of father is a God-sanctioned, God-designed, and God-instructed role, we ought to be seeking to excel in fulfilling the important duties our Heavenly Father has committed to our care.

Leadership Defined
Too often young men are instructed to be the heads of their families yet are given no instruction on how to lead. I vividly recall the frustrations I faced as a newlywed regarding this new role. Young men tend to focus more on the commands God has given to their new wife, specifically submission (Eph. 5:22), than they do the commands given to them. It is often not long before a cyclical pattern of animosity begins and the Lord's pattern for the home is soon forgotten.

Rather than focusing on the wife's role, husbands ought to focus on becoming godly leaders for their families that deserve praise and submission. It is a shame that many men do not have a desire to grow as the leader of the family. As John MacArthur rightly states,

> People who are content with what they don't know, happy to remain ignorant about what they don't understand, complacent about what they haven't solved – such people cannot lead. If you want to find a leader, look for someone who is asking the right questions and genuinely looking for answers (MacArthur, 40).

I pray that we can all purpose to ask the right questions about leading the home and genuinely look for godly answers.

Leadership is earned. God has appointed the husband as the head of the family. As Paul writes, "For the husband is the head of the wife, as Christ also is the head of the church. . ." (Eph. 5:23). While this position is one assigned by God, without effective leadership skills the husband can seriously damage the faith of his wife and children. John Maxwell, a world famous author on leadership, makes the observation, "True leadership cannot be awarded, appointed, or assigned. It comes only from influence, and that cannot be mandated. It must be earned" (Maxwell, 13). Leadership is influence. A man may be given the office of king, but that does not make him a leader. In fact, his leadership could be so poor that he loses his office because of it – much like Rehoboam (1 Kings 12:1-16). Is the same not true in the family? It is certainly possible that our marriages may end in unscriptural divorce even though the Master condemns it in Matthew 19:1-10.

Have we, as husbands, considered that we must earn the respect of our wives? While they are commanded to respect us, we may be putting a great stumbling block in their way if we are not laboring to be worthy of it!

Leadership is learned. How, then, does one become a great leader? Many labor under the false notion that we are either born leaders or we are not – that we have no say in the matter. While some have natural talents for leadership that assist them, anyone can learn to improve his leadership skills. Numerous biblical examples illustrate this point to us.

Although very little is known about Joshua's early life, he was mentored by Moses in preparation for the important position in which he would later be placed. Moses called upon him to assist in the battle with the Amalekites (Exod. 17:8-13) and, from that point on, Joshua accompanied Moses at every significant event. Joshua was not ready to lead the people in Exodus 17, but he was ready by the time he was announced as Moses' successor (Num. 27:18-20)!

Jesus developed the apostles into leaders, as well. Taking a tax collector, a zealot, fishermen, etc. at the beginning, Jesus trained these men to be ambassadors of the faith culminating in His charge, "Go into all the world and preach the gospel to all creation" (Mark 16:15). These men were not born ready for such a task – they had to be trained and equipped! Throughout the gospel we find this process taking place. They were sometimes rebuked, oftentimes challenged, warned concerning temptations, and shown by example from the Great Leader what leadership truly is. The same is true for fathers today. We may not currently be great leaders of the home – but we can improve!

Leadership cannot be outsourced. Are you interested in more effectively leading your home? Undoubtedly, some are not. I humbly suggest to the

Bible student that all husbands and fathers are called to be leaders. And not just leaders, but great leaders.

Was Joshua speaking out of turn when he said those famous words, "As for me and for my house, we will serve the Lord" (Josh. 24:15)? How could he speak for what his family was going to do? Not only is his headship of the family shown, but also his confidence in the influence he had with them. We should strive to have such a spiritual influence in our families that we can be equally as bold concerning their continued faithfulness. Increasing influence means improving leadership skills!

Paul gave the command to all husbands – you and me included – "each individual among you also is to love his own wife even as himself. . ." and also, "Fathers, do not provoke your children to anger, but bring them up in the training and admonition of the Lord" (Eph. 5:33; 6:4) Both of these passages illustrate the individual nature of the commands of God. God commands *me* to love my wife and He commands *me* to raise my children correctly. Knowing that such a task has been given to us, why would we delay our efforts to improve our leadership of the home?

Leadership requires trust. Trust and honesty are requirements of all Christians and all leaders as well. Jesus creates a mighty standard of honesty when He commands, "let your statement be, 'Yes, yes' or 'No, no'. . ." (Matt. 5:37). Jesus sets a foundation of stability and trust in the home by explaining,

> "For this reason a man shall leave his father and mother and be joined to his wife, and the two shall become one flesh." So they are no longer two, but one flesh. What therefore God has joined together, let no man separate (Matt. 19:5-6).

Husbands and wives should be able to trust one another to be faithful and loyal to the new union created by God. Our wives and children should also be able to trust that we will provide love and guidance to the home. In too many homes this is not the case.

A recent news editorial pictured the disconnect between husbands and wives in many homes well. A woman was married to a wealthy banker and she had been well provided for financially. However, she felt no love from her spouse. After years of emotional neglect, she decided to offer him a "resignation letter" from the marriage with a six month notice. After describing her financial blessings and luxurious vacations she remembers, "I wondered how many other women would jump at the chance of stepping into my shoes. Or would they – like me – [realize] that no amount of money can compensate for a loveless marriage?" (Cunningham). While her approach was not a scriptural one, her words can help husbands to understand what John Maxwell calls the "Law of Connection."

Any gospel preacher can attest to the truth of these words: "People don't care how much you know until they know how much you care" (Maxwell, 116). Any leader needs to understand this truth, especially leaders of a family. If our wives or children feel as though we do not care for them or for their souls we will lose the ability to influence them to righteousness. A husband must consider the spiritual strength of his wife, encourage her growth, and lead by example. If he does not do those things, she will assume he does not care about her spiritual condition. With children this truth is even more apparent. Do your children know that you care deeply about spiritual things? How many fathers treat the Lord and His church carelessly through sporadic attendance and prioritizing entertainment over worship? Do these same men expect to influence their children spiritually? Our children need to know that we care about the Lord, their souls, and our own souls or they will not care what we "know" about God and His word!

In further explanation Maxwell says, "You develop credibility with people when you connect with them and show that you genuinely care and want to help them. And as a result, they usually respond in kind and want to help you" (Maxwell, 116). There is biblical truth in these statements. Remember what Jesus told the apostles:

> A new commandment I give to you, that you love one another, even as I have loved you, that you also love one another. By this all men will know that you are My disciples, if you have love for one another (John 13:34-35).

We strive to practice this teaching in Christ's churches. We understand that evangelism will not be successful if the body of Christ is not a picture of love to those outside. They should see us and want those bonds of connection as we have. They should see from our examples that we care about one another and also for them.

This principle stands true in our homes. If we want credibility with our families, they need to know that we love them. We need to show our love to them. Only then will we be able to lead them as God desires.

Leadership requires servitude. If we are to learn about leadership from the greatest leader, Jesus, then we must learn to be servants to those we seek to lead.

> [Jesus] got up from supper, and laid aside His garments; and taking a towel, He girded Himself. Then He poured water into the basin, and began to wash the disciples' feet and to wipe them with the towel with which He was girded. . . . [Jesus said,] "If I then, the Lord and the Teacher, washed your feet, you also ought to wash one another's feet" (John 13:4-5, 14).

The washing of His disciples' feet not only shows the humility of our Lord but also His understanding of leadership. Max Dawson observes,

> [Jesus'] way of leading stands in stark contrast to the leadership style of the world. . . . Jesus taught servant leadership. Jesus' leadership was not merely based on having authority; it was based on having a servant's heart (Dawson, 51).

Servitude is a necessary characteristic for the one who seeks to lead. If we are unwilling to serve others we may ask why we want to be leaders in the first place. We are not to seek after selfish gain and disregard the needs of others. As Christians, we are seeking to be a light that leads others to Christ.

As one author writes, "Servant-leaders are *healers* in the sense of *making whole* by helping others to a larger and nobler vision and purpose than they would be likely to attain for themselves" (Greenleaf, 240). In other words, our leadership is about seeking to attain good for the people we lead. Without this understanding of leadership we may confuse "leading" with "lording."

Leadership requires vision and purpose. "Leading" carries with it the assumption of a destination. Real leadership requires vision and purpose. Whether in the workplace, on the battlefield, or in the home, the leader needs a goal and a reason for accomplishing the goal in order to be effective and unite the people. What goal is greater than receiving an eternal heavenly reward alongside our wife and children? Our vision is to "be at home with the Lord" (2 Cor. 5:8)!

Being a father is not simply about raising "successful" children by worldly standards. We are seeking to instill in our young ones a love for the Lord, a thirst for His word, and sure footing on the path to eternal life. Our struggle is knowing how to accomplish this mighty task. All of the instruction the Scripture gives to fathers is meant to equip us for this good work. We are also blessed to be able to learn to apply the scriptural instruction in our homes by studying the good examples of spiritual men like Joshua and Peter.

Peter as a Family Leader

Most often, when we discuss the apostle Peter, we are referring to his work in preaching the gospel for the Lord, his mistakes during the Lord's ministry, or the growth of his faith. However, a character study of Peter has other excellent lessons for us as well. Consider briefly his growth as a leader in the pages of Scripture and his application of those principles to the home.

Peter as a leader. Peter, then called Simon, first heard of Jesus through his brother, Andrew. Hearing Andrew's news, "We have found the Messiah," Simon went to meet the One who had stirred his brother's interest. Scripture tells us, "Jesus looked at him and said, 'You are Simon the son of John; you shall be called Cephas' (which is translated Peter)" (John 1:40-42). The word "Peter" simply means "rock." MacArthur observes,

> This young man named Simon, who would become Peter, was impetuous, impulsive, and overeager. He needed to become like a rock, so that is what Jesus named him. From then on, the Lord could gently chide or commend him just by using one name or the other (MacArthur, 35).

It was some time later that Jesus called Peter to leave behind his work as a fisherman to follow Him (Luke 4:10). Although Peter was outspoken and bold at this point in life, he was not nearly the leader that he would become over the following years.

Peter learned how to be a leader from the Great Leader Himself. Jesus knew His plan for the disciples from the beginning and sought to prepare them for the task. As Jesus sat with Peter after the resurrection, He reaffirmed the importance of the coming work that Peter and the apostles would have to do. John recounts the scene: "So when they had finished breakfast, Jesus said to Simon Peter, 'Simon, son of John, do you love Me more than these?' He said to Him, 'Yes, Lord; You know that I love You.' He said to him, 'Tend My lambs'" (John 21:15). As the account continues Jesus asks twice more if Peter loves Him. In frustration, Peter finally says, "Lord, You know all things; You know that I love You" (John 21:17). Peter's frustration is understandable. It was, in his mind, as if Jesus was doubting his love. However, the Lord was actually explaining to Peter that his love for Jesus should drive His care for Jesus' sheep. We should also note that, just as Peter had denied the Lord three times (Matt. 26:34), he was asked to affirm His love three times. Peter was to be a leader in the faith of Christ. He would touch many lives and bring many to the Truth. His motivation must be pure. Jesus had been teaching Peter this lesson throughout His ministry. We can see from Jesus' example, as Peter did, that spiritual leadership requires a love of truth, a love of souls, and a willingness to suffer.

The love of truth Jesus instilled in Peter and the apostles stands in sharp contrast to the power hungry religious leaders of their day. One example is regarding the baptism administered by John. The chief priests and the elders of the people came to Jesus in order to question the authority by which He worked miracles. A truth seeker would have known the obvious; miracles are a confirmation from God of the word that is spoken (Heb. 2:3-4). However, these men were not sincere. Matthew records,

> Jesus said to them, "I will ask you one thing, which if you tell Me, I will also tell you by what authority I do these things. The baptism of John was from what source, from heaven or from men?" And they began reasoning among themselves, saying, "If we say, 'From heaven,' He will say to us, 'Then why did you not believe him?' But if we say, 'From men,' we fear the people; for they all regard John as a prophet" (Matt. 21:24-26).

The "reasoning" of these supposed leaders considers the response they would be given from either Jesus or the people, but they never stop to consider what is truth! Peter and the disciples were to take the lesson as well: never let your love of power become stronger than your love of truth. Eventually the disciples learned the lesson. Does a husband and father not need the same lesson? Warring with family for power in the home may not be the best way to attain the influence that leaders seek.

Another lesson was shown to Peter and his disciples repeatedly: love should drive the quest for souls. The Scriptures reveal that Jesus' presence, preaching, and suffering were all rooted in His love of man. This fact is in sharp contrast to the religious leaders of Jesus' day. It is not unfair to characterize the scribes and Pharisees as racist and hateful. The Jews so despised the Samaritans that they would not speak to them or even travel through Samaritan lands! Jesus had little concern for these hateful traditions of men. Not only does Jesus have an entire conversation with a Samaritan woman (John 4:7-26), but John also tells us that He even spent two days preaching the good news in a Samaritan city (John 4:40-43)! The Lord's disdain for Jewish animosities is also apparent during His visit to Tyre and Sidon. A woman came to Him seeking relief for her demon-possessed daughter. The disciples, annoyed with her pleading, asked Jesus to send her away. This opportunity is used as a teaching example for the future apostles to all mankind. Jesus informs the woman in their presence, "It is not good to take the children's bread and throw it to the dogs" (Matt. 15:26). These harsh words picture the common Jewish thinking of the time. When the woman responds with kindness and humility, Jesus says of her what the Jews would have ignored and what His disciples would have overlooked, "O woman, your faith is great; it shall be done for you as you wish" (Matt. 15:28). Truly, the disciples left that table with a deeper understanding of Jesus' love for souls. Does a father not need the same instruction? Our leadership of the home is not to be rooted in anything but love for the souls of those under our care. Our wife and our children have souls that can be lost. When we speak to them, let it be in a manner that can win them for Christ.

Besides these things, Jesus was willing to suffer for the truth and showed His disciples that they must have the same fortitude. Jesus repeatedly explains throughout His ministry that suffering and death await Him at the hands of the Jews. However, such a fate was not for Him alone. He tells the twelve beforehand,

> . . .beware of men, for they will hand you over to the courts and scourge you in their synagogues; and you will even be brought before governors and kings for My sake. . . .You will be hated by all because of My name, but it is the one who endures to the end who will be saved. . . .Therefore everyone who confesses Me before men, I will also confess him before My Father who is in heaven (Matt. 10:17-18, 22, 32).

Jesus was not seeking to discourage their preaching, but rather to encourage them to stand strong in the face of it! Matthew records the words Jesus tells Peter concerning his fate:

> "Truly, truly, I say to you, when you were younger, you used to gird yourself and walk wherever you wished; but when you grow old, you will stretch out your hands and someone else will gird you, and bring you where you do not wish to go." Now this He said, signifying by what kind of death he would glorify God. And when He had spoken this, He said to Him, "Follow Me!" (John 21:18-19).

Peter understood from this point forward that loving truth and loving souls sometimes leads to suffering. All Christians should remember this principle. Do not husbands need to have the same fortitude in the home? Our wives and children will not be perfect, just as we ourselves are not perfect. We will be tempted to cast aside love and replace it with bitterness. It is for this reason Paul instructs, "Husbands, love your wives and do not be embittered against them" (Col. 3:19). We will sometimes have to suffer for walking peacefully and with love towards our families. We must be willing to suffer in whatever way is necessary so that what is good can be victorious through us.

Peter learned in these ways and many others what it takes to be a spiritual leader of Jesus' flock. We honor Peter by recognizing that, as best we can see, he applied these principles to his home as well.

Peter leading the home. Scripture tells us very little of Peter's family. Extra-biblical sources shed little more light on the topic. However, the little we have is very beneficial for those who seek to learn from him about family leadership. We can see from these writings that Peter was married, continued to care for his wife while doing the work of an apostle, gave godly advice to others on leading the home, and offered a glorious vision and purpose for his family.

The New Testament plainly reveals to us that Peter was married. Luke comments in passing, "[Jesus] entered Simon's home. Now Simon's mother-in-law was suffering from a high fever, and they asked Him to help her" (Luke 4:38). If Peter had a mother-in-law then he must have had a wife. Immediately we can see a point of application for modern husbands concerning the care and concern of in-laws. We do not know if his mother-in-law was in his home permanently or temporarily, but we do see that Peter extended his love and concern to the mother of his wife in the same manner he would towards his wife. Not only is he showing love towards one in need (James 2:15-16), but he is revealing how he leads his wife. Certainly her respect for Peter grows by witnessing his concern, especially when Peter asks the Lord for assistance.

There can be no doubt that being asked to leave work behind made the life of a disciple difficult. Life must have become immensely more difficult when Jesus sent the apostles on to the work after His ascension. From the first sermon Peter preached on the day of Pentecost (Acts 2) until just a short while later the number of Christians in Jerusalem grew to be about 5,000 men (Acts 4:4)! There was surely a great deal of demand placed upon Peter and the other apostles in seeking to ground these new converts. Not only that, but also it was not long before there were issues arising that increased demand on the apostles to be in organizational disputes – a task which was promptly assigned to a newly appointed group for the task (Acts 6:1-6). In such a frenzy of responsibility it would be easy for a husband to forget about his wife and give himself completely to his work. While we do not know if Peter had children at this point, if they were grown by the time his work was beginning, or if they were still under his roof, we can be assured that, if Peter children, he would remember their needs – just as he did for his wife.

Paul records for us Peter's efforts to balance his work for the Lord with family by asking the Corinthians, "Do we not have a right to take along a believing wife, even as the rest of the apostles and the brothers of the Lord and Cephas?" (1 Cor. 9:5 – Cephas is the Aramaic name for Peter). Thus we see that Peter did not leave his wife behind for his work. He even took her along in his preaching! The Lord's command to "go into all the world and preach the gospel" (Mark 16:15) did not nullify Peter's responsibilities towards his wife. Paul even acknowledges, "but one who is married is concerned about the things of the world, how he may please his wife, and his interests are divided" (1 Cor. 7:33-34). And rightly so! It can be difficult for men today to strike the appropriate balance between work and family. It is wise for us to remember that if an apostle of Christ can still seek to fulfill his wife's needs then so can we!

The truth is that Peter never separated his faith, his work, and his family. They were all one in the same. He explains to all Christian husbands that the same should be true for them. "You husbands in the same way, live with your wives in an understanding way, as with someone weaker, since she is a woman; and show her honor as a fellow heir of the grace of life, so that your prayers will not be hindered" (1 Pet. 3:7). Peter sought to be understanding towards his wife. It is difficult to be in submission, yet Peter commands it of Christians to "every human institution" (2:13), servants to masters (2:18-20), and wives to husbands (3:1-6). Are these tasks not difficult at times? Truly it is difficult at some points for a wife to be submissive to her husband – especially unbelieving husbands. Therefore, Peter says that husbands need to be "understanding" towards them. Certainly the concept is one of patience and love. He instructs us to show our wives "honor as a fellow heir." In Christ, there is "neither Jew nor Greek, there is neither slave nor free man, there is neither male nor female. . ." (Gal. 3:28). Therefore, we should treat our wives as sisters in Christ, seeking to remove stumbling blocks from their paths instead of placing them. Although in heaven there will be no marriage (Mark 12:24-25), both we and our wives will be judged by God according to how we conduct ourselves "in the body" (2 Cor. 5:10). Does it not logically follow that our primary responsibility as husbands and fathers is to assist in conveying our families to heaven? Peter certainly believed so. Peter says that failing to be godly and responsible will even hinder our prayers.

Little else is given in Scripture regarding Peter's marriage, but there is more to consider regarding the vision and purpose that drove Peter to lead his family. When we last read from Peter he is preparing for his death. He writes,

> I consider it right, as long as I am in this earthly dwelling, to stir you up by way of reminder, knowing that the laying aside of my earthly dwelling is imminent, as also our Lord Jesus Christ has made clear to me. And I will also be diligent that at any time after my departure you will be able to call these things to mind (2 Pet. 1:13-15).

Even as the day of his departure looms closer, Peter is showing the leadership skills he learned from Jesus. In this hour he might have been seeking for pity or some way of escape. Instead, he shows the servant's mind his Lord had taught him. He is seeking the spiritual good of his brothers and sisters in Christ. Despite the lack of biblical testimony about the events following Peter's words, the early Christians maintained traditional accounts of his passing. While their words cannot be verified, it stands to reason that the earliest writers had little cause to misrepresent the death of an apostle. It is said that Peter was arrested and carried to Rome in order to face trial before the emperor Nero. Just as Paul records in 1 Corinthians 9:5, Peter had his wife with him when arrested. Nero was ramping up his persecution against the Christians and now had both Peter and his wife in custody. While any man may speak boldly of his willingness to give his own life for a righteous cause, it becomes more difficult to speak boldly about the death of our loved ones. Peter's wife faced trial before he did and he watched as her sentence of death was announced. In a moment of such emotional strain we gain an understanding of the vision and purpose with which Peter had lead his home. Clement of Alexandria recounts,

> They say, accordingly, that the blessed Peter, on seeing his wife led to death, rejoiced on account of her call and conveyance of home. He called to her very encouragingly and comfortingly, addressing her by name and saying, "Remember the Lord!" Such was the marriage of the blessed and their perfect disposition towards those dearest to them (Clement).

Peter's vision for his home was not nearly as focused on this life as it was the next. Perhaps the last words his wife ever heard were reminders of why we are Christians and why we are willing to "count it all but loss." Our faith is not about this life but about the next. Are we leading our homes in a way that reminds our wife and children of this fact daily? Are we constantly calling out to our wives through our actions to "remember the Lord"? Do our children see in their parents a "perfect disposition towards those dearest to them"? If not, I pray that they can begin to see it in all of our homes today.

Peter learned how to be a leader from Jesus Christ Himself. Those lessons enabled him to lead many souls to Jesus as an apostle and to lead his home in a way that serves as a good example for all of us. Seeing a good example and becoming a good example are separate things.

Applying Godly Leadership Principles to Your Home

How do we apply the principles of leadership and Peter's good example to our own homes? We must understand some important and difficult truths if we want to become family leaders as the Lord wants: It takes time, learning, and love.

Becoming a family leader takes time. Having the desire to improve my leadership of the home does not equate to an over-night change. Although we may immediately implement improvements to our standard way of operating, lasting change will only appear over a longer term. If we seek to be perceived by our wife and children as a leader, then it will take time to retrain their minds to view us in this way. If I have been leading without the feelings of my wife in mind then it will take longer than a week to change her perception of me. It may even take years! Jesus trained the twelve for about three years before sending them out to preach the gospel to all the world. Joshua was trained by Moses for nearly a lifetime before he led the people into Canaan. Why would I then imagine myself capable of effectively leading my home after hearing a sermon or reading a paper? Only through patience, incremental goal setting, and diligent review of ourselves can we expect to develop into godly leaders of the home.

Many times we stumble as a husband because we base our behavior, focus, and leadership on the perception we have of our wife's role. While we need to encourage her to fulfill her duty to her God and her husband, we want to become better leaders even when she is stumbling in her responsibilities. Our improvement will likely spur her on to improvement as well.

Consider the advice Peter gave to wives with unbelieving husbands as an example of patience in marriage:

> In the same way, you wives, be submissive to your own husbands so that even if any of them are disobedient to the word, they may be won without a word by the conduct of their wives, as they observe your chaste and respectful behavior (1 Pet. 3:1-2).

Consider the difficulty that anyone would have in implementing Peter's (and the Holy Spirit's) advice! A wife, especially one who was not raised in a godly home, has a great challenge in fulfilling her role. Do we not also think that leading the home is a challenge? A woman who is struggling to learn how to be submissive and to win her husband "without a word" has a difficult work that will take time to learn. Do we think that implementing good leadership principles in our homes will be "quick and easy"? If so, we are sorely mistaken.

We must patiently invest the time necessary if we want to leave a lasting legacy in our families of godly leadership as Joshua did. Joshua knew at the end of his life that he had taught his family well (Josh. 24:15). It may take us a lifetime, also.

Becoming a family leader takes learning. It needs to be emphasized again that becoming a successful leader takes learning. Time by itself will not accomplish the goals we set for our family as godly men, just as time alone will not make one a faithful person. We know Psalm 119:105 well: "Your word is a lamp to my feet and a light to my path." Scriptural principles should be our cornerstone.

We also need to learn from the successful ones around us the skills necessary to lead godly homes. Even the apostle Paul recognized that experienced husbands and wives should be taking the lead in teaching the young. As he writes to Titus,

> Older men are to be temperate. . . .Older women are to . . . encourage the young women to love their husbands, to love their children, to be sensible . . . being subject to their own husbands, so that the word of God may not be dishonored. Likewise urge the young men to be sensible. . . (Titus 2:2-6).

The implication is that older men and women have something valuable to teach from experience to the newlyweds. We need to be encouraging older ones to take this responsibility seriously in our churches.

In every other area of life – business, trades, sports, etc. – we look to the successful to teach their keys of success to the less experienced. Yet, all too often we neglect seeking marital advice and instruction on home leadership from those who have done it so well before us! We would be spared much heartache if we would humble ourselves in the sight of the Lord and older, godly men in order to learn how to lead.

Are you investing the time necessary to become a great leader of the family? A husband and father is capable of impacting countless souls through the influence he has with his family such as future children, spouses, friends, and co-workers. We ought to take such a thought seriously and approach our homes as devoted leaders who seek to serve those entrusted to our care in a way that will equip them to lead others as well.

Becoming a family leader takes servitude. We often hear that "marriage is an institution." What does that mean? Robert Greenleaf, an author and lecturer of servant leadership, says,

> An institution is a gathering of persons who have accepted a common purpose, and a common discipline to guide the pursuit of that purpose, to the end that each involved person reaches higher fulfillment as a person, through *serving and being served* by the common venture, than would be achieved alone or in a less committed relationship (Greenleaf, 250).

Have you considered that your duty as a husband is to serve your wife in order to assist her in reaching "higher fulfillment" as a Christian? We cannot accomplish that goal without becoming her servant, just as the apostles could not lead others to Christ without becoming servants to those they taught (1 Cor. 9:19-25). The merely authoritarian view of the husband's role is not effective leadership by any standard. Greenleaf also points out, "When someone is moved atop a pyramid, that person no longer has colleagues, only subordinates" (Greenleaf, 76). What a sad state our homes are in if our wives view themselves as mere subordinates to us! May we serve in such a way that they see our love – and re-choose us as their leaders day by day!

Becoming a family leader takes love. All of our efforts to influence our families is doomed to failure without a sincere love for our wives and children. A gospel preacher once studied with a man whose marriage was failing. The man exclaimed, "I would die for her!" That may have been the case, but he was unwilling to live for her. Our culture's understanding of "love" has been thoroughly polluted by selfishness, lust, and greed. However, this misunderstanding has appeared throughout man's history.

We are told, "Absalom the son of David had a beautiful sister whose name was Tamar, and Amnon the son of David loved her" (2 Sam. 13:1). Amnon had the type of "love" that many today have which is driven by selfishness rather than the good of another. He raped his half-sister as soon as he found opportunity. Soon thereafter we read,

> Then Amnon hated [Tamar] with a very great hatred; for the hatred with which he hated her was greater than the love with which he had loved her. And Amnon say to her, "Get up, go away!" (v. 15).

This account may seem unbelievable, but how often do we see the same event, in principle, play out in marriages today? All who marry speak of their love for one another. All who marry desire one another. Yet, most marriages in this country end in divorce! The hatred that grows becomes stronger than the love that united – then families divide. This selfish love is not the type of love godly leaders should have towards those under their care. Consider the love God commands us to have towards our wife and children.

"Husbands, love your wives. . ." (Eph. 5:25). Paul's statement is simple, but fulfilling the command in the way God desires is not always as simple. The word Paul uses, *agape,* means "love, i.e. affection or benevolence" (Strong's Greek). William Barclay goes further, defining it as "unconquerable benevolence" and "undefeatable good will" (Barclay). L. A. Stauffer says, "*Agape* is benevolent and good even when it is undeserved" (Stauffer, 24). The world tells us that "love" is the feeling we have when we are around someone we care about. God tells us that love is the choice we make to do good even when we are tempted to do otherwise. A husband will be tempted to act selfishly, be embittered towards his spouse, and lord his will over the family. We will then be tempted to covet our neighbor's wife when the butterflies we felt in our stomachs on the wedding day fail – as though the problem was with our wife rather than in ourselves. It is for these reasons and others we are enjoined by the Lord to choose a better way.

Agape is a love that can be commanded – even contrary to emotional desire. Jesus uses this type of love in the Sermon on the Mount to describe how we should behave towards those who wish us harm:

> But I say to you, love [*agape*] your enemies and pray for those who persecute you, so that you may be sons of your Father who is in heaven. . . . For if you love those who love you, what reward do you have? Do not even the tax collectors do the same? (Matt. 5:44-46).

Jesus says that we can choose to treat a person differently than they treat us. Is the same lesson not true regarding our wife? We are to seek her good and be benevolent towards her even when she may be acting in a way that does not deserve respect. This love is not just a commandment of God, but a need of the wife. Our *agape* gives her stability and security. It is an essential part of leading the home. Just as a husband needs the respect of his wife in order to be fulfilled, she needs this unconditional benevolence from her husband in order to be fulfilled. We must tend to her needs if we seek to influence her. Paul continues in Ephesians 5 to use two illustrations that prove the point.

The apostle commands husbands to love their wives "just as Christ also loved the church" (Eph. 5:25). Is the leadership and headship of Jesus a burden to the church or a blessing to it? We know it is a blessing. Jesus "gave Himself up for [the church]" (Eph. 5:25). It was for our interest that He sacrificed. It was to better our condition. There was no selfishness in His motivations. All Jesus did was "so that He might sanctify her" (Eph. 5:26) and "present to Himself the church in all her glory" (Eph. 5:27). If Jesus' example of love towards the church is the manner in which we should love our wives then we have a great task before us! Are we leading our homes in a way that will bring about the good of our wives? Do we speak to them in such a way that will help to save their souls or do we incite them to despise our headship? Our leadership should cause them to love our headship of the home. A husband's poor leadership can cause a wife to despise Christ's order for the family and cause both husband and wife to wander into sin. These things ought not be so. If we will love our wives as Christ loves the church then she will love and respect us as the church loves and respects Jesus.

Next, Paul commands husbands to "love their own wives as their own bodies" (Eph. 5:28). Our natural inclinations cause us to preserve and care for ourselves. We should extend this instinct to our wives. "He who loves his own wife loves himself" (Eph. 5:28). Paul continues, "for no one ever hated his own flesh, but nourishes and cherishes it" (Eph. 5:29). Sometimes word studies are beneficial in understanding the author's purpose. The word for "nourishes" (*ektrephō*) means "to bring up to maturity. . ." (Strong's Greek). Just as we care for ourselves in order to come to maturity, we should be doing the same for our wives. It is not that they are incapable of nourishing themselves. Rather, as the head of the home we are seeking to be a blessing to their efforts. We should create an environment for them that encourages positive spiritual, emotional, and physical health. Good leaders in every field seek to nourish their followers. We should as well!

"Cherishes"(*thalpō*) is defined as, "to warm, hence to cherish" (Strong's Greek). Just as a hen gathers her chicks in order to warm and protect them, just as we seek warmth and protection from the cold, so our wives should find in us someone who will cherish them. Both literally and figuratively, we should wrap them in a warm embrace through the storms and trials of life. If we do so, we will love them as ourselves and we will find a person who loves our headship *because* of our leadership.

Loving our wives as we ought is at times a challenge. It tends to be easier to feel in our hearts love for our children, but equally difficult to properly express. Only the most selfish of men lack the natural affection for their young. Such abandonment is rare amongst God's people though it is a growing epidemic in our society. Selfishness, though, is expressed repeatedly in action by many husbands towards their children despite the emotion fathers feel in their hearts. What does it profit, fellow fathers, if we love inwardly but outwardly are distant, cold, inconsistent, and resentful? This selfishness often becomes apparent through a lack of patience with our young. It is for this reason Paul says, "Fathers, do not exasperate your children, so that they will not lose heart" (Col. 3:21). Strong's Greek says "exasperate" (*erethizō*) means, "(to stir to anger); to stir up." Why would fathers have to be told not to exasperate their children? I formerly lacked understanding in this regard. Then my son became a toddler. The temptation to stir our children to anger and be overly heavy-handed with them comes easily. We must deny these temptations.

So many tasks are difficult in raising children and wear on the patience of a parent. Paul knows that fathers tend to lose their patience and become burdensome to the godly development of their children. Paul pointedly tells fathers that children can lose heart if they are overbearing or lack patience in raising their young! The spiritual side of the child is of greatest interest to Paul and it should be to us as well. What a sad fate for a child to refuse his father's teachings of God because of a father's exasperation. It can and does happen. May we strive to be patient and loving leaders for our children who balance both sides of our responsibilities to discipline and be patient. Let us look to our God for a perfect fatherly example as does the author of Hebrews. Regarding discipline we are told, "Those whom the Lord loves He disciplines, and He scourges every son whom He receives" (Heb. 12:6). We must discipline our children "diligently" or "promptly" as good leaders and loving fathers (Prov. 13:24). We relinquish our headship and leadership of the home when we outsource this responsibility solely to our wives.

Furthermore the author reminds, "we had earthly fathers to discipline us, and we respected them; shall we not much rather be subject to the Father of spirits, and live?" (Heb. 12:9). Discipline is necessary in order for our children to respect us. If only the mother disciplines, then only the mother will be respected by the young. It is for this reason we paid our own fathers respect. We are also reminded, "[Our fathers] disciplined us for a short time as seemed best to them, but He disciplines us for our good, so that we may share His holiness" (Heb. 12:10). We ought to be disciplining our children for their good not as a release of anger if we are to imitate God. What is our goal in discipline? Is it not to bring about respect for what is right? We are seeking, as God does, to bring our children to an understanding of holiness. Sometimes we need fewer "rules" for our children – those that point to holiness and respect – and those rules more strictly and consistently enforced. None of these biblical goals is easy to achieve. Yet, we should press on to the goal and endure the hardships necessary to make changes because, besides our wives and children, we have love for our God.

Our God is the maker and designer of the family unit. Our labor in our homes can be likened to our labor in His church. He designed the church and set in order the positions within it for the good of His children and the advancement of His gospel (Eph. 4:11-12). We are to behave properly in His church lest we become stumblingblocks to those we seek to edify (1 Tim. 3:15). He has entrusted us with His word so that we do not have to trust the wisdom of men to tell us the path to salvation (1 Cor. 2:1-5). Are these lessons not true in our homes as well? The Lord has designed the family roles: father, mother, and children. He has instructed on what is proper behavior in the home; we can decimate the lives of one another if we forsake His instruction. He has given His word to instruct us in these things so that we do not have to rely on the advice of fallible men and women alone. May we seek to bring God the glory in the church and in the home.

Final Thoughts

Sadducees came to Jesus questioning Him about marriage. They spoke an elaborate story concerning a woman who married a man with six other brothers. Her husband died before having a child and his brother married her to bring forth children for his deceased brother as the law of Moses stipulated for her benefit. However, this man died also. The situation repeated until all seven brothers had died and the woman died as well. They asked the Lord, "In the resurrection therefore, which one's wife will she be? For all seven had married her" (Luke 20:33). One can imagine the frustration the Lord must have had, knowing these men's hearts. The story was nearly an absurdity in its unlikeliness of occurrence and they were only interested in His answer in order to suggest that belief in a resurrection is ridiculous. However, Jesus speaks an explanation to them that will remove their confidence and silence them for a time. He says,

> The sons of this age marry and are given in marriage, but those who are considered worthy to attain to that age and the resurrection from the dead, neither marry nor are given in marriage; for they cannot even die

anymore, because they are like angels, and are sons of God, being sons of the resurrection (Luke 20:34-35).

The Lord's words serve as a worthy lesson for us as well. There will come a time in which we are neither married nor will we be given in marriage. One day our bodies will be changed and we will ascend to meet the Lord in the air, "and so we shall always be with the Lord" (1 Thess. 4:17). At that time, we will be only "sons of God" and will worship the Lord in His holiness. We should be leading our homes in a way that reflects this fact. My wife will not always be my wife, but I pray that she is always a child of God and that we are in our heavenly home together. I pray the same for my children. The loving embrace of the Lord is something to be longed for by us all, but embracing Him with our families could only add to the joy of the moment.

This end is the definition of successful leadership for us. We are husbands and fathers. We are God-purposed to help carry our families to this scene of final and eternal glory. All we do and all we are should be given to this end. I pray success for you and yours. I pray that our families can all meet in that place together.

Works Cited

Barclay, William. *Barclay's Daily Study Bible Commentary New Testament.* [Cd-Rom] Logos Research Systems Inc., June 1, 2001.

Bible, NASB(95).

Clement of Alexandria [c. 195], ANF 2.541.

Cunningham, Tessa. "The day I resigned from my marriage." *www.daily-mail.co.uk/femail/article-2212024.* October 2, 2012.

Dawson, Max. *Kingdom Leaders.* Florida College Press, November, 2011.

Greenleaf, Robert K. *Servant Leadership.* Paulist Press, New York/Mahwah, N.J. 2002.

MacArthur, John. *Twelve Ordinary Men.* Thomas Nelson, Inc., 2002.

Maxwell, John C. *The 21 Irrefutable Laws of Leadership.* Thomas Nelson, Inc., 2007.

Stauffer, L. A. *Family Life: A Biblical Perspective.* Guardian of Truth Foundation, 1989.

The Threat of Pornography: Making Sex an Idol

Ron Halbrook

But fornication, and all uncleanness, or covetousness, let it not be once named among you, as becometh saints; neither filthiness, nor foolish talking, nor jesting, which are not convenient: but rather giving of thanks.

Ron Halbrook was born in Indianola, MS in 1946, moved to Belle Glade, FL in 1951, and grew up and graduated from high school there. He preached for the Southside Church of Christ in Belle Glade in the summer of 1964. During his years at Florida College (1964-67), his preaching continued with the Central congregation near Live Oak, FL (fall 1965), the West Sixth St. church in Pine Bluff, AR (summer 1966), and the Hercules Ave. church in Clearwater, FL (1966-67).

During 1967-73 Ron labored with the Wooley Springs church near Athens, AL, taught high school at Athens Bible School, and finished a degree in history at Athens College (1969). He labored with the Broadmoor church in Nashville, TN 1973-78 (and completed a master's degree in church history at Vanderbilt University, 1979), the Knollwood church in Xenia, OH 1978-82 (with Mike Willis in a two-preacher arrangement), the church in Midfield, AL 1982-84, and the West Columbia, TX church in 1984-97. In August of 1997, he began work in a two-preacher arrangement with Andy Alexander at the Hebron Lane Church of Christ in Shepherdsville, KY. Andy moved to Bowling Green, KY in 2003 and Steven Deaton took his place at Hebron Lane in June 2004. This arrangement allows Ron to hold several gospel meetings and make four trips to the Philippines each year. He has made fifty trips to the Philippines since 1995.

Ron's articles have appeared in such religious journals as *Truth Magazine, Searching the Scriptures,* and *The Preceptor.* Other writing includes tracts (*Unity With Christ & Christians; Honorable Marriage, The Original Church of Christ*), booklets (*Trends Pointing Toward a New Apostasy; Understanding the Controversy*), and books (*The Doctrine of Christ & Unity of the Saints; Halbrook-Freeman Debate on Marriage, Divorce, & Remarriage*). Ron married Donna Bell in 1967. They have three children: Jonathan, David, and Deborah. Jonathan (married Tanya Bryant; children: Payton, Cole, Paige, Abbie), David (married Starla Page; children, Joel), and Deborah (married Jamie Williams; children: Timothy, Seth).

> For this ye know, that no whoremonger, nor unclean person, nor covetous man, who is an idolater, hath any inheritance in the kingdom of Christ and of God (Eph. 5:3-5).

The Ephesians were warned not to become obsessed with sexual desires so as to elevate sex to the status of a god, for this is only another form of idolatry. The idolatrous image of Pornography lures many souls into The Pantheon of Sexual Idolatry. Such idols are nothing in the end but mere expressions of man's rebellion against the true and living God. Men who worship them are cast into the abyss of utter darkness, far away from the God of love and the love of God.

Pornography is "the depiction of erotic behavior (as in pictures or writing) intended to cause sexual excitement,"[1] or as defined in a legal dictionary, "The representation in books, magazines, photographs, films, and other media of scenes of sexual behavior that are erotic or lewd and are designed to arouse sexual interest."[2] Our legal system says so-called soft-core pornography is protected by the First Amendment to the U.S. Constitution but not more explicit hard-core materials. The courts often flounder in applying laws against obscenity because they claim they cannot easily distinguish between what is soft and what is hard-core.

The Bible does not flounder in condemning all such materials as sinful and destructive to moral character, to homes, and to nations. The purpose of this study on the threat of pornography is to help us understand what sex can and cannot do by God's design. Our sexual nature fulfills its God-given purpose within boundaries revealed by God, but it is abused when its importance is exaggerated and elevated beyond those boundaries. We shall see that God's Word challenges us and equips us to walk in love in a sex-saturated society. Is it possible for those who have embraced the darkness of pornography to overcome it and to escape its devastation? Yes, we shall show that the gospel of Christ proclaims forgiveness of all sins and equips us to defeat the sin of pornography.

---

[1] Online edition of *Merriam-Webster Dictionary*, accessed March 24, 2013. *http://www.merriam-webster.com/dictionary/pornography*.

[2] The Free Dictionary, an online resource, accessed March 24, 2013. *http://legal-dictionary.thefreedictionary.com/pornography*.

God's Purpose for Sex:
What Sex Can and Cannot Do

"So God created man in his own image, in the image of God created he him; male and female created he them" (Gen. 1:27). Being made in God's image, we alone of all creatures on earth have the capacity to know God, to love God, and to obey God from the heart. How grand and glorious the thought that we were created to have fellowship with God, to be friends and companions of God!

Uniquely Express Marital Love, Commitment, and Companionship. The Father, the Son, and the Holy Spirit share a perfect fellowship in the Godhead. Likewise, humans fashioned as male and female share a blissful companionship in marriage. When God presented Eve to Adam, He spoke words which have echoed through the centuries in marriage covenants around the world, "Therefore shall a man leave his father and his mother, and shall cleave unto his wife: and they shall be one flesh" (Gen. 2:24). As husband and wife serve each other in the home, their hearts and hopes are united as "one flesh" – as if they were one person – symbolized in sexual intimacy and union.

Sexual intimacy is a physical union expressing unselfish love, fellowship, and companionship within the marriage relationship. It symbolizes a lifelong covenant and commitment to love each other "for better, for worse, for richer, for poorer, in sickness or in health, in adversity as in prosperity, and forsaking all others, to love and to cherish, 'til death do us part!" Sexual intercourse without this context and meaning abuses and perverts our sexual nature, doing great harm to both parties!

Produce Offspring in the Context of a Loving Family. "Lo, children are an heritage of the LORD: and the fruit of the womb is his reward" (Ps. 127:3). God designed our sexual nature to produce offspring within the marriage relationship in the atmosphere of unselfish nurturing love. The child conceived in the love of a husband and a wife is enveloped within their love. This is not love as a moment of selfish sensual lust but true, tender, committed, responsible love – love as unselfish giving and serving. Sensual love in conceiving a child is thus only one aspect of a comprehensive love shared by husband and wife, and extended to their child. And, thus God perpetuates the human race in the context of a loving family.

Reflect Reverential Fear of God. "Marriage is honourable in all, and the bed undefiled: but whoremongers and adulterers God will judge" (Heb.

13:4). When we discipline our lives to keep sexual expression within the confines of marriage, we reflect our love and respect for God who is the origin of all the blessings of marriage. We acknowledge that we will stand before Him in Judgment – we are accountable to Him in all things. Our sexual nature is not our invention, and solely our prerogative, but is utilized in submission to God and God's design.

Let it be clearly understood that God, not Satan, is the author of our sexual nature with all its attendant blessings. By God's power, God's wisdom, and God's love we are created male and female in order to share the marital fellowship of mutual love, service, and bliss as "one flesh" (Gen. 2:24). Satan can mar and destroy our companionship but cannot improve or enhance it.

It is God, and not Satan, who invites husbands and wives to share sensual love in Proverbs 5:18-19, "Let thy fountain be blessed: and rejoice with the wife of thy youth. Let her be as the loving hind and pleasant roe; let her breasts satisfy thee at all times; and be thou ravished always with her love." Satan, the consummate liar, seduces by offering the pleasure of a stranger, but the person so deceived falls into the pit of "utter ruin," is enslaved by the painful "cords of his sin," and dies "for lack of discipline" (Prov. 5:14, 22-23, NIV).

God, not Satan, guided Solomon to write "The Song of Songs" unabashedly celebrating sensual love in the context of marriage. By God's beautiful design, the bride invites her husband, "Let my beloved come into his garden, and eat his pleasant fruits," and he joyfully responds, "I am come into my garden, my sister, my spouse: I have gathered my myrrh with my spice; I have eaten my honeycomb with my honey." Their friends endorse and encourage their blissful union, "O friends; drink, yea, drink abundantly, O beloved" (Song of Sol. 4:16-5:1). All the joys of passionate love are gifts of God.

Cannot Satisfy Apart from God. In the name of sexual fulfillment, Satan deceives us into violating our sexual nature, making true fulfillment impossible! God did not create male and female as impersonal sexual machines or contraptions, but rather our sexual nature is tied to our whole being – interwoven with our physical, emotional, and psychological being.

William M. Struthers[3] is one of several neuroscientists who have studied

---

[3] Struthers, *Wired for Intimacy: How Pornography Hijacks the Male Brain.* Parts of the book are heavy with research materials, but this does not detract from the parts which explain more simply how both chemical and thought processes

the interplay of human conduct and brain chemistry. He points out that God wired our nature including the brain for an intimate relationship as husband and wife which includes sexual intercourse, but pornography short circuits the ability to develop and share intimacy by training the brain to enjoy a quick chemical "fix" void of intimacy. This perfunctory sexual experience without true intimacy leaves the deeper emotional and psychological nature of man empty and frustrated, while also training the mind to view people as disposable images.

Struthers explains that when we follow God's instructions "we are better able to appreciate the image of God in each person and have a healthy view of sexuality where we honor one another," then he goes further:

> This is not only a spiritual reality, but also a neurological one. When a husband and wife restrict themselves to each other, directing their sexual energies toward one another, they will find that they occupy each other's thoughts. They will find that they will be more closely bound to each other. This is God's plan for a husband and wife—that they will image God's exclusive love for His people as they exclusively set this part of themselves (their reproductive nature) aside for one another.[4]

In other words, when husband and wife share "their sexual energies" even the response of the brain draws them together emotionally and psychologically as one flesh or one person.

Violating God's plan simply cannot produce the same true intimacy and union that brings two people together as one flesh or one person. For instance, when a person views pornography, the brain triggers sexual arousal which seeks some outlet or means of fulfillment. Struthers continues,

> The unfortunate reality is that when he acts out (often by masturbating), this leads to hormonal and neurological consequences, which are designed to bind him to the object he is focusing on. In God's plan, this would be his wife, but for many men it is an image on a screen. Pornography thus enslaves the viewer to an image, hijacking the biological response intended to bond a man to his wife and therefore inevitably loosening that bond.[5]

---

are affected by pornography. There are two useful appendices of resources for recovering from pornography and sexual addictions.

[4] Struthers, "The Effects of Porn on the Male Brain," *Christian Research Journal*, 34, 5 (2011). *http://www.equip.org/articles/the-effects-of-porn-on-the-male-brain-3/* (accessed March 30, 2013).

[5] Struthers, "The Effects of Porn on the Male Brain."

In short, this person experiences a purely physical release of sexual energy without the possibility of intimate companionship and fulfillment of his sexual nature. "Like eating candy to satisfy hunger, pornography can feel like a healthy way to satisfy the drive for intimacy. In truth, it provides no nourishment whatsoever, and results in a greater degree of need."[6] The more the person returns to this experience, the more he trains his brain to crave something that will never satisfy his needs as a whole person. As this perverse craving grows, he becomes addicted to a sin that will torment and destroy him.

Satan seduces us with cheap counterfeits which cannot satisfy our sexual nature or needs. Sex apart from God and God's design is empty, void, disappointing, frustrating, and destructive. God's gift of passionate love in monogamous marriage cannot be matched by such crude cruel counterfeits as pornography, voyeurism, fornication, adultery, polygamy, rape, incest, pedophilia, necrophilia, homosexuality, and sex change. Salt water increases and inflames thirst rather than satisfying it. Exactly so, the sexual fetishes and obsessions offered by Satan inflame sexual desires beyond all hope of healthy fulfillment, enslaving and enraging the person so deceived.

Pornography erases from man's frame of reference the image of God in woman, reducing her to a mere impersonal object or toy for recreational convenience. This destroys the most meaningful and fulfilling dimension of sexual intimacy: husband and wife serving one another in mutual love and respect as "one flesh." The result is a downward spiral of frustration, deeper and deeper devaluation of the woman's real worth, and a dark and destructive self-loathing.

Pornography begins with visions and vistas of new-found freedom to enjoy great pleasure, but it is a horrific and heartless slave master of the soul without pity for its victim (see chart on next page). It is a lie, originating with Satan, father of lies. It is a fantasy, a mirage leading to unspeakable disappointment. It is an advertisement for fornication, which destroys the capacity for sexual fulfillment. It is salt water which only intensifies desire beyond hope of satisfaction. It is poison Kool-Aid, offering a momentary sweet taste but delivering the taste of death. It is a monster which devours its prey. It is a revolving door with no exit. It is a house of horrors with no escape. It is a spider's web which entangles the fool to receive deadly venom. It is simply a sin, like all sin, ending in the eternal torment of the

---

[6] Struthers, "The Effects of Porn on the Male Brain."

PORNOGRAPHY IS. . .

- **Pornography is** a lie–a lie built on a cascade of lies – a lie originating from the father of lies, Satan, our adversary and accuser.
- **Pornography is** a fantasy, a mirage promising great pleasure and happiness, but delivering unspeakable disappointment.
- **Pornography is** an advertisement for fornication, which, rather than fulfilling human needs, destroys the capacity to experience fulfillment.
- **Pornography is** salt water which cannot satisfy human thirst but only intensifies it beyond hope of satisfaction.
- **Pornography is** poison Kool-Aid: The momentary sweet taste transforms into the bitter taste of darkness, disappointment, and death.
- **Pornography is** a monster who will not be denied his prey.
- **Pornography is** a revolving door with no exit.
- **Pornography is** a house of horrors from which there is no escape.
- **Pornography is** a spider's web prepared for the foolish fly – the frustrating entanglement is followed by deadly venom.
- **Pornography is** a sin – like all sin, ending in the eternal torment of the lake which burns with fire and brimstone, i.e., the irrevocable absence of God's love, fellowship, and care.

---

lake which burns with fire and brimstone, which means the irrevocable absence God's love, fellowship, and care.

Pornography and Sex:
False Gods to Ancient and Modern Man

Satan successfully used fantasy to deceive mankind beginning in the Garden of Eden. God gave Adam and Eve every good blessing, but Satan claimed He deprived them of the best blessing of all: to taste the forbidden fruit of the tree of the knowledge of good and evil. First, he denied the penalty of sin and then he presented sin in all its false luster: "For God doth know that in the day ye eat thereof, then your eyes shall be opened, and ye shall be as gods, knowing good and evil" (Gen. 3:5). Of course, rather than blessing them, sin brought them to the depths of disappointment and despair as they experienced guilt, shame, and separation from God's fellowship.

Pornography offers sexual fantasies outside and beyond the passionate love shared in monogamous marriage. It depicts erotic behavior in order to induce sexual excitement. The word "pornography" is derived from the Greek term *pornographos*, writing about prostitutes (from *pornē*, for prostitute, and *graphein*, to write), and is obviously a close relative to the word fornication or *porneia*. Though pornography often leads to fornication, it alone does not meet the actual definition of fornication.[7]

Pornography and fornication were commonplace in ancient societies such as Babylon, India, Greece, and Rome often in religious contexts.[8] Cultic

---

[7] Halbrook, "Pornography and Fornication: Two Deadly Sins." This article explains that since pornography does not fall within the definition of *porneia*, pornography alone is not a legitimate ground for divorce and remarriage (Matt. 5:32; 19:9). The addictive and degenerate nature of pornography will often lead a man who views it to commit the sin of fornication, which is the only scriptural ground for divorce and remarriage (see Halbrook, "'Marriage Is Honorable:' A Study of Marriage, Divorce, and Remarriage," *Guardian of Truth*, XL, 12 (June 20, 1996):368-71, reprinted in tract form; "The Halbrook-Freeman Debate on Marriage, Divorce, & Remarriage" [Bowling Green, KY: Guardian of Truth Foundation, 1995]).

[8] The ancient Greek historian Herodotus recorded the Babylonian practice of religious prostitution as follows: "The foulest Babylonian custom is that which compels every woman of the land to sit in the temple of Aphrodite and have intercourse with some stranger once in her life. Many women who are rich and proud and disdain to mingle with the rest, drive to the temple in covered carriages drawn by teams, and stand there with a great retinue of attendants. [2] But most sit down in the sacred plot of Aphrodite, with crowns of cord on their heads; there is a great multitude of women coming and going; passages marked by line run every way through the crowd, by which the men pass and make their choice. [3] Once a woman has taken her place there, she does not go away to her home before some stranger has cast money into her lap, and had intercourse with her outside the temple; but while he casts the money, he must say, "I invite you in the name of Mylitta" (that is the Assyrian name for Aphrodite). [4] It does not matter what sum the money is; the woman will never refuse, for that would be a sin, the money being by this act made sacred. So she follows the first man who casts it and rejects no one. After their intercourse, having discharged her sacred duty to the goddess, she goes away to her home; and thereafter there is no bribe however great that will get her. [5] So then the women that are fair and tall are soon free to depart, but the uncomely have long to wait because they cannot fulfill the law; for some of them remain for three years, or four. There is a custom like this in some parts of Cyprus" (*The Histories* 1.99).

prostitution common in Canaanite religion was strictly forbidden to God's people (Deut. 23:17-18). Diana of the Ephesians was a goddess whose torso was covered in breasts. Having sex with a sacred prostitute at the Temple of Aphrodite in Corinth was considered an act of worship and a fertility rite.

As the sins of the fathers have been visited upon their children, the blight of pornography has afflicted mankind throughout the centuries. The invention of printing in the 15th century led to the rapid spread of pornography in the 16th-20th centuries, and the invention of photography in the 19th century led to vivid erotic pictures and films in the 20th-21st centuries. Historian Frederick Allen has observed that our technologies are "nothing more or less than plain expressions of our human nature" with its strengths and weaknesses. That is why,

> Every new information technology since the printing press has spawned pornography. By the early 1500s, half a century after Gutenberg, an Italian named Pietro Aretino was making his living in the business. Almost as soon as there were photographs, there were dirty photographs, and on a very large scale: A London pornographer busted in 1874 possessed 130,000 of them. As soon as there were movies, there were dirty movies.[9]

Allen noted major advances in 1953 with the introduction of Hugh Hefner's *Playboy Magazine* and in 1957 with the Supreme Court's ruling that nothing is legally obscene unless it is "utterly without redeeming social importance." "By 1972, when *Deep Throat* was released, hardcore was virtually mainstream."[10]

The coming of the age of computers and the internet in the 20th-21st centuries resulted in an explosion of pornography not far removed from the ancient ages when erotic images were worshiped as gods. Thousands of pornographic websites support multiple-billion dollar industries every year.

Marking the 50th anniversary of *Playboy Magazine* in 2003, R. M. Schuchardt admitted "the complete cultural victory of pornography in America today. Hollywood releases 400 films each year, while the pornography industry releases 700 movies *each month*." He then offered an even more graphic and pervasive example of the quantum change which had

---

[9] Allen, "When Sex Drives Technological Innovation," *American Heritage Magazine* 51, 5 (September, 2000), 19.

[10] Allen, *ibid.* Allen does not name the specific Supreme Court case, but it is *Roth v. United States* and its companion case *Alberts v. California*, 354 U.S. 476 (1957).

occurred in those fifty years: "Fifty years ago an American girl would have been ashamed to be seen in public with too little on. Now she's embarrassed to be seen with too *much* on – even if she's in church."[11]

Women bowing to the idol of sex. The fetish of sinful sexual fantasies ensnares both men and women. Hemlines have climbed while necklines have plunged as women have conformed to society's acceptance of pornography. Mary Quant, an inventor of the mini-skirt in 1965, explained that in dress fashion, "Pornography is great if it's good," and, "Good pornography is erotic but pleasing. Only ugliness is obscene." Sharing the view that women's fashions should attract attention to such erogenous zones as the hips or the breasts, she explained that "the crutch [crotch] is the most natural erogenous zone" and clothes should be designed "to lead the eye to it." Asked if there might be an aura "of vulgarity in cut-out and see-through dresses . . . giving an illusion of nothing beneath," she responded, "But I love vulgarity. Good taste is death, vulgarity is life."[12] Women who present themselves as vulgar obscene objects for the adulterous eyes of men should not be shocked when men treat them as nothing more than vulgar obscene objects.

Western culture has succumbed to these seductive dress fashions with very little resistance even among religious people. God covered Adam and Eve from their shoulders to their knees in modest "coats" or tunics, but both men and women have gradually reverted to the abbreviated "aprons" which barely cover from the waist to the mid-thighs.[13] This is evident from the

---

[11] Schuchardt, "Hugh Hefner's Hollow Victory," p. 50. This quotation about an American girl's sense of shame reflects the reality that a sense of shame is innate to mankind. The only question is in what direction it will be directed. Wendy Shalit commented in her book *A Return to Modesty*, "We are human beings, and we always are ashamed of *something*. We are ashamed of smoking, but not see-through clothes for young girls" (p. 61).

[12] Alison Adburgham, "Mary Quant talks to Alison Adburgham Tuesday 10 October, 1967." In another interview Quant infamously asserted the mini skirt is symbolic of a woman who wants to seduce a man: "Am I the only woman who has ever wanted to go to bed with a man in the afternoon? Any law-abiding female, it used to be thought, waits until dark. Well, there are lots of girls who do not want to wait. Mini-clothes are symbolic of them" ("Anything Goes: Taboos in Twilight," *Newsweek*, November 13, 1967, p. 76). Interview published in *The Guardian* (British newspaper published in London), *http://century.guardian. co.uk/1960-1969/Story/0,,106475,00.html* (accessed March 15, 2013).

[13] The aprons made by Adam and Eve covered the waist and upper thighs, whereas

prevalence of shorts exposing the thighs and all sorts of "mini" fashions.

Some people insist we should adjust to these fashion changes as mere fads and normal generational changes, but, actually, even ancient pagan moralists protested similar trends in their time as vulgar. When Romans rewove Chinese silk "into a flimsy gauze which left little to the imagination," there was an outcry:

> "I see clothes of silk, if clothes they can be called," wrote the philosopher Seneca (4 B.C.-A.D. 64), "affording protection neither to the body nor to the modesty of the wearer, and which are purchased for enormous sums, from unknown people." Pliny told of garments that "render women naked." Other writers waggishly referred to clothes "made of glass."[14]

Pornographic attire is not limited to prostitutes or to any one age of history.

Not only do women poison the atmosphere with pornography by wearing immodest dress, but also they fall victims to the sex god by participating in chat rooms. Men being more visual are more easily drawn to porn sites, while women being more social or verbal are drawn to sex-oriented chat rooms. Both practices generate harmful sexual fantasies which destroy character, homes, and souls. In addition, such devices as mobile phones are now widely used for "sexting," sending sexually explicit texts and photos, and women are heavily involved.[15]

Multitudes bowing to the idol of sex. All segments of modern society in western cultures including religious and political leaders bow in porno-

---

the coats or tunics made for them by God covered from their shoulders to their knees. The Hebrew term translated "apron" in Genesis 3:7 is *hagora*, meaning "girdle, belt, . . . loinclothes, . . . aprons" (Harris, *Theological Wordbook of the Old Testament*, 1:263; cf. Gesenius, *Hebrew and Chaldee Lexicon*, 260; Brown, Driver, Briggs, *Hebrew and English Lexicon*, 292). The term translated "coats," "tunics," or "garments" in Genesis 3:21 is *kuttonet*, meaning "a tunic. . . ; generally with sleeves, coming down to the knees, rarely to the ankles" (Gesenius, 420; cf. Harris, 1:459; Brown, Driver, Briggs, 509).

[14] Collins, *East to Cathay: The Silk Road*, pp. 44-46.

[15] Pamela Paul, "He Sexts, She Sexts More, Report Says," *New York Times*, July 15, 2011, *http://www.nytimes.com/2011/07/17/fashion/women-are-more-likely-to-sext-than-men-study-says-studied.html?partner=rss&emc=rss&_r=0* (accessed March 30, 2013).

graphic homage to the sex god.[16] Robert Bork's *Slouching Towards Gomor-rah* chronicles the descent of our society into the abyss of liberalism's amoral concepts of morality, including tolerance and acceptance of pornography. Correctly noting, "Pornography is basically propaganda for fornication," Bork explains that "rising affluence" undermines traditional constraints of religion, morality, and law.[17] The more people focus on consumerism, entertainment, and personal indulgence, the more religious teachers retreat

---

[16] Magazines such as *Playboy* and *Penthouse* reflect the popularity of pornography in western cultures but are illegal in China and in most Muslim countries in Asia and Africa. *Playboy* has had a religion editor in the past (see booklet publishing a debate between Anson Mount and William S. Banowsky, *Christianity and Hedonism, A Clash of Philosophies*, which says on the cover, "A discussion between Anson Mount, religion editor of Playboy Magazine, and Dr. William S. Banowsky, minister of the Broadway Church of Christ, Lubbock, Texas"). Religious leaders around the world especially in western cultures have found numerous pretexts to compliment such trashy magazines as aids to defeating Puritanism and establishing healthy attitudes toward sex. The circulation of *Playboy* has declined in recent years because pornography is so widely available through numerous mediums, especially the internet, but it recently expanded to publish *Playboy Israel*, a Hebrew language edition in Israel (where *Penthouse* flopped in 1989 because "observant Jews and Muslims live by strict modesty rules" and do not like even fully dressed women to appear in advertisements; Ian Deitch, "Playboy magazine launches Hebrew language edition," *Courier-Post*, March 5, 2013, *http://www.courierpostonline.com/viewart/20130305/ENT/303050038/Playboy-magazine-launches-Hebrew-language-edition* [accessed April 1, 2013]).

[17] Robert Bork, *Slouching Towards Gomorrah*, pp. 138, 8-9. Bork (1927-2012), former Solicitor General of the U.S. and Appeals Court judge, was nominated to the Supreme Court by President Ronald Reagan in 1987. Savage attacks by liberal Democrats against his judicial philosophy of originalism (cases involving constitutional law should be decided by the intent of the original framers of the Constitution, not by subjective or modern standards) led to his rejection by the Senate and to a new word in the English language: to Bork. In 2002 the *Oxford English Dictionary* added "Bork" as a verb: "To defame or vilify (a person) systematically, esp. in the mass media, usually with the aim of preventing his or her appointment to public office; to obstruct or thwart (a person) in this way." His conservative moral views played a role in his rejection. Senator Ted Kennedy complained that he would not uphold abortion and he did not believe in evolution. Liberal groups opposed him out of fear he might someday vote to overturn the Court's 1973 decision in *Roe v. Wade* which legalized abortion. It is tragic that someone with Bork's conservative moral values was demonized and rejected as a danger to our nation!

from proclaiming commands and prohibitions and turn to counseling and therapeutic themes.[18] The prophets of Jeremiah's day reassured and consoled the people, "saying, Peace, peace, when there is no peace," and God sadly said, "My people love to have it so" (Jer. 8:11; 5:31).

Religion gradually succumbs to liberalism's drift away from personal constraints "toward radical individualism and the corruption of standards."[19] To illustrate Bork's assessment, no one will admit moral standards are being lowered, but degenerate dancing is defended as harmless recreation, drinking alcohol and smoking marijuana as socializing, fornication and adultery as true love, homosexuality as an alternative lifestyle, and pornography as a legal right. "Modern liberals employ the rhetoric of 'rights'. . . to delegitimate the idea of restraints on individuals by communities. . . .Why there is a right for adults to enjoy pornography remains unexplained and unexplainable."[20]

During 1989-91 there was a controversy about the National Endowment for the Arts funding events which displayed such "art" as Andres Serrano's crucifix in urine and Robert Maplethorpe's homoerotic pictures. Bork points out that even cultural conservatives were reduced to protesting taxpayers' subsidies rather than insisting such pornographic displays "should not be shown in public, whoever pays for them."[21]

Of course, the big brouhaha is always over the supposed dangers of censorship. There is always censorship, but it just depends on *what values* are affirmed as to what is censored. If pornography cannot be censored, why should child pornography be censored, or threats against the President's life, or, the latest target, bullying. Secular humanists are trying to censor any mention of God, Christ, the Bible, such moral principles as defense of unborn life, and any number of other things not considered politically correct by liberal censors!

It goes without saying that the entertainment industry is the biggest purveyor of pornography, but the fact that the public consumes this filth as recreation shows how debased much of society is today. "Popular entertainment sells sex, pornography, violence, vulgarity, attacks on traditional forms

---

[18] Bork, p. 9.

[19] Bork, p. 61.

[20] Bork, p. 151.

[21] Bork p. 150.

of authority, and outright perversion more copiously and more intensely than ever before in our history."[22] Porn sales are about $3,000 per second and $10-14 billion per year in the U.S. – bigger business than professional football, baseball, and basketball combined[23] – almost $100 billion annually worldwide. Plenty of people are paying plenty of money for plenty of pornography.

Where have these trends led us? "Sex is now being made into the measure of existence" while "modesty, fidelity, abstinence, chastity, delicacy, and shame . . . are today ridiculed."[24] The spread of pornography through every phase and level of society is elevating sex to the status of a god.

Harmless or harmful? Paying pornographic homage to the sex god is not a mere harmless pastime. Humanistic secularism defends pornography as a victimless crime. Even *AARP Magazine's* "Modern Love" column advised that "levelheaded adults can enjoy erotic pictures in private without undermining their relationships, their immortal souls, or our republic."[25] To

---

[22] Bork, p. 126.

[23] "A recent article in the *New York Times Magazine* makes some comparisons to show how the $10 billion-a-year pornography business has become one of the most flush and vigorous in America: It's bigger than the combined revenues of all the professional football, baseball, and basketball franchises," says Janet M. LaRue in "Porn Nation" (*World and I* 16, 8 [Aug. 1, 2001]:44). LaRue, a lawyer with expertise in pornography law, is the Senior Legal Analyst with the American Civil Rights Union. The article she cited said, "The $4 billion that Americans spend on video pornography is larger than the annual revenue accrued by either the N.F.L., the N.B.A. or Major League Baseball. But that's literally not the half of it: the porn business is estimated to total between $10 billion and $14 billion annually in the United States when you toss in porn networks and pay-per-view movies on cable and satellite, Internet Web sites, in-room hotel movies, phone sex, sex toys and that archaic medium of my own occasionally misspent youth, magazines. Take even the low-end $10 billion estimate (from a 1998 study by Forrester Research in Cambridge, Mass.), and pornography is a bigger business than professional football, basketball and baseball put together" (Frank Rich, "Naked Capitalists: There's No Business Like Porn Business," *New York Times Magazine*, May 20, 2001, *http://www.nytimes.com/2001/05/20/magazine/20PORN.html* [accessed March 24, 2013]).

[24] Bork, p. 149.

[25] Hugh O'Neill, "What Are You Looking At?" *AARP Magazine* [American Association of Retired Persons], March & April 2004, p. 28.

the contrary, viewing pornography undermines the marriage covenant by violating a man's commitment to love his wife exclusively, which includes focusing his sexual passions on her alone. The wife's sense of self-worth and well-being are undermined by her husband's seeking out perverted fantasized images of other women as if his wife's realistic presence, personality, and sexual companionship do not satisfy his needs.

Research shows that wives whose husbands regularly turn to pornography feel they are "no longer sexually attractive to their partners" and they are "viewed more as sexual objects than real people."[26] Not only does the male dehumanize the female represented in the images as a mere plaything for his perverted desires, but also he devalues his wife as a companion capable of meeting his needs – she too is reduced to the status of a sex toy, an outdated broken toy. How can his wife feel, other than diminished and devastated?

A man typically hides his activities when viewing pornography, but inevitably the wife finds out. Her trust in him is destroyed. Her sense of security is destroyed both by the humiliating realization that he is attracted to images of other women and by the realization that he is not honest and open with her.

A vast body of research on pornography proves that it "puts one at increased risk for committing sexual offenses, experiencing difficulties in one's intimate relationships, and accepting rape myths (i.e. beliefs that trivialize rape or blame the victim for the crime)."[27] Rapists and child molesters often admit pornography played a role in their crimes.[28]

---

[26] Raymond M. Bergner and Ana J. Bridges, "The Significance of Heavy Pornography Involvement for Romantic Partners: Research and Clinical Implications," *Journal of Sex & Marital Therapy* 28, 3 (2002):193-206, cited in "Research on Pornography," a summary of over one hundred scholarly studies (published by The Aurora Center at the University of Minnesota).

[27] This conclusion reflects "a meta-analysis of 46 published studies on the effects of pornography" by Neil Malamuth, T. Addison, and J. Koss, "Pornography and Sexual Agression: Are There Reliable Effects and Can We Understand Them?" *Annual Review of Sex Research* 11 (2000): 26-94, cited in "Research on Pornography."

[28] A few examples cited in "Research on Pornography" include Edna Einsiedel, Social Science Report. Paper prepared for the Attorney's General's Commission on Pornography, Department of Justice, Washington, DC (1986). W. L. Marshall, "Pornography and Sex Offenders," in *Pornography: Research Advances and*

Ted Bundy was executed January 24, 1989 in Florida after raping and murdering 30-50 women and girls across our nation. In an interview with Dr. James Dobson the day before his execution, Bundy explained that pornography played a major role in his crimes. He started reading soft-core magazines he found randomly at age 12-13, and his habit gradually led him to hard-core and sexually violent materials. There is a natural progression as "you look for more potent, more explicit, more graphic kinds of material" until reaching "that jumping off point where you begin to think maybe actually doing it will give you that which is just beyond" viewing it. Speaking of people like himself who grew up in a normal loving religious home, he warned, "Pornography can reach in and snatch a kid out of any house today."[29]

The warning of Ted Bundy is truer today than it has ever been because of the tidal wave of pornography flooding all media outlets especially computers. Parents must assert their God-given duty to lead their children by carefully guarding them. Children should watch T.V. and use electronic media in open spaces of the home and in their rooms with the doors open. Parents should monitor what *has been viewed* as well as what *is being viewed* over the internet. As President Ronald Reagan said of the Soviet threat, "Trust but verify."

Parents should think twice about having such services as HBO (Home Box Office) available on the T.V.s in their home as the fare continues to degenerate. Devices such as TVGuardian and other filtering devices for electronic media should be utilized to prevent access to pornographic sites and materials.

Children who disobey parental rules in these matters should be disciplined, but this should include prayer and Bible instruction about why rules are necessary and healthy in life. There is no true "right of privacy" which prevents parents from guiding their children safely to adulthood – this

---

Policy Considerations, ed. Dolf Zillmann and Jennings Bryant, pp. 185-214 (Hillsdale, NJ, England: Lawrence Erlbaum Associates, Inc., 1989). Daniel Lee Carter, Robert Alan Prentky, Raymond A. Knight, Penny L. Vanderveer, and Richard J. Boucher, "Use of Pornography in the Criminal and Developmental Histories of Sexual Offenders," *Journal of Interpersonal Violence* 2, 2 (June 1987): 196-211.

[29] James Dobson, "Fatal Attraction: Ted Bundy's Final Interview," Pure Intimacy at *http://www.pureintimacy.org/piArticles/A000000433.cfm* (accessed March 29, 2013).

"right" is another popular myth of secular humanism which undermines parental authority.

Daily prayer and Bible reading as a family will help build character in each member of the family, which is the ultimate protection against pornography in all forms.

I am profoundly unimpressed by the claims that pornography is "a harmless pastime" and "a victimless crime" which ought to be protected by "pluralism" and "the right to privacy." My siblings and I were sexually molested by our own father and pornography played a role in his perverted desires. We knew exactly where his stack of magazines was hidden in his bedroom closet. Our scars testify that the harm is real, the victims are real, and the privacy is phoney.

An under-reported phase of suffering inflicted by pornography is the wrenching quandary faced by a wife who is faithful to her husband but who realizes his sin is discouraging, angering, tormenting, and introducing powerful temptations to their children. When she pleads with him to repent and to get help to no avail, how can she protect the children? I saw my mother weep and plead with my father to no avail. She did not know I occasionally visited the stack of magazines in the closet (though I later turned from them sensing there was something horribly wrong with them). She did not know these magazines contributed to my father molesting us (and we were too afraid to discuss it with her until after we were adults). None of us knew living in this environment would contribute to my brother and one of my sisters turning away from the church and the Lord. She did know she was terribly ashamed of the pornography in our home.

Should she have left and taken us out of this environment in an effort to create leverage which might have broken my father's stubborn will?[30] Such

---

[30] I am not implying that pornography is a scriptural ground for divorce and remarriage; I have argued at length that it is not (see my article "Pornography and Fornication: Two Deadly Sins"). Reflecting on the traumatic effects of pornography in our family, I am simply recognizing a husband's conduct can be so dangerous that a conscientious wife will be forced to wrestle with what options she has to protect their children and to communicate to him the seriousness of his sins. In exhausting every possible means to be both a good wife and a good mother, she may be forced to leave both to protect the children and to apply leverage in breaking his stubborn will and in bringing him to repent so that the family can be reunited in righteousness and peace. Does this mean she is returning

matters were not openly discussed by Christians in those days and her sense of shame was so deep it left her not knowing where to turn or what to do. I will not second guess her decision to stay because I know how sincerely she did the best she knew to do at the time, but no one could have known the utterly devastating and lifelong effects our living in that environment would have. I do not like to remember those days, but I mention this matter in order to illustrate the horrendous effects pornography can have–including the complex dilemmas faced by a godly wife who struggles to be faithful to her husband while also protecting her children from irreparable harm.

One of the finest young preachers I have ever known was consumed and destroyed by pornography. I spent hours and days trying to help salvage him and his marriage. After viewing pornography in his teenage years, he later thought getting married would automatically eliminate the sin. It did not. His progression alternated between promising himself to quit and returning to the pictures, gradually finding that grosser and more perverted pictures were necessary to sustain the thrill.

The habit is expensive, and he ran up $60,000 in credit card debt and stole from a community organization in which he was active. When pictures could no longer satisfy his increasingly perverted desires, he began to visit houses of prostitution. Finally, as the darkness and emptiness of sin frustrated and enraged his soul, he attempted suicide. In the end, he destroyed his marriage, his faith, and everything precious to him. His number is legion!

Through the internet the sex god offers a wide variety of pornography so depraved and perverted it shocks normal sensibilities. Referring to pedophile bulletin boards and sites depicting "bestiality, torture, bloodletting, and sadistic injury," Judge Bork gives a couple of gruesome internet examples of the graphic abuse and murder of two kidnapped children: "The castration of the 6-year-old boy is 'reported in loving detail' and occurs before he is shot. The 7-year-old girl is then repeatedly raped by nine men before having her nipples cut off and her throat slashed."[31]

The sex god in the end is Satan himself, and to embrace and consume pornography is nothing short of homage to Satan. Pornography with its sexual perversion cannot satisfy the needs of the body or the soul but only

---

wrong for wrong, or does it mean she is simply trying to prevent greater wrongs? That is her dilemma.

[31] Bork, *Slouching*, p. 135.

sears the conscience, dismantles a person's character, and torments his soul. Pornography's Anti-Agenda destroys faith in God by violating His Word; destroys males by reducing them to sexual machines and monsters; destroys females by reducing them to one-dimensional sex toys for the amusement of men; destroys children by preventing them from developing healthy attitudes toward their sexual nature and by making them objects of abuse; destroys families by destroying the bonds of love, trust, security, and self-

---

Pornography's Anti-Agenda
- **Anti-God:** destroys faith in God by violating His Word.
- **Anti-Male:** reduces men to sexual machines and monsters.
- **Anti-Female:** reduces women to one-dimensional sex toys.
- **Anti-Children:** prevents them from developing healthy attitudes toward sex and makes them objects of abuse.
- **Anti-Family:** destroys the bonds of love, trust, security, and self-worth.
- **Anti-Sex:** reduces sex to a selfish dehumanized perfunctory experience.
- **Anti-Morality:** demolishes moral principles and values.
- **Anti-Community:** attracts prostitutes, pimps, gangs, and mobs.
- **Anti-Nation:** destroys the moral character of a people and their leaders.

---

worth; destroys sexual fulfillment by reducing sex to a selfish dehumanized perfunctory experience; destroys morality by demolishing moral principles and values; destroys communities by attracting prostitutes, pimps, gangs, and mobs; and destroys nations by destroying the moral character of the people and their leaders.

Ephesians 5:1-21
Walking in Love in a Sex-Saturated Society
First-century Christians lived in a morally corrupt and depraved world. Gentile culture spawned sex-saturated societies, exalting sex to the status of a god without understanding the true nature of God or of sex as created by God. The love and light of the gospel of Christ pierced the darkness – souls were saved – Christians learned to live above the corruption of the world and to walk in the love of God – parents were saved and saved their children!

The love and light of the gospel still shine in our sex-saturated society today! This may be seen in a study of Ephesians 5:1-21.

Verses 1-2: Christ Our Perfect Example of God's Love

Be ye therefore followers of God, as dear children; and walk in love, as Christ also hath loved us, and hath given himself for us an offering and a sacrifice to God for a sweetsmelling savour.

We imitate God's love by living a life of love for others just as Christ loved us and offered himself for us on the cruel cross of Calvary. Having introduced the amoral culture of the Gentile world in chapter 4, verse 17, Paul now counteracts such depraved living by insisting that Christians fill their hearts and lives with unselfish love toward their fellowmen. This will be the basis of his appeal for a life of moral purity in the verses to follow. Satan transformed love into self-indulgence, but Christ exemplifies the true love which acts in self-denial and selfless concern for the welfare of others.

Verses 3-6: God's Wrath Against All Forms of Immorality

But fornication, and all uncleanness, or covetousness, let it not be once named among you, as becometh saints; neither filthiness, nor foolish talking, nor jesting, which are not convenient: but rather giving of thanks. For this ye know, that no whoremonger, nor unclean person, nor covetous man, who is an idolater, hath any inheritance in the kingdom of Christ and of God. Let no man deceive you with vain words: for because of these things cometh the wrath of God upon the children of disobedience.

This passage reminds us we must live a life of love and light in a world seduced and cursed by sexual immorality.

There is a stark contrast here between the Gentile and Christian mindsets. In the Greco-Roman world "fornication had long come to be regarded as a matter of moral indifference, and was indulged in without shame or scruple, not only by the mass, but by philosophers and men of distinction who in other respects led exemplary lives."[32] Yet, Paul says to Christians in one of the premier cities of the Greco-Roman world, "But among you there must not be even a hint of sexual immorality" (v. 3, NIV).

---

[32] S. D. F. Salmond, *The Epistle to the Ephesians*, p. 352. Some translations and commentaries put "all things are lawful for me" in 1 Corinthians 6:12 in quotation marks to indicate that Paul is quoting his opponent's argument that fornication is morally neutral (RSV, NIV, etc.).

Paul's warning against "covetousness" (Greek *pleonexia*[33]) is most interesting in this context. The basic meaning originally was "having more," then "receiving more," and finally "desiring more." "From the first literary examples on [,] it is not restricted to material possessions" but was used of such things as "hunger for power."[34] "It is self-seeking, or *greed*: in whatever direction this central evil tendency finds it employment."[35] Trench defines it as "the fiercer and ever fiercer longing of the creature which has forsaken God, to fill itself with the lower objects of sense" like a vessel "ever filling" yet never filled.[36] The objects of such improper cravings may be money, possessions, power, or carnal and sensual experiences.

Though often used in reference to desire for material possessions, *pleonexia* as covetousness or greed is used in Ephesians 4:19 and 5:3 and 5 in the closest association with fornication, lasciviousness, and uncleanness. This is a warning against becoming so obsessed and consumed with sexual desire that it replaces God. *The man who makes sex his god is emphatically and undeniably an idolater.*[37] Restraints are loosened on the road to sexual idolatry by degenerate dancing, lascivious touching, immodest dress, immoral songs, and pornographic movies, T.V. programs, and internet sites. As the heart becomes corrupted, the mouth will pour out foul, foolish, filthy speech.

Unnatural desires are stirred when pornographic pictures first tease the mind. If viewing them continues, a door is opened further inflaming the desires which leads to another door with the same result again. The web

---

[33] *Pleonexia* is defined as "*greediness, insatiableness, avarice, covetousness*, lit. 'a desire to have more'" (William F. Arndt and F. Wilbur Gingrich, *A Greek-English Lexicon of the New Testament*, p. 673).

[34] Kittel, *Theological Dictionary of the New Testament* (TDNT) VII: 266.

[35] Henry Alford, *The Greek Testament* III: 122.

[36] Richard Chenevix Trench, *Synonyms of the New Testament*, p. 79.

[37] Commentaries are divided in applying *pleonexia* in these verses to desire for material possessions or to insatiable sexual desires. Enthroning either certainly qualifies as idolatry. Many writers point to Matthew 6:24 where Jesus taught we must choose between God and mammon, but the context there is very different from Ephesians 4:19 and 5:3 and 5. W. E. Vine's *Expository Dictionary of New Testament Words* lists passages where the term refers to "possessions" and other passages where it refers to "sensuality" including Ephesians 4:19 and Colossians 3:5 ("covetousness, which is idolatry," which is parallel to Eph. 5:5, "covetous man, who is an idolater") (*Expository Dictionary* I: 253) .

of sin will entangle the viewer more and more as he attempts to hide his activities, tells outright lies, and goes through all sorts of contortions to cover his trail – searing his conscience again and again.

Shocked at times by his own conduct, he will wonder, "Is this really me?" Somehow he manages to put this despised alter ego or strange new person in a special compartment of his mind, so that he will not suffer the pain of confronting reality. To reassure himself that all is well, he may at times rail against "the plague of pornography which is destroying our nation." He goes through cycles of promising himself to quit (and promising his wife, if caught), but also needing more perverted images to experience the thrill when the craving returns.

Later when pictures lose their luster, he will commit fornication, and may find himself in houses of prostitution where he never dreamed he could have gone even in his worst nightmares. As the compulsion and obsession spins out of control, this once upright man may find himself involved with child pornography and incest – lying and stealing to cover the crushing debt generated by his filthy deeds – contracting sexually transmitted diseases and bringing them home to his wife – and losing his family. Many will try religion, doctors, and self-help programs to break out of the cycle, but like the drunk they return again to the downward spiral, dying at last of disease or suicide, only to spend eternity in torment with Satan who deceived them from the start!

Pornography is a house of horrors in this life and the next, which is why Paul warned in verse 6, "Let no man deceive you with vain words: for because of these things cometh the wrath of God upon the children of disobedience."

Verses 7-14: Reject and Rebuke Immorality, Shine as Lights

Be not ye therefore partakers with them. For ye were sometimes darkness, but now are ye light in the Lord: walk as children of light: (For the fruit of the Spirit is in all goodness and righteousness and truth;) proving what is acceptable unto the Lord. And have no fellowship with the unfruitful works of darkness, but rather reprove them. For it is a shame even to speak of those things which are done of them in secret. But all things that are reproved are made manifest by the light: for whatsoever doth make manifest is light. Therefore he saith, Awake thou that sleepest, and arise from the dead, and Christ shall give thee light.

It is not God's purpose that we should isolate ourselves from the world by avoiding all contact with sinners, but we must avoid participating in their sins or giving signs of approval of their sins. Paul represents "all carnal-mindedness, in word or deed, as unworthy of Christians; unholy things do not become saints; the kingdom of God, the fellowship of the saints, permits nothing unholy in it."[38]

Christians receive and reflect the light of the gospel of Christ in their conduct. Or, another way to say it, they bear the fruit of the Spirit by a life of goodness, righteousness, and truth. This life is not a mere theory or tradition but must be put into daily practical application if God is to approve and accept us as His saints.

The voices of Christians may be muted by the atmosphere and philosophy of the times in which they live. While not participating in the sins of our age, we may seek to avoid controversy by mouthing such politically correct mantras as, "Well, we may not agree with drinking, gambling, pornography, abortion, and homosexuality, but you cannot legislate morality. Anyway, these practices harm no one except those who engage in them and we must respect their right to privacy."[39] Actually, as such practices destroy a person's character, they spread all sorts of damage to society at large including abuse of family members, failed homes, stealing, mayhem, and murder. The fallout affects all of us.

To speak out against such sins as destructive to a nation's character is to risk being called "a Bible-thumping bigot" or "a demagogue" for violating modern platitudes about pluralism. We should not be deceived: Such charges are only designed to impose some *different set of values* giving license to destructive behavior. As Judge Bork noted, "All legislation 'imposes' a morality of one sort or another, and, therefore, on the reasoning offered, all law

---

[38] Hermann Olshausen, *Biblical Commentary on the New Testament,* V: 125.

[39] The Fourth Amendment to the U.S. Constitution protects our citizens in the following words, "The right of the people to be secure in their persons, houses, papers, and effects, against unreasonable searches and seizures, shall not be violated, and no Warrants shall issue, but upon probable cause, supported by Oath or affirmation, and particularly describing the place to be searched, and the persons or things to be seized." The framers of the Constitution never imagined the concept of protection from governmental abuse would be expanded into a nebulous "right to privacy" to legitimize pornography, abortion, and homosexuality. The same concept can be used to legitimize euthanasia, assisted suicide, all forms of child abuse, and even murder. "Modern liberalism's obsession with the autonomy of the individual is taking us to a culture of death" (Bork, p. 186).

would seem to be antithetical to pluralism."[40] The values of the Bible have been replaced by secularist humanist values in much of modern legislation.

While Christians should support legislation which encourages good character, we should not imagine that civil government can force people to have the right kind of heart. The moral force of the gospel alone can do that, which is why we must speak up and speak out regardless of what civil government does. That is why Paul said in verse 11, "And have no fellowship with the unfruitful works of darkness, but rather reprove them." "Withdrawal from these sins is not enough. . . .God's children cannot be neutral in the spiritual battle against all such sins. . . .We must **reprove** (*elegchete*) them, exposing them in both our words and in our lives."[41]

No right to privacy can protect pornography from the glorious light of the gospel of Christ. The light of truth and right must shine upon the ugly sinful deeds of the sinner if he is to be converted. Only in this way can he awake and arise to repent and follow Christ who is the light!

Verses 15-21: Guided by the Holy Spirit

See then that ye walk circumspectly, not as fools, but as wise, redeem-ing the time, because the days are evil. Wherefore be ye not unwise, but understanding what the will of the Lord is. And be not drunk with wine, wherein is excess; but be filled with the Spirit; speaking to yourselves in psalms and hymns and spiritual songs, singing and making melody in your heart to the Lord; giving thanks always for all things unto God and the Father in the name of our Lord Jesus Christ; submitting yourselves one to another in the fear of God.

To walk circumspectly is to walk carefully and cautiously, not easily deceived because we are focused on understanding and obeying the will of the Lord. "Like the aerialist on a high wire, the child of God watches his step with precision."[42] When the heart is filled with the Spirit of God rather than inflamed by intoxicants and filthy images, God strengthens our character so that we can well avoid the pitfalls of pornography. His instruc-tions revealed in Scripture open our eyes both to dangers on every hand and to opportunities to do good on every hand.

This paragraph in verses 15-21 draws a stark contrast between the ways

---

[40] Bork, p. 277.

[41] C. G. "Colly" Caldwell, *Ephesians*, p. 242.

[42] Caldwell, p. 246.

of the foolish sinner and the wise saint. Rather than joining with drunkards in singing songs of revelry and debauchery, we unite our souls and voices as the saints of God to sing songs of praise and thanksgiving to our Savior. Rather than manipulating and abusing our fellowman for selfish ends, we learn to live out God's love in our own lives by submitting to each other in mutual service.

The beautiful paragraph which follows in verses 22-33 demonstrates how husband and wife serve each other in mutual love. The husband's unselfish love is an expression of submission as he serves the needs of his wife. The wise man knows that his relationship to his wife is based on love, trust, security, and a sense of self-worth or well-being.

The foolish husband who views pornography destroys the love which binds his wife and him together. His selfishness and lust increasingly blind him to the value of his wife as he falls deeper and deeper into the pit of pornography. As myriads of obscene images fill his mind, he becomes increasingly incapable of focusing his affection and attention on his wife. He may be puzzled as to why he does not find his wife sexually attractive anymore, not realizing pornography has reprogrammed his brain and his thoughts to respond to perverted images rather than to her love.

The foolish husband who pursues pornography destroys the vital trust shared between his wife and himself. As his pursuit of pornography repeatedly requires him to practice manipulation, lies, cover-ups, and deception, the wife no longer knows when to believe him. His repeated apologies and promises to do better become meaningless as he returns again and again to his own vomit.

The foolish husband who consumes pornography destroys his wife's sense of security. He weaves a tangled web as he tries to defend himself and cover his tracks, alternately pretending to be the victim of her cruel suspicions, pitching temper fits to intimidate her, exaggerating her faults to throw her off the trail, threatening her, verbally abusing her, and even resorting to physical abuse. He may even pressure her to perform perverted acts he has seen in the distorted world of pornography. She now fears the man she once honored and cherished. Her once beautiful nest of security has become a thorny thicket of insecurity.

The foolish husband who fills his mind with pornography destroys his wife's sense of self-worth. She is tormented by her husband's preference for pornographic images over her own passionate love for him. She is made to feel unattractive, unable to satisfy, and never able to measure up to the airbrushed fantasies of pornographic images. Though deeply offended by her husband's evil conduct, she is also tormented by fears and feelings of being worthless, ugly, repulsive, and useless.

One of the most sobering lessons of my life is the result of observing wives whose husbands have been entangled in the sin of pornography, and trying to help these couples salvage their relationship. *The emotional devastation suffered by the wife is equivalent to the devastation she suffers when the husband commits adultery.* The impact on the bonds of love, on trust, on security, and on self-worth are the same. Saving a marriage devastated by adultery or by pornography is a long, hard road flooded with painful tears.

Overcoming the Sin and Devastation of Pornography

The gospel of Christ is still the power of God to save people who are guilty of all kinds of sins. "For I am not ashamed of the gospel of Christ: for it is the power of God unto salvation to every one that believeth; to the Jew first, and also to the Greek" (Rom. 1:16). In the first century it saved fornicators, idolaters, adulterers, homosexuals, thieves, covetous people, drunkards, revilers, extortioners, and such like (1 Cor. 6:9-11). People who murdered the Son of God were forgiven in Acts 2 and began to worship and to follow him. The gospel has the same power in our time to save all sorts of sinners, yes, including those who are guilty of the vile sins associated with pornography.

What does God's Word teach that helps overcome the sin and devastation of pornography?

1. Grow in Fellowship with God: Refresh the Soul, Rebuild Character. Man was created to have fellowship with God. Sin destroys this relationship. God sent His Son to die as the perfect sacrifice for our sins – for all sins! Paul preached the gospel in full confidence it is God's power to reconcile sinners to Himself: "Now then we are ambassadors for Christ, as though God did beseech you by us: we pray you in Christ's stead, be ye reconciled to God. For he hath made him to be sin for us, who knew no sin; that we might be made the righteousness of God in him" (2 Cor. 5:20-21). Sinners in the world receive forgiveness and reconciliation when they submit to Christ by faith, repenting of all sins, confessing him to be God's Son, and yielding to him in water baptism (Mk. 16:16; Acts 2:38; Rom. 10:10; Acts 22:16). Christians who have fallen back into sin may humble themselves to confess their sins, repent of them, and pray God's forgiveness (Acts 8:22-24; 1 Jn. 1:9-10).

When our souls are reconciled to God, we find joy and refreshment to our souls as we grow in fellowship with Him. Growing in fellowship with God rebuilds our character. We grow closer and closer to God by listening to Him in Bible study and pouring out our hearts to Him in prayer. We can draw near to God in prayer and in meditation on such passages as these:

Psalm 19:14
Let the words of my mouth, and the meditation of my heart,
be acceptable in thy sight,
O LORD, my strength, and my redeemer.

Psalm 27:13-14
I had fainted, unless I had believed to see the goodness of the LORD
in the land of the living.
Wait on the LORD: be of good courage,
and he shall strengthen thine heart: wait, I say, on the LORD.

Psalm 57:1
Be merciful unto me, O God, be merciful unto me:
for my soul trusteth in thee:
yea, in the shadow of thy wings will I make my refuge,
until these calamities be overpast.

Psalm 101:3
I will set no wicked thing before mine eyes:
I hate the work of them that turn aside;
it shall not cleave to me.

Psalm 119:9-11
Wherewithal shall a young man cleanse his way?
by taking heed thereto according to thy word.
With my whole heart have I sought thee:
O let me not wander from thy commandments.
Thy word have I hid in mine heart, that I might not sin against thee.

2 Timothy 2:22
Flee also youthful lusts: but follow righteousness, faith, charity, peace, with them that call on the Lord out of a pure heart.

1 Peter 1:15-16
But as he which hath called you is holy, so be ye holy in all manner of conversation; because it is written, Be ye holy; for I am holy.

1 Peter 2:1-3

Wherefore laying aside all malice, and all guile, and hypocrisies, and envies, and all evil speakings, as newborn babes, desire the sincere milk of the word, that ye may grow thereby: if so be ye have tasted that the Lord is gracious.

1 Peter 2:11

Dearly beloved, I beseech you as strangers and pilgrims, abstain from fleshly lusts, which war against the soul.

1 Peter 5:6-7

Humble yourselves therefore under the mighty hand of God, that he may exalt you in due time: casting all your care upon him; for he careth for you.

Many passages are directly designed to build strength of character, thus helping a person to exercise self-denial, self-discipline, and self-control in the face of temptation. We are inspired by the account of Joseph who fled from Potiphar's wife rather than submit to her seduction (Gen. 39:12), and by the declaration of Job, "I made a covenant with mine eyes; why then should I think upon a maid?" (Job 31:1). If Joseph could decide to flee a seductive situation and if Job could decide to control his eyes, who among us cannot make the same decisions? Jesus warns us not to feed our minds with adulterous images and intentions (Matt. 5:27-30). The instructions given in Ephesians 5:1-21 teach us how to walk in love in a sex-saturated society. It is possible to overcome the sin and devastation of pornography. If we are looking for help, God's Word will provide abundant help as we draw near to God through Bible study and prayer!

2. Seek and Follow Good Counsel. "Understanding what the will of the Lord is" requires first learning what God's Word teaches and then learning how to apply its principles to meet various challenges in life (Eph. 5:17). By His good providence, God makes available good counsel from any number of sources and wise men take advantage of them as is repeatedly taught in the book of Proverbs:

Proverbs 16:21

The wise in heart shall be called prudent:
and the sweetness of the lips increaseth learning.

Proverbs 24:5-6

A wise man is strong; yea, a man of knowledge increaseth strength.
For by wise counsel thou shalt make thy war:
and in multitude of counsellors there is safety.

Proverbs 27:6, 17

Faithful are the wounds of a friend;
but the kisses of an enemy are deceitful.

Iron sharpeneth iron;
so a man sharpeneth the countenance of his friend.

Men who have wide experience in life often develop great skills of insight and become sources of wisdom. Wise counselors provide instruction, and the right kind of knowledge is power – power to solve problems, power to defeat temptation, power to overcome obstacles, power to reach goals. Wise counselors can give constructive criticism and advice. Testing ideas with wise counselors can sharpen our own skills and character.

Where will we find wise counselors? Mature Christians including godly men and women, elders, deacons, preachers, and Bible class teachers can be helpful.

In addition, authors, books, and websites share materials reflecting their study and research on such issues as pornography. Here are just a few resources: 1. Many authors discussing family life and family issues in *God Give Us Christian Homes*.[43] 2. Steve and Bette Wolfgang, "Helping Christians Addicted to Pornography" in *The Inspiration and Authority of the Scriptures*. 3. Gale Towles, "Works of the Flesh: Sensuality" in *Great Texts of the New Testament*. 4. Stephen Arterburn and Fred Stoeker, *Every Man's Battle: Winning the War on Sexual Temptation One Victory at a Time*. 5. Shannon Ethridge, *Every Woman's Battle: Discovering God's Plan for Sexual and Emotional Fulfillment*. 6. Ted Roberts, *Pure Desire: Helping People Break Free from Sexual Struggles*. 7. James C. Dobson, *Straight Talk*. 8. Dobson, *Love Must Be Tough*. 9. John H. Court, *Pornography: A Christian Critique*.[44] 10. William Struthers, *Wired for Intimacy: How Pornography Hijacks the Male Brain*. 11. Websites with vast amounts of materials such as *www.covenanteyes.com/*.[45]

---

[43] There is no specific lecture on pornography, but many of the lessons deal with related principles and attitudes. For instance, my own lecture on being sexually molested refers to the role of pornographic materials (Ron Halbrook, "God Hears the Cry of the Weak," *God Give Us Christian Homes*, p. 337).

[44] Court writes from his perspective as a psychologist in analyzing and refuting eight major defenses offered to justify pornography.

[45] For instance, Luke Gilkerson. "Your Brain on Porn." CovenantEyes. January 9, 2012. Accessed March 23, 2013. *<http://www.covenanteyes.com/>*.

Pornography can become so addictive that a good professional counselor who deals with addictive behaviors may be necessary.[46] It is wise to first inquire whether he or she respects the Bible as the standard of moral conduct. Such counselors often have wide experience in dealing with the dangers of pornography.

3. Arrange Accountability. First and foremost we must recognize we are accountable to God who created us and who knows our every thought, word, and deed. "The eyes of the LORD are in every place, beholding the evil and the good" (Prov. 15:3). The principle Solomon stated is always true: "He that covereth his sins shall not prosper: but whoso confesseth and forsaketh them shall have mercy" (Prov. 28:13). We make ourselves accountable to God by freely confessing rather than trying to hide our sins including the sin of pornography. Daily prayers are needed like the prayer of David in Psalm 19:12-14,

Who can understand his errors?
Cleanse thou me from secret faults.
Keep back thy servant also from presumptuous sins;
let them not have dominion over me:
then shall I be upright,
and I shall be innocent from the great transgression.
Let the words of my mouth,
and the meditation of my heart,
be acceptable in thy sight,
O LORD, my strength, and my redeemer.

Pornography is especially insidious, dangerous, and destructive as willful or presumptuous sin. If it takes complete dominion over our souls, we become hopeless in our blind stubbornness like King Saul who was cast away from God.

Other levels of accountability will help us overcome the sin and devas-

---

[46] For information on counseling for addictive sexual behaviors, contact Art Adams via email at *artadams3049@yahoo.com*. He is a Christian and a professional counselor in Indianapolis, IN. The Meier Clinics in several large cities are run by conservative evangelicals. SA (Sexaholics Anonymous) and its counterpart S-Anon (for family and friends affected by sex addicts) meet in many communities. Pinegrove Treatment Facility at Hattiesburg, MS, run by Patrick Carnes, conducts workshops and several treatment programs for addictive sexual behaviors.

tation of pornography such as making ourselves accountable to our wife, to the elders of the church, or to some mature Christian friend. Periodic questions from them and reports to them will help. Another step is to put the computer in an open area where our use of it could be observed at all times. Software which blocks porn sites can be installed. Accountability could include calling or approaching godly people when we feel weak or tempted, or when we stumble, in order to seek their guidance and counsel.

Lest Satan Get An Advantage: Forgive the Sinner!

Paul admonished the church at Corinth to forgive the brother who repented of the brazen and disgusting sin of taking his father's wife – a sin which even Gentiles detested.[47] Promising to join them in this spirit of forgiveness, Paul urged the saints, "Confirm your love toward him. . . . Lest Satan should get an advantage of us: for we are not ignorant of his devices" (2 Cor. 2:8-11). The pull of pornography is powerful, and every possible countervailing power is required to overcome it. The love and forgiveness of fellow Christians is one of the greatest of those powers.

The brother or the sister who musters the courage to openly confess the sin of pornography bears a heavy burden of sorrow and shame. Our words of sincere encouragement, our body language of acceptance, and our extension of hospitality will confirm our love and forgiveness. This love which "beareth all things, believeth all things, hopeth all things, endureth all things," and "never faileth" gives the restored brother or sister renewed hope (1 Cor. 13:7-8). If we shun and isolate this person, Satan will take full advantage of his vulnerabilities.

Because of the addictive nature of pornography, we must be ready and willing to forgive "seventy times seven" if our brother or sister falls again and repents again (Matt. 18:22). This is part of the process of escaping the horrible slavery of Satan and sin.

Forgiving and loving includes reaching out to strengthen and stabilize our restored brother or sister. Inviting this person to associate with us, or even offering to make ourselves available day or night when temptations arise, may cost us time, money, and sleep – but this is how we get the advantage over Satan.

We may hesitate to truly forgive and show our love while we thank God and congratulate ourselves that we are "not as other men are," but we would

---

[47] For the background to this situation, see 1 Corinthians 5.

do well to remember the lesson of Jesus about two men who prayed: one a self-righteous Pharisee, the other a brokenhearted tax collector. "And the publican, standing afar off, would not lift up so much as his eyes unto heaven, but smote upon his breast, saying, God be merciful to me a sinner." Jesus observed, "This man went down to his house justified, rather than the other," then drew out this important lesson: "For everyone that exalteth himself shall be abased; and he that humbleth himself shall be exalted" (Lk. 18:10-14). Let us humble ourselves to love and serve the penitent sinner who humbles himself, that we may be exalted together in the eyes of the Lord.

Conclusion: Hope, Rest, and Peace with God

Without question or doubt, the sin of pornography like all other sins can be overcome through the power of the gospel of Christ. God forgives us when we submit to Him in Christ, and God instructs us to know that He alone is our God. We will not be deceived when Satan tries to seduce us with pornography to make an idol god of sex. We will learn to imitate God by walking in love in this sex-saturated society. As we find hope, rest, and peace in fellowship with God, the cruel demon of pornography is driven out from our hearts and souls.

Let our constant prayer be the prayer of Psalm 19:14, "Let the words of my mouth, and the meditation of my heart, be acceptable in thy sight, O LORD, my strength, and my redeemer."

Bibliography and Additional Resources

Adburgham, Alison. "Mary Quant talks to Alison Adburgham Tuesday 10 October 1967." Interview published in *The Guardian* (British newspaper published in London). Accessed March 15, 2013. *http://century.guardian. co.uk/1960-1969/Story/0,,106475,00.html.*

Alford, Henry. *The Greek New Testament.* Revised by Everett F. Harrison. 2 double vols. Chicago: Moody Press, 1958.

Allen, Frederick E. "When Sex Drives Technological Innovation." *American Heritage Magazine* 51, 5 (Sept. 2000): 19-20.

"Anything Goes: Taboos in Twilight." *Newsweek*, November 13, 1967, pp. 74-78.

Arndt, William F., and F. Wilbur Gingrich, *A Greek-English Lexicon of the New Testament.* Chicago: The University of Chicago Press, 1957.

Arterburn, Stephen, and Fred Stoeker with Mike Yorkey. *Every Man's Battle:*

Winning the War on Sexual Temptation One Victory at a Time. Colorado Springs, CO: Waterbrook Press, 2000.

Banowsky, William S. and Anson Mount. *Christianity and Hedonism, A Clash of Philosophies.* Austin, TX: Christian Chronicle, 1967.

Bork, Robert H. *Slouching Toward Gomorrah: Modern Liberalism and American Decline.* New York: ReganBooks, 1996.

Brown, Francis, S. R. Driver, and Charles A. Briggs, eds. *A Hebrew and English Lexicon of the Old Testament.* Oxford: Clarendon Press, [1906]. Reprint, [1951].

Caldwell, C. G. "Colly." *Ephesians* in *Truth Commentaries.* Ed. by Mike Willis. Bowling Green, KY: Guardian of Truth Foundation, 1994.

Collins, Robert. *East to Cathay: The Silk Road.* Tadworth: World's Work, 1971.

Court, John H. *Pornography: A Christian Critique.* Downers Grove, IL: InterVarsity Press, 1980.

Deitch, Ian. "Playboy magazine launches Hebrew language edition," *Courier-Post,* March 5, 2013. Accessed April 1, 2013. *http://www.courierpostonline.com/viewart/20130305/ENT/303050038/Playboy-magazine-launches-Hebrew-language-edition.*

Dobson, James. "Fatal Attraction: Ted Bundy's Final Interview." Pure Intimacy. Accessed March 21, 2013. *http://www.pureintimacy.org/piArticles/A000000433.cfm.*

_____. *Love Must Be Tough.* Nashville: Word Publishing, 1996.

_____. *Straight Talk.* Nashville: Word Publishing, 1995.

Ethridge, Shannon, and Stephen Arterburn, afterword. *Every Woman's Battle: Discovering God's Plan for Sexual and Emotional Fulfillment.* Colorado Springs, CO: Waterbrook Press, 2009.

Gesenius, Wilhelm, and Samuel Prideaux Tregelles. *Hebrew and Chaldee Lexicon to the Old Testament Scriptures.* Grand Rapids, MI: Eerdmans, 1957.

Gilkerson, Luke. "Your Brain on Porn." CovenantEyes. Jan. 9, 2012. Accessed March 23, 2013. *http://www.covenanteyes.com/.*

Halbrook, Ron. "God Hears the Cry of the Weak," in Mike Willis, ed.,

God Give Us Christian Homes: Truth Magazine Annual Lectures June 26-29, 2006 (pp. 333-348). Bowling Green, KY: Guardian of Truth Foundation, 2006.

_____. "'Marriage Is Honorable:' A Study of Marriage, Divorce, and Remarriage," *Guardian of Truth*, XL, 12 (June 20, 1996):368-371. Reprinted as tract under same title: Bowling Green, KY: Guardian of Truth Foundation, [1996].

_____. *The Halbrook-Freeman Debate on Marriage, Divorce, & Remarriage.* Bowling Green, KY: Guardian of Truth Foundation, 1995.

_____. "Pornography and Fornication: Two Deadly Sins." *Truth Magazine* XLVI, 13 (July 4, 2002):400-403.

Harris, R. Laird, Gleason Archer, and Bruce Waltke, eds. *Theological Wordbook of the Old Testament.* 2 Vols. Chicago: Moody Press, 1980.

Herodotus. *The Histories* trans. A.D. Godley Cambridge: Harvard University Press, 1920.

Kittel, G. and G. Friedrich, eds. *Theological Dictionary of the New Testament* (TDNT), 10 vols. Grand Rapids: Eerdmans, 1964-76.

LaRue, Janet M. "Porn Nation," *World and I* 16, 8 (Aug. 1, 2001): 44-49.

Olshausen, Hermann. *Biblical Commentary on the New Testament.* Trans. by A.C. Kendrick. Bowling Green, KY: Guardian of Truth Foundation, 2005 [orig. publ. New York, Sheldon: Blakeman & co., 1857-58].

O'Neill, Hugh. "What Are You Looking At?" *AARP Magazine* [American Association of Retired Persons]. March & April 2004, p. 28.

Paul, Pamela. "He Sexts, She Sexts More, Report Says," *New York Times,* July 15, 2011. Accessed March 30, 2013. *http://www.nytimes. com/2011/07/17/fashion/women-are-more-likely-to-sext-than-men-study-says-studied.html?partner=rss&emc=rss&_r=0.*

"Resource on Pornography." Aurora Publication, The Aurora Center: University of Minnesota. Accessed March 21, 2013. *Http://www1.umn.edu/aurora/pdf/ResearchOnPornography.pdf .*

Rich, Frank. "Naked Capitalists: There's No Business Like Porn Business." *New York Times Magazine,* May 20, 2001. Accessed March 24, 2013. *Http://www.nytimes.com/2001/05/20/magazine/20PORN.html.*

Roberts, Ted. *Pure Desire: Helping People Break Free from Sexual Struggles.* Ventura, CA: Regal, 1999.

Salmond, S. D. F., *The Epistle to the Ephesians*, in *The Expositor's Greek Testament*, ed. W. Robertson Nicoll, vol. 3 (New York : Dodd, Mead, 1897-1910; reprint, Grand Rapids: William B. Eerdmans, 1974.)

Schuchardt, Read Mercer. "Hugh Hefner's Hollow Victory." *Christianity Today* 47, 12 (Dec. 2003): 50-54.

Shalit, Wendy. *A Return to Modesty: Discovering the Lost Virtue.* New York, NY: The Free Press, 1999.

Struthers, William M. "The Effects of Porn on the Male Brain." *Christian Research Journal*, 34, 5 (2011). Accessed March 30, 2013. *http://www.equip.org/articles/the-effects-of-porn-on-the-male-brain-3/.*

_____. *Wired for Intimacy: How Pornography Hijacks the Male Brain.* Downers Grove, IL: InterVarsity Press, 2009.

Trench, Richard Chenevix. *Synonyms of the New Testament.* Marshallton, DE: National Foundation for Christian Education, 19 – [1855; rev. 1880].

Vine, W. E. *An Expository Dictionary of New Testament Words.* 4 Vols. in 1. Westwood, N.J.: Fleming H. Revell, 1962.

Willis, Mike, ed. *God Give Us Christian Homes: Truth Magazine Annual Lectures June 26-29, 2006.* Bowling Green, KY: Guardian of Truth Foundation, 2006.

_____. *Great Texts of the New Testament: Truth Magazine Annual Lectures June 23-26, 2008.* Bowling Green, KY: Guardian of Truth Foundation, 2008.

_____. *The Inspiration and Authority of the Scriptures: Truth Magazine Annual Lectures July 11-14, 2005.* Bowling Green, KY: Guardian of Truth Foundation, 2005.

Woman in the Home

Can I Be A Supermom?

Elaine Jordan

Introduction

In today's busy world, modern women often feel that we must be success-ful businesswomen; sexy wives; wonderful homemakers, and compassionate mothers. Adding to these roles, the idea that women must be all things to all people and the best at every measure makes a modern paradigm that can be crushing to women.

The Bible also provides us with high standards. The virtuous wife of Proverbs 31 is a high bar that Christian women reach for, but we sometimes find it to be more intimidating than the modern paradigm. This woman is a great wife, industrious homemaker, successful businesswoman, concerned community volunteer, supporting city leader, wise, strong, and honorable. The virtuous wife in Proverbs sets a higher standard than the modern para-digm, because the virtuous wife *fears the Lord*.

Elaine Jordan was born on April 13, 1955 to D. C. and Nancy Laws and is the oldest of three children. She met her husband, Ray Carpenter Jordan, in Knoxville, Tennessee and they married on February 14, 1986 during the middle of an epic ice storm. Ray and Elaine have two sons, Adam and Scott. Adam Jordan is serving in the Navy aboard the USS Hue City and Scott Jordan is attending graduate school for Physical Therapy.

Elaine graduated from East Tennessee State University in 1976 with a BS in Com-puter Science. She began her career as a computer analyst at Tennessee Valley Authority (TVA) and left TVA as the IT Manager at Browns Ferry Nuclear Plant in fall 1994. She founded her own company, Total Solutions, in May 1995 to perform contracting services for both gov-ernment organizations and private companies. In 2005, one of Total Solutions' employees became a partner and continues to manage the company allowing Elaine to re-tire from Total Solutions in January, 2010 to care for her mother who had ALS. Ray retired the following year and they moved to a farm in Pulaski, Tennessee.

Elaine Jordan has written two devotional books, *A Christian's Musing* and *Reflections*.

The virtuous wife is the biblical example of wisdom in action. The book of Proverbs teaches us about wisdom and often portrays wisdom as Lady Wisdom and her activities as the virtuous wife. Should we aspire to be like this wife of Proverbs 31:10-31 and does this example apply to us as modern women? I don't know all the answers and today's discussion will not cover all aspects of Lady Wisdom's virtues. My goal is to discuss the problems of working outside the home while being a Christian wife, homemaker, and mother. The virtuous wife can be our example as she is a wonderful wife, mother, and homemaker while making a profit from her fields and vineyards.

Today working outside the home is reality for many women and often a divisive issue among Christians. Even though we try very hard, we cannot be as successful as Lady Wisdom while we balance all the demands of our time and attention. Christian women need to be working women whatever their circumstances and face the same problems wherever they are working. We women certainly have a hard time measuring up to Lady Wisdom and the example she sets in Proverbs 31.

Today women work outside of the home for many reasons. Actually I don't like the term "working outside of the home," because it implies women who don't have a job outside the home are not working. Often working moms devalue their stay-at-home sisters. Stay-at-home women do have a job and are working every day. They just don't get a paycheck. Working women often get the benefits of stay-at-home moms when these mothers volunteer at school or are available for the working mothers as back-ups for their sick children. Stay-at-home women may be the ones who support our Christian brethren when they need a hand. Where we work shouldn't be the issue among Christian women. All of us should be working women.

So why do Christian women work outside of the home? For some, it is because their paychecks are necessary to pay the bills and to supplement what their husbands earn. Some of our sisters are single mothers responsible for supporting their households. Some need to work because unfortunate circumstances have turned their world upside down and money must come into the household. Some work to pay for extras for the household or to save for their children's college or their own retirement. Some women work to make a difference in the world, others to keep their credentials current, and others for self-fulfillment. Women choose or are compelled to work outside the home for many reasons.

I chose to work outside the home and was not compelled because my husband financially supported our family well. My husband and I are a working couple. Together we raised two sons who make us very proud. Our older son is serving in the Navy and the second is attending grad school for physical therapy. I worked outside the home until I retired. For sixteen years, I worked for TVA and my last position there was the Information Technology Manager at Browns Ferry Nuclear Plant. I chose to leave Browns Ferry to spend more time with our young sons and started my own company. This company performed services that government and commercial business contracted out. It started in a home office and grew to over 200 employees. I have retired, but my business is still running under my business partner's direction. After retiring, I have many personal projects and work with the Guardian of Truth Foundation to publish devotional material, so I still have interests "outside the home."

So yes, I combined being a Christian, wife, mother, homemaker, and businesswoman into one busy life. And yes, Proverbs is spot-on when the virtuous wife is said to *"rise while it is still night"* and *"her lamp does not go out by night."* Being a Christian woman requires work no matter what tasks you choose. All Christians must be industrious. In 2 Thessalonians Paul writes, *"we commanded you this: If anyone will not work, neither shall he eat"* (3:10). America's Puritan work ethic and the virtuous wife are powerful drivers for us to be workers and most understand that the Bible teaches that all of us must work. However, cramming a career, marriage, and homemaker into one life is hard for anyone.

So, at the outset, let me state our goal is not to be a Supermom like the lecture title suggests. The fact is there are no Supermoms any more than there is a Superman. Superman is a fictional character who was "faster than a speeding bullet, more powerful than a locomotive, and able to leap tall buildings in a single bound." But, there is no Superman! And, neither is there any Supermom! Every woman has only twenty-four hours in a given day and can only cram so much into any given moment of time. No time management skills guru can change this fact. Consequently, ordinary women have to make choices – choices guided by the revelation of God's word to frame her life, just like men must do. Our goal is to be the best Christian woman we can and today we are going to consider the virtuous wife for our example.

We know the virtuous wife has these attributes – her husband trusts her, she is a good homemaker, and she fears God. Let's discuss potential problems that working outside the home can have on our marriages, our homes, and our relationship with God.

Priorities Within Our Marriages

Having the correct priorities within our marriage is often hard for a busy, working woman. Even identifying the priorities is complicated in our current society with so many conflicting examples and demands. When we are not careful, we learn what marriage priorities should be from modern media which portrays husbands as bumbling fools, dedicated wives as simpletons, and successful business women as conniving cougars.

A Christian woman must balance her life to fulfill God's requirements, build her marriage, and accomplish her goals in the business world. This balance comes from understanding and managing our priorities which are God, our marriage, our children, and then everything else. Everything else includes our jobs, our clubs, our friends, everyone we know, and everyone else to whom we are related.

Ephesians 5:22-23 demonstrates these priorities well. *"Wives, submit yourselves to your own husbands as you do to the Lord. For the husband is the head of the wife as Christ is the head of the church, his body, of which he is the Savior."* In these verses, God clearly has the highest priority and the husband is the next priority for Christian women.

A lot of women get tied up with the words "submit to your husband" and are adamantly not interested in being a Stepford wife to any man. This is not what God intended. In following verses, He told husbands *"love your wives, just as Christ loved the church"* and *"love their wives as their own bodies. He who loves his wife loves himself"* (Eph. 5:25a, 28). A God-centered marriage has one leader for the family with two partners building a life together. Working outside our homes can devalue our home life to us and cause us to ignore what our real priorities should be.

God, then our marriage – those are our priorities. When we are busy working, our priorities can become upside down. Business deadlines, travel schedules, and ringing phones can become our motivators and the only things we think about. Our personal identities can be tied up with our business roles. Instead of being a Christian wife to my husband, I can be the business entrepreneur looking for the next big thing. It is not wrong to develop the next big thing. What is wrong is neglecting God and our husbands.

Yes, I know that I have not told anyone how to balance her priorities and the minutes of her life. But your heart knows where your true interests are. If your business challenges are the most important thing in your life with God and your marriage mixed in for good composition, then you already know your priorities are not right.

As we establish our priorities, we must be honest with ourselves, accept what we are, and not measure ourselves with someone else's ruler. Some women have the physical and emotional strength to be involved in many activities at the same time. They are capable of managing both a career and their home and may be more involved in the local church than some stay-at-home moms. Other women are not as suited to the pressures that working outside the home imposes on family life which they recognize as their priority. Every woman must learn to adjust to her unique strengths and limitations as she balances her life to fulfill God's requirements.

Godly women have God, their marriage, and their families as their life priorities.

Temptations in a Business Environment
Marriage is hard in any circumstance and a working wife often has a lot of temptations enticing her away from her marriage commitment. Long hours, business travel, and close working relationships between men and women can beguile two office mates into believing a love affair would hurt no one. We know this isn't the truth.

Ephesians 5:3-7 tells us the real truth. *"But among you there must not be even a hint of sexual immorality, or of any kind of impurity, or of greed, because these are improper for God's holy people. Nor should there be obscenity, foolish talk or coarse joking, which are out of place, but rather thanksgiving. For of this you can be sure: No immoral, impure or greedy person—such a person is an idolater—has any inheritance in the kingdom of Christ and of God."*

The danger of intimate association between business associates has led to many wrecked homes. A woman may come into the office and see her male co-worker sad or angry. They begin talking and he cries on her shoulder about how badly his wife is treating him. A perfectly legitimate relationship can change into a dangerous situation in the most innocent way – a touch, a subtle glance, a suggestive word, or a private joke. We can let our guard down in the workplace, because we spend so much time there and are not paying attention to the dangers.

Love affairs are never a good thing. Sexual immorality is condemned throughout the Bible and adulterers were stoned in Bible times. We cannot even say that love affairs between working people are a modern problem. Antony and Cleopatra were well known lovers in Roman times. Antony was married to Octavia, the sister of Octavius Caesar, and his infatuation with Cleopatra caused him to divorce Octavia to marry Cleopatra, Pharaoh of Egypt. This relationship caused a war and resulted in death to both Antony and Cleopatra.

Love affairs are not in God's design for marriage. There is never a way that a Christian woman can commit any sexual immorality and honor her marriage vows. This includes simple flirting or any type of intimate relationship with a male coworker that excludes or devalues your husband. This is *improper for God's holy people.* When your coworkers, either man or woman, become more important to you than your husband, you are not honoring God or your marriage.

Some business environments are not good for our marriages or us as a Christian, because the work environment itself is not godly! They can be filled with crude jokes and gossip which lead Christian women from godly lives. For example, being "in the know" about the office may mean knowing more than just office procedures. Being "in the know" may mean knowing all the ugly things in the coworkers' lives and indulging in idle gossip about them. Being a popular person in the office may mean telling crude or hateful jokes to entertain our coworkers or listening to them tell those same jokes. Remember in James 3:10, we are taught that from the tongue proceeds both blessing and cursing, but only blessings should be there! Don't let our presence in an ungodly business environment cause us to slip into gossip and foolish talk. Christians cannot participate in this type of office activity.

Some businesses are so intent on making a profit that business practices include lying, cheating, and stealing. Our jobs may ask us to participate in activities that look just a little askew and we don't notice that we are sliding toward sin. Marketing practices may include omission of a product flaw or exaggeration of a capability leading to total misrepresentation of our companies and ourselves. Poor business practices can demand profit over substance at all costs. Working in an ungodly business environment can seduce us into believing a strong bottom line for the company or a beautiful home, nice car, and retirement plan for ourselves are our most important goals, because greed has become our motivator.

There is nothing wrong with have having a strong bottom line, a beautiful home, nice car, and retirement plan. It is wrong when material wealth has all your attention and has become your idol. God has warned us that, when we are greedy and have let earthly wealth become our idol, He is not our first love, and we are not part of His kingdom. *"For of this you can be sure: No immoral, impure or greedy person – such a person is an idolater – has any inheritance in the kingdom of Christ and of God"* (Eph. 5:5). I am not saying that working outside the home will cause a Christian woman to become greedy and participate in shoddy business practices. However, godly women must recognize those enticements, avoid sin, and remember their priorities – God, marriage, and children.

Christian women must hold themselves apart from ungodly business practices and environments. When we find ourselves in a bad business situation, we must determine how we are going to get out of it. Remember Joseph fled from Potiphar's wife leaving his coat in her hand! Joseph chose jail rather than sin (Gen. 39:12, 20). Just because we need a job doesn't mean we need a job that will cause us to sin. A godly woman must guard herself against the temptations in her workplace, just like Joseph did.

Family Leadership

What happens when the wife is more successful than the husband in the business world? She can make more money, have higher professional status, or have more education than the husband. When the wife has more status or leadership in the business world, this can spill over into the marriage causing her to assume the leadership position there. Some women have more natural leadership capabilities than their husbands and leading the family is a natural outcome for them.

A woman asserting her leadership from the work environment into the marriage can happen in our marriages. Yes, God wants our families to have good leaders and has identified the husband as the leader. In Titus 2: 5b, He tells women to be *"obedient to their own husbands, that the word of God may not be blasphemed."*

A girlfriend told me a story to illustrate this command. When we are single women, we are paddling our own canoe. We have both oars and are responsible for the direction and speed of our canoe. We can go anywhere we want! When we marry, we agree to sit in the front seat of our husband's canoe with one paddle. He sits in the back with his paddle and directs the canoe. If the front seat follows the direction of the back seat, then the canoe glides smoothly through the water. When the front and back seats paddle separately or the front seat tries to guide the canoe, the canoe goes in circles. The canoe only operates smoothly when the back seat is guiding the canoe and the front seat pulls with the leadership. Both seats are working together in harmony in their canoe. Christian marriages are like this canoe and the husband sits in the back seat.

A godly man will recognize the skills of his wife and utilize them to the greatest benefit of his family. Some women are more skilled in managing the finances than the man and the husband might ask his wife to take charge of this aspect of the household, for the benefit of all members of the family. He will appreciate the wisdom of his godly wife and consult her before making decisions that affect all of the family. A young woman should be looking for a man who has judgment enough to appreciate the contribution she can make the home when she is looking for a mate.

As I said earlier, a God-centered marriage has one leader for the family with two partners building a life together. Remember Jesus submitted to God's will in the Garden of Gethsemane. He said, *"not My will, but Yours, be done"* (Luke 22:42b). Both Jesus and God are deity and members of the Trinity, but Jesus submitted to God's plan. We, as Christian women, should also submit to God's plan. Remember Ephesians 5:23 tells us that the husband is the head of the household and Christ is head of the church. When we follow the leadership of our husbands, we are not allowing the word of God to be blasphemed. A godly woman follows the leadership of her husband.

As with the woman of Proverbs 31, a husband can trust his virtuous wife because she. . .

- Knows her life priorities are God, her marriage, her family, and then everything else
- Avoids ungodly temptations in her work environment and
- Follows her husband's leadership.

Shortchanging Our Homemaker Responsibilities
Working outside the home can cause a Christian woman to shortchange her role as homemaker. The woman's attitude and personality as the homemaker sets the tone for the household. My husband taught our sons, "When Mama isn't happy, nobody is happy." My husband wasn't teaching that Mom was the leader of the household, but that she establishes the character and qualities of the household. Wives and mothers create a restful, nurturing home or a chaotic, discouraging house.

The management of the household is a role given to women. In 1 Timothy 5:14, the management of the household is identified as the responsibility of the woman. Different translations use terms, such as, ruling the household, taking care of their homes, and guiding the house. Clearly God wanted women to create homes for their families.

When working mothers focus on material priorities, such as fancy houses, new cars, and savings accounts, the tendency of the household is to measure everything with dollar signs. When work is always the biggest priority for Mom, real priorities of God, marriage, and family slide into oblivion. When unproductive activities, such as television or Facebook, command an inappropriate amount of time, then the whole household swims against the tide of inattention. Nothing is necessarily wrong with a big house, new car, a savings account, work deadlines, television, or Facebook. The issue is how the mother mixes these concerns with real priorities that have lasting consequences. A working mom must manage her household so that God is honored and family members are nurtured.

In Titus 2:5, women are told to be homemakers so the word of God is not blasphemed. In 1 Timothy 5, young widows are counseled to marry, to have children, to manage their homes, and to give the enemy no opportunity for slander. How we Christian women run our households does matter. Our actions and our households must glorify God, build God's kingdom, and strengthen our families. Inattentiveness on our part to the real priorities of life can give nonbelievers reason to doubt or discredit God's word. This does not mean the house is immaculately clean every day and every meal is home cooked – not at all. This means Christian homes are managed with God as the priority. Working women cannot give up the management of their home because they also work outside the home. The role of homemaker is too important for that.

We women sometimes do not put an appropriate value on mundane homemaker duties. If home life is not valuable, then why do marketers use images of children and mothers making cookies and families eating meals together to sell their products? They do that because they know a strong home life is one of the most desirable things for all humans. People who were not lucky enough to have loving homes as children often have bitterness, instead of love, in their hearts. Those with strong homes have a solid base to face the world and all its problems. Even worldly leaders know this. William Ross Wallace said that the hand that rocks the cradle is the hand that rules the world.

Putting our homemaker duties into a high priority does not mean the homemaker cannot use outside help to perform those services. The virtuous wife in Proverbs did not give up the management of her home when she guided her servants to perform domestic chores. Sarah, Leah, and Rachel did not give up the management of their homes when Hagar, Bilhah, and Zilpah performed domestic chores. Neither is a godly women giving up the management of their home, when they use a cleaning service, eat at a restaurant, or use a daycare service. This is no different than the husband using a yard service, mechanic, or carpenter to help with his household duties. A godly woman may make a conscious decision to hire someone to do a job she is perfectly capable of doing so that she has more time with her husband and children when she is at home. Her time may be better spent reading to her children than cleaning the bathroom. Or the godly woman may hire someone to do jobs that she can no longer do due to her declining health or other priorities of her time. She is managing the household to create a restful, nurturing home.

Earlier we discussed how each woman has different strengths and limitations as she works on her priorities of God, marriage, and family. The fact is there are only twenty-four hours in every day. A person can only fit so much into those hours without something suffering from not being given enough time and attention. What is enough attention from the mother's point of view may not be enough attention from the husband's or child's point of view. One must meet the needs of those to whom she committed herself when she married and became a mother. Do not be deceived by the quality time versus quantity of time cliché. A godly woman cannot neglect her homemaker responsibilities!

Time Away From Home
Sometimes mothers with jobs outside the home feel that they are short-changing their husbands and children because they are away from them during working hours and do not stay home all the time. This may be due to our ideas of a "Beaver Cleaver" mother from a 1950s television show. Mrs. Cleaver was always home with her pearls and apron on. Remember our female ancestors worked hard in their homes, in their fields, and in their stores. They sewed, spun, and hoed. They have worked throughout history without worrying about whether they should be stay at home or not. The issue isn't working away from home, but the management of the home.

No woman can spend 100% of her time with her husband or children and this shouldn't be her goal. Going back to the virtuous wife in Proverbs

31, did she take her children with her everywhere like a mama duck with all her ducklings tagging along behind? Did this virtuous wife have her children with her as she sought wool and flax, worked with her hands, went to the market, took care of her servants and the poor, bought land, planted vineyards, sold merchandise, spun yarn, made clothes, and supported her husband? Not always. However, she was responsible for her children and household 100% of the time and oversaw that they had appropriate care when they were not with her. The virtuous wife used her time productively by rising early and working long hours to accomplish all her duties.

Managing time is important no matter whether the woman works outside the home or is a stay-at-home mom. As the homemaker of the family, the woman is the center of home management ensuring that important activities preempt the urgent or insistent activities. Sometimes we know what our family priorities should be, but have trouble making them our daily priorities and to appropriately involve our household. We feel we have to be all things to all people and to enable our family members to do or have everything they dream. We set ourselves up for stressful lives and questionable objectives. This problem is not unique to the mother working outside the home, but is a problem for every woman.

Step back and look at your daily activities. Does your "busyness" support what you believe your priorities should be? No one can perform this review for you; however you, your husband, and your family live with the consequences of your "busyness." Your time away from home is not the problem. Managing your time so that your important homemaker duties are done is the problem. Godly mothers manage their time so as to be good homemakers.

Teaching and Training our Children
Success in the working world can make secular education for our children to have more value than teaching them about God. We all want our children to have the best possible education to provide them with the knowledge, skills, and abilities to succeed, but so has every parent throughout time. For example, the Apostle Paul was from an influential Jewish family with Roman citizenship who could provide the best for their son and so Paul was sent to the school of Hillel. Paul sat at the feet of Gamaliel to learn theology, law, and leadership. Gamaliel was on the Sanhedrin council, a Pharisee, and *a teacher of the law held in respect by all the people* who taught the

most promising young Pharisees to become rabbis.[1] Also according to the custom of New Testament times, Paul was taught tent making for a trade. (Acts 5:34; 18:3; 22:3). Paul's mother wanted the best for her children – just like we want the best for ours.

The biggest point to learn from Paul's mother is that she taught Paul to have a zeal for God. She wanted the best for Paul and taught him to love and fear God. Paul was demonstrating his zeal for God when he was persecuting the early Christians. This same zeal is why God counted Paul faithful and put him into the ministry (1 Tim. 1:12).

Teaching our children to know God has been emphasized to godly parents throughout time. In Deuteronomy 6, we are told to teach the greatest commandment to our children.

> You shall love the Lord your God with all your heart, with all your soul, and with all your strength. And these words which I command you today shall be in your heart. You shall teach them diligently to your children, and shall talk of them when you sit in your house, when you walk by the way, when you lie down, and when you rise up.

We can teach our children to love God when we talk with them, when we are working, when we are traveling, when we are relaxing, when we getting up in the morning and going to bed at night. We must teach our children to love God all day, every day. Yes, we are responsible for sending our children to school to learn math, history, science, and literature. However, teaching our children to love God with all their heart, soul, and strength is the most important lesson to teach them.

Our example teaches them as much as our words do. When our job is the most important thing in our life, this lesson is not lost on our children. Our children may know us better than we know ourselves. It is certainly clear to them when the parents attend church only to be seen by others or perform good deeds for the praise of others or your work is the most important thing to you. Notice verse 6 says the *words should be in your heart*. We cannot teach our children well when we do not live in a manner honoring God. Our children will not miss the lesson we are really teaching, when our jobs are more important to us than God, our marriage, or our family. It does not matter what you say when you act a different way. Godly women must teach their children to love and honor God.

---

[1] *Manners and Customs of Bible Lands,* Fred H. Wight, Moody Press (1953), 116.

Disciplining our Children

Discipline is hard for all mothers no matter where they work. However, a mother who works outside the home may give away the control of discipline to others. This is never the right thing to do. Teaching our children right from wrong with appropriate discipline is ours to do, not the school system's responsibility or our child care providers. These entities may support us or provide reinforcement of our training, but it is the Christian parents' responsibility to train and discipline our children.

Discipline is hard to do properly for any parent. Sometimes we think we love our children too much to cause them any tears or disappointment. I have seen parents throw in the towel and give up on discipline for their children. Proverbs has many verses to encourage parents about their children's discipline.

- Proverbs 13:24b – the one who loves her children is careful to discipline them.

- Proverbs 19:18a – Discipline your children, for in that there is hope

- Proverbs 29:15 – A rod and a reprimand impart wisdom, but a child left undisciplined disgraces its mother.

Discipline is a controversial subject for all parents and a divisive issue in our society. We have child counselors promoting new fads, theories, and methodologies for raising and disciplining children. Today there are parents whose goal is to provide only positive reinforcement for their children's self esteem and view discipline as a negative to be avoided. A whole generation has been raised with Dr. Spock and his relaxed attitude of childrearing and discipline. Sometimes a working mother may avoid discipline as too hard or would rather be a friend to her children than a mother.

Remember God said, *"Those whom I love I rebuke and discipline"* (Rev. 3:19a). In Hebrews 12, the author (perhaps Paul) writes,

Endure hardship as discipline; God is treating you as his children. For what children are not disciplined by their father? If you are not disciplined – and everyone undergoes discipline – then you are not legitimate, not true sons and daughters at all. Moreover, we have all had human fathers who disciplined us and we respected them for it. How much more should we submit to the Father of spirits and live! They disciplined us for a little while as they thought best; but God disciplines us for our good, in order that we may share in his holiness. No discipline seems pleasant at the time, but painful. Later on, however, it produces a harvest of righteousness and peace for those who have been trained by it.

Loving, Christian parents discipline their children to teach them right from wrong and to encourage proper behavior and attitudes. If God disciplines those whom He loves, parents must discipline their children whom they love. True, neither the parent nor the child will enjoy the discipline, but all will enjoy the child who has learned well. This disciplined child can grow up to be a wonderful young adult who loves God and his parents.

Often we are unsure what our discipline should be. We have so many experts with books, televisions shows, and college degrees who claim to know more on the subject than we do. Our discipline methods must be appropriate for each child without undue harshness and must be in their best interest. Appropriate discipline is not always physical, is certainly not unreasonably severe, nor does it ridicule the child. Parents may find it necessary to discipline each of their children differently, too. A verbal reprimand may be sufficient for one child, timeouts for one, and spanking for another. It is also important that the discipline is appropriate for the child's misdeed and age. Spankings are not the only discipline method. I did spank my two sons, but that is not the only punishment that I used. Other methods may work better for a particular child or in a particular situation and parents must use appropriate disciplinary methods. Remember Proverbs teaches that an undisciplined child is a disgrace and not loved. Providing discipline to teach our children is part of being a mother. All discipline must be controlled and not delivered in anger. Undue harshness has a negative effect on our teaching, is discouraging to our children, and teaches them to hate. We cannot fly into a rage and rant vicious things to our children and consider that to be appropriate discipline. All we have taught is hate.

* *"Do not provoke your children to wrath, but bring them up in the training and admonition of the Lord"* (Eph. 6:4b).

* *"Do not provoke your children, lest they become discouraged"* (Col. 3:21b).

These verses demonstrate that a balance is necessary to nurture, train, teach, and discipline our children. As we are disciplining our children, they must understand that we love them and God loves them. They must know they are *dearly loved children* (Eph. 5:1).

Working outside the home may make it easier for us to let bad behavior slide or to expect someone else to discipline our children, because we don't have time or don't want to be unkind to our children. We are not our children's best friend. We are their mothers. Godly women cannot shirk their responsibilities to teach and discipline their children.

As with the woman of Proverbs 31, a Christian woman,

* Recognizes the importance of being a homemaker
* Manages her time well
* Teaches her children to love God and
* Disciplines her children appropriately.

Fearing God

The last verses of Proverbs 31 make the last point for this lesson. We have seen that the virtuous wife is a good wife, mother, homemaker who works hard inside and outside the home and throughout the city.

> She watches over the ways of her household,
> And does not eat the bread of idleness.
> Her children rise up and call her blessed;
> Her husband also, and he praises her:
> "Many daughters have done well,
> But you excel them all."
> Charm is deceitful and beauty is passing,
> But a woman who fears the Lord, she shall be praised.
> Give her of the fruit of her hands,
> And let her own works praise her in the gates.

The virtuous wife of Proverbs 31 performs all her duties of wife, mother, and homemaker, makes business decisions, takes care of the poor, is involved in the community, and supports her husband's city leadership – all while she fears and respects our Lord. The godly wife knows God is first no matter where she is working. This is the truth that we must remember.

Sometimes we get so busy with the details of life that we forget to spend time with God. Just think how quiet time in prayer and reading your Bible calms your inner self and strengthens you. Spending time with God is an investment in yourself which prepares you for everything and everyone else.

Our modern culture tells us to invest in ourselves by taking care of ourselves first, to stay beautiful and young looking, and to be self sufficient without dependence on anyone or anything else. We are told that we are working hard and deserve to spoil ourselves and are spending our own money anyway. If you believe modern media, everyone can have anything as long as she wants it bad enough and works hard enough. Our modern culture and media are not teaching us the truth.

"A woman who fears the Lord, she shall be praised." That is the truth. Time with God is the investment in yourself and a godly woman honors God. There are many wonderful examples of working women in the Old and New Testament. These women used their daily opportunities to praise and honor God.

Queen Esther was a follower of God and her bravery saved the Jewish people from the vengeance of Haman. Queen Esther displayed courage and conviction when she approached King Ahasuerus to save the Jewish people from Haman's plot to destroy them. *"Who knows whether you have come to the kingdom for such a time as this?"* (Esth. 4:14b) was her Uncle Mordecai's question. Sometimes our opportunities to honor God are His providence and we must use those opportunities. Queen Esther demonstrated her faith in God and saved her people from annilation. Godly women must use their opportunities to show others their faith in God.

Priscilla and Aquila (Acts 18:24-27) were tentmakers and heard Apollos who *spoke and taught accurately the things of the Lord, though he knew only the baptism of John.* Priscilla and Aquila took him aside and taught him the *way of God more accurately.* Here Priscilla, a working woman, and her husband take their opportunity to teach an acquaintance about God. Priscilla and Aquila interrupted their moneymaking activities to teach Apollos about baptism. Another time, they risked their lives for Paul (Rom. 16:3-4) and supported the spread of the gospel. Honoring God was more important to this working couple than making their living at tentmaking or to taking the safe path with their lives. This working couple worked hard to spread the good news of Christ wherever they were working. We working women must also take time and the risk to teach others and to spread the good news of the gospel.

A great multitude of devout Greeks and leading women became Christians when Paul and Silas were in Thessalonica (Acts 17:1-4). The term "leading women" in these verses indicates these were prominent women who either held leading positions in the city or were the wives of leading officials. There is evidence that women of Macedonia often exercised considerable influence, worked outside the home[2] and were prominent in the church. These women would have used their positions and influence to spread the gospel and to encourage the Christian community in Thessalonica. Paul commends women often in his writings. For example, in Romans 16, he

---

[2] *Truth Commentaries: Acts,* Johnny Stringer (1999), 348.

commends Phoebe, Priscilla, Mary, Junia, Tryphena, Tryphosa, and Julia for their work in spreading the gospel message. These women are examples to us today because fearing and honoring God was their highest priority. These early Christian women were workers for Christ wherever they found themselves, just as we must be.

Of course, any list of New Testament working women must include Lydia (Acts 16:11-15). Lydia's business was selling expensive purple dye from the city of Thyatira. Lydia lived in Philippi, a Roman outpost, which was located on the Egnatian Way, Rome's primary artery to the east. The Egnatian Way made it easier for Rome to move troops throughout the empire and allowed trading along the road. Lydia would have had contact with men and women from all around the known world as she was selling her purple dye and she had authority over all her marketing and selling processes. Lydia clearly was a successful and prosperous businesswoman. Her devotion to God led to all her household becoming Christians and was the beginning of the church in Philippi. Not a shabby reputation for a working woman! Lydia could do this because God was her priority. We women today can have a similar influence on our household and business acquaintances when they can see God in our lives.

A Christian woman fears and honors God just like the wife of Proverbs 31, Queen Esther, Priscilla, Lydia, and all those Greek and early Christian women. She lives her daily life as a shining light for all to see and is an example for others to follow. A working woman uses her situation for others to see Christ in her.

You don't have to do something big to make a difference. You may not even know what influence that you are having. I am certain others can see God in your example when God has priority in your life. When I retired from my business, I had employees tell me what an influence I had on them. Use your opportunities to talk about God to others. You may be the person God has put in their path like Queen Esther was there for the Jewish nation. You may be the one to put someone on the right path like Priscilla did for Apollos. Use your opportunities to show others your honor for God. A godly woman fears and honors God wherever she is working.

Conclusion

Christian working women face many problems when they combine God's requirements for being a wife, homemaker, and mother with a career. Our goals as Christian women must be directly measured against the priorities of a working woman. Our real priorities are God, husband, family. No matter where a woman works each day, God is the first priority. Women who fear God shall be praised! Her life won't be simple. Her life won't be dull. No matter the details of her life, the people in her life will praise her when they will see God in her life.

Mother's Role in Spiritual Training

Becky Romine

During the time of Joshua, God fulfilled a promise that He made to Abraham years earlier. In Joshua 11:23, we read of this fulfillment:

> So Joshua took the whole land, according to all that the LORD had spoken to Moses, and Joshua gave it for an **inheritance** to Israel according to their divisions by their tribes. Thus the land had rest from war.

God gave the Israelites a gift, a special possession. He provided them an inheritance of land for His people to dwell in, to worship Him in, and of which they were to be good stewards. This land was a gift from God that the people could call their own. In Psalm 127:3, Solomon records these words:

> Behold, children are a **heritage** from the LORD, the fruit of the womb a reward.

This word "heritage" in Psalm 127 comes from the same Hebrew word that is used in Joshua 11 as "inheritance." In the same way that God gave a gift and possession to the children of Israel, He gives parents a beautiful gift and possession when He blesses them with their children who are to be loved, cherished, and nurtured. Along with this blessing comes the responsibility to raise these children to honor, obey, and glorify God and to help them reach the goal of living with God in heaven someday. He has entrusted

---

Becky (Norris) Romine, daughter of Benjie and Mary Jane Norris, was born and raised in Russellville, Alabama. She attended Florida College where she met her husband, Brent Romine. After graduating from the University of Alabama in Huntsville, she worked as a computer programmer until her first child was born. Becky and Brent have three children, Brock (17), Baylee (15) and Beth (12). They returned to Madison, Alabama in 2009 after spending several years in Atlanta, GA, Chelmsford, MA and Alexandria, VA. She now assists her husband in his new engineering company.

us with the duty of guiding precious souls as they begin their life journey.

We also read in Psalm 127:4,

> Like arrows in the hand of a warrior are the children of one's youth.
> Blessed is the man who fills his quiver with them!

Have you ever considered comparing your child to an arrow? A warrior draws back his bow, and shoots the arrow in a path aimed at a target. He ensures he can clearly see the target, moves away from any obstacles in his path, and shoots the arrow in the direction to hit the target. Of course, our "target" is the eternal goal of reaching heaven, of spending forever with our Creator who loves us, and we long to guide our "arrows" to that destination. Henry Wadsworth Longfellow wrote, "I shot an arrow into the air, It fell to earth, I knew not where." Do we as mothers keep our eye on the target when we train and encourage our children? Do we assist in identifying and moving the obstacles that may keep our children from "hitting the target"? Do we point our children in the direction they should be aimed? How sad it will be if our arrow falls to the earth missing the mark! Instead, how happy we will be if we can see our children headed in the direction of heaven! How wonderful it will be if we can watch our children becoming more like Him and serving Him!

God has blessed us, as mothers, with the responsibility of training, nurturing and preparing our children to serve Him and to be a powerful influence for good in the world. Timothy, Paul's "beloved (spiritual) son," had a sincere faith (2 Tim. 2:6). He was well-spoken of by the brethren in Lystra and Inconium (Acts 16:2), and he was known for "his proven worth that he served with (Paul) in the furtherance of the gospel like a child serving his father" (Phil. 2:22). This sincere faith of Timothy serves as an example to us thousands of years later. This faith first dwelled in Timothy's grandmother Lois and his mother Eunice. Timothy knew the sacred Scripture from childhood. From the time he was very young, his mother and grandmother ensured Timothy was learning God's Holy Word. (2 Tim. 3:5) What a magnificent thought that the strong faith and spiritual training of Lois and Eunice influenced the young man, Timothy, to make a significant impact on the spread of the gospel during the early church. The influence of your faith and spiritual training of your children could make a significant impact on the salvation of their souls and on the spread of God's kingdom today.

Our Father, who prepared us for good works (Eph. 2:10), does not leave us without the tools to accomplish His purpose. He provides us with instructions and guidance to fulfill the role we have as a spiritual example and teacher of our children. In the book of Deuteronomy we read of Moses' final instructions to the people of Israel before they entered the Promised Land. His words were a reminder of God's Law and the guidelines and teachings the people would need as they settled in the land that God had promised. Moses reminded the people of God's glory and greatness when He appeared to the people on the fiery mountain of Mt. Sinai and recalled the words God spoke when He said, "Oh, that they had such a heart in them that they would fear Me and always keep all My commandments, that it might be well with them and with their children forever" (Deut. 5:29). What were the people to do that it might be well with their children? Fear God and keep all His commandments! Likewise, we should fear God and keep all His commandments and guide our children to do the same.

How do we accomplish this? What can we do to reach this goal? In the very next chapter of Deuteronomy, God gives instruction regarding the foundation of obedience, specifies our motivation to serve Him, and describes the methods we can use to teach His commands to our children.

Foundation of Obedience

Now this is the commandment, the statutes and the judgments which the Lord your God has commanded me to teach you, that you might do them in the land where you are going over to possess it, so that you and your son and your grandson might fear the Lord your God, to keep all His statutes and His commandments which I command you, all the days of your life, and that your days may be prolonged. O Israel, you should listen and be careful to do it, that it may be well with you and that you may multiply greatly, just as the Lord, the God of your fathers, has promised you, in a land flowing with milk and honey.

Hear, O Israel! The Lord is our God, the Lord is one! You shall love the Lord your God with all your heart and with all your soul and with all your might. These words, which I am commanding you today, shall be on your heart. You shall teach them diligently to your sons and shall talk of them when you sit in your house and when you walk by the way and when you lie down and when you rise up. You shall bind them as a sign on your hand and they shall be as frontals on your forehead. You shall write them on the doorposts of your house and on your gates (Deut. 6:6-9).

Moses started with an acknowledgement of the one, true God and exhorted them to love Him with all of our being. He also states that the words he spoke to the children of Israel were the commandments, statutes, and judgments that God had commanded. He tells them "the words which I command you today shall be in your heart" (Deut. 6:6). Moses instructed them to "listen" to God's Word in verse 3 and "hear" in verse 4. They were to hear and acknowledge, "the Lord is God, the Lord is one." They were to teach of the holiness of God.

God also reveals these things to us through Asaph in one of the Psalms. Psalm 78 instructs us to give ear to God's Law and incline our ears to the words of His mouth.

> Listen, O my people, to my instruction;
> Incline your ears to the words of my mouth.
> I will open my mouth in a parable;
> I will utter dark sayings of old,
> Which we have heard and known,
> And our fathers have told us.
> We will not conceal them from their children,
> But tell to the generation to come the praises of the Lord,
> And His strength and His wondrous works that He has done.
> For He established a testimony in Jacob and appointed a law in Israel,
> Which He commanded our fathers
> That they should teach them to their children,
> That the generation to come might know, even the children yet to be born,
> That they may arise and tell them to their children,
> That they should put their confidence in God
> And not forget the works of God,
> But keep His commandments,
> And not be like their fathers,
> A stubborn and rebellious generation,
> A generation that did not prepare its heart
> And whose spirit was not faithful to God.

What is our foundation for obedience to God and for teaching our children to serve Him faithfully? God's Holy Word serves as the foundation of our faith and the faith of our children. We should diligently study and incline our ear to fill our heart with His word. His Word is "a lamp to our feet and a light to our path" showing us the way to heaven (Ps. 119:105). We cannot expect to teach our children and guide them spiritually unless we are full of His Word ourselves! But as busy mothers, how do we find the time and energy to study, meditate, and dwell on God's Word? Stephen Covey in his book, "The Seven Habits of Highly Effective People," lists one of the habits to "Begin with the end in mind." When we think of and meditate on the eternal goal, the spiritual salvation of our soul and that of our children, we will begin to look for every opportunity to spend time in His Word.

What are some ways we can study God's Word and strengthen our foundation with our busy lives as mothers?

- Love the one, true God with all your being.

- Make a habit of reading your Bible daily.

    ○ Find a time that works for you and schedule that time. Read your Bible aloud. Although you need some quiet time to study, let your children see you read your Bible. They watch and imitate you.

- Select verses that have a special meaning to you and memorize them. That way you will always have those verses with you in your heart.

- Download and listen to sermons or spiritual podcasts while you are driving, running errands or going for a walk or run, etc.

- Attend Ladies' Bible classes.

- Teach a Bible class.

    ○ You will increase your own knowledge as well as your students.

- Pray!

Motivation To Serve God and Teach our Children

Both Deuteronomy 6 and Psalm 78 describe the reasons for holding to God's Word and teaching our children. These scriptures encourage us by giving us motivation to provide spiritual guidance. In Deuteronomy 6:2, we read that the Israelites were to keep God's statues along with their sons and grandsons all the days of their life **that your days may be prolonged**. God had many blessings in store for the people of Israel if they remained faithful to Him. He would send the rain for abundant crops, their offspring would be blessed, their enemies defeated. Although God does not guarantee us abundance in material goods today, He does promise us that He will provide us with every necessity we need (Matt. 6:25-34) and guarantees us "peace that passes understanding" if we pray with thanksgiving and trust in Him (Phil. 4:7). Don't we want the days of our children to be prolonged? Don't we want them to have the most fulfilling and joyful life they can have through their love of God? Don't we want them to be filled with peace and contentment? We see several other reasons for making God's Word known to our children in Psalm 78:5-8. We should "arise and declare them" to our children that they may "**set their hope in God.**" What a blessing to guide our children to set their hope in God! This hope will give them confidence, faith, and joy in spite of the disappointments of life that may come their way. Your children will be able to keep their eye on the target of heaven where they can be in His presence forever. God also wants us to teach His Word to our children that they will "**not forget the works of God**." Who of our children cannot recall the marvelous stories of the Ten Plagues, the crossing of the Red Sea, David and Goliath, and the miracles of Jesus. These stories in the Bible give our children a glimpse into the glory and power of God and His involvement with mankind. They will know of His omnipotence and believe that their God can do all things. They will rely on Him to accomplish great things in their lives and have faith that their God has the power to save them from their sins. Additionally, we teach our children spiritual truths that they may "**keep His commandments**." In order to be pleasing to Him, we are expected to obey and trust Him. We are to be holy as He is holy and become like Him. We teach and sing to our children at an early age that "obedience is the very best way to show that you believe." In verse 8 of Psalm 78, we read of another reason to teach our children and declare God's testimony. God eventually punished His people because they forsook Him and worshipped idols. He did not want future generations to "**be like their fathers, a stubborn and rebellious generation**." We do not want a selfish and prideful child, but rather one who loves God and wants to please Him. In Deuteronomy 8:2, God reminds the Israelites that the reason God led them in the wilderness forty years was to humble and test them. He wanted them to depend on Him. In Deuteronomy 8:11-17, God instructed them to beware of taking their blessings of the new land for granted. He warned them of becoming full and forgetting God, the source of their blessings. We are so blessed in our society with more than we need. We need to diligently remind our children of who provides for us and encourage them to be thankful and dependent on Him. We want our children to be filled with humility and have a servant's heart. We want children whose heart is right. *"For the eyes of the Lord move to and fro throughout the earth that He may strongly support those whose heart is completely His"* (2 Chron. 16:9). What a blessing if God found your children and strongly supported them because their heart completely belonged to Him!

Methods to Teach Our Children

We see that the foundation of our faith and that of our children is grounded in the Word of God. We understand why God wants us to teach our children because He wants us to set their hope in Him, to remember His works, to keep His commandments, and to be humble rather that rebellious. But how do we accomplish this teaching? With all the responsibilities of being a mother, how do we find time to instill in our children to "love the LORD with all their heart and soul"? God has equipped you with abilities and talents to enrich the lives of your children. We have a special kind of "mother love" to care for and nurture our children. We eagerly long to hold them affectionately, to meet their needs and support them. We must use our love and talents wisely to accomplish our goal. What is your goal as a mom? Is it to be the one who everyone says accomplished the most? The one whose child is a great athlete, a whiz at academics, and an accomplished musician while you have an immaculate house and cook gourmet dinners? (We know this is an impossible mission anyway.) While we certainly need to do our best in everything God has given us to do and do all to glorify Him, what is the MOST IMPORTANT goal? As a mother or grandmother, what is your goal for your children or grandchildren? When this life is over, and you look back, what is really important? Is it that they were the top-ranked tennis player on the high school team? That they drove the best car? That they were valedictorian? When you look at these achievements with an eternal perspective, with God's perspective, how significant are they? Is this what He cares about? What is really important? When we have a goal that we hope to achieve, we sometimes write a "mission statement." What is your mission statement? How would you answer this question: My hope for my children is _____? In addition to stating your goal, you must identify steps to take to reach that goal. How do you hope to accomplish this goal? What actions can you take? Note the steps described in Deuteronomy 6:

> These words, which I am commanding you today, shall be on your heart. You shall teach them diligently to your sons and shall talk of them when you sit in your house and when you walk by the way and when you lie down and when you rise up. You shall bind them as a sign on your hand and they shall be as frontals on your forehead. You shall write them on the doorposts of your house and on your gates (Deut. 6:6-9).

We should teach God's words which are on our heart (our foundation). We are told to be diligent about this. We can be diligent because this teaching process will become an integral part of our lives with our children. It will be a never-ending process. We will look for every opportunity to fill our children with God's Word. We should want to have the Word so deeply ingrained in our children that it fills every fiber of their being. We will talk of God's Word when we sit at the dinner table in our house, when we drive to school, when we go to bed at night and wake up in the morning. His Word should become a natural part of conversation that can occur anywhere at anytime of day. Life is full of teachable moments when a parent slows down to observe and relate life experiences to the Bible. This means that we should be available to our children. We should be interacting with them and discussing life with them.

When our children are young:

- Use Bible "board books" to share God's truths.

- Sing hymns as you rock them.

- Talk of God's blessings of food and shelter as you cook a meal and clean your house.

- Play Bible games (e.g., Bible Bingo or Bible Pictionary).

  ° I have fond memories of something I played with my children we called "Bible questions for candy." I had a pack of small sweet tarts and would reward each child with a piece if he answered the question correctly.

- Act out a Bible story or have your child illustrate a story with art supplies.

- At any age you can take a walk outside to discover the wonders of God's creation.

As your children get older:

- Read the Bible with your children.

- Quiz them on Bible facts.

- Be aware of the lessons they are studying for Bible class and discuss the lesson with them.

- Talk about Bible characters together and how their actions displayed their relationship with God.

As your children mature into pre-teens and teens, it can become more difficult to find time to spend with them.

- Use modern means of communication to connect with your teen on a spiritual topic. Send a text or an email with a verse or thought of the day.

- Ask them what they learned from that day's sermon.

- Your teens are greatly influenced by their peers at this age.

  ° Get to know the friends of your children.

  ° Host teen devotionals or singings in your house.

- Relate experiences from your teenage years and how you grew spiritually from them. (Yes, they will probably think your experiences are not relevant, and you are from the Stone Age!)

- Take time to listen to them, to understand them, to be empathetic to their heartaches and show how God understands and cares for them.

- Tell them constantly how much you love them and God loves them!

Children of all ages observe how we behave as parents and the model we set as a spiritual example. Let them see you reading and studying your Bible. Let them hear you joyfully singing praises to God. Do they observe you seeing to the needs of others, of maintaining patience in adversity, of saying kind words, of telling the truth in all things? Do they see in your life that you "love the LORD you God with all your heart and soul" and that you "love your neighbor as yourself"?

We cannot forget another tool God has provided to assist us in the spiritual training of our children: prayer. We should pray daily for our own spiritual knowledge and maturity. We should pray without ceasing that we glorify God in all we think and do and that we will be a wonderful example as a mother. We should also pray *with* our children. Pray with them before meals and before bed. Offer a prayer of thanksgiving when something wonderful happens. Pray with them when they are scared or troubled. Pray with them about the friendships they have and the choices they make for the future. Finally pray FOR your children. Let them know you are praying for them. Use the Bible itself, God's actual words, and incorporate them into a prayer. For example, take Matthew 4:4: "May __(child's name)__ not live on bread alone, but on every word that comes from the mouth of God," and "Surround __(child's name)__ with friends who will sharpen her as iron sharpens iron" (Prov. 27:17). The possibilities of things to pray for your child in this way are endless.

Conclusion

Have you considered that we do not know much about our family members of previous generations? We probably don't know where our great grandmother was born or what was the occupation of our great-great grandfather. It is difficult to remember what took place in times gone by. We don't remember much about the physical attributes of our previous generation, perhaps not even their accomplishments. There is not much we receive from them of a material heritage, but there is something that can certainly be passed down from generation to generation that affects the lives of all family members. That is our spiritual heritage! How you live your life today, the example you set today and what you teach your children today can affect multiple generations for good. You can influence your children and your children's children to serve God, to reach the goal of heaven and to take others with them. You can be like Lois and Eunice and have an impact on those who are not yet born because of your spiritual guidance today. Let us pray for God's blessing on us as mothers that we will have the strength and knowledge to carry out this task He has given to us. Let us treasure the gifts He has bestowed on us.

"Unless the LORD BUILDS THE HOUSE, those who build it labor in vain" (Psa. 127:1).

Adjusting to Widowhood

Ruby Hall

Our journey here on earth is filled with adjustments to the changes that we experience in our lives, *e.g.*, marriage, the birth of children and their leaving the nest, serious illness, loss of employment, disabling accidents, or death of a loved one. Whatever it is that affects our lives, we need to understand that God knows about it and that Jesus cares. "What a friend we have in Jesus, all our sins and griefs to bear." 1 Peter 5:6-7 tells us, "Therefore, humble yourselves under the mighty hand of God, that He may exalt you in due time, casting all your care upon Him, for He cares for you."

In addition, our brethren care. They "weep with those who weep" (Rom. 12:15). They will help us bear our burdens (Gal. 6:2). Two verses from the song, *Blest Be the Tie*, express this well:

Ruby Hall was born on April 18, 1938 to Sam and Neva Hinkle – the sixth child in the midst of ten boys. Both she and her husband, Bruce, attended Athens Bible School and graduated from there in 1956. They were married on July 5, 1957. They have four children, twelve grandchildren, and seven great-grandchildren. Bruce retired from the Kohler Company. After 49½ years of marriage, he passed away suddenly on January 6, 2007.

Ruby worked short assignments (2 years or less) for the Farmers Home Administration, NASA, and the Army at Redstone Arsenal. She graduated from Calhoun Community College and Athens College with a BS in Elementary Education. She spent nearly thirty years in her teaching career, most of which were in the sixth grade at Athens Bible School. She retired in 2001. She taught again at ABS for the school year 2009-2010 to allow her daughter-in-law to have a year off to be with her newborn son.

Ruby attends the Jennings Chapel Church of Christ where Bruce served as an elder for many years before his death. She has been active in teaching a variety of classes there. She also volunteers with Hospice of Limestone County, takes an oil painting class, and babysits a three year-old grandson.

We share our mutual woes,
Our mutual burdens bear;
And often for each other flows
The sympathizing tear.

When we asunder part,
It gives us inward pain;
But we shall still be joined in heart,
And hope to meet again.

The widow goes through a period of emotional trauma, but many people, especially Christians, will offer to assist her through this crisis. Even so, it is still very difficult trying to adjust to the death of a spouse who has been beside her for many years. Some of the problems of adjustment to this loss are loneliness, making decisions alone, finances, where to live, fear of living alone, planning the future, and, later on, whether to remarry. The age that a woman becomes a widow may determine the choices she makes to solve these problems. Every heart goes through the healing process in a different way and at a different pace.

After the death of my husband, our house began to overflow with grieving family and friends, most with a dish of food, to comfort one another in the loss of this good man. Our family soon had to take care of some immediate concerns. Many decisions had to be made. Who should be called? Who will conduct the funeral services? Who will serve as pall bearers? What songs will be used? Which pictures will we use for the family slide video? What about the casket? These were among the many questions that had to be addressed immediately to provide the funeral home with the information needed for the arrangements.

Hundreds of friends and family filed through the funeral home on the night of visitation to comfort us and share memories of their connection with him. We knew what it was like to stand together, sharing the load of this loss and the joys of having our family and friends by our side. Ultimately, our faith in God was our main source of healing and comfort.

Soon after the funeral, the reality of my being alone hit "like a ton of bricks." Contacts from family and friends dwindled away. I understood that they had to get back to the regular routine of their own lives. Also, if they had not experienced this same loss, they did not fully understand a widow's feelings and feared saying inappropriate words. I became the odd person out with couples because our society seems to be couple-oriented.

Eating alone became a hard adjustment to make as a widow. Fast-food eateries seem easier for me than a more formal setting. A widow can make adjustments to these difficulties by calling up a friend and asking her out to lunch, or by telling some of the couples that she is ready to be included in social gatherings. The friends may be waiting for a sign from her on how to approach the situation. Remember, they have not had her experience.

Besides struggling for emotional strength to face life alone, I faced many difficult chores to get my life in some sort of order. The list is endless: obtaining certified copies of the death certificate; getting the property retitled; designating another person for bank accounts and other jointly-held assets; changing the name on the car registration; updating all legal documents to remove the deceased, if necessary; designating Power of Attorney for myself; designating new beneficiaries of insurance policies or investments; contacting the life insurance company after the death; obtaining Letter of Testamentary; probating the will; and the list goes on and on. A good, understanding lawyer helped me through most of the legal work in a timely manner. The key here is to not let your frustration overtake you.

If you have experienced the loss of your mate by death, your road has been lonely and difficult. People will say, "Time will heal!" This is really not true. The tragic loss does not completely heal; we just adapt to the loss. Remember Paul's statement in Philippians 4:13, "I can do all things through Him that strengtheneth me." God's promises of blessings are always much greater than the demands He makes of us in this life. If we concentrate on counting our blessings instead of on the loneliness and self-pity, it will be easier to accept the tragedy and fill our lives with contentment.

On a personal note, I started my grieving period by thanking God for the blessing of allowing me to have a righteous man as a mate for almost fifty years; thanking Him for giving my children a loving father and godly example; thanking Him for this man who worked so hard to provide for his family; and thanking Him for all the other blessings He provided through this man. The time we had together was a gift from God. Feeling thankful and enriched for the time we had together has made my loss easier to bear. Thankfulness and self-pity do not dwell in the heart at the same time. As David said in Psalm 40:5, "Many, O Lord my God, are Your wonderful works which You have done; And your thoughts toward us cannot be recounted to You in order; If I would declare and speak of them, they are more than can be numbered."

There are two ways to get to the top of an oak tree: Grab the first limb and start climbing – or find an acorn, sit on it and wait. This old saying is true. That oak tree can represent every challenge, every obstacle and every goal in my life. My choice is either face it head on or wait around and hope something else changes the situation for me (Kelli Pellegrine, *Christianity Magazine*, August, 1991).

Several years ago we used this concept in one quarter of our ladies Bible class at the congregation where I attend. We studied the different attitudes that will help us to climb our oak tree in our service to God and others. The study stressed that each person is responsible for *her* own attitude and for how *she* climbs that oak tree.

We know that the death of the spouse cannot change, but we can change the way we accept the situation. Will I face the challenge head-on or will I wait around with a self-pity attitude and make excuses for not grabbing that first limb to start climbing the oak tree? I can learn to be a tree climber instead of an acorn sitter by a lot of prayer and patience, and with much practice. I pray that God will continue to help me climb my tree.

After we lose a mate, we can face the future with confidence if we have genuine faith as seen in Lois and Eunice (2 Tim. 1:5); if we have hope in Christ who does not disappoint us (1 Cor. 15:19); and if we have trust in the living God (1 Tim. 6:17). We can say with Paul, "For this reason I also suffer these things; nevertheless I am not ashamed, for I know whom I have believed and am persuaded that He is able to keep what I have committed to Him until that day" (2 Tim. 1:12). If we fail to put our complete faith, hope, and trust in God, we often become frustrated, confused, and depressed. Our hearts are overcome with feelings of loneliness, distrust, and even fear. We cannot handle this loss without God's help. When giving the great commission to His disciples in Matthew 28:20, Jesus said, ". . .observe all things that I commanded you; and lo, *I am with you always*, even to the end of the age." We must believe that He is *always* with us. We must choose to trust God instead of wallowing in self-pity. A life filled with self-pity produces fruits of resentment, fear, and much unhappiness.

Guilt feelings may enter into our thoughts after the death of the mate. Could I have done more? Should I have been aware of the illness earlier? Could I have made him more comfortable? There will never be satisfactory answers to these questions, and he would not want me to have this nagging feeling of guilt.

Should we feel guilty about complaining to God about our problems? Not necessarily! David wrote in Psalm 55:17, "Evening and morning and at noon I utter my complaint and moan and He will hear my voice." Again, in Psalm 142:2, he wrote, "I pour out my complaint before Him; I tell my trouble before Him." The psalmist was perplexed about his circumstances and discontentment, and he called upon God to relieve his suffering. But there is a line that we must not cross in our complaints to God. We must never forget that He is the Creator and Lord and that we are the creatures. Complaining because our lives are not as we would like is really blaming God for our troubles. Paul said, "I have learned to be content in whatever circumstance I am in" (Phil. 4:11). I heard this comment in a sermon recently, "Happiness is wanting what you have, not having what you want." We need to learn to cope cheerfully with our situation without complaining. We will be much happier if we can put this cheerful attitude into practice.

A widow may describe this as the worst time of her life and allow discouragement to consume her. Discouragement begins with negative thoughts; but she is the one who controls her thoughts. She can combat negative thoughts by counting her blessings, naming them one by one; by thinking about her many righteous friends; by meditating on the good things of life; by looking beyond herself; and by concentrating on being a servant to others. I cannot tell you that the last six years have been easy; but I can truthfully say that those years have been easier by concentrating on the aforementioned thoughts.

Death is the most certain thing about life. "It is appointed for man to die once" (Heb. 9:27). Whether the death of our spouse is sudden or after a prolonged illness, we need to think ahead about how we would react because it will leave us lonely and shaken. We do not want our faith weakened, but strengthened. Immediate grief is normal; but we should not overly "grieve as others who have no hope" (1 Thess. 4:13). We need to be prepared to accept our circumstances in life without bitterness and resentment. Often we are not willing to be content with our state in this life because we forget that "our citizenship is in heaven" (Phil. 3:20).

Loneliness has been called "the most desolate word in all human language." For the widow who buried her life's mate and now sets the table for one, the loneliness will still be there no matter how fast-paced her life. We are more lonely at certain times of the year – holidays, birthdays, anniversaries, and other special days that we shared. Loneliness, more or less, forces us to turn our concerns over to God when we are going under and there is nobody there. We take so many things for granted in this life. We need to be thankful for the ability to walk, to work, and to be able by God's grace to rise to see a new day.

One who strives to face life's difficulties alone, trusting only in self, will soon give up in despair or drown herself in self-pity. On the other hand, the faith that is centered on God recognizes and believes that God will "comfort us in all tribulation" (2 Cor. 1:3-4). Our Father will never leave us. He knows when we hurt. He will always listen. We need to search His word for light when the hour of our grief is so dark.

A woman who becomes a widow should not cease being a servant of the Lord, one who puts the Lord first in her life. If she uses her time of loneliness to be God's servant, there will not be much room for the self-pity and bitterness that many widows fall into in times of suffering. This can be done by placing the needs of others far ahead of self. She can do this by looking for good works to perform for others, *e.g.,* teaching the lost, ministering to the sick, helping the poor, volunteering for worthwhile organizations, or encouraging other lonely widows. One of the greatest ways we, as widows, can help others is with a word of cheer and hope. A person receives comfort when she is giving it. The cheerful countenance of a widow gives other widows encouragement and hope. Each one of us needs someone of whom we can say, "I can do it if she thinks I can." Charles Dickens wisely wrote, "No one is useless in the world who lightens the burden of it for someone else." We need to encourage all who come under our influence. "Be of good courage" (Isa. 41:6). Be an example by reaching out to others who care for you. All of us at some time seem to back away from telling our friends and other Christians, "I'm hurting today!" They are not mind readers – we need to share this information.

We know that grief is very real, but it is difficult to describe. Our brain is a complex organ. So many of our memories are stored in that organ just waiting for some incident to bring it to the surface again. We get to a point that we think we have worked through the grief and something "pops up" from this storehouse of memories that tells us that it is still there to some extent. It may even be something in a dream that kindles our memory.

We have already mentioned that no two widows respond to death in the same manner or heal at the same rate. The more dependent person will feel more helplessness than the more independent one. The more emotional one will express pain differently. A person with a history of depression may be more likely than others to feel agitated and fearful. The person with a strong social network will have others to help fill the emptiness. Most of all, the person with a strong faith, trust, and hope in God will look to Him for help and will heal more quickly than one with a weaker faith. The healthy personality with a strong dependence on God has a better chance of bouncing back.

From the beginning, God never meant for us to be alone. He gave us the ability to communicate and to share life, and He gave us the responsibility to care for one another (Gal. 6:1-2). When we start the grieving process, it is good to have someone to talk with about what we are feeling. We do not need to feel isolated at this time. Shedding tears is a blessing God has given to mankind. Tears can help us to find relief in our sorrow. It will help if we choose at least one person to whom we can talk freely and can cry with, if we feel like crying. The person needs to be someone who can be trusted as a confidant and preferably one who has experienced the same loss. She should also share the same religious convictions. We need to be reassured that the feelings we are experiencing are normal. It helps to know that someone is sharing our burden of grief because she has been through the same thing and knows what the feelings and thoughts are first-hand. Later, we can be the same type of friend to someone else. Such talks are an important way of working through grief to greater understanding, to readjustment, and to becoming a stronger person.

In my opinion, depression is one of the most dangerous results of grief. I have seen this result in several members of my family and friends. It is not a pretty picture. One friend is still in this state after many years. She constantly dwells on the memories of the deceased and relives the past over and over. It is as if going over the good times again and again will wipe away her loss; but it has only hindered the grieving process. She still dwells upon the loss almost exclusively, and the depression increases. Strength and courage have disappeared. If you feel yourself sinking in this manner, think of it this way: If you had died before your husband, how would you want him to react? I hope that you would want him to feel sorrowful for his loss, have fond memories of you, and try to get on with his life. Although some grief may always be present, it is controlled. Complete adjustment may never come, but we must adapt. What purpose will it serve for you to be unhappy forever? Who will benefit from this unhappiness?

Jeanie Campbell, a licensed mental health counselor who has practiced in the Seattle area for approximately thirty years, based her counseling on

Biblical principles. She had this to say in some of her writings about grief being a useful process:

> Feelings of anxiety or helplessness may show up as pain, dizzy spells, heart palpitations, headaches, neck or back pain in the body. A grieving person may become hyperactive, or full of nervous energy, or jittery. One may overwork to use up adrenaline, energy, or to distract oneself from one's thoughts and feelings. There may be dreams or nightmares.
>
> The event is real, and sad. You recognize a loss. What was there is no longer there. Depression includes sadness, tears, lethargy or fatigue, loss of pleasure, sleep disturbance, feelings of helplessness, inability to concentrate or focus, or being distracted. Some describe this as "the crash." The loss is real and overwhelming. One may be reminded again and again of the absence, and feel again and again the loss. One may be unable to work.
>
> The grieving person feels as if she has survived the loss. The grieving person begins to look ahead instead of back. She can enjoy memories of the lost person. She changes her life to reflect the absence of the missing person while retaining the good qualities and values, which she received from the relationship with her spouse.
>
> While grieving, she must attempt to go about her daily life and maintain some sense of normalcy of her usual schedule and lifestyle. This actually helps her recover from grieving. Make small decisions and let large decisions wait, if possible. If large decisions won't wait, consult someone you trust (used with permission).

The age of the widow determines some of the difficulties she will face during the grieving period. A young mother alone can feel completely overwhelmed with the task of raising the children. She may have to look for work, downsize her home, move in with her parents, or move to a different school district for the children, which in turn will create a new problem for children who are already unhappy.

Older widows may face financial loss, a move to another location to be near her children, or a residence in a health facility. Whatever the age or state of dependency the widow finds herself, many difficult adjustments will have to be made without the aid of her husband.

If you are one of the fortunate ones to still have your mate with you, please encourage him to work with you to get all of the financial and legal documents in proper order. If the unthinkable happens, this knowledge will make your adjustment much easier to achieve. Your husband will probably want to spare you from the worry of "hunting" for information.

Through pain and sorrow, in loneliness and depression, when friends do not understand the hurt, the Christian widow always has an all-caring and abiding friend in Jesus – "casting all your care upon Him, for He cares for you" (1 Pet. 5:7). As a mediator, Jesus makes it possible for our requests for help to reach "the Father of mercies and God of all comfort; who comforts us in all our affliction so that we might be able to comfort those who are in any affliction with the comfort with which we ourselves are comforted by God" (2 Cor. 1:3-4). In life's darkest hours, we are comforted with His words of assurance.

To be helpful, we must meet the needs of the one hurting. We must not let the hurt of the one we know and love to make us uncomfortable because she is not the same person at this time. We are told in God's word to love our brethren and show them compassion. "But whoever has the world's goods, and beholds his brother in need and closes his heart against him, how does the love of God abide in him? Little children, let us not love with word or with tongue, but in deed and truth" (1 John 3:17-18). We are to show kindness and tender affection (Rom. 12:10; Eph. 4:32; Col. 3:12) and to help and encourage the weak (1 Thess. 5:14; Acts 20:35; Rom. 15:1).

We, as children of God, need each other. We must, as Paul says in Galatians 5:13, "by love serve one another." That love should always be evident among us as we "consider each other to provoke unto love and good works" (Heb. 10:24). We certainly should make every effort to be the support system for the new, grieving widow. We should use our tongues, hearts, ears, and hands to offer solace, sympathy, and mercy. God wants something from us besides opening our doors and letting people sit on the furniture. We must open our hearts to sharing, listening, caring, and giving.

The loving memories that I have of my husband did not die with him. They will be there for me for the rest of my life. They are no longer the burden of early grief, but a source of real comfort and joy.

Everything that happens to me will test my character. I will either become stronger or weaker. If I endure the suffering of my loss with strength, I will concentrate on what is happening *in* me and not what is happening *to* me. I will be able to accept the reality of the death with a healthy attitude. I need to remember that my life here is a journey, not a home. I need to learn from God to turn heartaches into blessings on this journey with the hope of an eternal home to come.

Because of my loss, I can now feel that I have received a gift from God to be able to help and comfort, with understanding, those who lose a spouse.

I hope and pray that when the end of my life comes that I have just worn out from climbing my oak tree and not rusted out because I was caught still sitting on my acorn waiting for my oak tree to grow. "I beseech you therefore, brethren by the mercies of God, that you present your bodies a living sacrifice, holy, acceptable unto God, which is your reasonable service" (Rom. 12:1). The Bible has been my anchor for hope and comfort. The Scriptures give so much hope and new life to a grief-stricken soul.

Other Resources

Becton, Randy. *Everyday Comfort.* Grand Rapids: Baker Books, 1993.

Flatt, Bill. *Growing Through Grief.* Nashville: Gospel Advocate, 1989.

Head, Margaret. *Can Grief Be A Blessing?* Morris Publishing, 1984.

Jamerson, Joyce. *Will You Wipe My Tears?* Spiritbuilding Publishing, 2008.

Tope, Betty. *Calming the Storms of Life.* Athens, AL: Guardian of Truth Foundation, 2012.

Wright, H. Norman. *Experiencing Grief.* B&H Publishing Group, 2004.

Yancey, Philip. *Where Is God When It Hurts?* Grand Rapids: Zondervan Publishing House, 1977.

_____. *Accepting Bereavement.* Nashville: 21st Century Christian.

Raising Godly Children

Developing Character in Children

Bobby Graham

Character is the sum of the mental and moral attributes distinguishing one person from another. While many persons might possess some of the same attributes, different individuals will manifest those attributes to varying degrees and in different proportions. In the end, it is the combination and balance of those attributes which makes each person the individual that he

---

Bobby Leon Graham was born August 30, 1946 to Mary and Leon Graham, Florence, Alabama. He spent most of the years growing up under preaching of Curtis Flatt and Franklin T. Puckett. Bobby's father served as elder at College View for thirty years. His father is now at Helton Drive congregation (for the last twenty years); his mother is deceased.

Bobby graduated from Coffee High School in 1964, attended Florida College two and one-half years, graduated from Athens College and finished a Master's Degree in Education. He has done schoolwork at Athens Bible School for thirty-four years, serving as teacher, assistant principal, and principal; he still teaches Bible and conducts elementary chapel.

Bobby began preaching in 1962 while still in high school once per Sunday and increased to twice per Sunday after a few months. He preached through college in Florida and Alabama. He married Karen Ruth Hodge from Akron, Ohio, in November 1967. They have three children: Richard; Mary Katherine who is married to Darren Winland (preaches in Limestone County, AL) and has two children; and Laura Ruth who is married to Jeremy Paschall (preaches in Cullman, AL). All three are faithful Christians.

Bobby has preached at Somerville Road in Decatur with Granville Tyler, three churches in Limestone County; Richmond, VA (West End); Trinity, AL; Huntsville, AL (Chapman Acres). He wrote for *Gospel Guide*, edited by Billy Norris, for forty-one years. He helped train several young preachers from the North Alabama area and Canada for many years. He has served as an elder in two congregations, has stressed in his own work "mission meetings" in destitute fields, making many trips to New England and Northeastern states and also such work in the mountains of VA and KY. He has made fourteen preaching trips to Belize. Currently he works with Old Moulton Road church in Decatur and writes Q & A column in *Truth Magazine*.

is. Because the individual human is made in divine likeness to God (Gen. 1:29-27), he can choose to be the person whom God wants him to be.

Some individual characteristics are inherited, but most of them are learned and developed. One's potential to speak is inherited, but he learns how to speak and what to speak. The laziness of an uncle, the temper of the father, the moodiness of the mother, an aunt's shyness, as well as the sulkiness, fears, and optimism seen in different people – all such are learned, not inherited (Duvall, 8). Traits of character are likewise learned. The responsibility of the son is distinct from that of the father (Ezek. 18:1-24). No parent is responsible for the offspring in the sense that one will be held accountable for the moral progress or lapses of another. Seeds of character are early planted in a child, and the formation of character is first the God-given responsibility of the parent and later of the maturing child, to the degree of his own responsibility and accountability. Notice this analysis of individual responsibility presented by the Old Testament prophet Ezekiel in chapter eighteen:

1. Sin does not accrue, for each person is responsible for his own sins (18:1-4).
2. The righteous person shall not die (18:5-9).
3. The father's righteousness does not accrue, for it does not protect a wicked son from death (18:10-13).
4. Every individual bears responsibility for his own righteous conduct or evil conduct (18:14-20).
5. Just as one can repent of his evil and do good, so can a righteous person turn from his goodness to practice evil (18:21-24). In other words, change is possible in one's character.

These verses certify that moral determinism (character being divinely predestined, controlled by Adamic sin, or caused by earlier actors [parents]) is not embedded in our psyche, that our "corrupt nature" (moral depravity inherited from Adam) does not forbid repentance, and that each responsible individual is accountable to God for himself (free will in free moral creatures). These clear principles must guide us in training our children, as well as the children as they mature into accountable beings.

Developing character means that character is the result of teaching and training, not inheritance (though ancestral influence contributes to character formation). It is taught, not caught. An individual's values, dreams, convictions, philosophy of life, and religion make him what he is (Duvall, 16).

Because forming character comes under the umbrella of instruction and guiding the child's experiences, it also comes within the job description of parents. They are the principal developers of character in children. No one – the preacher, the elders, the church, the school teacher, the principal, the school, the government, or the "village" of a broader society – has the God-given responsibility which parents have. We do not by the previous statement suggest that no one else contributes to a child's character, but that nobody can substitute for parents in the divine plan of character development.

Infants and very young children are not susceptible to much of the teaching and training needed by older children; but they can begin to learn broad ideas, which later can be filled out as they are connected to principles and precepts. The preschool child has a conscience; but he is still not accountable, despite his recitation of certain facts. As that child moves into the middle years, he can become quite moralistic, applying the rules in a harsh, rigid way (Stone and Church, 414). Not even this rigid insistence on moral behavior means the child is accountable, though it does aid in character development.

God's Brilliant Contribution on Character Development

Because God knows character that is worth having and worth developing in children, it is essential that we look first to what He says on this subject. Perhaps the divine mandate given to Israelite parents in Deuteronomy 6 is the best place to begin our examination. It was there that the Lord of heaven and earth sought to direct them in their guidance of their children in the formation of the kind of character that would cause God to bless them with long life in their land and success in their role as a model for the nations.

> Now this is the commandment, and these are the statutes and judgments which the LORD your God has commanded to teach you, that you may observe them in the land which you are crossing over to possess, that you may fear the LORD your God, to keep all His statutes and His commandments which I command you, you and your son and your grandson, all the days of your life, and that your days may be prolonged. Therefore hear, O Israel, and be careful to observe it, that it may be well with you, and that you may multiply greatly as the LORD God of your fathers has promised you – "a land flowing with milk and honey."
>
> Hear, O Israel: The LORD our God, the LORD is one! You shall love the LORD your God with all your heart, with all your soul, and with all your strength. And these words which I command you today shall be in your

heart. You shall teach them diligently to your children, and shall talk of them when you sit in your house, when you walk by the way, when you lie down, and when you rise up. You shall bind them as a sign on your hand, and they shall be as frontlets between your eyes. You shall write them on the doorposts of your house and on your gates. So it shall be, when the LORD your God brings you into the land of which He swore to your fathers, to Abraham, Isaac, and Jacob, to give you large and beautiful cities which you did not build, houses full of all good things, which you did not fill, hewn-out wells which you did not dig, vineyards and olive trees which you did not plant – when you have eaten and are full – then beware, lest you forget the LORD who brought you out of the land of Egypt, from the house of bondage. You shall fear the LORD your God and serve Him, and shall take oaths in His name. You shall not go after other gods, the gods of the peoples who are all around you (for the LORD your God is a jealous God among you), lest the anger of the LORD your God be aroused against you and destroy you from the face of the earth. You shall not tempt the LORD your God as you tempted Him in Massah.

You shall diligently keep the commandments of the LORD your God, His testimonies, and His statutes which He has commanded you. And you shall do what is right and good in the sight of the LORD, that it may be well with you, and that you may go in and possess the good land of which the LORD swore to your fathers, to cast out all your enemies from before you, as the LORD has spoken. When your son asks you in time to come, saying, "What is the meaning of the testimonies, the statutes, and the judgments which the LORD our God has commanded you?" then you shall say to your son: "We were slaves of Pharaoh in Egypt, and the LORD brought us out of Egypt with a mighty hand; and the LORD showed signs and wonders before our eyes, great and severe, against Egypt, Pharaoh, and all his household. Then He brought us out from there, that He might bring us in, to give us the land of which He swore to our fathers. And the LORD commanded us to observe all these statutes, to fear the LORD our God, for our good always, that He might preserve us alive, as it is this day. Then it will be righteousness for us, if we are careful to observe all these commandments before the LORD our God, as He has commanded us.

Analyzing What God Said

First, the Lord affirmed the essential nature of what He here says about training children in character development (v. 1). Second, He tied such matters to the often absent virtue of fear (reverence) of God, shown in submission to divine authority (v. 2). Third, these matters were connected to obedience to God (v. 3). Fourth, the prolonging of their days in the land promised them and their growth in accord with promises earlier made to

Abraham were dependent on this development of character (vv. 2-3). Fifth, parental responsibility in this area was shown to result from love for God and their heartfelt adherence to the principles (vv. 5-6). Sixth, their urgency was underscored by the diligence of parents in inculcating such character in children (v. 7). Seventh, teaching as the fundamental work of parents in developing character must occur based on parents' own example (vv. 7-9). Eighth, the right kind of character produces the right kind of behavior (vv. 10ff). Ninth, specific attributes of character are here implied as integral to desirable character: gratitude, reverence, fidelity, loyalty, and endurance (vv. 10-15). Tenth, character development results in faithfulness to God (vv. 17-24). Eleventh, righteousness of life is the final effect of character development (v. 25).

These words of divine instruction regarding parental attempts to develop character in their children are far superior to any that men have written or might later write. In an age when many parents clamor over the latest manual devoted to child-rearing and when bookstore shelves are brimming with how-to-do-it books for parents, is it not remarkable that nothing written since Moses wrote Deuteronomy even approaches the wisdom found in Deuteronomy six? Does it not become obvious that man's Maker spoke here? He knew what He spoke of, because He created human beings. The Manual came from the Maker!

John Rosemond's Bill of Rights for Children
Having just affirmed God's ways to be higher than man's, it might seem strange to some that we would next insert writings from man. Our reason for doing so is that the writer of the following words spoke from the foundation of divine revelation. Unlike many who assert children's right to be independent of parental influence, he believes the Scriptures are God-breathed and relevant to training children by parents. Pay close attention to what he says:

> Because it is the most character-building, two-letter word in the English language, children have the right to hear their parents say, "No" at least three times a day.

> Children have the right to find out early in their lives that their parents don't exist to make them happy, but to offer them the opportunity to learn the skills they – children – will need to eventually make themselves happy.

> Children have a right to scream all they want over the decisions their parents make, albeit their parents have the right to confine said screaming to certain areas of their homes.

Children have the right to find out early that their parents care deeply for them but don't give a hoot what their children think about them at any given moment in time.

Because it is the truth, the whole truth, and nothing but the truth, children have the right to hear their parents say, "Because I said so" on a regular and frequent basis.

Because it is the most character-building activity a child can engage in, children have the right to share significantly in the doing of household chores.

Every child has the right to discover early in life that he isn't the center of the universe (or his family or his parents' lives), that he isn't a big fish in a small pond, that he isn't the Second Coming, and that he's not even – in the total scheme of things – very important at all, no one is, so as to prevent him from becoming an insufferable brat.

Children have the right to learn to be grateful for what they receive, therefore, they have the right to receive all of what they truly need and very little of what they simply want.

Children have the right to learn early in their lives that obedience to legitimate authority is not optional, that there are consequences for disobedience, and that said consequences are memorable and, therefore, persuasive.

Every child has the right to parents who love him/her enough to make sure he/she enjoys all of the above rights (*http://rosemond.com/2011/ bill-rights-children-poster*).

Some very basic principles useful to parents are found in the God's Word and likewise reflected in Rosemond's writings. Parents who use them will rear children to know and serve God.

1. Submission to parental authority
2. The wise use of "No" is not negative in its effect on a child
3. Increasing independence of children as maturity allows it
4. Controlled protest
5. Parents – not buddies
6. Parents the final court of appeal
7. Learning responsibility by being responsible
8. The wisdom of occasionally deflating the child's ego
9. Loving a child by doing what he needs instead of what he wants and teaching him gratitude for such treatment
10. Childhood as a time of life for learning subordination to legitimate

authority, disregard of which always entails undesirable consequences for the training of the child in obedience

11. Parents' consistent efforts to provide this kind of character development for their children

Such strategies will succeed when applied by parents who love God and honor the Scriptures. Generations of dysfunctional parents have produced generations of dysfunctional children. When parents do not know what they should do with children or how to do it, they perpetuate their problem in generations to come. For this reason the God of Abraham, Isaac, and Jacob sought to ensure, as much as He could in moral beings possessing the power of free will, a posterity which would remain close to God and aloof from the world. His work did not fail, but Israel and Judah failed fully to apply what God gave them. In an entirely separate strain of Bible history, the nations strayed from Jehovah because they forgot God/put Him out of their knowledge, resulting in their wholesale abandonment of character development in their children (Rom. 1:18-32). God's words are practical only when people practice them. Will we repeat the same old mistakes of earlier generations, or will we rise to the challenge to train our children?

What God Expects of Parents

Children, obey your parents in the Lord, for this is right. Honor your father and mother, which is the first commandment with promise: that it may be well with you and you may live long on the earth. And you, fathers, do not provoke your children to wrath, but bring them up in the training and admonition of the Lord (Eph. 6:1-3).

Children, obey your parents in all things, for this is well pleasing to the Lord. Fathers, do not provoke your children, lest they become discouraged (Col. 3:20-21).

Now for the third time I am ready to come to you. And I will not be burdensome to you; for I do not seek yours, but you. For the children ought not to lay up for the parents, but the parents for the children (2 Cor. 12:14).

But if any widow has children or grandchildren, let them first learn to show piety at home and to repay their parents; for this is good and acceptable before God. . . .But if anyone does not provide for his own, and especially for those of his household, he has denied the faith and is worse than an unbeliever. . . .If any believing man or woman has widows, let them relieve them, and do not let the church be burdened, that it may relieve those who are really widows (1 Tim. 5:4, 8, 16).

Nurturing in the Chastening and Admonition of the Lord

And, ye fathers, provoke not your children to wrath: but nurture them in the chastening and admonition of the Lord (Eph. 6:1, ASV).

1. Zerwick and Grosvenor say that Paul's use of *paideia* means discipline or training (590). The word derives from its root *pais*, meaning a child. As used by Paul the word "covers all the agencies which contribute to moral and spiritual training" (Vincent, 865).

2. Fathers must lead in this task, because they lead in the home according to divine mandate. Mothers, as helpers suitable to whatever task requires their assistance, also lend a helping hand. Parents must act in unity so as not to confuse children with different expectations and varying standards.

3. The area of their nurturing is "the chastening and admonition of the Lord." "Instruction or training" is included in *chastening*, and "bringing into the mind or warning" is done in *admonishing* (Vincent, 865).

4. To do what the Lord would do or wants done is signified by "of the Lord." One must study the Bible intently to learn what the Lord wants done in training children. For this reason, what has already been emphasized from Deuteronomy 6 is paramount in importance.

5. J. H. Thayer adds a dimension here by saying that *paideia* involves the whole training and education of children, relating to the cultivation of the mind and morals of the child, including commands, admonitions, reproof, and punishment (473). The suggestion of morals identifies the substance of which character is formed.

6. The parents of Jesus responsibly developed Him in the area of character, because He "advanced in wisdom and stature, and in favor with God and man" (Lk. 2:52). The total development of the child —mental, physical, spiritual, and social—was their attention as they did the work indicated by *paideia*. Luke's observation that Jesus was "subject to his parents" in Luke 2:51 shows the role of the parents as the leaders in character development. The world has God in heaven to thank for the gift of Jesus Christ, but we must not forget that Joseph and Mary played their part well in providing the kind of childhood development which gave the world the kind of human being Jesus became. One has to wonder whether such devotion to divine duty as Jesus showed would today be found in the modern family. Would our contemporary Jesus

turn aside from the mission that brought Him to earth, because of the lack of family training?

7. In one sense all parents receive a gift from God in their children, and they then are responsible for training the child to love God and man (Psa. 127:3). The child must be viewed as a heritage from God before he can be trained "in the chastening and admonition of the Lord."

Building Character in a Child

Unless the LORD builds the house,
They labor in vain who build it;
Unless the LORD guards the city,
The watchman stays awake in vain.
It is vain for you to rise up early,
To sit up late,
To eat the bread of sorrows;
For so He gives His beloved sleep.
Behold, children are a heritage from the LORD,
The fruit of the womb is a reward.
Like arrows in the hand of a warrior,
So are the children of one's youth.
Happy is the man who has his quiver full of them;
They shall not be ashamed,
But shall speak with their enemies in the gate (Psa. 127:1-5).

Drawing from this great passage, we learn some outstanding principles to guide us with our children:

1. Humility befits parents as they work to train their children, because they will eventually realize that they can never do the job alone. They need the help of God. He must be involved in the building of this "house." To leave Him out of the work is to work in vain, for nothing. Early hours, long hours, and remorse over wasted efforts amount to nothing. Put God in charge of this effort!

2. They also must understand that "through wisdom is a house built, and by understanding it is established" (Prov. 24:3).

3. God's heritage must be accepted gratefully as a reward from the Lord and trained for their mission in life, the serving of God and neighbor.

4. The moral training of children (character development) must be supervised by parents, not left to chance or to the school, in a manner similar to a warrior's preparing an arrow for flight toward its target.

5. The target for all character development/moral training by parents must be their fitness for divine service leading to eternal life (Eccl. 12:13-14).

6. Influence in future generations depends upon proper development of character.

Some Brief Principles to Use in Character Building

God First: Put love for God above all else, because it all crumbles without its center in Jesus Christ (Matt. 22:37-39).

Honesty: Make your word your bond (Eccl. 5:4-5; Eph. 4:25).

Personal Responsibility: You made the mess, so you clean it up (Gen. 3:12-13).

Helpful Discipline: I am disciplining you for your own good (Heb. 12:10). Rearing a child without controls is like building a house without a floor. The child has no limits, no guidelines, no firmness, no assurance, no confidence, and no framework or foundation for character development.

Respect for Older People: Show respect for your elders with courteous forms of address and helpful acts for them (Heb. 12:9; 1 Pet. 5:5).

Importance of Modesty: Cultivate respect for self and for other by stressing that what one wears affects both the wearer and the watchers ("What do you have on?" 1 Tim. 2:9).

Warning Signs for Parents

When should parents give even more attention to their task? Are there ways in which children signal us that they need even more help? Psychologist Robert Hare has devised a list to alert parents (Website: healthvsmedicine). We should watch for the following signs in the family:

1. Glib And Superficial Charm – the tendency to be smooth, engaging, charming, slick, and verbally facile. Psychopathic charm is not in the least shy, self-conscious, or afraid to say anything. A psychopath never gets tongue-tied. They have freed themselves from the social conventions about taking turns in talking, for example.

2. Grandiose Self-Worth – a grossly inflated view of one's abilities and self-worth, self-assured, opinionated, cocky, a braggart. Psychopaths are arrogant people who believe they are superior human beings.

3. Need For Stimulation or Proneness To Boredom – an excessive need for novel, thrilling, and exciting stimulation; taking chances and doing things that are risky. Psychopaths often have a low self-discipline in carrying tasks through to completion because they get bored easily. They fail to work at the same job for any length of time, for example, or to finish tasks that they consider dull or routine.

4. Pathological Lying – can be moderate or high; in moderate form, they will be shrewd, crafty, cunning, sly, and clever; in extreme form, they will be deceptive, deceitful, underhanded, unscrupulous, manipulative, and dishonest.

5. Cunning and Manipulativeness – the use of deceit and deception to cheat, con, or defraud others for personal gain; distinguished from Item #4 in the degree to which exploitation and callous ruthlessness is present, as reflected in a lack of concern for the feelings and suffering of one's victims.

6. Lack of Remorse or Guilt – a lack of feelings or concern for the losses, pain, and suffering of victims; a tendency to be unconcerned, dispassionate, coldhearted, and unempathetic. This item is usually demonstrated by a disdain for one's victims.

7. Shallow Affect – emotional poverty or a limited range or depth of feelings; interpersonal coldness in spite of signs of open gregariousness.

8. Callousness and Lack of Empathy – a lack of feelings toward people in general; cold, contemptuous, inconsiderate, and tactless.

9. Parasitic Lifestyle – an intentional, manipulative, selfish, and exploitative financial dependence on others as reflected in a lack of motivation, low self-discipline, and inability to begin or complete responsibilities.

10. Poor Behavioral Controls – expressions of irritability, annoyance, impatience, threats, aggression, and verbal abuse; inadequate control of anger and temper; acting hastily.

11. Early Behavior Problems – a variety of behaviors before age 13, including lying, theft, cheating, vandalism, bullying, sexual activity, fire-setting, glue-sniffing, alcohol use, and running away from home.

12. Impulsivity – the occurrence of behaviors that are unpremeditated and lack reflection or planning; inability to resist temptation, frustrations, and urges; a lack of deliberation without considering the consequences; foolhardy, rash, unpredictable, erratic, and reckless.

13. Irresponsibility – repeated failure to fulfill or honor obligations and commitments; such as not paying bills, defaulting on loans, performing sloppy work, being absent or late to work, failing to honor contractual agreements.

14. Failure to Accept Responsibility for Own Actions – a failure to accept responsibility for one's actions reflected in low conscientiousness, an absence of dutifulness, antagonistic manipulation, denial of responsibility, and an effort to manipulate others through this denial.

15. Juvenile Delinquency – behavior problems between the ages of 13-18; mostly behaviors that are crimes or clearly involve aspects of antagonism, exploitation, aggression, manipulation, or a callous, ruthless tough-mindedness.

Another source (Children, Youth, and Family page, website of Dane County, Wisconsin Department of Health and Human Services) supplies this slightly different list:

1. Changes in normal activities or behaviors which cannot be explained by the normal issue of adolescence.

2. Changes in the teen's appearance.

3. Changes in friends or peer group.

4. Staying in the bathroom for a prolonged period of time, which could indicate the beginning of an eating disorder or drug use.

5. Problems at school, such as cutting class, slipping grades, or fights with classmates.

6. Indifference to hobbies or school activities they previously enjoyed.

7. Refusing to do chores.

8. Missing curfew, staying out all night.

9. Creating a chaotic and hostile environment at home.

10. Defying authority and breaking rules at school, home, in the community.

These informative lists are compiled by specialists in the field, but they accurately reflect what our own experience verifies and what Bible teaching implies. A quick reading of the lists readily reminds us of the Bible's teaching concerning fundamental virtues and attributes of character needed by all. It should be apparent that the absence of these Biblical attributes in a life invites their opposites into prominence in one's life, because moral vacuums do not stay long unoccupied.

Children Learn What They Live
by Dorothy Law Nolte, Ph.D.

If children live with criticism, they learn to condemn.
If children live with hostility, they learn to fight.
If children live with fear, they learn to be apprehensive.
If children live with pity, they learn to feel sorry for themselves.
If children live with ridicule, they learn to feel shy.
If children live with jealousy, they learn to feel envy.
If children live with shame, they learn to feel guilty.
If children live with encouragement, they learn confidence.
If children live with tolerance, they learn patience.
If children live with praise, they learn appreciation.
If children live with acceptance, they learn to love.
If children live with approval, they learn to like themselves.
If children live with recognition, they learn it is good to have a goal.
If children live with sharing, they learn generosity.
If children live with honesty, they learn truthfulness.
If children live with fairness, they learn justice.
If children live with kindness and consideration, they learn respect.
If children live with security, they learn to have faith in themselves and in those about them.
If children live with friendliness, they learn the world is a nice place in which to live.

The Role of Discipline in Character Development

Children are born with abilities and inclinations, but they lack the self-control needed to harness all of these powers and potentials. The importance of their acquiring this discipline or mastery of self is seen in different examples. Horses or mules can be harnessed so that their powers and potentials are effectively applied to the pulling of the Queen's carriage or the farmer's plow. Similarly, the rocket's engine provides power, but a guidance system is needed to propel the missile to its destination. Even a rifle must be aimed if the power of the gun is to kill the deer. Without such control (discipline), neither the rifle, the horse, nor the rocket will have its desired effect. Parents face a similar, but much more important, responsibility of training their child so that he gains the discipline needed for harnessing his own powers and propensities.

Because parents face hurdles and perils in their effort to develop character in the child, they must remember that he is a learner/disciple and must fit their training of the child to a disciple. Training or treatment suited to a disciple is what we call the discipline applied by parents to the child to cultivate his internal discipline. Discipline includes whatever means are useful to help the child to develop attributes of character that will prove useful to him in ordering his life and to control them in the balance that is helpful.

Before a person can become a leader of others (through the formation of his character), he must first exercise discipline over himself. Only then will he be able to harness (discipline) all the passions and inclinations of his personality. The proper use of all such depends on his mastery of self. Internal (self) discipline, however, develops as a result of external discipline.

External and Internal Discipline
Briefly stated, external discipline is first encouraged or applied by another person (Prov. 19:18; 29:15-17); but internal discipline is formed within the person. The mild reproof, the stern look, and the swat to the "seat of learning" have the design of encouraging the child to grow in his own discipline. Both external and internal discipline have a proper function in establishing order and control in the child. The younger the child, the more need there is for external means of control, while the objective for maturing children is their growing capacity to order themselves. Order in one's life is both intentional and practical—intentional, because there must first exist the desire or purpose to bring order to one's life, and practical, because he must control his thoughts, words, and actions by regular practice. When one has translated his purpose to discipline himself into his practice of it, the internalizing of self-control has been achieved.

Ingredients of Discipline
Integral to the formation of character through the achieving of self-discipline are the following ingredients:

1. **Parental influence:** Firm guidance by precept and example must be present from respected superiors, the two parents (Gen. 18:19; Deut. 6:7ff). This ingredient is sorely missing in many instances today! Undisciplined youth lacking in desired character development is the result.

2. **Example:** Clear, consistent behavior and fair discipline also should be present (Ezek. 16:44).

3. **Discipline and instruction of the Lord:** Clear and consistent Biblical

goals and methods are crucial (Eph. 6:4); this involves such training (restraints, reproofs) as God would give.

4. **Correction harmonious with the Scriptures:** In the mind of the child it must be compatible with parental love (Prov. 3:11-12; 13:24) and related to the mistake (Prov. 22:15; 23:13-14).

5. **Desired effect:** A growing sense of responsibility for ordering one's life indicates the development of self-discipline, which is so essential to character formation (Lam. 3:27).

Disciplining in Love

Because the chastening and admonition used for children should be regulated by what the Lord wills (Eph. 6:4), love must always guide all disciplining of them. A powerful work written by James Dobson more than forty years ago, *Dare to Discipline*, has provided a counter-argument to the liberal approach earlier advocated for several years by Dr. Benjamin Spock and others. While most of what Dobson wrote deserves our attention and needs emphasis by parents, we must limit our present consideration of his work to this summary, covered in chapter one, "Teaching Respect and Responsibility to Children":

1. Children learn what they are taught, whether by parental neglect or affirmation of correct instruction and discipline, because they do not inherit the needed attitudes and understandings.

2. Parental affection and warmth must undergird efforts toward discipline, but love does not eliminate the need for guidance, instruction, and discipline.

3. Requiring children to inhibit their behavior and restrain their impulses is not hurtful to them, but helpful.

4. When children do not receive training in respect or responsibility to parents, they will demonstrate neither of these virtues in later life.

5. When parents stress the relationship of their children to them, they prepare their children for attitudes in other relationships.

6. Respectable conduct by parents is necessary in early childhood for the children to imitate parental attitudes and conduct during adolescence.

7. Hardheaded refusal to obey parents should be handled with physical discipline; pain purges the "dross."

8. Children need and want control in their lives, but parents must demonstrate that they have earned the right to control them by their example, instruction, and discipline.

9. Harsh, oppressive, unloving, and whimsical punishment antagonizes, exasperates, and discourages children. On the other hand, children must know that their flagrant disregard/challenge of parental boundaries set out of love for them will bring regret.

10. Punishment is what parents do *for* their children, not *to* them. They will lose control when they are unwilling to correct and control them.

11. During adolescence all instruction, training, and discipline of earlier life merges; any unresolved matter from those earlier years will erupt later.

12. While parental authority will sometimes be challenged, proper handling of childish infractions will garner respect and even affection after the "heat of the moment" has passed.

13. Discipline must be aimed at the objectionable behavior for the child's benefit.

Conclusion

Surely the priceless heritage of our children is reason enough to prompt in all a continuing effort to address the need for moral education in the home. Possibly the focus of this study will also equip us with the attitudes, ideas, and skills that we need. Bible study and prayer, as well as daily walking with our God, moreover, tower above all other considerations! What are we doing for our children? What could we be doing? What will we do? The future of our families, our congregations, and our nation depends, in part, on what you and I do.

Bibliography

Dane County, Wisconsin Department of Health and Human Services. Website: www.danecountyhumanservices.org/family/Delinquency/signs_and_symptoms.aspx.

Dobson, James. *Dare to Discipline*. Wheaton, IL: Tyndale House Publishers, 1970.

Duvall, Evelyn Millis. *Family Living*. New York: The Macmillan Company, 1961.

Hare, Robert. Website: healthvsmedicine.blogspot.com/2006/01/signs-and-symptoms.html.

Stone, L. Joseph and Joseph Church. *Childhood and Adolescence: A Psy-*

chology of the Growing Person. New York: Random House, 1968.

Thayer, Joseph Henry. *Greek-English Lexicon of the New Testament.* Grand Rapids: Zondervan Publishing House, 1965.

Vincent, Marvin R. *Word Studies in the New Testament.* Wilmington, DE: Associated Publishers and Authors, 1972.

Zerwick, Max and Mary Grosvenor. *An Analysis of the Greek New Testament.* Rome: Biblical Institute Press, 1981.

The Legacy of Our Children

Stan Adams

Legacy is defined as "1. A gift by will especially of money or other personal property: bequest; 2. something transmitted by or received from an ancestor or predecessor or from the past. . . .Examples of legacy: She left us a legacy of a million dollars. He left his children a legacy of love and respect" ("Legacy").

It is our task in this lecture to discuss the legacy of our children. There

---

Stanley Warren Adams was born on August 26, 1952, the third of four living children born to Wiley (faithful gospel preacher) and Wilma Hobbs Adams (deceased July 28, 1990). His brothers, Keith and Art, labor in part-time preaching efforts and his sister, Paige, is married to Jim Deason, who is a full-time preacher and elder in Cullman, Alabama. Stan has been blessed to be the husband of Carla Schoonmaker Adams, a true blessing from God. They married on February 20, 1976 and are the parents of three sons. Jared Wade is married to Tracy with two daughters, Ashlyn (14) and Micaiah (9); Shaun Wesley, father of Anna Beth (7) and Tyler (5); and Matthew Warren who is married to Erin.

Stan attended Florida College from 1970-74 and continued his education at Montevallo University in Alabama. He worked in furniture sales for three years and preached part-time for the Bloomfield church in Macon, Georgia before beginning his first full-time work with the Elliottsville Church of Christ in Alabaster, Alabama in 1977. He has subsequently labored as a full-time evangelist in Calera, Alabama; Lake Jackson, Texas; Edna, Texas; Pensacola, Florida; and presently preaches for the Newton Church of Christ in Newton, North Carolina which has a very successful bi-monthly television program that reaches five states. He has held meetings in Alabama, Arkansas, California, Colorado, Florida, Georgia, Indiana, Kentucky, Maryland, Mississippi, Missouri, North Carolina, South Carolina, Ohio, Oklahoma, Pennsylvania, Tennessee, Texas, Virginia, and West Virginia. He also writes the "News and Notes" column for *Truth Magazine* and co-edits an on-line periodical, *Apostolic Doctrine* with John Gentry. He also edits a monthly bulletin for the Newton Church of Christ, *The Beacon,* and has written articles for *Truth Magazine* and *Searching the Scriptures.* Stan would like to thank his wife, all of their sons, and John Gentry for their feedback and editing skills with his lecture.

are two ways to approach this subject; one is our children as our legacy and the other is what we leave our children. The former is the result of the latter. To a large extent what our children become depends largely on how we have done our job in pointing them in the right direction. Our job is to point them, and it is their job to follow our direction.

The theme for this lectureship is *Building Strong Homes*. The legacy many have left to their children is sadly one of divorce, abuse, and sin. Although children can overcome their raising and rise above wicked, broken homes, it is inherent on all of us who call ourselves Christians to do all we can to direct the next generation (our children) in the right paths. We can teach them, encourage them, and direct them, but we cannot apply God's word for them. They must take up the mantle and stand for truth themselves. Let us look at what the Bible teaches regarding a legacy.

The Bible has much to say about what we leave our children, and most of it pertains to what we leave them spiritually. After all, this is the greatest legacy. Take the time to reflect on the following Bible verses. "God wants to use every family for His purpose. The inheritance we accumulate and leave **for** our children is not as important as the personal legacy we leave **in** them" (Sachem).

Legacy God Gave to Mankind
And God blessed them, and God said unto them, Be fruitful, and multiply, and replenish the earth, and subdue it: and have dominion over the fish of the sea, and over the fowl of the air, and over every living thing that moveth upon the earth (Gen. 1:28).

Legacy of the Home
Therefore shall a man leave his father and his mother, and shall cleave unto his wife: and they shall be one flesh (Gen. 2:24).

But if from thence thou shalt seek the Lord thy God, thou shalt find him, if thou seek him with all thy heart and with all thy soul (Deut. 4:29).

Honour thy father and thy mother, as the Lord thy God hath commanded thee; that thy days may be prolonged, and that it may go well with thee, in the land which the Lord thy God giveth thee (Deut. 5:16).

Legacy of the Father
Now these are the commandments, the statutes, and the judgments, which the Lord your God commanded to teach you, that ye might do them in the land whither ye go to possess it: That thou mightest fear the Lord thy God, to keep all his statutes and his commandments, which I command

thee, thou, and thy son, and thy son's son, all the days of thy life; and that thy days may be prolonged. Hear therefore, O Israel, and observe to do it; that it may be well with thee, and that ye may increase mightily, as the Lord God of thy fathers hath promised thee, in the land that floweth with milk and honey. Hear, O Israel: The Lord our God is one Lord: And thou shalt love the Lord thy God with all thine heart, and with all thy soul, and with all thy might. And these words, which I command thee this day, shall be in thine heart: And thou shalt teach them diligently unto thy children, and shalt talk of them when thou sittest in thine house, and when thou walkest by the way, and when thou liest down, and when thou risest up. And thou shalt bind them for a sign upon thine hand, and they shall be as frontlets between thine eyes. And thou shalt write them upon the posts of thy house, and on thy gates (Deut. 6:1-9).

Individual Responsibility to Apply Truth Taught
The fathers shall not be put to death for the children, neither shall the children be put to death for the fathers: every man shall be put to death for his own sin (Deut. 24:16).

Commitment of the Righteous Home
And if it seem evil unto you to serve the Lord, choose you this day whom ye will serve; whether the gods which your fathers served that were on the other side of the flood, or the gods of the Amorites, in whose land ye dwell: but as for me and my house, we will serve the Lord (Josh. 24:15).

Spiritual Legacy of Prophets
And it came to pass, when they were gone over, that Elijah said unto Elisha, Ask what I shall do for thee, before I be taken away from thee. And Elisha said, I pray thee, let a double portion of thy spirit be upon me. And he said, Thou hast asked a hard thing: nevertheless, if thou see me when I am taken from thee, it shall be so unto thee; but if not, it shall not be so (2 Kings 2:9-10).

Generational Legacy
We will not hide them from their children, Shewing to the generation to come The praises of the Lord, and his strength, And his wonderful works that he hath done. For he established a testimony in Jacob, And appointed a law in Israel, Which he commanded our fathers, That they should make them known to their children: That the generation to come might know them, even the children which should be born; Who should arise and declare them to their children. . . (Psa. 78:4-6).

Legacy to Grandchildren
But the mercy of the Lord is from everlasting to everlasting upon them that fear him, And his righteousness unto children's children; To such as

keep his covenant, And to those that remember his commandments to do them (Psa. 103:17-18).

Legacy of Children (A Blessing)

Lo, children are an heritage of the Lord: And the fruit of the womb is his reward (Psa. 127:3)

Wise Son Listens to Instructions and Law

My son, hear the instruction of thy father, And forsake not the law of thy mother. . . (Prov. 1:8)

Legacy of Righteousness

Trust in the Lord with all thine heart; And lean not unto thine own understanding. In all thy ways acknowledge him, And he shall direct thy paths (Prov. 3:5-6).

Legacy from Father and Mother to Child

My son, keep thy father's commandment, And forsake not the law of thy mother. . . (Prov. 6:20).

Legacy of a Good Family Name

The memory of the just is blessed: But the name of the wicked shall rot (Prov. 10:7).

Legacy of Earthly Goods

A good man leaveth an inheritance to his children's children: And the wealth of the sinner is laid up for the just (Prov. 13:22).

Legacy of Discipline – Instruction – Pointing the Right Way – Spiritual Emphasis

He that spareth his rod hateth his son: But he that loveth him chasteneth him betimes (Prov. 13:24).

Train up a child in the way he should go: And when he is old, he will not depart from it (Prov. 22:6).

But lay up for yourselves treasures in heaven, where neither moth nor rust doth corrupt, and where thieves do not break through nor steal: For where your treasure is, there will your heart be also (Matt. 6:20-21).

And thou shalt love the Lord thy God with all thy heart, and with all thy soul, and with all thy mind, and with all thy strength: this is the first commandment (Mark 12:30).

Now if any man build upon this foundation gold, silver, precious stones, wood, hay, stubble; Every man's work shall be made manifest: for the day shall declare it, because it shall be revealed by fire; and the fire shall try every man's work of what sort it is. If any man's work abide which he hath built thereupon, he shall receive a reward. If any man's work shall be burned, he shall suffer loss: but he himself shall be saved; yet so as by fire (1 Cor. 3:12-15).

Legacy of Good Character
Let no corrupt communication proceed out of your mouth, but that which is good to the use of edifying, that it may minister grace unto the hearers. And grieve not the holy Spirit of God, whereby ye are sealed unto the day of redemption. Let all bitterness, and wrath, and anger, and clamour, and evil speaking, be put away from you, with all malice: And be ye kind one to another, tenderhearted, forgiving one another, even as God for Christ's sake hath forgiven you (Eph. 4:29-32).

Legacy of Godly Relationship
Therefore as the church is subject unto Christ, so let the wives be to their own husbands in every thing. Husbands, love your wives, even as Christ also loved the church, and gave himself for it; . . . .For this cause shall a man leave his father and mother, and shall be joined unto his wife, and they two shall be one flesh. This is a great mystery: but I speak concerning Christ and the church. Nevertheless let every one of you in particular so love his wife even as himself; and the wife see that she reverence her husband (Eph. 5:24-25, 31-33).

Legacy of Obedience
Children, obey your parents in the Lord: for this is right. Honour thy father and mother; (which is the first commandment with promise;). . . (Eph. 6:1-2).

Legacy of Unselfishness
Let nothing be done through strife or vainglory; but in lowliness of mind let each esteem other better than themselves. Look not every man on his own things, but every man also on the things of others (Phil. 2:3-4).

Legacy of Godly Service and Character
Put on therefore, as the elect of God, holy and beloved, bowels of mercies, kindness, humbleness of mind, meekness, longsuffering; Forbearing one another, and forgiving one another, if any man have a quarrel against any: even as Christ forgave you, so also do ye. And above all these things put on charity, which is the bond of perfectness (Col. 3:12-14).

Legacy of Proper Authority
Children, obey your parents in all things: for this is well pleasing unto the Lord (Col. 3:20).

Legacy of Obedience and Blessing
But continue thou in the things which thou hast learned and hast been

assured of, knowing of whom thou hast learned them; And that from a child thou hast known the holy scriptures, which are able to make thee wise unto salvation through faith which is in Christ Jesus (2 Tim. 3:14-15).

Legacy of Righteousness Benefits Others

For we have great joy and consolation in thy love, because the bowels of the saints are refreshed by thee, brother (Phile. 7).

Legacy of Marriage as God's Arrangement

Marriage is honourable in all, and the bed undefiled: but whoremongers and adulterers God will judge (Heb. 13:4).

Everlasting Blessing of the Gospel Legacy

Elect according to the foreknowledge of God the Father, through sanctification of the Spirit, unto obedience and sprinkling of the blood of Jesus Christ: Grace unto you, and peace, be multiplied. Blessed be the God and Father of our Lord Jesus Christ, which according to his abundant mercy hath begotten us again unto a lively hope by the resurrection of Jesus Christ from the dead, To an inheritance incorruptible, and undefiled, and that fadeth not away, reserved in heaven for you, Who are kept by the power of God through faith unto salvation ready to be revealed in the last time. Wherein ye greatly rejoice, though now for a season, if need be, ye are in heaviness through manifold temptations: That the trial of your faith, being much more precious than of gold that perisheth, though it be tried with fire, might be found unto praise and honour and glory at the appearing of Jesus Christ: Whom having not seen, ye love; in whom, though now ye see him not, yet believing, ye rejoice with joy unspeakable and full of glory: Receiving the end of your faith, even the salvation of your souls. Of which salvation the prophets have inquired and searched diligently, who prophesied of the grace that should come unto you: Searching what, or what manner of time the Spirit of Christ which was in them did signify, when it testified beforehand the sufferings of Christ, and the glory that should follow. Unto whom it was revealed, that not unto themselves, but unto us they did minister the things, which are now reported unto you by them that have preached the gospel unto you with the Holy Ghost sent down from heaven; which things the angels desire to look into. Wherefore gird up the loins of your mind, be sober, and hope to the end for the grace that is to be brought unto you at the revelation of Jesus Christ; As obedient children, not fashioning yourselves according to the former lusts in your ignorance: But as he which hath called you is holy, so be ye holy in all manner of conversation. . . (1 Pet. 1:2-15).

All of these passages teach the value and blessing of a godly legacy. While it is true, according to Proverbs 22:1 and Ecclesiastes 7:1 that a good earthly name is more valuable than gold, it is our spiritual name that we need to be most concerned about. Many families seem to pride themselves more on their earthly family name to the neglect of their spiritual family name (Christian). Children should not be taught to obey us so that they do not embarrass the earthly family. They should do right so they do not disparage and mar the name of Jesus.

What is the present day picture of the legacy we are leaving our children? Each generation strives to leave the next generation better off in every way than the previous generations. For the first time in the United States, we are facing leaving the next generation worse off than ever. Recent signs indicate that we will leave the next generation economically broke, morally perverted, and spiritually weak. It seems as if even the freedoms all earlier generations enjoyed may not be the legacy of the next generations.

Psalm 11:3 says, "If the foundations be destroyed, what can the righteous do?" The answer is that the righteous must continue to do righteously. We must remember that the path of the righteous is a narrow one, and few there be that find it. We cannot fold to the pressures of a decadent society. The righteous remnant of God's people must continue to wage the battle against evil. We must start in our own homes.

As a society, the foundations for our godly homes are under attack. Same-sex marriages, decadence on the computer and the TV, and humanism in every facet of our society threatens the core of our existence on this earth. But in the midst of such unrighteousness, we can still raise godly children and leave them a great spiritual legacy if we will stand firm. In fact, the many challenges we face may serve to make our homes stronger if we unite them against evil. One legacy we can leave to our children is that of seeing us fight against every evil thing. Too many want to raise their children to never know battle, but when we as Christians forget how to fight the good fight, we have lost ourselves and our legacy to another generation.

Will our country become a nation of relics and ruins regarding the church? Will we compromise the principles of truth to such a point that we lose our identity as God's people in this country? In the future will we be a place like Asia Minor is today, where there are ruins of a once great stronghold for God's people, but there is not sound congregation anywhere to be found? I trust this will not be the legacy we will leave our children, but it could happen.

Is a generation arising among us that will despise everything good (Ps.

78:8; Prov. 30:11-14)? If it could happen during the time of Israel, it can happen today. How does it happen? How does a generation depart from their legacy of faith?

It happens gradually. Israel did not intend for their children to one day pass their children through the fire. Through a series of compromises with evil and idolatry, Israel and Judah eventually digressed to the point that God rejected them as His people. Judah should have learned from her sister Israel, but she repeated and chose the same course of destruction as Israel. Let us realize that their demise was in spite of God and not because of Him. God did not cause Israel to fall; they did that all by themselves. God pled with them, warned them, disciplined them, suffered long with them, and did all that He could to lead them in the right paths, but they would not serve Him and became hardened to His pleas through the prophets. Through their own rebellion they fell. It has continued this way from the beginning. Each generation is responsible for its own actions.

In the midst of all the departures in the Old Testament, we see bright spots like Daniel, Azariah, Mishael, and Hanani (Shadrach, Meshach, and Abed-nego). These young men were taken from their country and placed in a foreign, wicked environment, yet they did not bend or bow to evil. They maintained their righteousness before God. Where did they get such strength? Although they were responsible for their own actions, they learned to pray at home, and they learned trust in God at home. Yes, they likely had parents who practiced and took seriously the Lord's command in Deuteronomy 6:1-6. The same can happen today. Our homes can be strong and we can leave our children a strong spiritual legacy.

We must also consider that even in the midst of ungodliness there are those of character who arise to serve God even though they have not been the beneficiaries of a righteous legacy. A case in point is that of Hezekiah whose father, Ahaz, was wicked but Hezekiah turned out good, perhaps from the godly influence of Isaiah (2 Chron. 28:24-26). Consider also Hezekiah's son, Manasseh who started off wicked but turned back to God once he was humbled by the heathens (2 Chron. 33). Perhaps Hezekiah's words and wisdom surfaced later when he turned to God. We must also factor in Ezekiel 18:14 which teaches that someone can overcome his wicked raising or ignore his righteous raising. While a godly legacy is of tremendous value, the lack of one is no excuse for a person to be ungodly. My mother, several gospel preachers, and others I have known are examples of those who have overcome the legacy of their raising and have chosen on their own to be people of integrity and honor. They would be the first to argue the value of a godly legacy. If you are one who has not had the blessing of a godly legacy, you can begin now to build one. It is hard to overcome one's difficult raising, but many have done so. Someone must start a family legacy of honor and obedience, why not you?

We have many examples in the Old Testament and the New of people who managed to rear godly children and leave them with a godly legacy of faith: Moses and Timothy, and our Christian ancestors who died in the arena of Rome for the faith. They are our ancient legacies. In the Lord's church today we have many ancestors of faith, who held the line and preached the truth without fear or favor of men. These preachers, elders, and brethren sacrificed friendships for truth and we enjoy the blessings we have today due to their love, respect, and defense of it. Many gospel preachers of the past have made it possible for those who preach today to enjoy the level of monetary support that they do. Those who preach today must be careful that they do not let the blessings of sufficient support move them to complacency and false comfort in the places they preach. None of us need get so comfortable in local works that we will refuse to preach what needs to be preached. As my dad advises, we should all keep a bag packed, in case the truth causes some to run us off. God will provide for His own. There are good brethren who will step up and support the preaching of the truth; it is our job to preach it without fear of favor of men and to preach each lesson as if it were our last. As Foy Smith stated years ago, ". . .preach the gospel as a dying man to dying men." Our love for souls must be more important than our comfort here on this earth. The truth cannot be for sale.

How do we leave a godly legacy? We cannot do it by compromise. All digression occurs little by little. Compromise is one of the devil's most deadly weapons. Just a little compromise here and there will not harm, he would have us believe. This is how generations arise that know not God (Judg. 2:10).

Those who are my age or older were raised by a generation who loved their country and knew what sacrifice was all about. They honored God and revered His word. We enjoyed a time when kids could be kids and moms did not work outside the home and dads were hard workers. It was a time when the entire family schedule did not revolve around the activities of the children. Dad was the head of the house, mom was the queen, and the children were subjects. Everything was not handed to us; we had to be inventive and actually get a paper route to have extra money. Many of us were raised poor but did not realize it until we got older because we had parents who did not whine about the sacrifices they made. We were raised by servants with spirits of service. That generation has been called the Greatest Generation. But this Greatest Generation spawned the Baby Boomer Generation which has spawned the Me Generation who will spawn the Entitled Generation. We can see even today that generational attitudes about legacy have an effect.

I appreciate the legacy my parents and grandparents passed on to me. I was privileged to know my great-grandfather Adams and great-grandmother Stotesberry. They, along with my grandparents and parents, left behind a great legacy of faith and respect for truth that lives on today in our family. How long it will last rests, to large degree, on what is done with this legacy by the next couple of generations. All of my ancestors that I remember came up the hard way. I always knew my family was not rich in this world's goods, but they possessed a greater wealth and passed an appreciation of that on to us. They passed on the great stories of previous generations. Memaw could really tell some stories about the past. My dad developed her talent and His children and grandchildren are blessed to have those stories live on today. They passed on to us that peace does not come free. This is true in society and in the Lord's church. Someone paid a price for what we take for granted. When it has come time to take a stand for truth, we learned lessons about how to fight with love but firmness. We learned that families do not come first, the Lord does. We learned that right is always right and you do not bother to look about as to who is with you before you make your stand for truth. If you are with the Lord, that is all that matters. Make sure you are on the right side. We learned that when you are wrong integrity insists that you admit it and repent. From my dad and mom I learned the beauty of true love and devotion to one another as husband and wife. My mom taught us that you do not have to yell to get your point across. She never raised her voice to any of us, but commanded quiet strength with dignity in all she did, even when she corrected us. My dad taught us how to love our children spiritually. He sacrificed many opportunities to hold meetings because he felt that evangelism started at home and at the time he was needed more at home. He knew the Lord had other servants who could preach the word and did not give that job to him only. Dad and mom taught us that the only thing that would separate us as a family was walking away from the Lord and that, if that happened, there could be no compromise, but, if true repentance took place, we would be whole again and the past would be put aside. This is some of my legacy. I realize we could all sit for days and compare our legacies, but we all realize that those who were part of those legacies had flaws and were not perfect. But we respect them and their legacy because they were striving to be. If we were found to be in error, it was in spite of them and not because of them. My father is still preaching the gospel full time and has said he wants to wear himself out doing so. He has also said he does not want to live long enough to undo any good he may have done. This is a good thing for all who preach to remember as we preach the word and stand firm for what is right.

The legacy we are leaving our children is under attack. We have been under siege for many years, and what we are seeing today is the result of years of gradual departure from the old paths. Humanism and secularism have overrun the borders of our homes and the few shots that have been fired have fallen on empty, hard hearts. The devil is roaming at will in many of the homes of Christians. He first came as a visitor and now he owns the hearts of our children and many of us. We have heard his roaring in the soft voice that calls for a kinder and gentler approach and for an end to this right and wrong thing. You can compromise with the world, he tells us, and we, like Eve, fall for his deceits.

In the Lord's church, Satan has convinced many that compromise is the way to truth. He has convinced many that to take a strong stand is to be mean-spirited and that love disallows all conflicts. The cry of David to Israel in 1 Samuel 17 – "Is there not a cause?" – has been lost in the empty noise that comes from many pulpits. Those of us who were raised on the true gospel are witnessing a departure from the faith in our generation, and, sadly, many of us have fallen prey to the seductions of Satan. We have taken the teeth out of our sermons and are more concerned with how our "presentation" comes across than whether we are teaching the truth. Little talks have replaced gospel sermons. This is the legacy our children are growing up on and it is time for all who fill pulpits to wake up and go back to the "old paths" wherein is the right way. Generations fed on that gospel changed the world for Christ, and it will continue to happen as long as we do not sell out and apologize for that truth.

If things continue to go the way they are, then we will leave as a legacy to our children a secularized church, and the home as God would have it will be a rarity, instead of the rule.

What can the righteous do to leave a godly legacy in the midst of a wicked world? Prepare them for what they are going to face. Let them know that a broken home need not be a destroyed one.

What does God want us to teach our children as we get up, go through the day, and lie down at night? Share with them the stories of their ancestors of faith. Let them know that doing right is not always popular, but it is always the right thing to do.

Teach them courage. Teach them to have faith. Teach! Teach! Teach! This will take our time and will require of us work! Work! Work!

Let them know they will be responsible to pass on these teachings and to implement them in their lives. Let them know it is possible to pass on legacies successfully. I am the fourth generation in my family of Christians. I was taught right. But anytime I ever messed up it was my choice, and I did what I did in spite of my raising, not because of it. There will never come a time when Satan will let up or back off of us because of who we are or how our ancestors served. He will ramp up his efforts to stop the generational chain of faith. He does not fight fair and he will own our children and grandchildren if we give in.

We need to teach them that they are accountable for their own direction. We can teach them properly, but we cannot heed and obey for them. Brethren, it is high time we stop blaming ourselves and beating ourselves up when we do all we can to rear godly families only to see them not heed the warnings of wisdom and fall away. When we have warned the evil one to not go down that road and he goes down it anyway, he will answer for his own sins (Ezek. 3:18-21; 22:3-9). God (the ultimate example to all fathers) taught, pled with, suffered long with, disciplined, and lovingly chastised His people throughout time, and still His children departed. He sent them prophets to warn them, and the people blamed God for making things too hard on them. God did not, nor should we, beat Himself up and consider Himself a failure when those He taught did not heed His words of wisdom He spoke. God was not held accountable for the evils of His children, nor should we today be held accountable for those who disobey (even our own children) when we have done all we can to guide them in the right paths. Remember the prophet Ezekiel who was looking for a man who would stand in the hedge and fill the gap, but he could find none (Ezek. 13:5; 22:30)? Was it God's fault no one stepped up? Of course not. It was the disobedient, deluded peoples' fault.

Certainly the Bible does speak of some sins that affect people unto the third and fourth generations (Gen. 15:16; Exod. 20:5; 34:7). Today we know that divorce can have such an effect. The scars of divorce keep on for several generations. But in Ezekiel 3:18-21 and 33:3-9, we read that it is everyone's responsibility to personally apply the warning given. A sinful life does have an impact on a legacy (would you name your daughter, Jezebel)? Let us all remember that the way we behave in this life impacts those we are around (especially our families). Thankfully God's Word is powerful enough to move even the most stubborn to repentance and godliness.

How long are we accountable for our children? If they return, is it all our doing? At what point are they accountable for their own sins? How many households is a man responsible for? Brethren, I urge us all to restudy these things and realize it is possible for godly men and women to rear up ungodly children (Ezek. 18:4-20), and it is also possible for ungodly people to raise up godly children. We all agree that in the last case the child is responsible for applying or not applying what his parents told him, so why not in the first case? Let's be very careful not to bind where God has not bound, or loose where He has not loosed. If we are not careful, we can indict God for the disobedience of His children and will have to redo our lessons on the prodigal to show that the father (who was just and perfect) must have done something wrong to cause his boy to go live riotously (actually, both sons disrespected their father in their own way).

We see that dysfunctional families are not unique to our generation. Abraham, Isaac, and Jacob had their own failures in their families. Every time God's marriage laws were not respected, chaos and division came. There is truly nothing new under the sun.

We continue to read throughout the history of Israel of families that withstood the temptation to fold to the sin around them. These are bright spots of faith for all of us and help us to realize that no matter how bad or bleak it gets, it is possible to raise godly children and have godly homes in the midst of a wicked world.

Look at the example of Jesus and His parents on this earth. Luke 2 tells us that He grew in "wisdom, in stature, and in favor with God and man." This tells us that Jesus was trained by His family intellectually, physically, spiritually, and socially. This is our task today. Moses was taught diligently by his mom and sister, and that teaching overrode every effort made by his Egyptian teachers to lead him away.

Imagine what it was like to be a young family in the church at Corinth, Ephesus, or Jerusalem. These areas were full of idolatry. The towns were full of wickedness, but still we know that there were godly brethren in all of these places. Did they have to deal with division? Did they have to deal with false brethren? Of course they did; just as we do today. Let's remember and take heart that even "if the foundations be destroyed," there will always be a remnant of the righteous who will reach down and take the torch from the previous generation and will fight the good fight, keep the faith, and inherit the riches God has waiting for us all.

Our question is, will we survive and thrive in the midst of a wicked world? Will we live compromising lives or will we hold fast to sound words? Will we let our children know of the generations that preceded them (family and spiritual) that allow them to enjoy the things they have today?

What are you leaving behind to help your family?

> God wants to use every family for His purpose. The Old Testament reveals God's primary purpose for the family. God's promises and teachings were handed down from one generation to the next generation through the family. God is telling His story of restoration and redemption through the family. For many Christian families this concept has become lost and muddled. American families get sidetracked when it comes to the things that really matter. The stuff we accumulate becomes the pursuit of our ambitions. What we give or do for our children takes priority over what we leave behind. Parents forget the importance of leaving a legacy (Sachem).

I love to watch track relay races, especially the 4x400 meter relay. Even a casual observer of such a race realizes that. . .

> When it comes to relay races, the victory does not necessarily come to the fastest and most impressive runners. The victory goes to the team that was the most successful in passing the baton from runner to runner. You can be the fastest and most impressive individual runner in the world but if you fail to successfully pass the baton to the next runner the race will be lost. When you fumble the baton you lose the race (Krell).

Many world-class relay teams have lost races that were theirs for the taking due to poor passing of the baton to the ensuing runner. In spiritual legacy it is the same. One runner finishes his race and passes the baton of faith to another to continue down the track. So it has gone spiritually from Abraham to Isaac to Jacob to Joseph to the judges, prophets, kings, apostles, early Christians, and finally to us. Across these many generations the baton is passed from over 4000 years ago to you and me in the 21st century. We have a great spiritual legacy to pass on to the next generation. It is the gospel of Christ. It is powerful, and it changes lives and conquers nations. May none of us let the mantle of faith fail on our watch. Let us make sure that we do not raise up a generation that knows not God.

Works Cited

Krell, Keith. "Passing the Promises (Genesis 25:1-18)." *Bible.org.* Bible.org, 2005. *<http://bible.org/seriespage/passing-promises-genesis-251-18>* Accessed 12 Dec., 2012.

"Legacy." *Merriam-Webster.com.* Merriam-Webster, 2012. *<http://www. merriam-webster.com/dictionary/legacy>* Accessed 12 Dec., 2012.

Sachem, John. "Bible Verses About Family Legacy: God Uses the Family for His Purpose," *Yahoo! Voices.* Yahoo! Inc., 9 Feb 2010. *<http:// voices.yahoo.com/bible-verses-family-legacy-5443437.html>* Accessed 12 Dec., 2012.

Wisdom in Child-Rearing

Mark Mayberry

Introduction

Sacred Scripture focuses upon eternal and exalted themes, such as the redemptive plan that was in God's mind before the foundation of the world, foreshadowed over long ages past, but revealed and realized in the person of Jesus Christ. Yet, the Word of God also has immediate and practical benefit. It teaches us how to live from day to day. The Bible sets forth God's pattern for the home. It is a guide-book for the work of parenting, an instruction manual for child-rearing, containing relevant examples of success and failure.

Christians recognize that the Mosaic Law was taken out of the way, nailed to the cross, and is no longer binding (Eph. 2:14-16; Col. 2:13-14).

Mark Mayberry, the son of Donald Mayberry and Ruth Hutcheson Mayberry, was born on February 23, 1957 in Nashville, Tennessee. Raised in Middle Tennessee, Mark spent most of his childhood in Clarksville, where he obeyed the gospel and was a member of the South Clarksville Church of Christ. He met Sherelyn Finley while attending college in Florida. They were married in 1978. After moving to Texas, the Mayberrys lived in Groveton (79-81), Tyler (81-86), and Cooper (86-91), laboring with faithful brethren in each community. In 1991, they moved to Clarksville, Tennessee and spent seven years working with the Warfield Boulevard congregation. The family moved back to Texas in 1998, to the city of Alvin, which remains their home. They continue to work and worship with the Lord's church that assembles at Adoue Street, where he also serves as one of its elders. Mark is also a Board Member of the Guardian of Truth Foundation. Mark and Sherelyn are blessed with two wonderful sons: Nathan and Ryan. They have been encouraged by good brethren in each place where they have lived, particularly by those godly elders who diligently watch in behalf of their souls. They are also thankful for their extended physical families, most of whom are loving, faithful Christians.

However, the Old Testament contains much that is worthy of remembrance and reflection, especially in reference to the present subject (Rom. 15:4; 1 Cor. 10:6-11).

The Blessings of a Godly Home

Solomon said, "A good man leaves an inheritance to his children's children, and the wealth of the sinner is stored up for the righteous" (Prov. 13:22). What sort of inheritance are we leaving for our children and grandchildren? Is it material? Is it spiritual? Will our offspring continue to share a relationship with God? Will our descendants be grounded in the most holy faith (Psa. 102:28)?

The 127th Psalm affirms the importance of a God-centered home, saying "Unless the Lord builds the house, they labor in vain who build it. . . ." The blessings of hearth and home include contentedness, companionship, and the delight of children.

The 128th Psalm declares that the benefits of reverential fear are bestowed upon husbands, wives, children, and grandchildren. God-ordered homes are graced with happiness and harmony, productiveness and prosperity.

The Curse of an Ungodly Home

Lack of Leadership. Many parents fail to provide leadership, and are dominated by their offspring. Isaiah described a similar judgment that fell upon ancient Israel, in which God rendered them leaderless: "I will make mere lads their princes, and capricious children will rule over them. . . . Their oppressors are children, and women rule over them. . ." (Isa. 3:4-5, 11-12). Woe unto the land (or family) whose leader is a mere lad (Eccl. 10:16).

Numerous homes suffer from another form of role reversal. God's Word affirms that the husband is the head of the wife, and the wife should be subject to her husband (Eph. 5:22-33; Titus 2:3-5). Feminists reject this structure, labeling it patriarchal, oppressive, and outdated. This radical reordering of the family has progressed for decades, to the disadvantage of children and the detriment of society.

Lack of Discretion. Many parents evidence a lack of discretion. Children cry out, "That's not fair!" when they feel that their "rights" have been violated. Parents may provoke such a response if they do not follow the path of fairness. By showing favoritism, Isaac and Rebekah contributed to the alienation that existed between Esau and Jacob, and their descendants

(Gen. 25:28). Jacob manifested similar misjudgment with equally sad results (Gen. 37:3-4). Warning against this kind of failure, Paul said, "Fathers, do not provoke your children to anger. . ." (Eph. 6:4) and again, "Fathers, do not exasperate your children. . ." (Col. 3:21).

Lack of Discipline. Many parents evidence a lack of discipline. Perhaps the most tragic example of failure is that of Eli – a good and godly man who served as High Priest and Judge; yet he was a lax father who exercised no control over his sons, Hophni and Phinehas. Because he did not back his verbal rebukes with a vigorous response, Eli proved an ineffective disciplinarian. Additionally, his moral authority was compromised because he personally benefited from his sons' scheming behavior (1 Sam. 2:12-17, 22-29). They brought divine judgment on themselves because of their iniquity; sadly, Eli shared in his sons' shame because he did not (effectively) rebuke or restrain them (1 Sam. 3:10-14; 4:10-18).

Lack of Stability. Many homes evidence a lack of stability. Divorce imposes a terrible burden upon children who are deprived of a fully functional family. Whenever the divine pattern of marriage is ignored (i.e., one man being joined to one woman for life), complications ensue and heartache follows. During the last holiday season, it was widely reported that a "dad" was the tenth most popular Christmas list request for children.

> When it comes to Christmas, it might be safe to assume children will ask Santa for an extensive list of toys, games and treats. But a survey of their typical lists for Father Christmas has shown many have more serious concerns, requesting "a Dad" instead. A study of 2,000 British parents found most children will put a new baby brother or sister at the top of their Christmas list, closely followed by a request for a real-life reindeer. A "pet horse" was the third most popular choice, with a "car" making a bizarre entry at number four. Despite their material requests, the tenth most popular Christmas wish on the list was a 'Dad.' . . . A request for a "mum" reached number 23 on the list [Hannah Furness, "A dad is tenth most popular Christmas list request for children," *The Telegraph*, 23 December 2012, http://www.telegraph.co.uk].

Consequences. Parental failure may result in temporal consequences. The effects of sin are often long-lasting, bringing a curse upon successive generations: "He will by no means leave the guilty unpunished, visiting the iniquity of fathers on the children and on the grandchildren to the third and fourth generations" (Exod. 34:6-7; cf. Num. 14:18; Deut. 5:9). Divine judgments sometimes fall upon future generations (Exod. 17:8-16; Deut.

25:19; 1 Sam. 15:1-3); pathological behaviors, substance abuse, and welfare dependency may have similar multi-generational effects.

Parental failure may result in eternal consequences. A lack of leadership, discretion, discipline, and stability in the home may pull our children down the road to hell. Are we teaching self-indulgence or self-denial? Do we take up Jesus' cross on a daily basis, or do we crucify the Son of God afresh and put Him to an open shame? Do we wish to save our lives (for sin and self), or are we willing to lose it (for the sake of Christ)? Are we seeking to gain the world at the cost of our soul? Do we confess Christ daily, or do we deny Him before men? How we answer these questions will determine our destiny, and impact our children's hope of heaven (Matt. 16:24-27; Mark 8:34-38; Luke 9:23-26).

Homes Are Successful When Parents Follow Divine Wisdom

We must distinguish between the wisdom of God and the wisdom of the world. What is meant by wisdom? The Greek word *sophos*, translated "wisdom," refers to one who is "skilled" or "wise" [Thomas]. It pertains "(1) to knowing how to do something in a skillful manner; (2) to understanding that results in wise attitudes and conduct" [BDAG]. *Nelson's New Illustrated Bible Dictionary* offers the following comments on wisdom, defining it as the "ability to judge correctly and to follow the best course of action, based on knowledge and understanding." The essence of Biblical wisdom is that we humble ourselves before God, reverently submitting to His authority, being obedient to His counsel and commands.

Secondly, what do we mean by the world? This term has three distinct meanings in Scripture, identifying (1) the physical realm, created by God, reflecting His glory and power; (2) the realm of mankind, made in God's image, being the object of His love; (3) the realm of Satan and sin, in rebellion against God, being the object of His wrath.

This sinful world is subject to the wrong master. The kingdoms of the world are the rightful possession of Jesus Christ (Psa. 2:1-11; 1 Tim. 6:13-16; Rev. 11:15; 17:14), but the world is presently dominated by Satan, the Great Usurper (Matt. 4:8-10; Luke 4:5-8; 2 Cor. 4:3-4; 1 John 5:19).

The world pursues the wrong kind of philosophy and is filled with the wrong kind of wisdom. Its philosophy, as reflected by the Judaizing and Gnostic heresies, sets aside the will of God, adding to, subtracting from, and otherwise changing heaven's message (Gal. 4:9; Eph. 2:1-2; Col. 2:8, 20-23). Its wisdom reflects a repudiation of God's word and ways. Exchanging the truth of God for a lie, God gave them over to degrading passions and demeaning doctrine (Rom. 1:18-23; 1 Cor. 1:18-31; 3:18-20). Accordingly, the world and its ruler are under divine judgment (John 12:27-32; 14:29-31; 16:7-11; Rev. 20:10-15).

What relationship should God's people share with this sinful world? While we live in the world, we must remain distinct from the world (John 15:18-20; 17:14-16; 1 Cor. 2:6-16). Resisting the world's evil influence (John 17:14-17; 1 Cor. 5:9-13; James 4:4-10), we seek to be an influence for good (Matt. 5:14-16; Rom. 10:14-18; Phil. 2:14-16).

This has special application to our present subject; the world offers egregious counsel when it comes to child-rearing. Christians must not allow the modern entertainment media to define the roles of husbands and wives, parents and children. Furthermore, godly parents will reject advice from the modern class of helping professionals when their counsel conflicts with the Lord's will.

While many ridicule the Christian faith and Biblical principles of godly living, "Yet we do speak wisdom among those who are mature; a wisdom, however, not of this age nor of the rulers of this age, who are passing away; but we speak God's wisdom in a mystery, the hidden wisdom which God predestined before the ages to our glory" (1 Cor. 2:6-7). Let us build our homes upon the solid foundation of divine wisdom, following the sound principles set forth in the pages of Sacred Scripture (Prov. 24:3–4).

Homes are Successful when Parents Fulfill Their God-given Duties
Parents must Love their Children
1. Storgē Love. Parents should manifest natural affection toward their children, as communicated by the Greek word *storgē*. It describes the special love and affection that is shared in a home. It communicates the love of parents for their children, the love of children for their parents, the love of brothers and sisters, the love of kith and kindred.

This word appears twice in Sacred Scripture, but only in its negative form, *astorgos*, describing individuals who are "without natural affection/unloving" (Rom. 1:31; 2 Tim. 3:3). Thomas defines *astorgos* as a compound of the negative prefix and *storgē* [family affection], meaning "without natural affection" [794]. BDAG say it is descriptive "of one who is lacking in good feelings for others, thereby jeopardizing the maintenance of relationships (e.g. political and familial) that are essential to a well-ordered society."

Additionally, it appears in the compound *philostorgos*, occurring once, describing those who are tenderly/dearly devoted to one another (Rom. 12:10). Thomas defines *philostorgos* as a compound of *philos* [beloved, dear, friendly] and *storgē* [family affection], meaning "tenderly loving" [5387]. BDAG say it is descriptive of "loving dearly" (Rom. 12:10). In extra-Biblical literature, Josephus employs this latter term in relating David's grief upon hearing of the death of his son Absalom (*Antiquities* 7.252; cf. 2 Sam. 18:33).

Sadly, our modern society is cursed by a lack of natural affection. Abortion destroys the lives of countless innocent unborn babies. Millions of children are raised in broken homes, without the companionship and guidance of their dads and/or moms. Many suffer at the hands of abusive parents, step-parents, live-ins, or (temporarily) significant others.

Addressing the Macedonian disciples, Paul twice alludes to this quality, by saying, "But we proved to be gentle among you, as a nursing mother tenderly cares for her own children" (1 Thess. 2:7), and again, "You know how we were exhorting and encouraging and imploring each one of you as a father would his own children" (1 Thess. 2:11).

To raise godly children, it is essential that we manifest the qualities associated with *storgē*. They need our tender affections. They need the encouragement and exhortation that comes from loving parents. They need our time and attention, protection and provision. They need the security of knowing they are dearly-loved and deeply-cherished.

2. *Phileō Love.* Parents should love their children with friendly affection, as communicated by the Greek words *philos/phileō.* This is the love of affection and shared values, the love of friendship and fealty, the love of loyalty and allegiance, the love of merit and appreciation. It reflects our positive response to the good qualities seen in another person. We share this love with family, friends, and brethren.

Thomas defines the root adjective *philos* as "beloved, dear, friendly" [5384]. BDAG say it "(1) pertains to having a special interest in someone; (2) substantively, [it is descriptive of] one who is on intimate terms or in close association with another." Bauer also notes Aristotle's definition: "one soul inhabiting two bodies."

Friends offer blessings (Acts 10:24). They offer protection (Acts 19:31). They offer assistance (Luke 7:6; 11:5, 6, 8; Acts 27:3). They offer sympathy and shared joy (Luke 15:6, 9, 29; John 3:29). Loving families must do the same.

Believers must be friends of God (James 2:23), and also friends of one another (3 John 15). However, we must not be friends with the world (James 4:4). Godly families live by the same principles.

Thomas defines the verb *phileō* as from *philos* [beloved, dear, friendly], meaning "to love" [5368]. BDAG say it means "(1) to have a special interest in someone or something, frequently with focus on close association; (2) to kiss as a special indication of affection."

God loves His Only Begotten Son (John 5:20), and the disciples of Christ (John 16:27). Believers must love the Lord Jesus (1 Cor. 16:22), and also one another (Titus 3:15). Our love for Christ must exceed the love we have for our parents (Matt. 10:37), and even the love we have for life itself (John 12:25). In like manner, Christian parents seek to instill such values in the hearts of their children.

Significantly, *philos* also appears in various compound forms, signifying both positive and negative qualities. Disciples are obligated to be lovers of God, lovers of good, lovers of mankind, lovers of strangers, and lovers of honor. Parents are obligated to teach these same values to their children.

Several compound words have special significance to our study. When Paul said, "*Be devoted* to one another in brotherly love; give preference to one another in honor" (Rom. 12:10), he employed the Greek word *philostorgos*, which (see above) is descriptive of the tender love shared within a close family.

Writing to Titus, the inspired apostle said "Older women likewise are to be reverent in their behavior, not malicious gossips nor enslaved to much wine, teaching what is good, so that they may encourage the young women to *love their husbands*, to love their children, to be sensible, pure, workers at home, kind, being subject to their own husbands, so that the word of God will not be dishonored" (Titus 2:3-5). He employs the Greek word *philandros*, which signifies a wife's love for her husband, and also *philoteknos*, which communicates a mother's love for her children.

Finally, the New Testament oft speaks of "brotherly love" (Rom. 12:10; 1 Thess. 4:9; Heb. 13:1; 1 Pet. 1:22; 2 Pet. 1:7). Here the Greek word is *philadelphia*, identifying "the love of brothers." In extra-Biblical occurrences, this term is used in the literal sense of love for siblings, i.e., blood brothers or sisters. In Scripture, it is employed in the transferred sense of mutual affection that is shared by fellow-Christians. When parents teach their children to love one another, the physical home becomes a proving ground, a place of development, wherein we prepare our children for eventual membership in God's spiritual family, the church.

3. Agapaō Love. Parental love must also be with purpose and principle, as communicated by the Greek words *agapē/agapaō*, the most exalted form of love, not based upon emotion, but an act of the will that seeks the highest good of another

The noun *agapē* signifies "love" or "goodwill" [Thomas]. BDAG say this term, which has left little trace in polytheistic Greek literature, refers to "the quality of warm regard for and interest in another. . . ." The verb *agapaō* means "to love" [Thomas]. BDAG say it means "(1) to have a warm regard for and interest in another, (2) to have high esteem for or satisfaction with something; (3) to practice/express love."

Agapē love is the abiding principle in a healthy marriage. It is not born of a lover's need, nor does it have its source in the love object. *Agapē* does not exist in order to get what it wants but empties itself to give what others need. Thus, the Bible says, "Husbands love your wives" (Eph. 5:25-33; Col. 3:18-19).

Wives should respond with warm affection. Older women are to teach the younger women to love their husbands and to love their children (Titus 2:3-5). As noted earlier, *philandros*, translated "love their husbands," describes a wife who is affectionate toward her husband; *philoteknos*, translated "love their children," depicts a mother who is fond of her children.

In the New Testament, a husband is commanded to *agapeō* his wife while a wife is commanded to *phileō* her husband and children. Certainly a man should also *phileō* his wife, and a woman should also *agapeō* her husband and children. However, the emphasis is significant. As head of the home, a husband is responsible for its overall values and direction. Therefore, he should unselfishly seek the highest good of each member of that household. In contrast, a wife sets the emotional tone in a family. She should show fondness and affection toward her husband and children. In summary, the husband provides loving-leadership while the wife provides tender-affection.

Adam failed to provide spiritual leadership of his family (cf. Gen. 3); today, many men are similarly negligent, with equally tragic results. A husband deficient in loving leadership may (occasionally or often) show affection toward his wife and children, but they will have little respect for him as the head of the house. Based on a sense of mushy sentimentality, a father may allow those under his charge to pursue a course that is inconsistent with their highest spiritual good. Such behavior is a betrayal of parental duty.

Depending upon circumstances, a godly husband and father must be strong enough to say "No!" and caring enough to say "Yes!" Acting as the protector of his family, he will help them avoid physical and spiritual dangers. Acting as their benefactor, he will pursue activities and associations that further their physical, spiritual, and emotional well-being.

Parents must Teach their Children

1. Through Example. Parents should teach their children by setting the proper example (Deut. 4:40; 31:12-13; Jer. 32:38-40). Christ's challenge, "You are the salt of the earth" and "You are the light of the world" has special application to the family (Matt. 5:13-16). Salt serves as a preservative; do we exercise a similar effect in the lives of those we love? As candles provide physical illumination, our words and deeds should reflect the glory of the Father. Jesus said, "If you love Me, you will keep My commandments" (John 14:15; cf. 15:10-11). Is our example helping or hindering our children?

2. Through Precept. Parents should teach their children through precept, stressing the authority of divine revelation (Deut. 4:1-2, 9-10; 6:4-9; 11:18-21; Isa. 38:18-19). Before Israel crossed into the Promised Land, Moses reminded his countrymen of the demands of the Covenant. They must obey God's statutes and ordinances. Avoiding the sin of adding to or subtracting from the Law, they were to faithfully keep the Lord's commandments. Israel was reminded of the revelation given at Mt. Sinai: "Assemble the people to Me, that I may let them hear My words so they may learn to fear Me all the days they live on the earth, and that they may teach their children."

Deuteronomy 6:4-9 is especially noteworthy: "Hear, O Israel! The Lord is our God, the Lord is one! You shall love the Lord your God with all your heart and with all your soul and with all your might. These words, which I am commanding you today, shall be on your heart. You shall teach them diligently to your sons and shall talk of them when you sit in your house and when you walk by the way and when you lie down and when you rise up. You shall bind them as a sign on your hand and they shall be as frontals on your forehead. You shall write them on the doorposts of your house and on your gates" (cf. also Deut. 11:18-21).

Making the most of the brief time they are allotted to train their children, fathers will tell their sons of God's faithfulness (Isa. 38:18-19; Eph. 5:15-16). Worthy wives and mothers will do the same (Prov. 31:26-31). Divine truths that we have heard and known, which our fathers have told to us, must not be concealed, but faithfully communicated to our children and grandchildren (Psa. 78:1-4).

The present generation should praise God's works to the next, telling of His greatness, declaring His mighty acts and wonderful works (Psa. 145:3-6), and also His devastating judgments (Joel 1:1-7). Lois and Eunice instilled such conviction in the heart of young Timothy, passing along their sincere faith, convincing and convicting him in the truth, pointing him to the Sacred Writings (2 Tim. 1:5-7; 3:13-17).

Children evidence a natural curiosity, constantly asking, "How? What? When? Why?" Devoted parents and grandparents will utilize such opportunities, providing Biblically-based answers that affirm God's power, purpose, and prerogatives (Exod. 12:23-27; 13:6-9, 14-16; Josh. 4:1-7, 19-24).

Parents must Discipline their Children
1. Instructive Discipline. Parents have an obligation to instruct their children in the word and ways of God. For Israelites, this specifically applied to the Passover and the Feast of Unleavened Bread, which commemorated their deliverance from the land of Egypt (Exod. 12:23-27; 13:11-16), and to the memorial stones taken from the Jordan, that commemorated their crossing into the land of promise (Josh. 4:4-7, 19-24). More generally, they were required to teach God's testimonies and statutes to their children (Deut. 6:1-9, 20-25).

Instructive discipline is a key to raising godly children: "Come, you children, listen to me; I will teach you the fear of the Lord" (Psa. 34:8-14, esp. v. 11). Elsewhere, David said, "The law of the Lord is perfect, restoring the soul; the testimony of the Lord is sure, making wise the simple. The precepts of the Lord are right, rejoicing the heart; the commandment of the Lord is pure, enlightening the eyes. The fear of the Lord is clean, enduring forever; the judgments of the Lord are true; they are righteous altogether. . . . Moreover, by them Your servant is warned; in keeping them there is great reward" (Psa. 19:7-14).

The 119th Psalm asks, "How can a young man keep his way pure?" The answer: "By keeping it according to Your word. With all my heart I have sought You; do not let me wander from Your commandments. Your word I have treasured in my heart, that I may not sin against You..." (Psa. 119:9-16).

Paul's admonition to his son in the faith is also relevant to our sons in the flesh. Timothy was commanded, "Continue in the things you have learned and become convinced of, knowing from whom you have learned them." Further, he was reminded that "from childhood you have known the sacred writings which are able to give you the wisdom that leads to salvation through faith which is in Christ Jesus." Finally, the apostle affirmed the power of divine revelation: "All Scripture is inspired by God and profitable for teaching, for reproof, for correction, for training in righteousness; so that the man of God may be adequate, equipped for every good work" (2 Tim. 3:14-17).

2. *Corrective Discipline.* Corrective discipline must be applied when instructive discipline fails to achieve its purpose. The rod represents corporal punishment (Prov. 13:24; 22:15; 23:13-14; 29:15). While corrective discipline may seem severe, it is in reality an expression of love (Prov. 3:11-12, 24; Heb. 12:4-11; Rev. 3:19). When corporal punishment is employed in a timely and appropriate manner, the benefits and blessings are great (Prov. 13:24; 19:18; 22:15; 23:13-14; 29:15).

Properly administered discipline, both of the instructive and corrective varieties, leads to life. Proverbs 6:23 says, "For the commandment is a lamp and the teaching is light; and reproofs for discipline are the way of life." It leads to honor. Proverbs 13:18 says, "Poverty and shame will come to him who neglects discipline, but he who regards reproof will be honored." It leads to peace. Proverbs 29:17 says, "Correct your son, and he will give you comfort; he will also delight your soul." It leads to knowledge. Proverbs 12:1 says, "Whoever loves discipline loves knowledge, but he who hates reproof is stupid." It leads to understanding. Proverbs 15:31-32 says, "He whose ear listens to the life-giving reproof will dwell among the wise. He who neglects discipline despises himself, but he who listens to reproof acquires understanding."

Nevertheless, when discipline is neglected, especially during the impressionable years of youth, the results are often disastrous. Society will eventually impose its harsh sentence, with far less compassion than when discipline is administered by loving parents. Furthermore, the prospect of life-altering correction diminishes once one has acquired the habits of rebellion.

While Proverbs 22:6 says, "Train up a child in the way he should go, even when he is old he will not depart from it," let us recognize that this passage, like other principles set forth in the Book of Proverbs, is a generalization, and not an absolute rule. Exceptions exist. Each individual is a creature of choice, the possessor of a free will. Good sons and daughters may come from bad families, and vice-versa (cf. Ezek. 18).

Some will not hear (Prov. 13:1) or heed (Prov. 10:17). Those who reject discipline are fools (Prov. 15:5), straying from the words of knowledge (Prov. 19:27), bringing shame to themselves and their parents (Prov. 13:18; 29:15). They will suffer the consequence of their folly (Prov. 1:24-26; 1:30-31; 5:11-13; 7:22-23; 10:13-14; 15:10; 15:32; 16:22; 26:3; 29:1).

Homes Are Successful When Children Fulfill Their God-Given Responsibility

1. Honoring Parents. Children must honor their parents. This fundamental principle is set forth in both the Old and New Testaments (Exod. 20:12; Lev. 19:3; Deut. 5:16; Eph. 6:2). Under the Mosaic Law, the penalty for dishonoring one's parents was severe, being counted as a capital offense (Exod. 21:17; Lev. 20:9; Deut. 27:16; Prov. 20:20). Correspondingly, Jesus sternly denounced those who paid lip-service to God, but refused to honor their parents by providing for them in their age and infirmity (Matt. 15:1-9; Mark 7:9-13). The inspired apostle said such individuals have denied the faith and are worse than unbelievers (1 Tim. 5:3-4, 7-8, 16).

2. Obeying Parents. Children must obey their parents. In the Proverbs, sons (and daughters by inference) are repeatedly admonished to hear and heed their parents' instruction (Prov. 1:8; 1:15; 3:1, 21; 4:1, 10; 5:7; 6:20; 7:1, 24; 8:32; 23:19, 22). The inspired apostle Paul echoed these sentiments, saying, "Children, obey your parents in the Lord, for this is right" (Eph. 6:1) and ,"Children, be obedient to your parents in all things, for this is well-pleasing to the Lord" (Col. 3:20).

Conclusion

God's pattern will work; hence, let us work God's pattern. Let us resolve to be like the patriarch Abraham, of whom it is said, "For I have chosen him, so that he may command his children and his household after him to keep the way of the Lord by doing righteousness and justice, so that the Lord may bring upon Abraham what He has spoken about him" (Gen. 18:19).

In conclusion, please permit a few personal observations as we summarize this lesson.

Parents should love their children, evidencing natural affection, the love of friendship, and the love of principle and purpose that seeks their highest good. Sherelyn and I enjoyed being around our boys, spending a great deal of time together in work, worship, play, and travel. Because we homeschooled our children, thus enjoying a greater degree of flexibility, my wife and sons often accompanied me when I was away in Gospel meetings. This helped broaden their association with fellow-Christians, creating lasting friendships, and cultivating a love for the brotherhood of believers.

Parents should teach their children. In raising our children, we engaged in regular, daily Bible study. Sherelyn and I endeavored to set the right example before our children. We sought to avoid inconsistency, especially regarding our choices of entertainment, movies, music, and television. We emphasized the need for modest attire, both in public and around the house. We encouraged our children to cultivate friendships with fellow-Christians, and our home was open to their companions. This helped us provide a controlled environment, and also impressed them with the importance of hospitality.

Parents should teach their children to listen to instructions, with the expectation that they respond the first time. Let us avoid the trap of vain repetition. Don't nag or needle; don't harp or harangue. Shun saying, "If you don't straighten up, I'm going to threaten you!" When a child misbehaves, warn them once, and if a positive response is not forthcoming, implement appropriate corrective measures. Stick with it until the child submits and obeys.

Parents should discipline their children. Mothers and fathers should manifest maturity even when their children do not. If kids misbehave, we should not respond in kind. Corporal punishment is no excuse for adults to merely vent their frustrations. Instead, let us maintain self-control, calmly and deliberately dealing with troublesome situations as they arise.

Our goal as parents was to help our children achieve self-sufficiency. From an early age, we tried to instill a sense of responsibility in their hearts. We played together, and we also worked together. They had chores. They were expected to help around the house, in cleaning, mowing, and maintenance. In time, expectations grew and responsibilities increased. Both participated in various building projects and home renovations. Our boys learned the value of hard work. We held them accountable for their actions, stressing the need for honesty and integrity.

Our sons both obeyed the gospel at an early age. As they grew, they began participating in the worship services, leading in singing, serving the Lord's Supper, praying, and presenting lessons from God's Word. Through the grace of God, and the application of the gospel to their lives, they have grown to responsible manhood, and are a continuing source of joy to their parents. May God similarly bless all parents who endeavor to raise their children in the nurture and admonition of the Lord.

May we be blessed with Christian homes: "Homes where the Bible is loved and taught, homes where the Master's will is sought, homes crowned with beauty Thy love hath wrought – God give us Christian homes! God give us Christian homes!" (Baylus B. McKinney [1949], "God Give Us Christian Homes," *Psalms, Hymns and Spiritual Songs*, Munfordville, KY: Sumphonia Productions, 2012, Song # 553).

Sources

BDAG = Frederick William Danker, ed., *A Greek-English Lexicon of the New Testament and Other Early Christian Literature, 3rd ed.* (Chicago, IL: The University of Chicago Press, 2000).

NASB = Unless otherwise noted, all Scripture quotations come from *New American Standard Bible: 1995 Update Edition* (LaHabra, CA: The Lockman Foundation, 1995).

NIBD = R. F. Youngblood, F. F. Bruce, R. K. Harrison, eds., *Nelson's New Illustrated Bible Dictionary* (Nashville, TN: Thomas Nelson Publishers, 1995).

Thomas = Robert L. Thomas, *New American Standard Hebrew-Aramaic and Greek Dictionaries: Updated Edition* (Anaheim: Foundation Publications, Inc., 1998).

Resources

Because We Love You, edited by Mike Willis.

Courageous Living: Co-Parenting, by Wilson Adams.

Family Life: A Biblical Perspective, by L. A. Stauffer.

God's Plan for Parenting, edited by Kevin Maxey.

Good Homes in a Wicked World, by Irven Lee.

Harmony in the Home, by Mike Willis.

The 1979 Florida College Annual Lectures: The Godly Family in a Sick Society, edited by Melvin Curry.

The 2006 Truth Magazine Lectures: God Give Us Christians Homes, edited by Mike Willis.

Conclusion

Let's Build Strong Homes

Michael Richardson

We live in a day and time where there has been a lot of change due to advances in technology. I stand amazed at how quickly technology is upgraded and how short a life span many products have. There is a different mindset about what should be repaired versus what should be replaced. It was not too long ago one could easily find shoe repair and typewriter repair shops. Now those are difficult to find because the attitude is that, instead of repairing things, it is easier and sometimes less expensive to replace them. It has become apparent that this attitude has seeped into many other aspects of life.

Danger of Replacing Instead of Rebuilding

In these times it must be established that, although culture may change, God stays the same. "For I am the Lord, I change not" (Mal. 3:6). In Hebrews 13:8 the Hebrew writer states, "Jesus Christ is the same yesterday, and today, and forever."

Michael Richardson was born August 19, 1975. He was extremely blessed to be adopted by Don and Eileen Richardson of Dickson County, TN. He is grateful for the godly example they set and the training and discipline he received in his upbringing. His mother, Eileen, passed away in 2009.

Mike attended Florida College (1993-1995). While there he met and later married Mary Yates Richardson of Birmingham, AL. Mike and Mary are blessed to have two sons, Jackson (9) and Sam (6).

Mike was extremely blessed and ever grateful for his very close relationship with Robert Jackson who Mike considered a father, mentor, and friend. Mike worked two summers with the Jackson Heights church in Columbia, TN, under Ken Weliever and a summer with the Eastside church in Shelbyville, TN, with Frank Butler.

Mike began full time work in 1996 with the Main St. Church of Christ in Chapel Hill, TN and spent a year there. Then he began work with the Central Church of Christ in Charlotte, TN, and was there from 1997-2008. From 2008 to the present he has been working with the Campbell Road Church of Christ in Madison, TN (a suburb of Nashville).

Also, God's standard does not change. "The grass withers, the flower fades, but the word of our God stands forever" (Isa. 40:8; 1 Pet. 1:22-25). We must never think that man has the right to change what God has revealed to be His standard. We have seen religious leaders change God's standard to conform to the desires of man, instead of changing man's desires to conform to God's standard (Rom. 8:29; 12:1-2). When we conform God into the image we want Him to have instead of allowing Him to conform us into His image, we trade true faith in the true God for a false sense of spirituality. This leads to false security and a lack of self-sacrifice needed to be true disciples (Matt. 16:24).

The Threat of the Crumbling Home

The home is the cornerstone and basic unit of society. Throughout history the home life has been subject to strife and struggle, because marriage and parenthood are difficult and require constant humility and self-sacrifice. In other words, it takes hard work to make a successful family. We don't like hard work. We want a quick fix. If our Iphone, for example, is an older model, we want to replace it with the newest version, because advertisers can hide a new model's defects. When we apply this attitude to marriage, the ramifications of changing are not so simple. Besides trading for something just as flawed, we also break homes, hearts, vows, and God's standards.

Due to the deterioration of the home we see many people living shattered and bruised lives. It is no wonder there are so many depressed people and psychological problems in our day. There is hardly a family today in our nation that is not touched by the decay of the home life in one manner or another.

Some of the Issues That Cause the Home to Crumble

So why has the home life spiraled into decay and why are so many homes are broken?

We'll use a building as an example. What would cause a building to crumble or fall? A building may not be constructed according to the correct pattern, through carelessness, laziness, or lack of knowledge. Inferior materials may have been used to build the structure. A building may deteriorate due to a failure to maintain it. A foundation not built on solid ground can weaken the structure. Also, outside influences – storms, flood, etc. – can chip away at the building, and a strong storm can knock it off its foundations. "Except the Lord build the house, they labor in vain" (Ps. 127:1). Too often, we leave out the very One who should be the foundation of not only our homes but our lives. Now consider this great truth: Only God, who instituted and ordained the home, can give the necessary instructions to build that home. The home begins to fall when man ignores God's word, and what should be a strong, solid foundation is soon turned to rubble by man's interference with God's divine plan. The home is a divine institution, ordained by God for the well-being of His people. The question is: Will we follow His pattern for the home, or ignore His plan?

No home can stand without God as a rule. If we do not follow the plan God has given for the home life, then, like the builder of the building taking shortcuts, it will come back to hurt us. Too many young people get married without being prepared for this great step in life. Many are just too immature. They spend more time preparing for the wedding celebration than they do for the marriage. They want the fancy wedding day, but do not put consideration into the lifelong commitment. One man in Nashville, TN, said many years ago, "God wanted a taste of heaven on earth, so He made the home." Then he said, "The devil wanted a flavor of hell on earth, so he introduced discord into the home." Instead of going to the guidebook God gave in the Bible, they go to other, secular resources. It is not wrong to read other materials on marriage, nor is it wrong to seek counsel. However, when you are building something, it is always best to go back to the blueprint. God's blueprint for marriage gives different roles to men and women. The apostle Paul, in Ephesians 5:22-33, gives God's pattern for marriage. We need to understand the roles God has given us. No one is inferior in personhood. We all are created by God with an eternal soul. We must not confuse difference of roles with inequality. God has ordained that wives are to submit to their own husbands as to the Lord. Notice it is the job of the wife to submit. It is not the place of the husband to make her subject to him. Husbands have been instructed to love their wives as Christ loved the church. This is the blueprint of God for marriage.

Some build with inferior materials. Selfishness, thoughtlessness, and pride weaken the structure of marriage. Some neglect their marriage and fail to maintain the home. Distracted with social media and other forms of individual entertainment, couples no longer depend on each other on a day-to-day basis. Families seldom meet around the supper table anymore. If you do not communicate and grow together, then you will grow apart.

Society and outside influences also attack the structure of marriage. The sanctity of sex in marriage is under attack. The divorce rate appears lower today, but that is a skewed statistic due to the fact that many no longer bother to marry, they just live together as if they were married. They may have children, share the bills and responsibilities, but do not make the commitment to stay true to one another. We have lost the concept of the sanctity of marriage. Our permissive society encourages premarital and even extramarital relations. The lack of any form of self-control regarding sex has become a great problem in the moral makeup of our land. "Marriage is honorable among all and the bed undefiled, but fornicators and adulterers God will judge" (Heb.13:4). Sex is sanctified in the bed of marriage. Any other time, it is sinful. Another societal factor is the homosexual movement. The attitude over "gay rights" has changed greatly in our land. Now people are bringing their sin into public view and calling it an acceptable lifestyle. Opponents of gay marriage are ridiculed as backwards, prejudiced, and hatemongers. Young people think it is the "moral" thing to be "tolerant" of homosexual marriage. Moral standards are now being influenced by society rather than by God.

Financial issues can also attack the home from outside. Husband and wife should agree on financial goals and work together toward them. Too often, money problems will drive a wedge of stress and blame between a husband and wife. Or the desire to increase status and position will cause dissatisfaction with one another. Jobs can become too important. When work takes up too much time or when husband or wife puts a job before the interests of his or her family, relationships will be affected. Working, whether at a job or inside the home, is a vital part of life, but should be balanced and prioritized correctly.

Illness can also place stress on a marriage. How many who say "in sickness and in health" really mean it? Caring for a parent, child, or spouse can be an exhausting, time-consuming, and expensive prospect. If one's spouse becomes permanently disabled in some way, requiring much care, it can seem hopeless and dreary. God's way is to submit in love to duty. Society's way is to declare that the individual's needs should come first and a spouse who can't give enough should be discarded.

The relationships between parents and children are also breaking down. In Ephesians 6:1-3, children are instructed to obey their parents in the Lord and to honor their father and mother. If children do not respect parental authority, they will not respect any other kind of authority. Parents have begun putting the children's desires above the family's needs. How many times have marriages failed due to spouses arguing over parenting styles and decisions. How often are children given toys and entertainment in place of direction and example? Parents neglect to discipline their children or to discipline in the correct manner. "And you, fathers, do not provoke your children to wrath, but bring them up in the training and admonition of the Lord" (Eph. 6:4).

The Results of Broken Homes

One does not need to look far to see the impact of broken homes on society. We see it in our schools where children show no respect for those in authority. Many children act with disdain towards teachers and others who have jurisdiction over them. We witness the results of broken homes in society when we consider how many Americans with the attitude of being entitled because we have failed to teach children the value of self-discipline, patience, and working for a purpose. Many people feel they are "owed" something just because they were born an American. Children should expect (if both parents are alive) a father and mother training them up in the admonition of the Lord. However, a society that feels entitled to have at a young age what it took their parents years to work for is a community of people who will not follow God's word to work and provide for their own. "For even when we were with you, we commanded you this: If anyone will not work, neither shall he eat" (2 Thess. 3:10). And, "But if anyone does not provide for his own, and especially for those of his household, he has denied the faith and is worse than an unbeliever" (1 Tim. 5:8).

We witness the home's breakdown in crime and other acts of rebellion. We see the lack of concern for human life and how desensitized Americans have become in regard to violence.

Another place we see the home's decay is in the local church. The world is not becoming more like the people of God, but God's people are beginning to act more like the world and are no longer living holy and sanctified lives. We see where "churches" appeal to the carnal side of man instead of his spiritual needs. Many individuals who have religious influence in our land see the problems in the home, and instead of going back to the Book to repair the home they seek to replace the family with entertainment and social teachings. Religious leaders today strive to be politically correct and popular, rather that teaching the whole counsel of God. Budget-driven and institutionalized churches prefer to tell members that God wants them to be happy (in the world), rather than teaching them how to be holy and set apart, which doesn't always lead to worldly happiness. "For the time will come when they will not endure sound doctrine, but according to their own desires, because they have itching ears, they will heap up for themselves teachers; and they will turn their ears away from the truth, and be turned aside to fables" (2 Tim. 2:26). That time is now.

What Is Needed

First, more preaching is needed on the home life and the roles and responsibilities of each family member. We need to go back to the pattern God has given and build on the solid foundation.

> Therefore whoever hears these sayings of Mine, and does them, I will liken him to a wise man who built his house on the rock: and the rain descended, the floods came, and the winds blew and beat on that house; and it did not fall, for it was founded on the rock. But everyone who hears these sayings of Mine, and does not do them, will be like a foolish man who built his house on the sand; and the rain descended, the floods came, and the winds blew and beat on that house; and it fell. And great was its fall (Matt.7:24-27).

We need to learn to spend time together in the home. Spouses need to be devoted to one another. Spouses should not neglect their marital duties. "Let the husband render to his wife the affection due her, and likewise also the wife to her husband" (1 Cor.7:3). How many marriages could be saved if couples remembered this command in Scripture?

We need men to step up and lead the home and be the kind of husbands God has directed. We need men to love their wives as themselves and be concerned with the souls of their family. We need fathers who discipline their children out of love and for the good of the child. Adam was silent when he should have spoken up and rebuked Eve before she partook of the forbidden fruit. The silence of Adam echoes through many homes today as men do not stand up to direct their families as God directed. When he wrote Titus, the young preacher, Paul instructed him what to preach in regard to the roles of each one in the home.

> But as for you, speak the things which are proper for sound doctrine: that the older men be sober, reverent, temperate, sound in faith, in love, in patience; the older women likewise, that they be reverent in behavior, not slanderers, not given to much wine, teachers of good things – that they admonish the young women to love their husbands, to love their children, to be discreet, chaste, homemakers, good, obedient to their own husbands, that the word of God may not be blasphemed. Likewise, exhort the young men to be sober-minded, in all things showing yourself to be a pattern of good works. . . (Titus 2:1-7).

We need women to remember God's direction to them (Titus 2:5).

Women need to remember they will stand in judgment before God regarding their obedience to His command to be subject to their husbands. We have a great problem today in that men do not want to lead and women do not want to submit, so homes end up with a nominal head and a *de facto* head. Anything with two heads is a monster. Sometimes a woman may want her husband to be a stronger leader of their home, and develop resentment because of his failure in her eyes. Women need to recognize that they are a primary source of encouragement for their husbands. Couples need to see how they can help each other fulfill the roles God has given them in the home. Failure to maintain proper roles can also spill over into the church. Men must strive to be good elders and deacons, rather than seeking to shirk these responsibilities. "The elders who are among you I exhort. . . . Shepherd the flock of God which is among you, serving as overseers, not by compulsion but willingly, not for dishonest gain but eagerly; nor as being lords over those entrusted to you, but being examples to the flock" (1 Pet. 5:1-2). Women must take care to stay in the roles God has given them in worship, without questioning His wisdom. All must be done in humility and in the spirit of putting others first—in the home, in the church, and in our dealings with the world.

We need parents who discipline their children out of love. I have heard some people say they love their children too much to discipline them. But really they love themselves too much as they don't like the feeling that comes with having to train their children by doing something they find unpleasant. In Hebrews 12:5-11 the man of God reveals the purpose of discipline in regard to God and man, using a parent disciplining a child as an example. "No chastening seems to be joyful for the *present*, but painful; nevertheless, *afterward* it yields the peaceable fruit of righteousness to those who have been trained by it" (Heb. 12:11). The statement, "This hurts me more than it does you" rings true many times, but it is the result of the discipline that we desire: for our children to live righteously before God.

We need parents who teach children and we need children to respect parental authority. We need to teach our children to pray and to study Scriptures. What is needed is to turn off the television and to spend time with each other and follow God's pattern.

CPSIA information can be obtained at www.ICGtesting.com
Printed in the USA
LVOW122018010713

340902LV00004B/8/P